Choose the Right Nursery

Education and Childcare Options for Under 5s

by Alison Falconer

The Stationery Office: London

Table information © Crown Copyright

This publication reproduces the Primary School Performance Figures for England, Scotland and Wales. This material is Crown copyright and is reproduced under licence from the Controller of Her Majesty's Stationery Office.

The Primary School Performance Figures for England, Scotland and Wales were originated by the Department for Education & Employment, the Scottish Office Education & Industry Department and the Welsh Office Education Department respectively. None of these three government departments, nor the Controller of HMSO, takes any responsibility for the accuracy of the Crown material as it appears in this publication; for the way in which the Crown material is presented; or for the views expressed in this publication. Any opinions, advice, judgements or conclusions offered in this publication are entirely those of the authors and not of the Crown.

British Library Cataloguing in Publication Data
A catalogue record for this book is available from the British Library.

ISBN 0 11 781996 4

Printed and bound by The Stationery Office Limited

1/99 402598 J0069489 19585

Published by The Stationery Office and available from:

The Publications Centre
(mail, telephone and fax orders only), PO Box 276, London SW8 5DT
General enquiries 0171 873 0011, Telephone orders 0171 873 9090
Fax orders 0171 873 8200

The Stationery Office Bookshops
123 Kingsway, London WC2B 6PQ, 0171 242 6393 Fax 0171 242 6394
68–69 Bull Street, Birmingham B4 6AD, 0121 236 9696   Fax 0121 236 9699
33 Wine Street, Bristol BS1 2BQ, 0117 9264306 Fax 0117 9294515
9–21 Princess Street, Manchester M60 8AS, 0161 834 7201 Fax 0161 833 0634
16 Arthur Street, Belfast BT1 4GD, 01232 238451 Fax 01232 235401
The Stationery Office Oriel Bookshop, The Friary, Cardiff CF1 4AA, 01222 395548
Fax 01222 384347
71 Lothian Road, Edinburgh EH3 9AZ, 0131 228 4181, Fax 0131 622 7017

The Stationery Office's Accredited Agents (see Yellow Pages)

and through good booksellers

Contents

For my daughters Caitlin and Isobel whose nursery education has been invaluable.

Acknowledgements

I would like to thank all the many people who have dealt patiently with my endless questions, and especially Rebecca Webster and the staff at City College Nursery.

Introduction

WHO NEEDS THIS BOOK?

Anyone looking for care and education for a child, at whatever age from birth to five, will discover a confusion of regulations, registrations, systems and philosophies. The nurseries and other institutions and individuals who provide services for this age group have developed differently to meet particular needs. This means that the picture of care and education on offer can be complicated and confusing. It also means there is a wide variety of services giving you the best chance of finding the care and education most suitable for your child.

This is not an 'advice' book. Most parents get too much of that already and are quite capable of choosing the best for their child when they have the information to base it on. This book aims to provide that information.

Note: the term 'she' for a childcare worker implies she or he, and the term 'parent' refers to a child's legal guardian, whoever that may be.

WHAT IS IN THIS BOOK AND HOW TO USE IT

Section One

Explains the government's Nursery Education Scheme – one of the largest influences on nursery education today.

Section Two

Helps you establish your priorities for the care and education of your child. This includes a chart for you to fill in that will provide you with your own checklist against which you can judge the different services on offer.

Section Three

Describes the main types of education and care available for the under-fives, including the rules that govern them. Each sub-section has a panel at the beginning, indicating the minimum age children are usually admitted, whether the service is offered school hours only or all day all year, a rough price guide, which body if any, regulates the type of care, and whether providers are likely to be part of the government's Nursery Education Scheme. This allows you to dismiss any type of provision that is totally unsuitable without reading further.

Section Four

Explains about the different types of inspections that are carried out and how they can inform your choice of an individual nursery or carer. It then takes you through the interviewing, recruiting, visiting and decision-making process, taking into account your own priorities and the way each sector is organised.

Section Five

Looks at what you can do if you are not happy with your choice. It also details the help available with the costs of childcare and education, and explains what happens if you think your child has special educational needs. This sections also gives you a glance at the future, with details of some of the government's plans and promises likely to affect the under fives.

Section Six

The Directory section provides you with: nurseries attached to primary schools, maps so you can find your local education authority; lists of ISIS, Montessori, Steiner nurseries; a directory, and a wealth of other useful addresses; and a reference chapter on qualifications so you can check what it means if the staff at your nursery have NNEBs, NVQs or countless other initials to their credit.

Section One

General Information

The Nursery Education Scheme

The government's Nursery Education Scheme that funds pre-school education for four-year olds, has had a major impact on all kinds of nurseries and pre-schools. The Nursery Education Grant (Pre-school Year Grant in Scotland) is worth about £1,100 a year for each four-year old and can be used in private nurseries, but it comes with strict conditions. The nursery accepting the grant must provide a curriculum that allows each child to make the most progress he or she can towards certain goals, whether he or she has special educational needs or is a high academic achiever. These goals are laid down under the snappy title of 'Desirable Outcomes for Children's Learning *on Entering Compulsory Education*' (England) or *Before Compulsory School Age* (Wales); (A Curriculum Framework for Children in their Pre-school Year in Scotland). Like most aspects of education, they are currently under review. Each nursery or pre-school in the scheme must also accept inspection by Ofsted (the Office for Standards in Education) in England, OHMCI (Office of Her Majesty's Chief Inspector) in Wales and HMI (Her Majesty's Inspectors of Schools) in Scotland on how well they are providing these goals.

The 'Desirable Outcomes' are given in full exactly as they are laid down because they affect most nurseries and pre-schools. Because they are 'outcomes', they describe children as they are expected to have become through a successful nursery education.

(see pages 7 & 12) For the Welsh version, see page 7; for the Scottish Curriculum Framework see page 12.

DESIRABLE OUTCOMES FOR CHILDREN'S LEARNING ON ENTERING COMPULSORY EDUCATION (ENGLAND)

Personal and Social Development

These outcomes focus on children learning how to work, play, co-operate with others and function in a group beyond the family. They cover important aspects of personal, social, moral and spiritual development including the development of personal values and an understanding of self and of others. They should be interpreted in the context of the values agreed by the adults, including the parents, involved with each setting.

Children are confident, show appropriate self-respect and are able to establish effective relationships with other children and with adults. They work as part of a group and independently, are able to concentrate and persevere in their learning and to seek help where needed. They are eager to explore new learning, and show the ability to initiate ideas and to solve simple practical problems. They demonstrate independence in selecting an activity or resources and in dressing and personal hygiene.

Children are sensitive to the needs and feelings of others and show respect for people of other cultures and beliefs. They take turns and share fairly. They express their feelings and behave in appropriate ways, developing an understanding of what is right, what is wrong and why. They treat living things, property and their environment with care and concern.

They respond to relevant cultural and religious events and show a range of feelings, such as wonder, joy or sorrow, in response to their experiences of the world.

Language and Literacy

These outcomes cover important aspects of language development and provide the foundation for literacy. Children must be helped to acquire competence in English as soon as possible, making use, where appropriate, of their developing understanding and skills in other languages. The outcomes focus on children's developing competence in talking and listening and in becoming readers and writers. Other areas of learning also make a vital contribution to the successful development of literacy.

In small and large groups, children listen attentively and talk about their experiences. They use a growing vocabulary with increasing fluency to express thoughts and convey meaning to the listener. They listen and respond to stories, songs, nursery rhymes and poems. They make up their own stories and take part in role play with confidence.

Children enjoy books and handle them carefully, understanding how they are organised. They know that words and pictures carry meaning and that, in English, print is read from left to right and from top to bottom. They begin to associate sounds with patterns in rhymes, with syllables, and with words and letters. They recognise their own names and some familiar words. They recognise letters of the alphabet by shape and sound. In their writing they use pictures, symbols, familiar words and letters, to communicate meaning, showing awareness of some of the different purposes of writing. They write their names with appropriate use of upper and lower case letters.

Mathematics

These outcomes cover important aspects of mathematical understanding and provide the foundation for numeracy. They focus on achievement through practical activities and on using and understanding language in the development of simple mathematical ideas.

Children use mathematical language, such as circle, in front of, bigger than and more, to describe shape, position, size and quantity. They recognise and recreate patterns. They are familiar with number rhymes, songs, stories, counting games and activities. They compare, sort, match, order, sequence and count using everyday objects. They recognise and use numbers to 10 and are familiar with larger numbers from their everyday lives. They begin to use their developing mathematical understanding to solve practical problems. Through practical activities children understand and record numbers, begin to show awareness of number operations, such as addition and subtraction, and begin to use the language involved.

Knowledge and Understanding of the World

These outcomes focus on children's developing knowledge and understanding of their environment, other people and features of the natural and made world. They provide a foundation for historical, geographical, scientific and technological learning.

Children talk about where they live, their environment, their families and past and present events in their own lives. They explore and recognise features of living things, objects and events in the natural and made world and look closely at similarities, differences, patterns and change. They show an awareness of the purposes of some features of the area in which they live. They talk about their observations, sometimes recording them and ask questions to gain information about why things happen and how things work. They explore and select materials and equipment and use skills such as cutting, joining, folding and building for a variety of purposes. They use technology, where appropriate, to support their learning.

Physical Development

These outcomes focus on children's developing physical control, mobility, awareness of space and manipulative skills in indoor and outdoor environments. They include establishing positive attitudes towards a healthy and active way of life.

Children move confidently and imaginatively with increasing control and co-ordination and an awareness of space and others. They use a range of small and large equipment and balancing and climbing apparatus, with increasing skill. They handle appropriate tools, objects, construction and malleable materials safely and with increasing control.

Creative Development

These outcomes focus on the development of children's imagination and their ability to communicate and to express ideas and feelings in creative ways.

Children explore sound and colour, texture, shape, form and space in two and three dimensions. They respond in a variety of ways to what they see, hear, smell, touch and feel. Through art, music, dance, stories and imaginative play, they show an increasing ability to use their imagination, to listen and to observe. They use a widening range of materials, suitable tools, instruments and other resources to express ideas and to communicate their feelings.

DESIRABLE OUTCOMES FOR CHILDREN'S LEARNING BEFORE COMPULSORY SCHOOL AGE (WALES)

Language, Literacy and Communication Skills

Competent use of language is the most fundamental of human skills. It is a decisive factor in mastery of other areas of learning. The acquisition of language in early childhood is a complex process. If a child has a wide range of language experiences, that mastery should become well established and the child's intellectual, emotional and social learning will be enhanced.

By the time they are five, the nursery experiences that children have had should enable them to:

listen to a good story;

listen, respond to, and recall songs, nursery rhymes, poems and jingles;

communicate needs;

ask questions and listen to responses;

relate the broad thrust of the story;

re-tell their own experiences, broadly in the order in which they occurred;

discuss their current individual and group play and refer to their intentions;

express opinions and make choices;

identify and explain events illustrated in pictures;

choose a book and hold it the right way;

understand that written symbols have sound and meaning;

understand some of the functions of writing;

enjoy marking and basic writing experiences - using pencils, crayons, etc;

use marking implements for a range of purposes: painting, drawing, writing, scribbling.

Personal and Social Development

Children of nursery age will be learning about themselves. They will be learning about relationships with other children and with adults, and about the responsibilities that are involved. They will be learning about the world outside the family, about how people live and work, about the past and about people and places outside their direct experience, including people from different cultures and backgrounds. They will be learning about standards of good behaviour and developing appropriate attitudes.

By the time they are five, the nursery experiences that children have had should enable them to:

feel confident and be able to form relationships with other children and with adults;

demonstrate care, respect and affection for other children and adults;

begin to show sensitivity to others and to those with difficulties;

concentrate for lengthening periods when involved in appropriate tasks;

explore and experiment confidently with new learning opportunities;

acknowledge the need for help and seek help when needed;

begin to take responsibility for personal hygiene (for example, washing hands after using the toilet, before handling food and so on) ;

dress themselves, if given time and encouragement;

take turns, share and begin to exercise self -control;

understand that all living things should be treated with care, respect and concern;

respond positively to a range of new cultural and linguistic experiences.

Mathematical Development

Beginning to understand mathematical processes and concepts is the foundation of numeracy. Children need to see the processes in action. For example, they need the concept of number to be visual, concrete and practical. They need to see it done and do it themselves. In order for mathematical ideas to be meaningful, they must first be understood in the context of an activity.

By the time they are five, the nursery experiences that children have had should enable them to:

use mathematical language in relevant contexts: shape, position, size and quantity;

recognise and recreate basic patterns;

recall a range of number rhymes, songs, stories and counting games;

sort, match, order, sequence, compare and count familiar objects;

begin to understand mathematical concepts such as "less" and "more";

begin to understand the mathematics of money;

begin to recognise numbers and begin to match number to sign and sound;

Knowledge and Understanding of the World

Children should have experiences of other cultures, of past events, of the work people do, of the use of money, of the environment, of animals and other living things. They should be encouraged to enjoy pulling, pushing, turning, experimenting, pouring, testing, digging, building and generally finding out how things work.

These will often be the experiences which will be the foundation of confidence in science and technology and its enjoyment.

By the time they are five, the nursery experiences that children have had should enable them to:

talk about home and where they live;

begin to understand about different places such as the countryside and the town;

have a basic understanding of the seasons and their features;

begin to understand the idea of time: meal times, times of the day (morning, bedtime), sequencing (yesterday, today and tomorrow);

identify some kinds of workers by characteristics of work: dentist, doctor, farmer, teacher, postal worker, factory worker, mechanic...,

have a basic understanding of the purpose and use of money;

begin to find out about outcomes, problem solving and decision-making;

begin to understand the use of a variety of information sources (for example: books, television, libraries, information technology);

begin to appreciate the importance of the environment:

begin to understand about food and where it comes from;

begin to appreciate the differences in and uses of a range of materials;

make choices and select materials from a range, exploring their potential, cutting, folding, joining and comparing.

Physical Development

Children of nursery age need to understand the concepts of health, hygiene and safety. They need to begin to understand the importance of diet, rest and sleep.

They will be developing physical control, mobility, awareness of space and a range of manipulative skills. They will need a range of experiences and should have access to safe and stimulating outdoor play.

By the time they are five, the nursery experiences that children have had should enable them to:

have an awareness of their own bodies and their growth;

move confidently, with increasing control and co-ordination;

use a range of small and large equipment with increasing skill and confidence (for example: bikes, balls, climbing frames...);

handle small tools and objects with increasing control and for appropriate purposes (for example: pencils, paintbrushes...);

understand, appreciate and enjoy the differences between running, walking, skipping, jumping, climbing and hopping;

understand and respond to suggestions about spatial relationships (for example: behind, underneath and below, on top of and above...).

Creative Development

Children of nursery age will be continually developing their imagination and creativity. Their ability to communicate and express that imagination and creativity will also be developing. Children with limited mobility or sensory impairments should not be excluded but may need alternative strategies for creative expression.

By the time they are five, the nursery experiences that children have had should enable them to:

respond to and enjoy rhythm in music and music-making with a range of instruments and with their voices;

use a range of materials to create representational images (pictures, drawings, constructions...);

make choices about colour and medium;

respond to suggestions for dance and imitative movements;

discuss work in progress and completed (for example: painting, instrument-making...);

begin to enjoy role play and imaginative drama;

begin to observe and appreciate the work of others;

begin to differentiate sounds without visual clues (for example: animals, instruments, voices).

A survey of inpsection reports

A major survey of nursery inspections by Ofsted compared how well the different categories of providers succeeded in delivering the 'Outcomes.' The survey covered inspections of 9,796 institutions that took place between 1 June 1997 and 31 March 1998. It included playgroups and pre-schools; private nursery schools; independent schools; local-authority day nurseries; private day nurseries; and a general category of 'others'. There was also a break down by educational approach between Montessori and High/Scope.

The most effective providers overall were independent schools, where 86.3% promoted the outcomes successfully and only 0.1% were poor. This compared with 75.4% of Montessori nurseries (0.7% poor), 74.3% of private nursery schools (0.6% poor) and 71.3% of High/Scope institutions (0.5% poor).

Very similar results in the high sixties were recorded for local-authority day nurseries, 67.6% (0.3% poor), private day nurseries, 66.6% (0.7% poor) and 'others', 68.7% (0.5% poor).

Only 49% of playgroups and pre-schools achieved this standard with 1.6% judged poor.

The report concluded that playgroups were more often constrained by staff who lacked training and experience and by lack of resources and problems with accommodation.

Most institutions were found to successfully promote the desirable outcomes in general and only 1% were considered poor.

'Personal and social development' was delivered most successfully overall, the weakest being 'knowledge and understanding of the world.'

The emphasis on planning for language and literacy and for mathematics was best in independent schools (about 92%) and private nursery schools (about 75%). This is not surprising considering the emphasis of these institutions on traditional academic subjects. Only 53% of playgroups gave these areas what Ofsted considered a high enough priority. Nine per cent of playgroups were actually graded poor in planning for language and literacy and 10% in planning for mathematics.

Independent schools also came out top for the quality of teaching and assessment of children's progress in relation to the desirable outcomes (73%). Local-authority day nurseries and private nursery schools were not too far behind at 60%. Private day nurseries did slightly less well at about 54%, and 42% of playgroups were successful in these areas.

The weaknesses most commonly noticed in assessing pupils' development related to a lack of clear targets rather than staff making poor judgements.

Reception classes did well in the survey despite having a lot of bad press about their unsuitability for four-year olds. Provision was judged to be satisfactory or better in 90% of reception classes inspected, and 96% of nursery classes. The quality of teaching was satisfactory or better in 95% of all classes, and the report pointed out that this often reflected the expertise teachers had in planning for the desirable outcomes developed from experience of the National Curriculum.

NATIONAL CURRICULUM

One of the main purposes for setting these 'outcomes' is so that children starting school already have a have a foundation in the areas covered by the national curriculum. Once they are at primary school, the subject areas become more specific and extend from the six subjects of the 'outcomes' to nine subjects at Key Stage 1 of the national curriculum in England and ten in Wales.

Personal and social development relates to English: speaking and listening (or Welsh and English).

Language and literacy relates to English: speaking and listening, reading and writing (or Welsh and English).

Mathematics leads to, well, mathematics.

Knowledge and understanding of the world relates to geography, history, science and technology.

Physical development to physical education.

Creative development leads to art and music.

THE CURRICULUM FRAMEWORK FOR CHILDREN IN THEIR PRE-SCHOOL YEAR (SCOTLAND)

The Curriculum Framework in Scotland is seen as a set of guidelines rather than an imposed curriculum, but it is still that case that only nurseries that subscribe to it can be funded through the Pre-school Year Grant. Its basic requirements are set out below:

In emotional, personal and social development, children should learn to:

- develop confidence, self-esteem and a sense of security
- care for themselves and their personal safety
- develop independence, for example in dressing and personal hygiene
- persevere in tasks that at first present some difficulties
- form positive relationships with other children and adults and begin to develop particular friendships with other children
- become aware of and respect the needs and feelings of others in their behaviour, and learn to follow rules
- play co-operatively and share resources
- become aware that the celebration of cultural and religious festivals is important in people's lives
- develop positive attitudes towards others whose gender, language, religion or culture, for example, is different from their own
- care for the environment and for other people in the community

In communication and language, children should learn to:

- listen to other children and adults during social activities and play

- listen with enjoyment and respond to stories, songs, music, rhymes and other poetry

- listen and respond to the sounds and rhythm of words in stories, songs, music and rhymes

- pay attention to information and instructions from an adult

- talk to other children or with an adult about themselves and their experiences

- express needs, thoughts and feelings with increasing confidence in talk and non-verbal language

- take part in short and more extended conversations

- use talk during role play and re-tell a story or rhyme

- use language for a variety of purposes eg to describe, explain, predict, ask questions and develop ideas

- use books to find interesting information

- recognise the link between the written and spoken word

- understand some of the language and layout of books

- develop an awareness of letter names and sounds in the context of play experiences

- recognise some familiar words and letters, eg the initial letter in their name

- use their own drawings and written marks to express ideas and feelings

- experiment with symbols, letters and, in some cases, words in writing

In developing their knowledge and understanding of the world children should learn to:

- develop their powers of observation using their senses

- ask questions, experiment, design and make and solve problems

- recognise patterns, shapes and colours in the world around them

- sort and categorise things into groups

- understand some properties of materials eg soft/hard, smooth/rough

- understand the routines and jobs of familiar people

- become familiar with the nursery/centre and places in the local area

- become aware of everyday uses of technology and use these appropriately (scissors, waterproof clothing, fridge, bicycle)

- be aware of daily time sequences, and words to describe/measure time eg snacktime, morning, first, next, clock
- be aware of change and its effects on them eg their own growth, changes in weather, trees, flowers
- care for living things eg plants, pets at home
- be aware of feeling good and of the importance of hygiene, diet, exercise and personal safety
- develop an appreciation of natural beauty and a sense of wonder about the world
- understand and use mathematical processes such as matching, sorting, grouping, counting and measuring
- apply these processes in solving mathematical problems
- identify and use numbers up to 10 during play experiences and counting games
- recognise familiar shapes during play activities
- use mathematical language appropriate to the learning situations

In expressive and aesthetic development children should learn to:

- investigate and use a variety of media and techniques such as painting, drawing, printing and modelling with fabrics, clay and other materials
- express thoughts and feelings in pictures, paintings and models
- use role play or puppets to recreate and invent situations
- use verbal and non verbal language in role-play
- listen and respond to sounds, rhythms, songs and a variety of music
- make music by singing, clapping and playing percussion instruments
- use instruments by themselves and in groups to invent music that expresses their thoughts and feelings
- move rhythmically and expressively to music
- participate in simple dances and singing games

In physical development and movement children should learn to:

- enjoy energetic activity both indoors and out and the feeling of wellbeing that it brings
- explore a range of different ways in which they can use their bodies in physical activity
- express ideas and feelings and respond to music and imaginative ideas in rhythmic and expressive movement

- run, jump, skip, climb, balance, throw and catch with increasing skill and confidence

- co-operate with others in physical play and games

- develop increasing control of fine movements of their fingers and hands

- be safe in movement and in using tools and equipment

The framework is designed to help children move easily on to school. The five categories of the pre-school curriculum lead on through emerging literacy and numeracy to the five to fourteen curriculum. *Emotional, Personal and Social Development* leads to Personal and Social Development and Religious and Moral Education; *Expressive and Aesthetic Development and Physical Development and Movement* lead to Expressive Arts; *Communication and Language and Knowledge and Understanding of the World* lead to English Language, Mathematics, and Environmental Studies.

Baseline Assessment

A new level of assessment was introduced in September 1998 for all children in their first half-term of primary school in England. This is called 'baseline assessment' and is designed to find out how much children already know, understand and can do when they arrive at school. A national pilot scheme was introduced in Wales on a voluntary basis in 1998, prior to is becoming compulsory in 1999, and its introduction is planned for Scotland.

The aim is to help teachers plan most effectively for each child and provide a starting point so the school can monitor how the child is progressing as he or she moves on. It may also help teachers identify any particular learning needs. The school can choose its own way of doing this, as long as the scheme is approved by the Qualifications and Curriculum Authority, but it has to include:

- language and literacy – focusing on children's developing skills in talking, listening, reading and writing;

- mathematics – looking at understanding of numbers and use of mathematical language;

- personal and social development – assessing children's ability to work, play and co-operate with others.

Some schemes also include knowledge and understanding of the world and physical and creative development. The school may also take into account any records passed on from a child's nursery.

Schools are expected to incorporate the assessment into normal school activities so it does not seem like a test, and you can expect to be invited to discuss the assessment afterwards with your child's teacher.

The reason this information appears in a book about pre-school education is because, although it may not seem like a test to pupils, it may to parents. The fact that CD-ROMS based on these assessment subjects are being published, and that government literature advises parents not to prepare children for the assessment, indicates that they all expect some parents to want to do just that with their pre-school children. Nurseries may come under pressure to prepare children for this just as they are coming to terms with delivering 'desirable outcomes'.

Parents who do prepare their children may be defeating the object. If a child is crammed full of information to 'do well' in the assessment he or she may appear to need less help than his or her school mates and may also become bored covering ground that less 'prepared' children need to cover. At worse, if children gain any impression from their parents that primary school is a place at which to succeed or fail at this young age, their first experience could be one of trepidation, rather than excitement at all the new opportunities on offer. This is far more likely to affect their long-term attitude towards learning, and therefore their success at school, than whether they outshine fellow pupils at the age of nearly five.

Section Two

What You Want For Your Child

Defining Your Priorities

A huge amount of research has been carried out into early childhood education, so you might think it would be possible to say with scientific certainty what is best for young children. However, if you are already a parent you will probably have agonised over plenty of 'well researched' scientific subjects already, so you will be aware that science is seldom as scientific as it seems when it comes to providing answers to seemingly straightforward questions.

In this case there is evidence to support a whole range of theories that often conflict and sometimes sound simply bizarre.

There is evidence of babies being taught to recognise their letters before six months, but also that children are not capable of focusing their eyes sufficiently to read easily until they are around seven; that early formal education can damage enthusiasm for learning – and that it doesn't. There is even evidence that spinning children around can help the connections in their brains.

Educational thought is also subject to fashion as one theory becomes dominant, then seems to go too far and be replaced by a swing in the other direction. In the sixties there was a move towards 'child-centred learning' on the basis that each child was an individual and that streaming and other assessments sent unhelpful messages of failure to a large number of children. The idea was that children should not be taught in whole classes but 'facilitated' to learn by their own co-operative discovery. These ideas had already been pioneered successfully by educators such as Maria Montessori. However, where they were applied wholesale to the state sector, problems arose and basic skills such as reading and writing appeared to suffer.

The backlash has meant the introduction of prescribed activities at all levels of schooling from the National Curriculum to the 'desirable outcomes of children's learning' at age four, with formal 'literacy hours' at primary schools and an emphasis on whole-class teaching and the phonics approach to reading (i.e. learning sounds and then how to put them together in words).

In the same way, mothers have been told (on the basis of 'research') that their children will be 'damaged' if they don't stay at home and look after them, and also that they will lose out if they are not sent off to nursery.

The truth is that research is usually undertaken in specific circumstances – in order to deal with a problem, such as crime for example, or to try out a theory. Whether one approach is 'better' than others has to be judged against what it is trying to achieve.

Children emerge as successful confident adults from a variety of starting places. Your child is an individual with his or her own needs, and probably part of a family with its own requirements. You are in as good a position as anyone to decide what those are, and by sitting down and thinking them through carefully, you are far more likely to end up with a successful arrangement that suits you.

Creating a Checklist

The tick boxes below should help you focus on the most important factors to you and eliminate some types of education and care before you get too embroiled in the detail. You can also use this section to help you choose between individual providers later on. Some considerations will be absolute, such as the amount of day care provided if you are working, or the cost if you are on a tight budget, others will be very important and some less so. The most effective way of using this section is to grade your answers. You may choose an 'x' to mark an absolute, for example, and then have a priority system of one to five (choose five as the most important). Any categories that do not apply, strike out, any other factors add in.

Age of child/children   Under two ☐   two-and-a-half to four ☐   four to five ☐

Work-day cover   Full-time childcare all year round ☐

Flexible childcare ☐

Term-time care only ☐

Limited sessions ☐

Reliability (no unexpected withdrawal of cover) ☐

Location   Near to home ☐

Near to work ☐

Cost   Must be free ☐

Maximum of _____

Should be covered by allowance in benefits ☐

Should accept government's Nursery Education Grant ☐

Benefits to child   Socializing with other children ☐

Access to space, materials and equipment ☐

Family-style care ☐

Sense of being part of local community ☐

Continuity of care ☐

An individual relationship with single carer ☐

Not dependent on trusting unmonitored carer ☐

Qualified carers/educators ☐

Regulated and inspected by local authority ☐

Provides strong academic start ☐

Works towards 'desirable outcomes for children's learning' ☐

(This is the government's pre-school curriculum designed to lead into the National Curriculum – more information p 5–15)

(see pages 5–15)

High staff/child ratio ☐

Emphasis on protecting/enjoying childhood ☐

Day-to-day parental involvement ☐

Special needs of any kind

Particular diet ☐

Long-term medication ☐

Wheelchair access ☐

Physical disability ☐

Special educational needs ☐

Other considerations:

_____ ☐

_____ ☐

_____ ☐

If you have completed this section, you should have a list of priorities that you can use to fill in the chart on the next page, or create your own if your priorities are very different.

The right hand column of the chart allows you to score each priority (for example, you may have decided that cost is a '5' priority so that goes in the box, whereas you have decided that the desirable outcomes deserve only a '1').

All the types of pre-school education and care listed in the next section of this book have a summary panel at the beginning of the entry with a guide to the age at which children are generally accepted, the hours usually offered, an indication of costs (although these tend to vary considerably across the country), who the inspecting authority is where appropriate, and whether the sector is likely to be part of the nursery education scheme. This should allow you to identify at a glance some providers who fail to meet your 'absolute' requirements. Cross these off your chart.

What you want, compared with what there is

	Day nursery	Nursery school	High/ Scope	Montessori	Steiner Waldorf	Nursery unit (state primary school)	Nursery unit (independent school)	Pre-school (playgroup)	Nanny	Childminder	Priority
Flexibility											
Reliability											
Cost											
Socializing with other children											
Access to space, materials and equipment											
Family-style care											
An individual relationship with single carer											
Qualifications											
Regulated and inspected by local authority											
Provides strong academic start											
Works towards 'desirable outcomes'											
High staff/child ratio											
Parental involvement											
Special educational needs											
Total											
Essentials (eg, take child of 18 months)											

As you read more about the different types of care, you can add a score for the extent to which each meets your needs. A low score means it is not very satisfactory, so against 'cost' a day nursery may score only '2' if you feel it is expensive, but may score '4' for delivering the desirable outcomes. If you added up the scores for a day nursery without reference to your priorities, you could end up with a high score that isn't appropriate to what you want for your child. The priorities column balances this out by reminding you that cost was very important and desirable outcomes weren't.

(If you enjoy numbers, you could multiply the score box with the priority box: so cost 2 x its priority 5, would give you 10; desirable outcomes 4 x priority 1, would give you 4. A total of 14. A childminder who scored 4 on cost but only 0 on desirable outcomes, would score 4 x 5 = 20 plus 0, a total of 20, indicating that, according to your own priorities, a childminder might be more suitable. However, this may sound more scientific than it is, and the numbers are only to give you a rough guide.)

One final point – putting numbers in boxes can never deal with the less practical but equally real concerns you may have. If a particular approach seems right for your child, you may be prepared to accept all sorts of inconveniences, and learning about it may change your priorities. That's fine. The purpose of this book is not to create a neat and interesting chart, but for you to consider what you want, learn about what's available and come to your own conclusions.

Section Three

What There Is

Private Nursery Schools

Age from	Open	Cost	Regulated	Nursery Scheme
c3	Term time	From c£400 per term	Social services	✓

(Please note: this panel is a rough guide for quick reference. Costs in particular can vary considerably across the country and between individual providers. 'Nursery Scheme' also covers Pre-school Year in Scotland.)

By far the largest number of free-standing nursery schools are privately run. They are generally open for the length of the school day during term time and provide places to children from around three to five.

What they teach

(see p.5)

Most nursery schools are part of the government's nursery education scheme and must therefore provide access to the Desirable Outcomes for Children's Learning. (The equivalent is the Pre-school Year scheme in Scotland where nurseries must offer the Pre-school Curriculum Framework – see p 5 for more detail.)

Each school should have a clear plan of how it intends to deliver each part of the curriculum. For example, they may teach mathematics through rhymes and counting games, or include sorting and matching objects, and recognising patterns. They may approach language and literacy through sharing and even learning stories, or they may use a formal reading scheme such as Letterland or Finger Phonics.

Schools that are part of this scheme are inspected regularly by Ofsted (OHCI in Wales) and reports are publicly available on how well they are delivering the 'Desirable Outcomes'. Nurseries that are part of the similar Scottish scheme are inspected by HMI which also makes all reports publicly available.

(see p.11)

A recent survey by Ofsted (see p 11) put private nursery schools second only to nursery departments of independent schools for the emphasis they gave to language and literacy and mathematics. This reflects their tendency to stress traditional 'academic' subjects.

All private nursery schools also have to be registered with, and inspected by, the social services department (social work department in Scotland) of their local authority. This department checks that staff are properly qualified, have had no convictions that make them unsuitable for work with children and that there are enough staff for the number of children. They also enforce space requirements, health and safety standards and check that there is a good balance of activities on offer.

Nursery schools must have classes of no more than 26 children. The person in charge of the school must have a Teaching Certificate and the nursery assistant must also hold an appropriate qualification.

Staff ratio

There must be two members of staff to every 20 children, or to 26 if the head doesn't teach and is excluded from the ratio. Some will have better staff ratios than this. The social services department may also require a higher staff ratio when children with disabilities or special needs are being cared for.

Other requirements include having written policies covering key issues such as health and safety, discipline, complaints, record keeping, equal opportunities and special needs.

Inspections take place annually. Inspectors are looking for adequate space and staffing, a suitable range of books and play equipment for imaginative, creative, messy and physical play. They will also expect staff to show that they plan a balance of activities for children. (See p 72 for the sort of report these inspections produce.)

(see p.72)

Some nursery schools have only 'sessional' registration, however, which means they cannot offer more than four hours continuous care. Children can attend either morning or afternoon sessions but cannot continue from a morning to afternoon session without a break away from the school.

The staff and space requirements are the same for sessional nurseries but other requirements such as meals, rest areas for children and so on are less stringent because of the far shorter time spent at nursery.

Moving on

In some areas, private nurseries have suffered because of the development of nursery classes attached to primary schools, in others, the government's Nursery Education Grant has provided a significant boost in areas where there is no state provision.

If you live in an area where there is a choice, it may seem preferable for your child to attend a nursery class at the primary school you have chosen so he or she can make lasting friendships, but, especially in rural areas, it may also be the case that many of the children from any one private nursery school will go on to attend the same primary school.

Most nursery schools also prepare children for future schooling in either the private or state sectors, so may suit you if you want to keep your options open at this stage.

Under the Nursery Education or Pre-school schemes, each child's progress should be recorded by staff and a portfolio of work collected so this can be passed onto the child's primary school where ever it is if the parent approves.

Special needs

What is on offer for children with special needs depends on the individual nursery, but nurseries accepting the government's Nursery Education Grant, and which have suitable facilities, have to look on applications from children with special educational needs as favourably as any other applications. Your local authority may also be able to support your child in attending the nursery of your choice. (See pp 108, 110.)

(see pages 108, 110)

The High/Scope Approach

Age from	Open	Cost	Regulated	Nursery Scheme
3 years or *c*6 weeks	Term time or full day care	Depends on type of care	Social services	✓

(Please note: this panel is a rough guide for quick reference. Costs in particular can vary considerably across the country and between individual providers. 'Nursery Scheme' also covers Pre-school Year in Scotland.)

The High/Scope Educational Research Foundation in Michigan gained international media attention when it published its long-term study of the effects of high quality pre-school education. The news that it dramatically cut crime rates among the under-privileged group studied and provided a considerable net gain in terms of the cost to the state, made headlines and affected government policies around the world. The UK now has its own High/Scope Institute and more than a hundred trainers. The High/Scope approach can be found in private nursery schools, day nurseries and state run nursery classes.

Research

The research studied the lives of 123 African Americans born in poverty and statistically at a high risk of failing at school. At ages three and four they were divided into one group which received the pre-school programme and another group which received none. Ninety-five per cent of the original participants were then contacted at the age of 27 and interviewed. Further information about them was gained from school, social services and arrest records.

By then, 7% of the pre-school education group had been arrested five or more times compared with 35% of the other group, 7% were arrested for drug dealing, compared with 25% of the other group.

They were also better paid, with 29% earning $2000 or more a month (1992) compared with 7% of the group without the pre-school education. Almost three times as many owned their own homes and more than twice as many owned second cars.

They did better all the way through school, gaining significantly higher achievement scores at 14 and literacy scores at 19. Seventy one per cent graduated from high school or gained certification compared with 54% for the other group.

The men also stayed married for nearly twice as long as the group without pre-school education and five times as many of the women were married when interviewed. Fifty-seven per cent of these women's children were born out of wedlock, compared with 83% for the other women.

An analysis of the saving that would have been made from welfare, schooling, the justice system, crime victims and the recuperation of taxes on higher earnings, compared with the cost of providing the pre-school programme put the return at seven dollars and sixteen cents for every dollar invested.

Approach

The emphasis of the High/Scope approach is on 'active learning' and the aim is to produce children who are decision makers and problem solvers; who can plan, initiate, and reflect on work chosen by themselves; work effectively individually, with other children and with adults; and develop skills and traits that enable them to become successful students in later education.

To achieve these aims, High/Scope says children need to act on their own innate desire to explore; ask and search for answers to questions about people, materials, events and ideas that arouse their curiosity; and solve problems that stand in the way of their goals and generate new strategies.

There is a strong belief in training and the involvement of parents, so that adults extend their expectations for the children. Active learning is seen to depend on positive adult-child interaction – adults sharing control with children, focusing on their strengths, forming relationships, supporting children's play and adopting a problem-solving approach to social conflict. The child should be able to express thoughts and feelings confidently and direct conversation. Adults should use encouragement, appreciation and a problem-solving approach rather than a child-management system based on praise, punishment and reward.

The physical setting is seen as having a major impact, so there is a strong emphasis on planning the layout of the nursery and selecting appropriate materials. Play space should be divided into specific interest areas with a plenty of easily accessible materials for children to choose themselves. Storage should be on low shelves, stacking boxes and trays with a variety of labels children can understand so they can find, use and return items themselves.

A consistent but flexible daily routine is important so that young children can anticipate what happens next and have a great deal of control over what they do during each part of the day. An example of the routine in a part-time nursery is given by the Institute as:

9.00	Greeting's circle
9.10	Planning groups
9.25	Work time
10.10	Tidy-up time
10.20	Review groups
10.30	Snack time
10.45	Outside time*
11.00	Small-group time

    11.25   Large-group time

    11.35   Lunch time

* In some settings there may be opportunities for outside time throughout the routine.

Great importance is given to the 'plan-do-review' process. When children express their intentions, whether it is a grunt and a point, a sentence or detailed discussion, High/Scope call it planning. Children are then thoroughly involved in the 'doing.' According to High/Scope, effective development comes about when children are actively involved with people, materials, events and ideas. 'Children need time for trial and error, generating new ideas, practising and succeeding.' Children act on their intentions (or 'do') during their work time.

The High/Scope approach also calls for time to be set aside for children to reflect on their experiences. 'Through this process they begin to match words to their actions and construct memories and insights they will modify as their understanding increases', according to High/Scope. Thus the 'review' element.

Curriculum

The curriculum lists what High/Scope consider 'key experiences' for young children's construction of knowledge.

Creative Representation

- Recognising objects by sight, sound, touch, taste and smell

- Imitating actions and sounds

- Relating models, pictures, and photographs to real places and things

- Pretending and role playing

- Making models out of clay, blocks, and other materials

- Drawing and painting

Language and Literacy

- Talking with others about personally meaningful experiences

- Describing objects, events and relations

- Having fun with language: listening to stories and poems, making up stories and rhymes

- Writing in various ways: drawing, scribbling, letterlike forms, invented spelling, conventional forms

- Reading in various ways: reading storybooks, signs and symbols, one's own writing

- Dictating stories

Initiative and Social Relations

- Making and expressing choices, plans, and decisions
- Solving problems encountered in play
- Taking care of one's own needs
- Expressing feelings in words
- Participating in group routines
- Being sensitive to the feelings, interests, and needs of others
- Building relationships with children and adults
- Creating and experiencing collaborative play
- Dealing with social conflict

Movement

- Moving in nonlocomotor ways (anchored movement: bending, rocking, swinging one's arms)
- Moving in locomotor ways (nonanchored movement: running, jumping, hopping, skipping, marching, climbing)
- Moving with objects
- Expressing creativity in movement
- Describing movement
- Acting upon movement directions
- Feeling and expressing steady beat
- Moving in sequences to a common beat

Music

- Moving to music
- Exploring and identifying sounds
- Exploring the singing voice
- Developing melody
- Singing songs
- Playing simple musical instruments

Classification

- Exploring and describing similarities, differences, and the attributes of things
- Distinguishing and describing shapes
- Sorting and matching
- Using and describing something in several ways
- Holding more than one attribute in mind at a time
- Distinguishing between "some" and "all"
- Describing characteristics something does not possess or what class it does not belong to

Seriation

- Comparing attributes (longer/shorter, bigger/smaller)
- Arranging several things one after another in a series or pattern and describing the relationships (big/bigger/biggest, red/blue/red/blue)
- Fitting one ordered set of objects to another through trial and error (small cup-small saucer/medium cup-medium saucer/big cup-big saucer)

Number

- Comparing the number of things in two sets to determine "more," "fewer," "same number"
- Arranging two sets of objects in one-to-one correspondence
- Counting objects

Shape

- Filling and emptying
- Fitting things together and taking them apart
- Changing the shape and arrangement of objects (wrapping, twisting, stacking, enclosing)
- Observing people, places, and things from different spatial viewpoints
- Experiencing and describing positions, directions, and distances in the play space, building, and neighbourhood
- Interpreting spatial relations in drawings, pictures, and photographs

Time

- Starting and stopping an action on signal
- Experiencing and describing rates of movement
- Experiencing and comparing time intervals
- Anticipating, remembering, and describing sequences of events

The curriculum is pretty much in line with the government's Desirable Outcomes For Children's Learning (Curriculum Framework in Scotland) (see p 5), so you could expect a nursery or group offering the High/Scope approach to be registered to accept Nursery Education/Pre-school Year Grant for four-year olds.

Quality/training

At present, the High/Scope Institute accredits people rather than nurseries or pre-school groups. Staff who have successfully completed its Curriculum Implementation Course (which takes six full days of training generally over six months or a year) can then have an evaluation visit at their nursery/group. If the curriculum is being implemented satisfactorily, they will be accredited and the nursery can say it is using the High/Scope approach. The Institute expects to introduce a second part to the course in 1999. This part will be optional but will qualify those who successfully complete it to train others within their own nursery.

The Institute also offers a Training of Trainers Course that involves 35 days of intensive training, generally organised as seven weeks over an eight month period. Those who successfully complete it will be endorsed by High/Scope to train other staff.

There are plans to introduce a system of evaluation that will accredit particular nurseries or groups. Initially the institute will identify around 20 that can demonstrate best practice. Progress is already being made towards setting the criteria for accreditation, so it may soon be possible to identify accredited High/Scope providers.

Special needs

High/Scope created their approach in response to the special social needs of a group of children. Because the trainers, rather than the nurseries, are accredited by High/Scope, however, the ability to take children with special needs will depend on what the needs are and the nature of the nursery, although those nurseries accepting the government's Nursery Education Grant must look on applications from children with special needs equally favourably where they have suitable facilities. Your local authority may also be able to support your child in attending the nursery of your choice. See pp 108, 110.

(see pages 108, 110)

Montessori Nurseries

Age from	Open	Cost	Regulated	Nursery Scheme
c2½	Term time or full day care	From c£400 per term	Social services	✓

(Please note: this panel is a rough guide for quick reference. Costs in particular can vary considerably across the country and between individual providers. 'Nursery Scheme' also covers Pre-school Year in Scotland.)

There are hundreds of nursery schools and some day nurseries across Great Britain and worldwide operating under the Montessori name. They claim to follow the educational principles established by Italy's first female doctor of medicine, Maria Montessori, who first set up a nursery for slum children in 1907.

Dr Montessori saw her method as a response to a child's natural inclination to work and learn. The emphasis was and is on respect for the individual child, and on creating a physical environment and social structure where a child can learn independently under the guidance of a trained adult. This adult is known as a director or directress, rather than a teacher, to reflect the role of directing a child's exploration of subjects, rather than teaching information.

A great deal of importance is placed on the child's physical surroundings – even down to the correct height for shelving – and on equipment which the child learns through manipulating in order to solve problems (for example, specially-designed Montessori rods that allow young children to work with very high numbers).

According to the Association Montessori Internationale, which was set up by Dr Montessori to continue her work: 'Montessori classrooms provide a prepared environment where children are free to respond to their natural tendency to work. The children's innate passion for learning is encouraged by giving them opportunities to engage in spontaneous, purposeful activities with the guidance of a trained adult. Through their work, the children develop concentration and joyful self-discipline. Within a framework of order, the children progress at their own pace and rhythm, according to their individual capabilities.'

Maria Montessori saw the transformation of children from birth to adulthood as occurring through a series of developmental planes, each lasting six years. In the first six years, children are described as: 'sensorial explorers, constructing their intellects by absorbing every aspect of their environment, language and culture' – hence the importance of creating a suitable physical environment and using equipment that can be touched and seen, rather than purely verbal information. This extends to the 'graceful walk' expected of class directors and the gentle voices they are expected to use with the children.

From aged three to six, she described children as possessing 'the absorbent mind'. She believed that in these years only was the child's mind able to absorb all aspects of the environment – physical, mental and spiritual – without effort or fatigue.

Most Montessori schools in Great Britain take children of roughly this age, usually from around two-and-a-half to six, classified as Casa dei Bambini (which simply means 'baby house'). The philosophy covers the whole of a child's development from birth to adulthood at 24, however, and there are an increasing number of schools opening worldwide for children at the next stage, from six to twelve.

Special needs

(see pages 108, 110)

The concentration on the abilities of an individual child mean children with special needs may well be accommodated but, as with all nurseries, it will depend on the needs and the facilities of the individual school. (See pp 108, 110) for how your local authority may be able to help your child attend the nursery of your choice.)

Curriculum

Children aged around three to six could expect to experience a broad array of subjects – bearing in mind that children choose their own activities from the range on offer. All the subjects are offered using a range of senses, touching, seeing, smelling, tasting, listening, and where appropriate, are aided by the use of specially-designed materials.

Practical life

Activities include many of the tasks that children are used to seeing (and sometimes taking part in) at home – washing and ironing, doing the dishes, etc. Children are expected to learn 'to interact convivially and with grace and courtesy'. They are expected to develop muscular co-ordination, learn to work at a task from beginning to end, and develop their will, self-discipline and concentration.

Language

Children should experience 'rich and precise' language in their Montessori environment. The idea is that children will become aware of the properties of language by being allowed to discover and explore these for themselves, rather than being taught. This sounds very laissez-faire, but expectations for achievement are high. Children are expected to learn to write and, as a consequence to read '... never remembering the day they could not write or read in the same way that they do not remember that once upon a time they could not walk'.

Geography, history, biology, botany, zoology, art and music

These are seen as extensions of sensory and language activities. The aims are spiritual as well as educational. Children learn about other cultures past and present in order to encourage an innate respect and love for the environment and create a sense of solidarity with the rest of humanity. Experiences with nature are designed to inspire a reverence for life.

Mathematics

Materials are used to help children understand abstract mathematical concepts.

Quality

Anyone can open a nursery and give it the Montessori name, whether they adhere to the philosophy and methods wholeheartedly, or have hardly heard of them. In many areas the Montessori name carries weight and could lend credibility to a commercial venture with little else to recommend it.

The Association Montessori Internationale therefore operates an approvals system. Here, this operates through Montessori Education UK. Schools approach the organisation for accreditation, and are inspected by trained assessors with a minimum of five-years experience. A list of schools that have been accredited can be found on pp 243, 244. As accreditation is taking place all the time, addresses of more accredited schools can be obtained from the organisation by sending a stamped addressed envelope to: Montessori Education UK, 21, Vineyard Hill, London SW19 7JL.

(see pages 243, 244)

It takes some time to get assessors out to schools, so some may not be on the list because they are awaiting assessment, or for other reasons not associated with being 'sub-standard'.

Another check point is the qualification of the director/directress. Diplomas are awarded by the AMI and its authorised institutions worldwide. This is simply called an AMI Diploma and should be for an appropriate age group. The Maria Montessori Training Organisation, 26 Lyndhurst Gardens, London NW3 5NW, is the affiliated training centre in the UK, but staff could receive the same level of training at approved institutes worldwide. The AMI diploma takes an academic year to complete full time.

The Montessori Society has also produced a list of questions to help parents check schools for themselves. It follows:

The environment
- Is the room attractive?
- Are the materials in good condition?
- Are the materials visible and easily accessible to the children?
- Does the room seems orderly and well-cared for?

The adults

- Are they comfortable and relaxed?

- Do they speak softly and gently to the children?

- Do they move slowly and gracefully?

- Do they respond appropriately to the children?

- Do they treat the children with respect and courtesy?

- Do the children obey instructions cheerfully and readily?

The children

- Do they choose their own activities?

- Do they show periods of intense involvement with their work?

- Do they handle materials carefully and replace them after use?

- Do they work on their own or in small groups?

- Do they show initiative?

- Are they able to solve their problems for themselves?

- Do they work harmoniously and co-operate with one another?

- Do they ask for help when they need it?

- Do they seem to be happy in the school?

The answers should be 'yes'.

Finally, however, if a school calls itself a Montessori nursery but meets few of the criteria, it may still be a perfectly good nursery school for parents who are not committed to the Montessori approach. Some schools may even have developed away from these principles to meet the demands of local parents. Such a nursery might still be worth considering but would have to be assessed alongside other nursery schools in the area.

Steiner Waldorf Schools

Age from	Open	Cost	Regulated	Nursery Scheme
c3^1/$_2$	Term time	From c£400 per term (some bursaries)	Social services/ DFEE/HMI*	not yet

(Please note: this panel is a rough guide for quick reference. Costs in particular can vary considerably across the country and between individual providers. 'Nursery Scheme' also covers Pre-school Year in Scotland.)

* DFEE: Department for Education and Employment; HMI: Her Majesty's Inspectors of Schools

Austrian philosopher and educationalist, Rudolph Steiner, opened his first school in 1919. The school was for children of workers at the Waldorf-Astoria cigarette factory in Stuttgart, and was opened at the request of its owner. Now there are more than 730 Steiner Waldorf Schools worldwide, including around 40 kindergartens across the UK.

Kindergartens generally take children from three-and-a-half to six, although many have playgroups attached to them for children from two-and-a-half. These lead on to lower schools from around six to 14 and upper school from 14 to around 19.

The stated aim of a Steiner education is 'to produce individuals who are able, in and of themselves, to impart meaning to their lives', educating the whole child, 'head, heart and hands'.

The emphasis of the philosophy is on the value of childhood and the importance of an education that is appropriate to a child's development. Education is to develop the potential of the individual child, rather than to fulfil economic or governmental requirements.

Rudloph Steiner summed this up: 'We shouldn't ask: what does a person need to know or be able to do in order to fit into the existing social order? Instead we should ask: what lives in each human being and what can be developed in him or her? Only then will it be possible to direct the new qualities of each emerging generation into society. Society will then become what young people as whole human beings, make out of the existing social conditions. The new generation should not just be made to be what present society wants it to become!'

The schools follow the belief that contemporary life puts pressure on children to grow up as quickly as possible, 'fast-tracking' them past the full benefits of each stage of development. There is no 'academic' content to activities in kindergarten but the children learn through imitation, play and creative expression.

Curriculum

Each school is expected to be involved with its local community and respond to the needs of children and parents, so no two schools would expect to share an identical curriculum. They would share the same educational philosophy and beliefs about child development, however, so teaching for different age groups is likely to be quite similar.

An emphasis on languages extends to the kindergartens where French and German are often experienced by the children through songs and rhymes. Activities would include lots of creative play, painting, drawing, modelling, crafts, singing, listening to stories, puppet plays, baking, woodwork, gardening, caring for the home and 'eurhythmy'. This latter is a feature of all Steiner schools and is a form of dance-like movement that is used to express music and speech – specific movements corresponding to notes or sound. The idea is to improve co-ordination and strengthen the ability to listen.

A close relationship with nature and the seasons, expressed through the celebration of seasonal festivals, is also a feature of the schools. Stories, verse and artistic activities are related to the seasons. The oral tradition is valued and traditional fairy tales and ring games are used in kindergartens with songs, stories and poems learnt by heart.

Parental involvement is encouraged, and the relationship with the teacher is a key aspect for the child in the early years. Once a child goes into a lower school at around six until he or she is 14, he or she would expect (ideally) to be taught by the same class teacher throughout.

Television is considered generally undesirable for young children, taking them away from the real world and quashing their imaginations. Computer use is also discouraged.

The belief that childhood should not be rushed, leads to the most controversial aspect of a Steiner Waldorf education – the introduction of formal academic studies later than traditional schools. Children are not taught to read until they are seven or eight, although writing is taught first and letters are introduced when they are six. Children do not use text books until they are around eleven, although they create their own workbook once they are six, which expresses what they learn in their main lessons. GCSEs and A levels are generally taken a year later.

Christopher Clouder, director of the Steiner Waldorf Schools Fellowship, claims that this is an advantage to children going onto traditional higher education both because they gain a love of learning and because they take their exams when they are best able to cope with them developmentally.

He says that at 16 children are generally going through emotional turmoil. By 17 exams are just something else that need to be done and are not such a problem. Those taking A levels at a Steiner school are still learning a broad range of subjects as well. He says that universities appreciate the extra year of maturity, the wish to learn that a Steiner education instils, and the ability to take responsibility.

Moving on

This is, of course, a long way to be thinking ahead when you are making decisions for a pre-school child, but the different pacing of academic studies means transfer to a state or standard independent school at some points can be problematic. From kindergarten to a primary school at five shouldn't be, but at six, when the Steiner kindergarten years run out, the child could be a year behind his or her new classmates in reading. Transferring during any of the first four grades of a Steiner lower school is recognised as potentially problematic because of this, although by the time a child is ready for a state high school he or she could expect to transfer without significant difficulties.

Special needs

The ability to take children with particular special needs depends on the particular kindergarten or school and its particular staff, so it is worth asking. Children with severe behavioural difficulties can only be catered for in Steiner special schools, which depend on the referral of the local authority. Severely handicapped children can gain a Steiner education within Camphill communities where children and staff live side by side. These are separate operations to the mainstream Steiner schools and kindergartens.

Quality

Rudolph Steiner Waldorf schools, unlike Montessori, are guarded by a copyright on the name. This is held by the Steiner Waldorf Schools Fellowship, which holds lists of member schools (fully-approved) and developing schools, which don't quite meet all the standards of the member schools but are working towards them. These schools may be ones that have been established more recently. Other schools, described as 'initiatives', are in the early stages of working towards recognition. All the approved schools listed are vetted by the Fellowship. Because each school is self-governing and should relate to its local community, this process involves advisors spending some time in the schools working with teachers and writing reports.

Both the title Rudolph Steiner Waldorf School and Waldorf or Steiner Education are protected by the copyright, but this still has to be policed nationally, and schools may get round it by calling themselves 'inspired by' Rudolph Steiner. A list of schools approved by the Fellowship can be found in the directory at the back of this book and can be obtained from: Steiner Waldorf Schools Fellowship, Kidbrooke Park, Forest Row, East Sussex RH18 5JA. As schools may pass through the approvals process at any time, do check with the Fellowship if there is not one listed near you.

Each school is run by a college of teachers who meet once a week (there is no head teacher), and a Council of Management (of parents, teachers and an administrator) – which takes legal responsibility for the school as its charitable trust. Each school listed by the Fellowship has to be owned by a charitable trust and cannot run to financially benefit anyone.

Each school has a stated grievance procedure. Any question or complaint about the running of the school is first taken up by the college of teachers. If it can not be dealt with by them, it goes to the Council of Management and finally to the Fellowship.

Kindergarten teachers can take a diploma recognised by the Fellowship and accepted by some social services departments for early-years registration. The diploma can be taken in two years' part-time study with a year's full-time practical element, or in one year full-time including some foundation elements. Teachers of older children would generally have teaching certificates as well as a Steiner Waldorf qualification, with upper-school teachers also expected to be graduates in their own specialties. Degree courses in Steiner education are common in the US and a course for middle-school teachers has just been introduced in Britain at Plymouth University.

Funding

(see page 5)

Steiner schools are state funded in many countries, although not in the UK. However, all kindergartens have been asked by the Fellowship to apply for approval for the Nursery Education (Pre-school Year) Grant. In at least one case this has already been granted. Ofsted inspectors are welcomed in the schools but the kindergartens do not ascribe to the 'desirable outcomes' or aspects of the curriculum framework (see p 5 for an explanation of these), which form a key element of the qualification for receiving the grant.

As this book goes to press, efforts are being made in the House of Lords to extend definitions to include a variety of approaches to pre-school education within the government's funding and inspection strategy. By the time you read this, your local Steiner kindergarten (if you have one) may be able to provide a local authority subsidised place for your child and an Ofsted inspection report – it is worth asking the school.

Finally, the aim of the Steiner Waldorf movement is that children should not miss out because of their parents' inability to pay the fees and in many cases bursaries are available through the school. Sibling discounts are also common.

Pre-schools and Playgroups

Age from	Open	Cost	Regulated	Nursery Scheme
c2^1/$_2$ (for pre-school)	Term time (some day care)	From c£2.50 per session (pre-schools)	Social services	✓

(Please note: this panel is a rough guide for quick reference. Costs in particular can vary considerably across the country and between individual providers. 'Nursery Scheme' also covers Pre-school Year in Scotland.)

The vast majority of all voluntary providers of pre-school education and care are affiliated to the Pre-school Learning Alliance, (formerly known as the Pre-school Playgroups Association). These are mainly pre-schools or playgroups offering five, two-and-a-half-hour sessions a week, but they also include a significant number of parent and toddler groups and some full day-care providers.

The Pre-school Playgroups Association was set up in the early sixties by parents who were running their own groups because of the lack of state nursery provision. The Pre-school Learning Alliance (PLA), as it has become, claim that more children now attend its member groups than any other form of pre-school provision. They are still strongest in rural areas where state nursery provision is limited.

The philosophy that underpins their work is founded on the belief that parental involvement in the education of the pre-school child is vitally important to its success. The stated aim of the PLA is summarised: 'to enhance the development and education of children primarily under statutory school age by encouraging parents to understand and provide for the needs of their children through community groups'.

Included in the PLA's wider aims is: 'the personal development of adults involved in providing for children by means of community groups', which is supported by providing training to 40,000 adults each year, many of them young parents. This reflects the belief that: 'Parents who have come to see themselves as learners create in their children a positive and confident attitude to the world of education', and that parental reinforcement at home of what is leant in the group makes that learning more effective.

The PLA is a charity run by elected volunteers who employ staff. So parents are involved in all aspects of the organisation from national to individual group level. The PLA believes this promotes responsibility to the community as a whole, and many playgroup or pre-school leaders go on to become school governors or councillors. This sense of responsibility is reflected in group fund-raising, which is often expected to provide additional funding and keep fees to parents low.

In Wales, Mudiad Ysgolion Meithrin offers pre-school education in Welsh.

Types of provision

The latest membership survey (1997) showed the type of education and care member groups had to offer.

Pre-schools, playgroups and under-five groups

Generally five sessions a week of two-and-a-half-hours a session for children from around three. Most of the children were under four and the average attendance was three sessions a week. Fees varied across the country and type of group but a rough average per session was around £2.50 (1997), far less than the cost of sending a child to a session at a private nursery school. The highest percentage of these groups was in villages.

Opportunity pre-schools are mainly or solely for children with special educational needs and generally operated on the same basis as other pre-schools.

Full day care

These groups offered an average ten-hour day, five days a week, broken down into two five-hour sessions a day, and most children attended for five sessions a week. Average fees (1997) were £9 per session, which reflects the higher demands made by social services departments on groups registered to provide sessions longer than four hours at a time, and the reduced day-to-day involvement of parental volunteers where working parents are catered for. Most of these groups were in country towns or suburban areas. Full day-care groups usually took children from around six months.

Extended day-care groups tended to provide the same sort of service as full day-care groups. Extended day care simply means that they are registered for sessions more than four-hours long.

Parent and toddler

Parent and toddler groups generally opened for one two-hour session a week only, which meant they did not have to be registered with social services which, in turn, meant they didn't have to be inspected by them.

Quality

All of these groups, other than parent and toddler, have to be registered with the social services department of the local authority and meet their space and staffing requirements. They must also provide an appropriate play curriculum. The number of children in one room must not exceed 26 and there must be one member of staff for every four two-year olds, or eight three or four-year olds. Half of these staff must be qualified.

According to the PLA's 1997 survey, however, there was an average ratio of one to seven children at pre-schools, one to five in under-five groups and almost one to four in full day-care groups.

Pre-schools (which, for this purpose include all the different categories above except parent and toddler groups,) can choose to be accredited by the PLA. If they are, they will be able to display an accreditation certificate. This means, among other things, that they have an adult-child ratio of only one to five.

The accreditation process takes place in three stages, and a certificate is valid for three years. It costs member groups £400.

Stage one is a self-assessment in which the group accumulates written evidence of its standards of practice and compares them with those required by the PLA. This evidence is in the form of policy documents, inventories, newsletters, menus and so on, and written observations of practice and the quality of teaching. (There are nearly 300 aspects of quality that have to be addressed by a full day-care group.) Where the group does not already reach the standards required, action plans have to be drawn up with a schedule for implementation. This self-assessment generally takes between four and nine months.

Stage two involves visits to the group by an independent PLA assessor. This person will check the portfolio of evidence, observe the group in practice and talk with parents and staff to make sure the group lives up to its self-assessment. If there are any areas that need attention, these must be improved on before there is a further visit.

Stage three is the final accreditation by the PLA's national accreditation panel. This panel verifies the work of assessors and monitors standards so that the same are applied consistently throughout the country.

After this, groups are required to report annually in writing to the panel to ensure that standards are being maintained and improved.

Many pre-schools are also registered to receive the Nursery Education (or Pre-school Year) Grant, which means they have to deliver the 'Desirable Outcomes' (or Curriculum Framework in Scotland) (see p 5) and are subject to inspection by Ofsted/OHMCI/HMI.

(see page 5)

Training

The PLA is allowed to grant qualifications under the terms of the Further and Higher Education Act 1992, and courses leading to its qualifications are available through colleges and adult-education centres, as well as through the PLA. Staff working in pre-schools may have these or other relevant qualifications.

The main qualifications on offer from the PLA are:

Diploma in Pre-school Practice – involving 220 hours class time, the same again on assignments and 200 hours work in an early-years setting.

Certificate in Pre-school Practice – requiring 120 hours class time, the same again on assignments and some experience during the course working in an early-years setting.

Experienced Playleader's Course – for people with long experience of pre-school work, it involves 120 hours class time, the same again on assignments and at least 120 hours work in an early-years setting during the course.

Special Needs Certificate – designed for special educational needs co-ordinators and involving 61 guided-learning hours, the same again on assignments and work in an early-years setting while studying.

Despite the PLA providing a wide range of training for members, some pre-schools still struggle to meet their registration requirements of half the staff being qualified.

Private and non-PLA playgroups

Not all playgroups or pre-schools are community-run. A small minority are run by private individuals, although these are seldom run for profit. Not all community playgroups or pre-schools choose to belong to the PLA either, although many will share some aspects of its approach. Those that do not, have to be judged on an individual basis. They still have to be registered with the local authority and meet its criteria for space, staffing and appropriate curriculum, and they still tend to cater for the same age group.

Nursery Units Attached to Schools

Age from	Open	Cost	Regulated	Nursery Scheme
c2¹/₂	Term time	State – free Independent – from c£300 per term	State – LEA Independent – DFEE/HMI	✓

(Please note: this panel is a rough guide for quick reference. Costs in particular can vary considerably across the country and between individual providers. 'Nursery Scheme' also covers Pre-school Year in Scotland.)
* DFEE: Department for Education and Employment; HMI: Her Majesty's Inspectors of Schools

The introduction of the Nursery Education Scheme/Pre-school Year, has led to an increase in the number of state primary schools opening nursery units or classes. There are also a considerable number of nurseries attached to independent schools.

STATE SCHOOLS

Nursery units or classes attached to state schools provide all free places. Some admit children from three but this will depend very much on the school and the education authority which funds it. At present these authorities are only obliged to find places for four-year olds. Hours offered are generally a minimum of five two-and-a-half-hour sessions a week during term time.

Reception classes

(see page 11)

Some schools take children straight into reception classes at four, and this has a received a lot of bad press with accusations that they have grabbed the new money available without providing education and care suitable for such young children. However, a recent report by Ofsted following a survey of 9,900 nursery-education providers (for more detail see p 11) found that their work compared well with traditional nursery schools or playgroups.

Curriculum

(see page 5–15)

Children will be provided with access to the desirable outcomes for children's learning in England and Wales, and the pre-school curriculum framework in Scotland, detailed on p 5–15. This could be provided in a number of ways and not necessarily divided into one outcome or another. Emotional, personal and social development could include role-playing, games, dressing up, or taking turns using equipment that is also improving physical development. Ethnic cookery can support mathematics as well as knowledge of the world. Good nurseries will also allow some time for learning through concentrated activity.

Quality

(see page 72)

(see page 71)

State nursery units/classes are inspected by Ofsted (the Office for Standards in Education) in England and OHMCI (Office of Her Majesty's Chief Inspector) in Wales and HM Inspectors of Schools in Scotland in the same way as schools. Inspection reports have to be made available to parents on request. English reports are also published on the Internet on the Ofsted web site (see p 72), and Scottish reports are available from the appropriate divisional office of the HMI. (For more information on how inspections work and how to understand the reports they produce see p 71.)

Staff ratios/ qualifications

State nursery classes must have two members of staff to 26 children between three and five-years old, or one to 24 children if the head is additional and also teaches. One member of staff has to be a qualified teacher and the other at least a qualified nursery assistant.

Moving on

The primary school that you want your child to attend is bound to be a major consideration when you look at nursery classes or units attached to schools. Your child will probably spend a year in a nursery unit part-time, compared with around six or seven years full-time in his or her next stage of education. If the primary of your choice has a nursery class, that does not mean you should feel pressured to send your child there when you would rather have him or her at home or in some other form of childcare. However, if a nursery class appeals to you, then there will be obvious advantages to applying for the one at your chosen school. The nursery's way of doing things will fit in with the school's way and your child will have the chance to meet others who will be going on to the same school.

Applications

Applications can be made directly to the nursery in England and Wales, so you can have several applications open at once. This may give you some breathing space while you have a look around and make your choice, and allow you a fall back if your first choice is not available. Many nurseries keep lists of interested parents, but these do not operate as priority waiting lists. If someone applies later than you but lives nearer to the nursery or meets some of the nursery's other criteria, then that person will be given priority.

In Scotland, parents should apply direct to their local authority for their child's pre-school year place, regardless of the type of place they are looking for, as long as it is to be wholly or partly funded by the Pre-school Year Grant. If you want a place with additional hours of childcare (for example, a place in a private day nursery), you should let the authority know and they will try and arrange this. In some parts of Scotland there are also centres where Gaelic is spoken.

Admissions policy

The government is committed to providing a nursery or reception-class place for all four-year olds, but in doing this through a full range of private and voluntary providers as well as state nursery classes. Local education authorities (LEAs) have a responsibility to ensure that children are matched to places that best meet their needs. However, in England and Wales, the authority may leave it entirely up to individual heads to allocate places, getting involved only if parents complain that places have been allocated unfairly or outside the stated admissions policy of the school.

Nurseries are encouraged to give priority to children with special educational needs and to those from socially and economically-deprived families. Other considerations may be how close the child lives to the school, and whether brothers and sisters have places.

Because nursery children are under statutory school age, LEAs are not obliged to have an appeals procedure for parents whose children are not given places in the nursery of their choice.

INDEPENDENT SCHOOLS

Of the schools affiliated to the Independent Schools Information Service (ISIS) throughout the UK, 849 currently offer nursery places. They are generally part of all-age schools that take children from two or three to 16 or 18, or of pre-preparatory schools that take them from two or three to seven. Pre-preparatory schools are often attached to preparatory or junior schools that take children from seven to eleven or 13.

The appeal of independent schools is generally their concentration on academic success and their frequent ability to offer smaller classes in good, well-equipped classrooms. That doesn't mean that two-year olds are expected to take formal lessons, but that expectations are high and that they are taught within a framework geared to academic achievement.

A survey of junior/preparatory schools in 1996 showed that significantly more pupils reached higher levels than the national average in English, mathematics and science at key stage-two tests for eleven-year olds. However, this does not allow for the fact that many independent schools select their pupils for academic ability in the first place. Staff ratios are likely to be higher, but staff may not be any better qualified than those in the state sector.

(see page 11)
A recent report by Ofsted (see p 11) indicates that planning an appropriate range of activities in the six areas of learning covered by the government's desirable outcomes, and assessing children's progress, is most comprehensive and detailed in independent schools. They also scored well on the organisational aspects of providing the curriculum, and on planning for language, literacy and mathematics.

(see page 5)
Many independent schools are registered to accept the government's Nursery Education (Pre-school Year) Grant for four-year olds, which means they have to provide access to the Desirable Outcomes for Children's Learning (or Curriculum Framework in Scotland) (p 5) and are inspected by Ofsted, OHMCI, or HMI.

There are also some specialist independent schools with nurseries for children with special needs or particular talents or which provide a particular religious education or follow a particular philosophy. Some Waldorf Steiner nurseries are part of independent Steiner schools, for example.

Quality

Independent schools in Scotland have always been inspected by HMI in the same way as the state schools. In England and Wales, however, if schools have 'Accredited by the Independent Schools Joint Council' (ISJC) in their literature, they have signed up for a voluntary inspection system and been subject to inspections every ten years lasting two-

and-a-half days by inspectors working for the ISJC. Schools are evaluated in relation to their: aims, administration, organisation and management, curriculum, staffing, premises, resources, quality of teaching and learning, assessment of pupils, recording and reporting of progress.

Discussions are currently underway to create an inspections service that would satisfy Ofsted without a separate inspection taking place. This is unlikely to happen before 2000 however.

Moving on

A key factor if you are considering a nursery attached to a private school is the sort of education you want for your child later on. There is nothing to stop you from sending your child to a pre-preparatory school until he or she is five and moving him or her into the state sector. However, five is not such a natural breaking point in the private system, with pre-preparatory schools taking children until they are seven, and all-age schools geared up for children staying in the private system. Nurseries attached to schools are integral to the school system, so changing from a nursery attached to one school to a different primary school can be difficult enough, but changing from the private to the state system at the same time could add its own problems on top. If this is what you want to do, it would be even more important to visit and appreciate how a state primary school operates before you are committed to the independent school nursery.

Financial planning

If you are considering putting your child through a full independent school education, then financial planning may be needed well before he or she is due to start even nursery school. A lump sum put into trust before your child's first birthday could reduce the cost by up to 50% compared with paying as you go. Some independent financial advisers specialise in this market and it pays to seek advice as early as possible.

Admissions

Many schools operate waiting lists for nursery places and some are selective even at this stage. Three-year olds can be asked to undertake assessments away from parents where they may be asked to identify their name from a list of similar ones, count, or carry out other tasks of a semi-academic nature more or less appropriate to their age. This is by no means the general approach however, and each school will have its own policy. Applications are generally made at least a year before the child is due to start.

EARLY EXCELLENCE CENTRES

Early Excellence Centres are being opened around the country as part of a government pilot project to combine pre-school education with day care and family services. There are 25 planned by the year 2000. As well as combining services to parents, the new centres have a role in training others who work with pre-school-age children.

The centres work on the principle outlined by the Department for Education and Employment: 'The government believes that in practice the provision of care and educa-tion are part of the same package ...' (*Nursery Education News*, News Sheet, March 1998). They involve the public, private and voluntary sectors working together to provide childcare, early education, family services and easy access to agencies working in health, training, and other specialist areas.

One of the first of these to be announced was the Pen Green Centre in Corby. It provides nursery education and childcare, out-of-school services including a homework club and youth club, training in parenting skills and family literacy and helps in the training of others who work with young children. These are the types of services that all the centres will aim to offer, but to a greater or lesser degree and appropriate to their communities.

The eleven centres that have been established so far are:

The ACE Centre, Chipping Norton, Oxon

Ashbrow Infant and Nursery School, Kirklees

Bridgwater College Children's Centre, Somerset

Coquet Early Years Centre, Amble, Northumberland

Dorothy Gardner Centre, Westminster

Ganneys Meadow Nursery School/Woodchurch Family Centre, Wirral

Hillfields Nursery Centre, Coventry

Pembury House and Woodlands Park Centres (working together), Haringey

Pen Green Centre, Corby, Northants

Reddish Vale Nursery School, Stockport

White City Early Years Centre, Hammersmith

However, more are being announced all the time. Your LEA should have information on any in your area.

Day Nurseries

Age from	Open	Cost	Regulated	Nursery Scheme
c6 weeks	All day, all year	From c£110 a week (more for babies)	Social services	✓

(Please note: this panel is a rough guide for quick reference. Costs in particular can vary considerably across the country and between individual providers. 'Nursery Scheme' also covers Pre-school Year in Scotland.)

Most day nurseries provide all-day, all-year-round care for the children of working parents, although a minority do shut during some school holidays.

Some take children from around six-weeks old, while others won't accept children under two. The staff ratio required is higher for babies and this makes it difficult for nurseries to break even on baby places. However, competition from state nursery units in schools for four to five-year olds and demand from mothers who wish to return to work after maternity leave, have encouraged an increasing number to open baby rooms.

Hours vary, with some opening for breakfast before eight o'clock and many staying open until around six. A few also offer a before and after-school service for older children. The day tends to be split into two or three sessions and charges are usually per session with a period of notice required. Some nurseries incorporate charges for meals in the fee per session where provided, others quote it as an additional cost. Many will cater for particular diets or allergies. Where nurseries are open long hours, they have to provide suitable meals, including a cooked lunch.

Nurseries vary in what they will provide. Many require items such as nappies, toothpaste, creams and lotions to be supplied by the parents. This can make a significant difference to the cost. Some will launder clothes that have become dirty during the day, although many will simply rinse items that are unhygienic and return dirty clothes with the child.

Some day nurseries are run by local authorities and voluntary organisations, although places are often restricted to parents on low incomes. Some are run by employers for their workforce, but most are run by private companies or individuals.

Unless they are run by a school – which is rare – all day nurseries have to register with their local authority social services department and are inspected annually. Parents should be informed about inspections and can ask to see the report.

There are strict national guidelines covering minimum staff ratios which are: children under two – three per adult; two-year olds – four per adult; three and four-year olds – eight per adult. No room may hold more than six babies under one-year old and no room may have more than 26 children in it.

As numbers of children tend to fluctuate, nurseries have to cope with the ratios either by employing casual staff for peaks or by keeping a level of staff higher than is always needed.

(see page 115)

At least half the staff on duty have to be qualified and national statistics indicate that around 61% of all nursery staff have a relevant qualification. (See p 115 for what the qualifications mean.) Acceptable qualifications depend on the position held. The nursery manager would be expected to have an NNEB or equivalent; a supervisor a qualification roughly equivalent to NVQ/SVQ level 3; and a nursery assistant NVQ/SVQ level 2.

A usual staff structure in a day nursery, depending on its size, would be a nursery manager, an officer in charge of each room in the nursery, and nursery assistants. You could expect a 'key worker' to be identified for your child, and that member of staff should always be able to discuss your child's daily activities and progress with you.

Social services inspectors check that day nurseries meet requirements for health, safety and adequate space, and also provide a suitable range of books and play equipment for imaginative, creative and messy play. They will also expect nurseries to show that they plan a balance of activities for children.

Nurseries have a series of written policies. Along with formal requirements, such as proper recording of children's attendance, child protection and health and safety policies, these often cover issues such as discipline, sickness (including which illnesses children will be excluded for and for how long) and what medicines will be administered. Their attitude towards the last two can vary considerably.

Nurseries largely take guidance from the Centre for Communicable Diseases and from doctors about particular childhood diseases such as chicken pox, measles, rubella and a huge list of others, all of which have their own isolation periods when children are barred from nursery. However, they have very different attitudes towards colds, head lice, and other minor ailments. They also have different approaches to non-infectious illness. It may be left entirely to the discretion of staff whether a child is thought too ill to benefit from nursery, or there may be other rules such as no children on a course of antibiotics, regardless of the condition that made them necessary.

Some nurseries will give prescribed medicines as long as you give written permission, others won't. Some will in some circumstances – such as giving long-term medication for conditions such as asthma – but not others. Attending nursery to give your child their medicine several times a day, even if it is only over a period of a few weeks, is a major commitment for a working parent, so this aspect of nursery policy can be very important.

Where day nurseries do score on the sickness front is that, except in very small operations, they won't close just because one member of staff is ill. This provides a reliability that more personal forms of childcare, such as a nanny or childminder, cannot.

As children are generally at nursery all day, they need time and space to rest and this will usually be worked into the children's routine. Babies need cots or prams to sleep in, but cushions or day beds are often provided for the toddlers and older children. Some nurseries allow children to watch videos at certain times in the day to relax, and if this is a concern it is worth checking an individual nursery's policy.

You would hope a day nursery could provide an area for outdoor play, although this isn't a legal requirement and it would be impractical for some inner-city nurseries. Where such an area exists, the social services department has to be convinced that it meets safety requirements. Where there is no outside area, the nursery is still obliged to make provision for physical play and may take children out to a nearby park or play area.

Many day nurseries are registered to accept the Nursery Education (Pre-school Year) Grant for four-year olds. This is available for each child starting at the beginning of the term after they reach four. It is paid directly to the nursery, which should then reduce the fees parents have to pay accordingly.

(see page 5)

In order to be allowed to accept this funding, the day nursery has to follow the government's desirable outcomes (or curriculum framework) with its four-year olds. (See p 5) However, each nursery may offer this in a different way. Many will have covered these areas of development within their normal programmes of structured play and creative activities, but the introduction of the funding linked to this requirement will have forced them to think coherently about the activities that support these areas of learning, including setting aside certain times for their older children to cover topics under the scheme.

Each child's progress should be recorded by staff and his or her work collected and made available to parents. This should result in a portfolio that is useful to the school the child moves on to.

Parents sending their child to a day nursery may face a dilemma when she or he becomes four if the school that they intend their child to go to has its own nursery unit. Nursery units often provide only part-time places for four-year olds and in no sense replace the work-time childcare a day nursery can offer. However, parents may be concerned that other children starting at the school will know each other and theirs will be 'left out'. Schools have to publish their admissions policies and then abide by them. However, there is anecdotal evidence that parents feel under pressure to accept a nursery place if they want a place for their child in an oversubscribed primary school, even if the school does not state that attendance at their nursery will be taken into account when they allocate places. (If the school admissions policy does not state it as a consideration, it should not be used to give priority to one child over another.)

On the other hand, moving a child from his or her familiar day nursery and introducing a secondary form of childcare to cover part-time state-school nursery sessions may be even more problematic, especially when your needs will change again once he or she attends school full-time. Working parents have to face such dilemmas all the time. The most important thing is not to feel pressured in any direction and make the decision you feel is best for you and your child.

Later on, if you feel a primary school has denied you a place unfairly, you can always appeal. If you get your request for a place in early and continue to liaise with the school of your choice, they are not likely to overlook you. If you decide to keep your child at day nursery, you may also be able to negotiate some visits or some trial sessions at the school before he or she starts, or find out if there are other children living nearby going to the school that you could invite round socially.

If you do decide to move your child to the school's nursery unit, make sure you check the admissions criteria of the school. You could put your child in the school nursery unit and still not gain a place in the primary school if other circumstances mitigate against you. Some children in nursery units will also find themselves split up from their friends by primary schools that have different intake dates depending on birthdays.

Workplace nursery

Employers will sometimes recognise the benefits of providing child-care facilities and offer places in workplace nurseries to their staff. The main advantage to the employers is their ability to keep expensively-trained staff. A special tax concession allows them to provide this service, whether free to staff or subsidised, without employees having to pay tax on the benefit.

A workplace nursery would generally provide all the same services as any other day nursery, tailored to the normal hours the company expects its staff to work. When the nursery is literally at the work place, it is easy for parents to drop children off and collect them, they know they are nearby in an emergency, and a working mother may be able to continue to breast feed her baby.

The capital costs of setting up a nursery from scratch can be substantial, however, and a common way forward is for employers to go into partnership with other institutions, employers or local authorities. This may mean that the 'workplace nursery,' is some distance away.

Companies in the service industries that set up these nurseries were hit by unprecedented redundancies a few years ago and many arrangements are under threat as they try to tighten their belts.

If your employer does not have an arrangement for staff, now may be a good time to for them to consider this, as there may be opportunities to buy places in existing nurseries in your area. Midland Bank, which is one of the largest employers offering nursery places, says that its childcare programme, including supporting these places, has helped them keep skilled staff. In 1988, only 30% of women returned after maternity leave, but by the end of 1997 the figure had risen to almost 80%.

Alternatively, existing nurseries that appear to be only for staff of particular companies or students of a college or university may actually have some community places available to members of the public. They are not likely to advertise these, so it is always worth enquiring.

Childminders

Age from	Open	Cost	Regulated	Nursery Scheme
c6 weeks	Agreed hours – can be flexible	From c£1.80 per hour	Social services	✗

(Please note: this panel is a rough guide for quick reference. Costs in particular can vary considerably across the country and between individual providers. 'Nursery Scheme' also covers Pre-school Year in Scotland.)

The title 'childminder' is probably a drawback to most of its best owners as it implies that a child will be watched over, hopefully kept safe, but not much else. In some cases this may be all that is provided but parents seeking the best of this form of childcare can expect a stimulating environment as well as a safe one, with equipment appropriate for the child's development, and a considered approach to the time spent in the minder's care.

Childminders come from all sorts of backgrounds and have a variety of reasons for taking on the work. Some are fully-qualified nursery nurses preferring to work in their own homes, some are people who simply enjoy being with children, and most of them are women. A vast proportion take it up once they have children of their own and your child may well be expected to fit into an existing family. This taking part in normal family life is often the reason parents choose a childminder for their children rather than a day nursery or other institutional care.

The possible variations on how a child might spend the day with a childminder are legion. The children in the childminder's care should be the focus of her or his attention, but the day may include collecting other children from school, visiting other families, mother and toddler or playgroup sessions as well as play and social activity within the home. According to Sue Griffin, Training Officer of the National Child Minding Association it is both the individual attention and the involvement with the local community that make using a childminder a good choice for many parents.

A childminder's own children must be included in the numbers she or he is allowed to mind. An individual can care for six children under eight where no more than three may be under five (i.e. school age) and no more than two under two-years old. Additional children over eight-years old can be cared for as long as the total is no higher than eight children under 14.

Childminders should be registered with their local authority's social services department. Prior to accepting them for registration, checks are made with the police and within the department to make sure there is nothing in the background of the applicant or anyone else in the home that would make them unsuitable to care for other people's children. This is dependent on the childminder telling the truth about her or his identity, however, and this is how Helen Stacey, the childminder who was convicted of the manslaughter of six-month old Joseph Mackin, avoided her previous convictions for prostitution coming to light. The social services department involved have since required more rigorous proof of identity but the loophole still exists in some counties as this book goes to press. If you are worried, ask your social services department how they are guarding against this happening again. But remember – cases like this get enormous publicity because they are *extremely* rare.

At least two home visits are made by a social services inspector to meet all members of the household and make sure the home is safe for young children. They look at the security of medicines and cleaning materials, for example, whether glass is protected, fires guarded and so on. They will often require safety measures to be put in place which they will then check on a second visit.

During the visits the childminder is expected to show an understanding of the physical, emotional and developmental needs of children. A wide range of toys, play materials and books appropriate to the ages of children to be cared for needs to be provided.

The childminder is given a certificate of registration once these inspections have been passed, so should be able to show it to you. The local authority social services department will also keep a list of registered childminders so you can always check with them.

Training

Some local authorities require childminders to complete a pre-registration course, some offer them but don't insist and some no longer offer these courses. Where minders have completed the course, they will have had a brief introduction to running their own business, a guide to health and safety issues, and an introduction to child-development issues.

The National Child Minding Association has been piloting a more substantial course in partnership with colleges and is about to introduce it nationally. This is a sixty-hour course validated by the Council for Awards in Children's Care and Education (CACHE) and will cover:

- taking the professional approach to childminding;
- relationships with parents;
- meeting children's needs;
- how children learn;
- managing children's behaviour;
- observing and assessing children's development and behaviour;
- keeping children safe;
- equal opportunities practice;
- protecting children from abuse;
- business aspects of childminding;
- providing for babies and for school-age children.

(see page 5)

Those whose assignments are assessed as satisfactory and whose attendance record is good enough will be awarded with a Developing Childminding Practice (Family Day Care) Stage One certificate, or DCP1. A Stage Two course award has also been developed to reflect a high level of skill, aimed at childminders who want to be able to deliver the Desirable Outcomes for Children's Learning. (See p 5 for details.) The hope is that childminders may then be able to register for the Nursery Education Grant for all four-year olds in their care. This course was piloted in the Autumn of 1998.

Some local authorities also require minders to have an up-to-date first-aid certificate. This involves attending a day-long course, which covers resuscitation techniques as well as basic first aid. The certificate is valid for three years.

(see pages 115–118)

On top of this, childminders may have any of the recognised child-care qualifications detailed on p 115–118.

However, only 30% of childminders have a relevant qualification, compared with 69% of staff working in nurseries.

Inspection

Local authorities are obliged to inspect each registered minder at least once a year to check that: services are being provided to an acceptable standard and children are properly cared for; facilities provided remain consistent with the information held on the register; and to encourage childminders to raise standards.

A report is then produced and the childminder is given a copy. A registered childminder should be able to show parents their latest report giving some indication of the quality of services provided.

While you are at work

Although some parents may use childminders to provide a short break each week, most do so to allow them to work outside the home. In those circumstances flexibility is often a major consideration. The flexibility offered by a childminder depends on the particular person and their other commitments but is likely to be greater than that offered by a day nursery.

Childminders are paid by the hour per child but with an agreement that should provide for a period of notice on both sides if arrangements are to be changed. A minder may be able to cope with an extra hour or so at the end of the day with little notice, although this may be charged at an extra rate, or may have a schedule that means an extra ten minutes would create impossible difficulties.

A childminder may accept responsibility for giving your child medicines, which some nurseries will not. She or he may even agree to care for your child if your child is ill, if yours is the only child she or he minds – or she or he may not, but at least this is something you can discuss with a childminder, whereas nurseries will have laid down sickness policies.

If the childminder is ill, however, you could find yourself looking for emergency cover or taking unwanted and probably ill-timed leave from work. Some childminders do get together on a local basis and may have agreements to take on each other's work when they are ill. If this is a possibility, parents would want to be sure that the alternative minder is also suitable.

Children with special needs

A carefully-chosen childminder whose home is suitable for the particular special needs of a child may be able to offer the personal attention such a child needs. Some local authorities will also recruit special teams of childminders who are given extra training to care for children with special needs as part of a community childminding scheme. You will need to check this with your local authority.

Fees

Fees vary considerably around the country but would generally be slightly lower per hour than a private day nursery in the same area. Some childminders offer cheaper rates for a sibling cared for at the same time. Childminders hope the government Nursery Education (Pre-school Year) Scheme may be extended in future to provide funding for four-year olds with qualified childminders who can show they are providing access to the desirable outcomes for children's learning (curriculum framework). (See p 5 for what these are.)

(see page 5)

A contract

Childminders are self-employed and should make a written agreement with parents about the services they will provide. This should include:

- a starting date;

- days and times they will be minding the child/children;

- the fee and the day of the week/month when payment is due;

- notice required to end the arrangement on both sides;

- items to be supplied by the parent or childminder (e.g., nappies, food, etc) and any additional costs for these items;

- any holiday/sickness arrangements. (Generally you will be expected to pay for a certain amount of time when the minder is allowed to take holiday, and for periods when your children are on holiday or not well enough to be minded, or when the minder is not well enough to care for them.)

If you want a minder to be flexible, you may write in any arrangement about fees for extra hours, or any agreement about whether the minder is willing to care for a sick child.

A written contract gives parents and minders a clear understanding of the services on offer, but can never legislate for the differences between people. One person's definition of 'too sick to look after the children', and another's may be sufficient to cause conflict later. Childminding is a very personal arrangement and parents need to feel that they are happy negotiating with an individual rather than an organisation – that they can be open about any problems or queries that may arise rather than suppressing them, not wanting to offend, and ending up removing their child from a situation in which the child was otherwise happy.

If a parent has a serious complaint about the care offered by a childminder, however, the social services department of the childminder's local authority will investigate and can remove a childminder's registration.

Nannies, Mother's Helps and Au Pairs

Age from	Open	Cost	Regulated	Nursery Scheme
c6 weeks	Hours agreed and flexible	From c£140 per week	✗	✗

(Please note: this panel is a rough guide for quick reference. Costs in particular can vary considerably across the country and between individual providers. 'Nursery Scheme' also covers Pre-school Year in Scotland.)

NANNIES

A good nanny can offer the most flexible form of childcare, selected especially to meet the particular needs of yourself and your child or children. The down side is that nannies are entirely unregulated.

Nannies care for children in their home, either coming in daily or living in. They often work long or flexible hours to cover the parents' work patterns and they take responsibility for every aspect of caring for the child. Nannies are often prepared to babysit and this can be agreed at the outset and written into their contracts.

A nanny should be able to plan your child's day with activities suitable to their stage of development and arrange social outings. She should also be able to respond to the tiredness, interests and so on of the child. The nanny should be aware of all aspects of child safety and be confident and competent to deal with emergencies in your absence. She should also be able to discuss all aspects of your child's development with you.

A nanny's role includes preparing meals for the child, so she should be capable of putting together a healthy menu plan. Other aspects of the child's physical care, such as keeping his or her room tidy and doing the child's laundry may also be included in the nanny's duties.

However, if you want a Mary Poppins just remember you never saw her with a Hoover in her hands! If you want other domestic duties undertaken then you should look for a mother's help, or a nanny/housekeeper rather than a nanny.

A daily nanny will need to eat during the time she is with your child so you will need to consider what meals you will provide (the nanny would obviously prepare these for herself). You may wish your nanny to take your child out in the car, or collect a child from school, in which case you will either need to provide a car or pay the nanny for the use of hers.

Being alone with children can be a very isolating experience, so many nannies will want to include some adult company in their day – visiting the homes where other nannies work, perhaps, or arranging outings for the children with other childcarers they know. This makes sense as long as the interests of your child are paramount and you know and approve of anyone being allowed into your home.

The nanny should keep you up-to-date on your child's development and talk to you about plans for the future. Therefore, it is important to allow some time regularly when she is contracted to be working for you when you will be free to talk over these issues in a relaxed way.

Living in

Nannies are the one form of childcare that you can move permanently into your own home. Obviously this is a big advantage if you want to be able to share night feeding of small babies, or if your work involves staying away from home. However, a nanny's duties do not extend to twenty-four hours a day, seven days a week just because they are under your roof!

Unless you live in a house with a separate guest wing, it is a big decision to have someone else living with you, just as it is for a nanny moving in with strangers. Part of your home will become her home. She will expect a degree of privacy, just as you will. You will need to consider how the arrangement would work from the moment the household wakes in the morning to the moment it wakes the next morning.

The nanny will need a bedroom but could you also offer her a bathroom? If she needs to share it with you, how would you feel with one more in the queue when you're trying to get to work in the morning? Would you feel relaxed hanging around in your old dressing gown and slippers in front of your employee? What about meals? Would you provide the nanny with meals as part of the family when you are all together? Would you take it in turns to cook or would you expect the nanny to cook her own meals and have her main meal with your child? How would you feel about her making herself snacks in your kitchen and how would you organise the shopping? Would she be able to bring friends to the house, and if so, which parts of it are in bounds? Would you expect her in by a certain time each evening? Would you provide her with a television/video/stereo in her room or allow her to bring these with her, or would you expect her to spend evenings in your sitting room? Can you provide a bedroom/sitting room separate enough from the rest of the house, so that music or television noise wouldn't disturb anyone, and yet near enough to the baby to be able to reach him or her easily when he or she calls? These are just a few considerations you need to think about, and once you've decided your views, you just need to find an individual nanny with the same views.

Special needs

Most substantial childcare qualifications include some aspects of caring for children with special needs. Your nanny may also be able to undertake extra training to help her understand the particular needs of your child. The advantages of employing a nanny for a child with special needs include the individual attention she is able to give and the fact that she is based in the child's home, so the environment is suitable.

Sickness

You could expect a nanny to look after a child with a normal childhood illness and give them any prescribed medicines. However, if you want your child to use alternative remedies, especially home concoctions or items not readily available over the counter, you would need to establish this with the nanny as they may not be prepared to take responsibility for administering them.

Your nanny will probably know other nannies and may be able to make an arrangement for cover if she is ill. However, this means your nanny covering for the other nanny's charges if she is ill. This sort of arrangement would need to be discussed at the outset. The nanny should continue to be paid during illness for up to 28 weeks (as long as she is earning more than £63 a week). The rate of Statutory Sick Pay is £57.70 a week and the employer can generally claim most of this back.

Agencies can often provide you with a temporary nanny at short notice, although for a considerable fee.

Qualifications

(see page 115)

There are no regulations about the qualifications a nanny should have but you could expect something equivalent to an NNEB, or National Diploma – requiring two-years study. (See page 115 for what the qualifications mean.)

Costs

Unlike childminders, nannies charge for their own time, rather than per child, although they may charge more if they are expected to look after children from more than one family. Employing a nanny becomes more economic the more children you have. If you have one child, a nanny is likely to be more expensive than a day nursery, a similar price if you have two, and a lot more economical if you have three. However you have to consider the extras involved. You may want to provide use of a car, petrol and costs for outings, meals and so on.

The table below shows the average weekly earnings for nannies and gives a rough guide to what has to be paid on top (correct for 1998/9), for a single person with a maximum personal allowance.

The average net weekly earnings of live-in nannies are roughly:

		Tax	NI	Total
Central London,	£182	£20.74	£25.90	£228.64
Outer London/home counties	£155	£14.80	£21.31	£191.11
Provincial towns/cities	£135	£10.80	£15.20	£161.00
Country	£132	£10.20	£14.75	£156.95

Average net earnings of daily nannies are roughly:

		Tax	NI	Total
Central London	£232	£32.24	£41.35	£305.59
Outer London/home counties	£200	£24.88	£28.96	£253.84
Provincial towns/cities	£168	£17.52	£23.52	£209.04
Country	£160	£15.80	£22.16	£197.96

Pay can also be affected by a concentration of demand for nannies and a lack of supply in particular pockets of the country.

You are also responsible for paying the nanny during any maternity leave, but statutory maternity pay is fully reclaimable.

These figures help to explain why (according to anecdotal evidence), a high proportion of nannies are paid 'cash-in-hand'.

You also need to consider the costs of recruiting a nanny. If you choose to use an agency, flat fees can range from around £135 to £500 or a percentage of the nanny's salary up to about 10% of a year's gross pay. It is generally cheaper to advertise if you are confident about selecting someone from scratch.

Employment

Apart from the cost, employing a nanny involves all the complexities of administering tax and national insurance.

There are companies that provide payroll services to parents employing nannies – providing payslips, deducting tax and national insurance, and keeping all necessary records. The cost of this service is in the region of £100 to £150 a year.

However, the Inland Revenue also operates a simplified scheme for domestic employment. Under this scheme, your local tax office PAYE (pay-as-you-earn) department, will supply you with simple charts so you can look up what you are thinking of paying your nanny net (i.e. the money she will get to keep each week) and one chart will tell you how much tax and another how much national insurance will have to be added. Alongside this is a working sheet for your calculations.

Once you have found a nanny and agreed a rate, the local office will take the details, prepare a tax code for the nanny and send you a pack of literature. You then send them the relevant amount of tax and national insurance each quarter. All you have to provide them with is the completed worksheet each year.

Nanny share

One popular way of cutting the costs of employing a nanny, is to find a family to share. No matter how close you are to someone as a friend, her or his approach to childcare might still be very different. Issues such as discipline, diet, whether you want the nanny to help teach your child to read, whose house should be used, whether the home-base parents are required to store some of the other child's toys, what activities you might want your children to attend, whose car might be used, how costs for petrol and food might be shared, and any other issues that are important to you should all be thoroughly discussed and ironed out before you consider recruiting together. Giving in on a point for the sake of agreement is only worthwhile if you are sure it will not lead to resentment later. A nanny can't possible provide the service you both want if you want different things.

Buying in to an existing arrangement has its pros and cons. You can see how the arrangement works and you choose either to fit in with it or not. You don't have so many choices but then, if the decisions are already made, you are not likely to resent them either. You should, nevertheless, interview the nanny and expect to see the references and other information on which the other parents selected her.

MOTHER'S HELPS

If you do want help with the housework as well as some childcare, a 'mother's help' is a possible solution. Mother's helps can be employed for light housework and looking after children. However, they are generally paid less than a nanny and people seeking these positions are less likely to be trained and experienced.

AU PAIRS

Unlike a nanny, an au pair is not an employee. Au pairs are allowed into the country to work with families for up to two years by a special arrangement with the Home Office, although a stay of six to twelve months is more usual, because they are seen as cultural visitors. They generally come to Britain to improve their English and experience life with a British family. Their work is restricted by the Home Office and they must be paid 'pocket money' as well as being provided with board and lodgings.

Au pairs are usually single girls between 17 and 27. The host family must give the au pair her own room and pay pocket money (generally between £35 and £60 a week) and can expect the au pair to work up to five hours a day, five days a week, with some baby sitting evenings on top. Travel expenses from and back to her home country are usually paid by the au pair, although the host family would expect to meet her from the airport, bus depot or station.

Suitable work would include light housework, such as vacuuming, dusting and tidying, getting children ready for school, making packed lunches and general childcare. Information about duties, free time, accommodation and pocket money has to be laid out by the host family and a full letter of invitation has to be sent to the au pair before she travels.

Au pairs should also be given time off for language classes and the host family is expected to help them enrol in a suitable language school. This brings up the obvious consideration that au pairs are unlikely to speak perfect English, which may be a major consideration if they are expected to care for children who do not speak anything else over an extended period.

Inevitably, by the terms of their stay in Britain, they will not provide the continuity possible with other forms of childcare, neither can they be expected to provide childcare over the full working day. If you would like your children to gain experience of another culture, however, they may have a lot to offer.

Childcare by Relatives

Relatives may be keen to offer their services in looking after your child while you return to work. This may seem like an ideal arrangement, and it can be. The relative, grandparent, aunt and so on may love the child in a way you would not expect from anyone outside the family. However, arrangements like this need just as careful consideration as any other childcare arrangement, or more so because of the added emotional complications that might arise out of your relationship with the relative who is offering their services. Being honest with each other is essential, but can be hardest when everyone's feelings have to be considered.

An elderly grandparent who is delighted with their new grandchild might feel exhausted and not so keen after a week's worth of dirty nappies, and bending and lifting with several pounds of wriggling baby. She or he may not have thought about the hassle of sterilising and preparing bottles or heating feeds. Looking after a baby, or even a toddler is a hard job so it is essential that whoever has made this generous offer knows the full story from the outset. Relatives may think they remember all this from their own parenthood, but if it was a while ago, they may need a few practice sessions without commitment from either side to remind them. It could be disastrous if they find they are unable to cope when you have just started a new job.

Make sure that you agree on issues of childcare that are important to you. The most common causes of disagreement are food, sleep and discipline. It is no good the relative saying she or he will do whatever you ask if you feel that a crying baby should be fed immediately and she or he believes that babies should be left at the end of the garden in their pram until they cry themselves to sleep. You may be at work worrying that her or his promise is not being kept. She or he may be doing as you ask, but feeling upset that her or his experience is not being valued; that you consider her or him incapable of bringing up a child satisfactorily. If one of your parents is the relative involved she or he may feel you are also criticising the way she or he brought *you* up.

If the child would be cared for in the relative's home, consider whether there are any dangers in the home they might not be aware of. Could you suggest tactfully that they would need a stair gate, for example, especially if the relative is already caring for her own small children without one?

Money

Close relatives can be paid for childminding without being registered. (Brothers and sisters, parents, aunts or uncles would be considered 'close'. Check with the local authority if you are considering a more distant relative.) Even if your relative has offered her or his services for nothing, if you could afford to pay something it might be worth considering this. As long as your offer would not be considered an insult, it might help you put the situation on a more professional footing. It shows your relative's work is valued and not taken for granted. It may prevent resentments building up as you are sharing the work but also sharing the rewards of your own return to work outside the home. It may mean you feel more able to ask your relative to do particular activities with your child, such as taking him or her to the park or reading to him or her.

Most problems can be solved if both parties are willing and prepared to be totally honest with each other. If you know you are not, then however much it may hurt someone's feelings initially, it would be better not to get stuck in an arrangement that threatens not only your childcare arrangements, but your wider family relationships. It is much better that relatives are around to help in emergencies and to provide a loving family for your child outside the working day, than a cheap form of childcare. If you hurt relatives' feelings with a refusal, you may well be able to win them round by asking them to babysit or inviting them to spend time with yourself and your child, but they should respect your choices for your child, just as they would expect their choices for their own children to be respected.

Staying at Home

If, having considered the options you decide that you would prefer to stay at home with your child, you may want to consider how you are going to provide the social activity that both of you will need, along with any other factors you noted in the 'what you want' section of this book that would not be easy to achieve at home.

You may be part of a close community where the majority of women stay at home with their children, in which case it may not be difficult to surround yourself with relatives and friends to give the child stimulation and yourself the adult company and occasional breaks you need. However, recent statistics indicate that more than 50% of mothers in Britain work outside the home. The statistics for fathers, had they been compiled, would be a lot higher, so being at home with a small child can be very isolating for both the adult and the child.

There are a whole series of voluntary and commercial activities generally available in bigger towns to help. These are just a few of the activities that might be available near you, they include:

Parent and Toddler groups
Parent and Toddler groups, voluntarily-run and usually held in church halls or community centres. These generally offer a selection of toys for the children and coffee and chat for the parents. Parents are often included on the rota for putting out toys, making coffee, etc. Fees generally cover costs and some have fund-raising events as well. These are often available even in small villages.

Park
Park. Even villages often have these as well and it goes without saying that they're great places for outdoor play and often useful for meeting other children and parents.

Music for Tots
Music for Tots groups are often run by members of the Pre-school Music Association, or by private music teachers. They are generally relaxed social groups where parents stay with their babies and small children while they take part in action songs and make 'music' with simple instruments. Fees from a pound a session up.

Pre-schools
Pre-schools. Although these have been included in the rest of the book as a form of child-care, they welcome parental involvement and one or more sessions a week could give your child access to messy or equipment-based activities that it might be difficult to provide at home. Cost is in the region of £2.50 per session.

Tumble Tots
Tumble Tots is a franchise operation offering physical play with trampolines and other gym equipment. There is an annual membership fee of £12.95, with fees per session varying across the country. Expect in the region of £3 per session. Parents are involved in

classes for children from walking to three-years old, although they are not from three to five. Gymbabes sessions with parents are run for babies from six months to walking.

Water Babies

Water Babies, or other swimming clubs for small children often operate at municipal pools or in school pools out of school hours. Some of these clubs allow the adult to get the child used to water and eventually teach him or her to swim. Others offer more intervention by a swimming teacher. Fees vary according to where they are and what's on offer.

Education at home

If you want to give your child an early education, there is help and support available from Education Otherwise, an organisation set up by and for parents who want to educate their children at home. Contact their enquiry line, tel: 0891 518303, or send an A5 stamped addressed envelope to: Education Otherwise, PO Box 7420, London N9 9SG.

Help with special needs

Your local education authority may be able provide help at home if your child has special needs. The Portage Scheme is a free home-visiting service for pre-school children with special needs that may be developmental or learning difficulties, or a physical disability.

The aim is to help parents teach their children new skills and can include giving advice and guidance, and may include the loan of toys and other learning resources. The trained home visitor (who is a volunteer) will select a task with the parent and work out the best way of helping the child achieve it. The parent agrees to practice the task with their child between visits and progress is recorded on a chart.

Contact your local education authority to see if they have a scheme available to you.

An occasional break

More and more activities for adults have crèches attached where you can leave your child to play under professional supervision while you swim, paint, gain a qualification or even shop. Sports centres, colleges and large shopping centres are the sort of places that may now offer this service. You need to check that you are happy with the arrangements for your child, however, especially that there is a good system for ensuring a child is only given back to its parent. Staff don't get to know children or parents who use the crèche only occasionally, so this is an important issue.

Costs

Staying at home with a child could be your most expensive option, although if you feel it is the best, then you will never feel happy doing anything else. When working out the cost, consider: loss of earnings, cost of social/educational activities or providing more toys/books at home, cost and availability of suitable transport so that you are not isolated.

Make sure you have thought about the company and support you might need. Your child's well-being is dependent on your own. Being miserable and lonely won't help and making friends when you are just getting used to coping with a baby or second child requires a lot of effort and determination.

Section Four

Choosing a Nursery or Carer

Inspectors and their Reports

Having produced a list of what you are looking for, you should be in a position to select one or several types of care and education that suit you. There are two basic kinds of inspection report that could help you choose between providers of the same type.

OFSTED

Ofsted is the Office For Standards in Education (for England). Its job is to improve standards of achievement and quality of education through regular inspections, public reporting and informed advice and it is independent of the Department for Education and Employment.

State nursery schools and classes are inspected by Ofsted in the same way as state schools. In 1996, Ofsted also started to inspect private nurseries funded by the state through the Nursery Education Grant. (See p 5)

(see page 5)

Ofsted had completed 15,300 nursery inspections by March 1998 and, of those, 99% were found to be acceptable.

How Ofsted works

Ofsted does not directly employ the teams of inspectors who visit nurseries. They work for independent contractors who have tendered for the work. The inspections are generally carried out by a Registered Nursery Inspector. Inspectors are people who are already qualified and experienced in the education of young children. They have to undergo an intensive training course on which they are assessed and, if they are successful, are registered for three years. Ofsted checks up on a sample of inspections to ensure standards are maintained. There is also a procedure for dealing with complaints by nurseries who are unhappy about the way inspections have been carried out.

Inspections

(see page 5)

Inspections are based on the way providers help children reach the 'desirable outcomes for children's learning' in: social development, language and literacy, mathematics, knowledge and understanding of the world, physical and creative development (see p 5), and usually last for one full day or shorter visits over two days. Visits might be longer for large nurseries.

The inspector assesses the quality of the planning and content of the educational programme, the quality of teaching and assessment of the children and its contribution to the children's attainment and progress, and the effectiveness of the nursery's partnership with parents. This begins before the inspection visit when the inspector looks at: a self-appraisal, that is completed by the nursery; a manager's form, that describes the set up of the nursery, its priorities and aims and the community within which it works; and any policy, information and promotional documents the nursery has produced.

The visit includes observing normal nursery activity and talking to staff, children and parents.

The inspector then discusses the findings with the nursery (although they are not negotiable) and puts together a report. This written report is sent to the nursery about four weeks after the end of the inspection visit and must be made available to parents as soon as possible and without charge. (Nurseries are allowed to charge enough to cover expenses if a copy is requested, however.) Ofsted also puts all inspection reports on its web site. The address is: http://www.ofsted.gov.uk/ (this covers English nurseries only). It aims to have all reports available through the Internet about twelve weeks after the inspection is completed. This provides a good opportunity to browse through reports in general and get a feel for the way they are written, as well as looking up particular nurseries.

The categories that have to be covered by the inspection are carefully laid out so that comparisons can be made relatively easily. Below is a sample headings sheet from a report as it appears on the Internet with examples of the sort of details that appear under each heading inside the report. Reports on the Internet are the same as the printed versions with only slight variations in style. The reports do not all conform strictly to the same style anyway, although the content covered is the same.

Nursery Education Inspection Report

Nursery name:

Nursery number:

Inspection details

This includes the name and address of the nursery, who the manager is, and what sort of nursery it is. This also includes the number of children, their ages, a little bit about the organisation of the nursery and the area it is in.

About the inspection

This provides some standard information about the purpose of the inspection, but also gives the name of the inspector, and the date of the inspection.

Main findings

This is effectively a summary of the findings of the whole report, highlighting the main strengths and weaknesses and the extent to which the nursery promotes all six 'desirable outcomes'. A judgement about whether standards are acceptable and the timing of the next inspection may appear in this section.

Key issues for action

The main point of Ofsted inspections is to improve the quality of nursery education, so even excellent providers are likely to have some points listed under this heading. Often these entries will suggest how providers can improve on these issues as well as listing them. For example: 'Make greater use of routine situations in the nursery to develop and reinforce mathematical skills and concepts', rather than asking the provider simply to improve the way mathematics is covered.

Providers have to draw up an action plan within 40 days of receiving the report, stating how they will address the key issues within the next twelve months, and this action plan has to be made available to parents. This plan should identify priorities to be dealt with immediately and give some detail about how issues will be tackled, for example, making a named member of staff responsible for a particular task with a deadline attached to each task. It should also explain how the success of the action taken can be judged. The action plan will then form part of the next inspection and the inspector will check it has been successfully carried out.

Outcome of the inspection

This gives a summary of the inspection results relating to each of the six 'desirable outcomes' and is useful in making quick comparisons. It lists each area and simply states whether it 'promotes desirable outcomes' or has 'some weaknesses', and so on.

The report states whether children's spiritual, moral, social and cultural development is fostered appropriately, and whether overall provision is acceptable. It is generally here that you'll find out how soon the inspector recommends a return visit. This is important. Despite the copious and precise guidelines laid down for inspectors, it is not possible to legislate away the individual style of writing of the inspector involved, so sometimes a negative report may not sound too bad when written by a positive person and vice versa. However, inspections are not cheap or re-inspections organised without the belief that they are necessary. The normal period for re-inspection is two to four years. The guidelines suggest that this is recommended if the provision for personal and social development, language and mathematics is likely to promote the 'desirable outcomes', and so is the provision for at least one of the other outcomes. If a re-inspection is recommended within one to two years, you can be sure that, although acceptable, the inspector had concerns about the quality of the provision. To put this in perspective, however, this judgement was made in 40% of inspections up to March 1998. This was the first time nurseries had to prepare for inspection so it will be interesting to see whether they will have learnt from the experience when the inspectors return.

The most serious judgement is that educational provision is not acceptable. Guidelines suggest that this would be the case if provision was 'poor' in the three areas previously mentioned – personal and social development, language and mathematics. If this happens, Ofsted will arrange its own visit to the nursery to corroborate findings, normally within two weeks of the initial inspection. If this inspection corroborates the inspector's findings the nursery's validation may be withdrawn, which means it would no longer be able to accept the Nursery Education Grant. Any provider in this situation would have the opportunity to make their case however.

An interesting aspect of these guideline is the priority given to three of the 'desirable outcomes' over the others. Creative development is clearly not seen as equally important for four-year olds as mathematics.

The educational programme

This section goes into detail on the strengths and weaknesses of provision of each of the six desirable outcomes. In many cases this is the part of the report that gives more of a feel for the nursery or pre-school. It is in this section you may learn that the class has a pet hamster or that children are given to riding around on trikes all day.

Planning of the educational programme

This is where the inspector considers the strengths and weaknesses of planning for all of the desirable outcomes. He or she is checking that there are proper systems in place to ensure a balance of learning in all areas, that it is clear what children are expected to learn from each activity planned, and that plans include the best way of deploying staff and grouping children for the activities. The inspector will want to know that planning is sufficient to build on learning that has gone on before, and that it does not fall apart if some staff are ill or on holiday.

Quality of teaching and assessment

The strengths and weaknesses of teaching and assessment
This section covers the type of relationship staff have with children as well as the way they encourage children to learn. The inspector should not take into consideration any preconceptions about teaching methods but assess whether the methods chosen by staff are effective, taking into account the purpose of the session, the number of children, their level of attainment and the resources available. However, guidance to inspectors in The Ofsted Handbook (1997 edition) states that a good mix of activities will involve practical activity and problem-solving, and that there should be sufficient time for children to learn through 'sustained involvement in concentrated activity'.

The organisation of these sections vary, with some addressing assessment separately further on. However, it is always an area that is covered in a report. The assessment section should look at the way children's attainment and progress towards the desirable outcomes is systematically assessed and recorded so that existing achievements can be built on. The guidelines suggest that assessment is better when parents are involved. Failure to keep good manageable records is a fairly common weakness among providers who are new to working with government agencies of any sort.

The strengths and weaknesses of equality of access and opportunity
This involves issues not only of race or gender, but of attainment and different rates of development. The inspector will look at the way groups interact and how staff deal with children who dominate groups or those who don't take part. The inspector will also check that children who are already ahead of the others are still challenged to make further

progress. This is where the inspector will note any children with special educational needs at the nursery or those with English as a second language and report on how these children are catered for. Regular assessment and monitoring of progress is particularly important for children with special educational needs, and children who do not speak English as their first language should expect to have time set aside so they can speak and listen in small groups, or one-to-one, to develop confidence and vocabulary.

The strengths and weaknesses of the learning resources and accommodation
The list of the 'basic' range of learning resources that providers should use in the guidelines to inspectors is a long one and it is not surprising that playgroups in temporary accommodation may struggle to provide them. They are:

- an attractive and comfortable place to sit, with a variety of books;
- a writing area with a variety of paper and tools to make marks and write;
- an imaginative play area with a variety of resources to promote and extend role-play;
- dry and wet sand, and a water tray, each with suitable equipment for filling, pouring, measuring and so on;
- growing and living things to observe and care for;
- collections of interesting objects to sort, count, feel and describe;
- equipment to promote early mathematical and scientific investigations;
- a variety of small and large construction equipment;
- cooking equipment and materials;
- a range of creative media such as paint, clay, wood and junk materials;
- simple musical instruments and tapes for listening to music; and
- artefacts and pictures that reflect both the local and the wider community.

However, inspectors are encouraged to focus on the impact the resources and accommodation have on teaching, and whether staff make effective use of what is available.

Partnership with parents and carers

This includes the sort of information parents are given about their children's activities and progress as well as their involvement in sessions or in visits. At a day nursery, the involvement of working parents during the day is likely to be limited by their own time constraints.

State nursery schools These are inspected under different guidelines to other nursery provision and their inspections result in reports of generally more than 30 pages compared with around five or six for private providers. Whole teams of inspectors visit the school and a typical contents list is included below.

Report contents

Main findings

Key issues for action

Introduction

Characteristics of the school

Key indicators

PART A: ASPECTS OF THE SCHOOL

Educational standards achieved by pupils at the school

- **Attainment and progress**

- **Attitudes, behaviour and personal development**

- **Attendance**

Quality of education provided

- **Teaching**

- **The curriculum and assessment**

- **Pupils' spiritual, moral, social and cultural development**

- **Support, guidance and pupils' welfare**

- **Partnership with parents and the community**

The management and efficiency of the school

- **Leadership and management**

- **Staffing, accommodation and learning resources**

- **The efficiency of the school**

PART B: CURRICULUM AREAS AND SUBJECTS

- **Desirable learning outcomes**

- **Language and literacy**

- **Mathematics**

- **Creative development**

- **Knowledge and understanding of the world**

- **Physical development**

PART C: INSPECTION DATA

Summary of inspection evidence

Data and indicators

Parental survey

These reports are in line with the sort of report you would see for a primary school, although they cover the same aspects as other nursery providers, teaching the same 'desirable outcomes'. The major difference is their level of detail, but they also use a different style of language. There are specific percentages given of teaching that is 'good', or 'satisfactory'. I have had some feedback from parents who are concerned at the term 'satisfactory', which they expect to mean 'only scrapes through above unacceptable'. In inspection-speak, however, satisfactory is applied strictly by its meaning. If teaching is satisfactory it is perfectly OK – it satisfies requirements.

Opportunity groups

Opportunity groups, primarily for children with special educational needs, are inspected by Registered Nursery Education Inspectors who have specialist expertise and have also undergone a training course specifically for the inspection of these groups. The principles underlying these inspections are the same as for other providers – how well the provider is helping children reach the 'desirable outcomes'. The reports are also on the same basis, the difference is simply in the recognition of the needs of children whose progress towards the outcomes may start at a different point and whose needs in making progress are more specialised.

In Wales, these inspections are carried out by OHMCI on the same basis.

In Scotland, nurseries are inspected by HMI to find out how well the curriculum framework is being delivered, whether learning is well planned, how well the children are assessed, and how effectively their progress is recorded and reported. They are also judged on how they handle equal opportunities and on their relationship with parents.

(see page 12)

See p 12 for details of the Curriculum Framework for the Pre-school Year.

LOCAL AUTHORITY INSPECTIONS

Social services departments of local authorities inspect all registered childminders, and all nurseries that are not part of a larger school. Reports can range from a brief update on an existing childminder to weighty documents on large day nurseries. They also vary according to the practice of the particular social services department.

Unlike Ofsted reports, these are not public documents. Parents of children at a nursery have a right to see its report and, as a potential customer, it is reasonable for you to expect to be allowed to see it. There is not the same requirement on the nursery to make it generally available however and, considering the potential size of the report, it is understandable if they do not want to supply copies. If you want the nursery to be helpful, you may have to be helpful yourself about calling in to look at it at a convenient time for them and being prepared to take notes. Also bear in mind that the most useful aspect of these reports is in comparing them and there could be quite a time commitment involved if you want to see several.

If you ask to see the report of a large day nursery, you may have to wade through a wealth of detail, including things such as the gap between towel pegs and whether there is coffee available in the staff room, before you can get an overall picture of the standard of care.

One nursery report from a typical social services department, for example, includes 20 sections with subsections detailing the condition of premises alone, including such information as security, the safety of heaters, electrics, glass, windows and floor covering, cooking and laundry facilities, pets, medicines and cleaning equipment, toilets and facilities for the children's rest – all things you might look at on a visit, but observed over a longer period by someone trained to look for potential hazards.

A report should also cover staffing ratios and whether staff have the qualifications required by the particular social services department. It will assess the nursery's policies and procedures and even tell you whether the menu is considered balanced.

One of its most interesting aspects is a description of the activities that took place during the inspection. You will be able to see the condition of toys for yourself on your visit, but you won't necessarily be able to tell how much the children get to play with them. The report should also give you an observation of the way the staff and children interact and how well children play together.

Although the detail of a report like this can seem tedious, it is also the detail that makes the report so valuable. A nursery may be able to put on a good show one day a year, but if it is slovenly the rest of the time, it will be hard to put all the small details right. It also ensures the report is more objective.

Childminders

Inspection reports on childminders need to be considered alongside their original registration document, which they should be able to show you. The annual follow-up reports can be quite short and based mainly on the childminder's answers to questions and a very brief look at the premises. They are very variable depending on the local authority and the individual inspector so it makes sense to check any information that is particularly important to you during your own visit.

Initial Enquiries

Now you are ready to choose between individual nurseries, childminders, nursery schools and so on, the first thing you need is a list of what is available. Details at the back of this book should give you a good start. Personal recommendation is also a good source if you know other parents in the same position. Don't be less rigorous in your checks with a recommended provider, however. Your child may have different needs to theirs and most parents of children in 'failing' schools think they are good schools.

(see pages 113–247)

A call to your local authority will provide you with a list of any day nurseries, nursery schools and classes that they run. At present, however, responsibility is split between departments. Social services departments are generally responsible for the care of young children. They run local authority day nurseries, and register and inspect pre-schools, private day nurseries, nursery schools and childminders. Education departments are responsible for state nursery schools and classes or nursery units attached to state schools.

The government is trying to remove this distinction between care and education for young children, however, believing that educators have a duty to provide care, and all carers to educate. All local authorities in England and Wales, in conjunction with their partners in voluntary and private nurseries, and social services departments have had to produce Early Years Development Plans that show how they will meet the government's commitment to provide nursery places for all four-year olds and further develop provision for young children. Those authorities who hadn't done so effectively before, had to work across these boundaries. It is therefore much more likely now that your authority will have a single information point on all the nurseries and pre-schools available in your area. Try looking in the council's social services department entry in the telephone book under childcare. They will also be able to give you lists of childminders.

(see page 5)

If your council doesn't have a single information point, the education department is now obliged to keep a list of all providers registered to accept the Nursery Education (or Pre-school Year) Grant for four-year olds (see p 5) as well as state nursery schools and classes. You may still miss out on some private providers that way. You can get information on: nurseries attached to independent schools from your regional office of the Independent Schools Information Service (ISIS) (see p 242 for addresses); Montessori Schools from Montessori Education UK (p 243); and Steiner kindergartens from the Steiner Waldorf Schools Fellowship (p 245).

(see page 242)

(see page 243)

(see page 245)

Some employers also offer staff the services of professional childcare consultants who hold lists of providers across the country and can help you find day care. However they tend not to include term-time nursery schools and local-authority nursery classes. Sometimes, other organisations, such as Training and Enterprise Councils (in England and Wales) or local enterprise companies (in Scotland), will hold lists. If not, you are left with the *Yellow Pages*. However, since private nurseries are trying to sell their services they are not in the business of hiding themselves.

Once you have a list of suitable providers, you may be able to eliminate some over the telephone. Telephone calls are good for quick answers to direct questions but you need to have a very clear list of initial questions.

Your questions will depend on your list of absolute requirements. If you have to have child-care from a particular date, your first question will be whether they have a place. If not, anything further at this point would be a waste of breathe.

(see page 22)

Once you have established which providers can meet all your absolute requirements, you can create your own list of possibles. It may be helpful to create your own chart rather like the one you filled in to compare the different types of care. (See p 22) Instead of the types of provision, you would put your list of possible providers along the top, with your list of priorities on one side. That way you can grade how well each provider fulfils each require-ment. However, this can only be a rough guide and a spur to memory. You will need to make fuller notes of your visit, including how you feel about such hard-to-quantify aspects as 'atmosphere'.

Further enquiries will depend on the sort of provision you are looking for.

Choosing a Pre-school or Nursery School/Class

(see page 5)

Ring and check first that they are likely to have a place available when you need one, if not, all other questions are immaterial. Also ask for all the written information they have available, including their last Ofsted report if appropriate. (See p 5.) The written information provided by a nursery school is likely to depend on whether it is attached to a school. This is largely because of the way they are regulated.

Private nursery schools that are not attached to schools and usually take children from about two-and-a-half should be able to provide you with a prospectus containing information such as the nursery's main written policies, including health and safety, record keeping, discipline and equal opportunities; it may include the names of permanent staff (or at least the head), their qualifications and experience and practical details such as opening times and fees.

A nursery attached to a school may have an entry within the school's prospectus – which may mean specific nursery information is limited – but is very helpful in giving you a picture of the way the nursery fits in with the school. If this is not the case, ask for the primary-school prospectus as well. If you are choosing a school at the same time as a nursery, it is important to look at the admissions policy, which should be contained in the school's prospectus. You need to know whether you could end up getting a nursery place but not a place in the school. It also makes sense to look at the school's results. These are published in 'league tables', which give the mistaken impression that you can look at a chart and see which school in your area is top and where the other schools fall. In fact they are listed alphabetically, but you can look up the school you're interested in and see how its results relate to the average. (For more detail see: *Choose the Right Primary School,* by Bob Findlay, The Stationery Office, London, 1998, £12.99.)

If a prospectus or leaflet indicates that something more is available on request, then request it. As with any other provision, the more written information you have before you visit a nursery, the more you will be able to concentrate on your observations. If one policy is particularly important to you, discipline for example, or medicines, then you can check on the telephone that this is covered in the prospectus. If it is not, they may offer to send you a separate policy document or explain the policy there and then.

Most private nursery schools (and some nurseries attached to independent schools) will be registered to accept the government's Nursery Education (Pre-school Year) Grant for four-year olds. If so, they should have an Ofsted report (OHMCI in Wales/HMI in Scotland). They should make a copy available to you on request, although they may make a small charge for photocopying. If you are connected to the Internet and live in England, you can look up reports of English nurseries you are interested in before you have even contacted the nursery. The reports are posted on the Ofsted Web site at: http://www.ofsted.gov.uk/ It usually takes Ofsted about twelve weeks after an inspection to get the report posted.

(see page 71)

(See p 71 for an explanation of Ofsted inspections and how they work.) If you don't have your own access to an Internet connection, you may be able to use one at a library or 'cyber café' where you should also be able to get help. Expect a fee to cover at least the telephone call you are making when you use the Internet.

(see page 75)

Local-authority nursery schools also have Ofsted (OCHMI/HMI) reports but these have a different format (see p 75). If you are looking for them on the Ofsted web site, call up the 'section 9/10 reports' mentioned. Separate nursery schools are listed under nurseries but those attached to schools are listed under their primary schools. They are inspected as if they were a seamless part of the school.

(see page 77)

A private nursery school should also have a copy of its last social services inspection report. This is unlikely to be made so readily available as they can be weighty and very detailed documents and there is no legal obligation to show it to you. (See p 77 for more information on these reports.) Existing parents do have a right to see them, however, so if you know any, asking them to take a look could be enlightening for them too.

Alternatively, the nursery might make it available to you to look at within the nursery. It is understandable if they want you to see their nursery in action first so you can put the report in context. They may feel very sensitive to even minor criticism in a report. If they are not prepared to let you see it at any point, however, you are bound to wonder what it says, and should be doubly sure you are satisfied with all aspects of the nursery yourself before you consider giving them the care of your child.

You should now be able to compare what written information you now have with your list of priorities and fill in some of the simpler aspects of your chart if you have made one, such as: Little Darlings Nursery School: location 4; staff/child ratio 4.

The next stage is the visit. Make sure you arrange this for a time when the nursery school will be functioning normally, (i.e. not when special events are on, or during a meal break). Make an appointment plenty of time in advance so that your request can reasonably be met – two weeks should be enough.

SEPARATE NURSERY SCHOOL

The person running the school could be a manager, a head teacher, or simply the teacher. You should have found this out from the prospectus, so when you ring to make an appointment, let the school know that you would like some time to talk with this person, as well as to be shown around the nursery.

NURSERY LINKED TO SCHOOL

It is quite likely, unless the school is particularly large, that the person with overall responsibility for the nursery will be the head teacher of the primary school. If this isn't clear in the prospectus, check when you call to make the appointment. Unless you have already decided on a different primary school without a nursery, it makes sense to see this process as one of finding out about the whole school, starting from the nursery through to the time children leave the school. Make an appointment to talk to the head and also to see round the nursery and the primary school.

Both

Think of your visit in two parts – one to ask direct questions, and one to observe how things work in practice. Turn up with a list of things you want to ask, and be aware that further questions are bound to arise once you have looked around.

If you are offered an open day/evening, that is fine for getting some of your direct questions answered and an introduction to the staff, but is in not adequate for assessing the teaching quality of a school.

It is useful if you can time your visits to different schools over a relatively short period to keep your general impressions fresh in your mind. Leave yourself plenty of time for each visit, however. Two in a day is plenty (three at the outside), otherwise you may have to skip questions or be too concerned about missing your appointment to concentrate fully on your observations.

Aim not to take your child with you on a first visit. It is impossible to look after a child and fully concentrate on what someone is saying, and it is not reasonable to expect staff to look after your child while you talk (although they may do so). A child may also prefer a school that you may reject in favour of one they liked less.

It is worth preparing a standard list of questions, based on your own priorities and on gaps in the information you have been able to gain before your visit. If you know any other parents, ask them about the nursery first, but don't take any questions off your list on the strength of their answers – there maybe developments on the way at the nursery they are not yet aware of. Add any concerns that arise from their answers to your list.

Some questions could be answered over the telephone, but one of the main points of questioning the person who is responsible for the nursery or school is to assess how well they manage it and this is much better done in person. You want to know how clear they are about their objectives and how they are carried out; how open and communicative they are in response to your questions; and how much they care about the needs of the individual child. Starting with general, open-ended questions will give you the chance to assess their priorities.

CREATING YOUR LIST OF QUESTIONS

Below are some aspects you may want to consider. They are not in order of priority, but designed to build up to some of the more difficult questions. That way, the head should not feel threatened by your questioning or need to be defensive. The open questions are in italics. Underneath are the direct questions you may want to cover. Ask any that are not covered by the head in her or his response to the first question. You will probably want to add your own questions according to your list of priorities or remove some you are not concerned about.

If you are visiting a nursery with a specialist approach, such as High/Scope, Montessori or Steiner, check the relevant section of this book first so that you are aware of what the nursery should be trying to achieve. Although most of the questions are still relevant, there may well be extra ones relating to their philosophy. The Montessori Society has also produced a guide for parents evaluating a Montessori nursery. See pp 37, 38 for their suggested questions.

Care and communication

How is the nursery school/class organised?

- you want to know whether the nursery is organised;

- how many children there are in a class;

- whether all staff are involved in planning activities, getting an idea of how they work together;

- what sort of records are kept about each child's progress and how often these are discussed with parents;

- whether parents are involved in activities or planning.

How do you manage discipline?
This would include:

- how parents are kept informed;

- how any bullying or fighting is dealt with;

- whether children are excluded from the nursery as a final sanction.

Physical well-being

(If there is not an outside play area) *How do children get fresh air and exercise? How do you deal with illness?*

- whether there is always a first-aider or nurse available;

- if there is somewhere for ill children to be kept separate while their parents are called for;

- what policies the school has about giving medication. Its stated policy about ill children may give staff some discretion – if you are working and this is important to you, find out what sort of symptoms have caused children to be sent home.

Education

What sort of routine/timetable do the children have?

- you want to know if the children do have a routine;

- whether smaller children have a rest time and how this is arranged;

- what meals or snacks, if any, are available;

- what 'extras' have to be paid for.

What do you teach children?
You want to know:

- whether they have a clear idea of the reason certain activities are chosen and what they expect a child to learn from them (this should include physical activities) and be appropriate to the age and ability of the children. (Where the school is run by the local authority or is part of the Nursery Education (Pre-school Year) Scheme, the head will almost certainly tell you about the desirable outcomes for children's learning/pre-school curriculum framework. Much of this information can be gleaned from their Ofsted (OHMCI/HMI) report, but it is worth hearing the head explain how they plan and vary activities so that a balance is achieved, even if a child only attends part-time.);

- how children are taught, e.g., in small groups, through individual project work, as a whole class or as a mixture;

- to what extent children can choose their own activities;

- what qualifications staff have if not in the prospectus.

What connections does the nursery have with primary schools in the area? (or its primary school if attached)
You need to know to what extent choosing this nursery school prepares your child for a particular primary school.

Physical safety

What sort of security do you have?
You should be able to tell how easy it would be to get into the nursery unnoticed. Some schools have hidden security cameras and, if so, you may want to know how closely these are monitored.

OBSERVATIONS

When you are shown round, make sure you are not rushed from room to room. Look out for the following:

On arrival

Could you get into the nursery unnoticed and harm or remove a child easily? (But bear in mind you are far more likely to get run over with your child on the way to nursery than for anyone to try to do this.)

Atmosphere

- are the staff fully involved with the children?

- how do they relate to the children and deal with any incidents?

- are the children purposefully involved in activities, or just milling around?

- do the children obey instructions willingly?

- do the children seem happy?

- is there a sense of calm/authoritarian control/chaos? (Silence is not a particularly good sign.)

Environment

- is children's work displayed on the walls?

- if so, is this work recent, or does it look like it's been there a while?

- is furniture the right size for children?

- is there equipment suitable for the age of the children present for: imaginative play (e.g., a home corner, dressing-up clothes); messy play (e.g., water, sand);

and creative play (e.g., paints and craft materials)? (If these things aren't evident, ask if there is any other equipment that is sometimes used.);

- are materials in cupboards and drawers that are clearly labelled?

- is the building bright and airy with plenty of space for the children? (This is an ideal unlikely to be fulfilled in most state primary schools, even though some excellent teaching is taking place. However, some cramped buildings have toilets leading into classrooms and classes are taught in rooms with little natural light and this does effect the quality of provision.);

- have staff made the best of what's there.

Hygiene Ask to be shown the children's toilets, and the food preparation area, if appropriate.

Outside
- is there a play area?

- is there equipment for climbing, balancing, kicking, riding? (Much of this will probably be in store at any one time, so ask what outdoor equipment the nursery has.);

- is the area clean, tidy and safe?

- if attached to a primary school, do small children have a separate area?

The first thing to do as soon as you leave the school is to write down your impressions, along with the answers to any questions that you didn't get to write down while you were looking around. If you are seeing a number of nurseries, it's easy to forget which features belonged to which.

Choosing a Day Nursery

A day nursery should be able to provide you with a prospectus containing information about permanent staff, their qualifications and experience; the nursery's main written policies, including health and safety, record keeping, discipline and equal opportunities; and practical details such as opening times and fees. They may send only a small summary document on initial enquiry, however, so if this is what arrives and it indicates that something more is available on request, then request it. The more written information you have before you visit a nursery, the more you will be able to concentrate on your observations. If food is especially important to you, ask if they could let you have a sample menu, and you can check on the telephone that their medicines or discipline policy or any other of particular interest to you is included in their prospectus. If not, they may be able to send you a copy of these alongside.

Day nurseries will generally be registered to accept the government's Nursery Education (Pre-school Year) Grant for four-year olds. If so, they will probably have an Ofsted inspection report (OHMCI in Wales, HMI Scotland). They should make a copy available on request, although they may make a small charge for photocopying. If you are looking at nurseries in England and are connected to the Internet, you can look up any reports you are interested in before you have even contacted the nursery. The reports are posted on the Ofsted web site at: http://www.ofsted.gov.uk/ It usually takes Ofsted about twelve weeks after an inspection to get the report posted. (See p 71 for an explanation of Ofsted inspections and how they work.)

(see page 71)

The nursery should also have a copy of the last social services inspection report. This is unlikely to be made so readily available. A report on a fair sized nursery could be in the region of 50 pages long. (See p 77 for details.) However, you may be able to see it at the nursery.

(see page 77)

You should now be able to compare the written information you have gleaned with your list of priorities and fill in some of the simpler aspects of your chart if you have made one, such as: Tiny Tots: staff qualifications 3 (out of 5); location 5; and so on.

The next stage is the visit. Make sure you arrange this for a time when the nursery will be functioning normally (i.e. not when special events are on, or if some children attend term-time only, not school holidays). Bear in mind, however, that the time of day that may be most convenient for you, for example, first thing in the morning, lunch time or late afternoon, will probably be the worst for the nursery as this is when they are accepting children for the day or dealing with the main meal. Check when snack times are too, as the nursery may be happy to show off their well-behaved children sitting quietly at tables eating, but it won't tell you much about their day-time activities.

Make an appointment plenty of time in advance so that your request can reasonably be met – two weeks should be enough.

You will need to make it clear that you would like some time set aside to talk to the nursery manager, as well as being shown round. Think of your visit in two parts – one to answer direct questions, and one to observe how the nursery works in practice. Turn up with a list of things you want to ask, and be aware that further questions are bound to arise once you have looked around. Ask if you will be able to see the last social services report while you are there, but you will need to leave plenty of time for this at the end of the visit.

If you are offered an open day/evening, that is fine for getting some of your direct questions answered and an introduction to the staff, but it is in not in any way adequate for assessing the quality of a nursery that depends heavily on the way the staff relate to the children and to each other.

It is useful if you can time your visits to different nurseries over a relatively short period to keep your general impressions fresh in your mind. If you do have to spread them over several weeks, your notes will be even more important. Leave yourself plenty of time for each visit, however. Two in a day is plenty, otherwise you may have to skip questions or be too concerned about missing your appointment to concentrate fully on your observations.

As with a nursery school, aim not to take your child with you on a first visit. It is impossible to look after a child and fully concentrate on what someone is saying. A child may also prefer a nursery that you do not. Of course it may not be possible to leave your child with someone else (if you had childcare you wouldn't be looking at day nurseries), but taking him or her on your first visit should be your last resort.

It is worth preparing a standard list of questions, based on your own priorities and on gaps in the information you have been able to gain before your visit. Some of these questions could be answered over the telephone, but one of the main points of talking to the manager is to assess how well she can manage. How clear is she about her objectives and how they are carried out; how open and communicative is she in response to your questions; and how much does she care about the needs of the individual child? Starting with general, open-ended questions will give you the chance to assess her priorities.

CREATING YOUR LIST OF QUESTIONS

Assuming you know about fees, hours and availability, below are some other aspects you may want to consider. They are not in order of priority, but designed to build up to some of the more difficult questions. That way, the manager should not feel threatened by your questioning or need to be defensive. The open questions are in italics. Underneath are the direct questions you may want to cover. Ask any that are not covered by the manager in response to the first question. You will probably want to add your own questions according to your list of priorities and remove some you are not concerned about.

Care and communication

How is the nursery organised?
- you want to know whether the nursery is organised;
- whether all staff are involved in planning activities, getting an idea of how they work together;

- if there is a key worker for each child (this person will be a vital contact point between yourself and the nursery);

- what sort of records are kept about each child's progress and whether these are shown to parents;

- staff/child ratio;

- staff turnover;

- whether parents are involved in activities or planning;

- how new children are 'settled'.

How do you manage discipline?
This would include:

- how parents are kept informed;

- how any bullying is dealt with;

- whether children are removed as a final sanction.

Physical well-being

What sort of routine do the children have?

- you want to know if the children do have a routine (It is generally agreed that dividing the day into predictable segments gives children a sense of security.);

- whether they have a rest time and how this is arranged (Some nurseries allow older children to relax in front of a video.);

- what sort of meals and snacks are provided;

- what 'extras' have to be paid for, e.g., food, nappies;

- what items parents provide.

How do you deal with illness?

- you want to know how promptly children with contagious or other illnesses are removed from the nursery;

- whether there is any facility to keep them separate while parents are called (i.e. how many seconds notice can you give your employer if you are called away);

- whether there is always a first-aider or nurse available to the nursery;

- what policies the nursery has about giving medication;

- what policies it has for excluding sick children. (Staff may well have some discretion on how the policy is implemented. If so, ask for examples of the sort of symptoms that have caused children to be excluded in the past.)

Education/activities   *How do you decide on suitable activities?*

- you want to know how they relate activities to child development;

- whether they have a clear idea of the reason certain activities are chosen and what they expect a child to learn from them (this should include physical activities such as balancing and throwing);

- how they plan and vary activities so that a balance is achieved, even if a child only attends some days;

- to what extent children can choose their own activities (encouraging independence is generally considered a good thing as long as children are not expected to take full responsibility for the structure of their day);

- if there is an outdoor play area, whether this is often used.

If you are interested in the 'desirable outcomes' ('curriculum framework'):

How does the nursery teach the 'desirable outcomes'/'curriculum framework' to four-year olds?

- you want to know whether this group of children has special sessions for concentrated study;

- how well the nursery understands what its trying to achieve;

- how well subjects are balanced.

You should get a good view of this from the nursery's Ofsted report.

What connections does the nursery have with primary schools in the area?

Physical safety   *What sort of security do you have?*

You should be able to tell how easy it would be to get into the nursery unnoticed. There may be a hidden security camera, however. If so, you may want to know how closely this is monitored.

What systems or policies do you have to prevent abuse of children?

Abuse by nursery staff, where they are seldom alone with children, is extremely unlikely and nurseries should have procedures which prevent this. Publicity about the recent case in Newcastle however, where some children were seriously abused, is likely to put this concern near the top of a parent's list. It seems that in the Newcastle case, police and social services checks had not been properly carried out on the staff involved and that children were largely taken out of the nursery for the abuse to occur.

You want to know:

- what policies the nursery has in place to prevent abuse;

- whether staff would take your child out of the nursery without notifying you (nurseries may ask you to sign a blanket permission, but if you don't they should agree to ask you permission before each trip);

- and whether all staff have had police and social services checks. (You can double check this with the social services inspection unit of your local authority.)

This issue is so emotive it is sometimes hard to keep it in perspective but any case like this should mean that practices are tightened up and the situation is *less* likely to happen.

OBSERVATIONS

Many of the features you would be looking for in a day nursery are the same as those you would look for in a nursery school but with added considerations due to the amount of time a child is likely to be there and because they are likely to be younger. Look out for the following:

On arrival

How easy would it be to get into or out of the nursery unnoticed?

Atmosphere

- are staff involved with the children, or talking to each other?
- how do they relate to the children and deal with any incidents?
- are the children purposefully involved in activities, or just milling around?
- do the children seem happy?
- is there a sense of calm/authoritarian control/chaos?

Environment

- is children's work displayed on the walls?
- if so, is this work recent, or does it look like it's been there a while? (displaying children's work lets them know it is respected);
- is furniture the right size for children?
- is there equipment suitable for the age of the children present for: imaginative play (e.g., a home corner, dressing-up clothes); messy play (e.g., water, sand); and creative play (e.g., paints and craft materials)? (If these things aren't evident, ask if there is any other equipment that is sometimes used.);
- are toys in cupboards and drawers that are clearly labelled and accessible to children?
- are babies separated from boisterous older children?
- are dangerous items all stored safely out of reach?

Hygiene

Ask to be shown:

- where your child would sleep during the day, if appropriate;
- where children eat (often in a play area cleared for the purpose);

- where nappies are changed (charts showing when children are due for a change are a good sign, as long as the one due an hour ago is actually ticked off !);
- the children's toilets.

Outside

- is there a play area?
- is there equipment for climbing, balancing, kicking, riding? (much of this will probably be in store at any one time, so ask what outdoor equipment the nursery has);
- is the area clean, tidy and safe?

Staff room

You may not need to see the staff area, but it's useful to know they have a quiet space where they can plan ahead, and discuss any frustrations away from the children.

Supplementary questions

The visit may well throw up supplementary questions. If you can see the manager again it is ideal to clear them up at the time. If you haven't seen the social services report, you could ask to see it now.

By the time you leave the nursery, your head will probably be spinning trying to sort out your impressions. The first thing to do is to write them down, along with the answers to any questions that you didn't get to write down while you were looking around. It's worth noting anything that comes to mind in the next day or two as well. If you are seeing a number of nurseries, it's easy to forget which one had the unattended crying baby, or the excellent mural.

GETTING A PLACE

Many nurseries of all sorts will have waiting lists, some several years long. Some private nurseries charge to be on their list. This is usually nominal but not refundable and is used to ensure they do not have a huge waiting list and still have empty places when they come to be allocated. You may still want to be on several lists so that you have options when you need them, especially in areas where there is a huge unmet demand for nursery places and when you want a place for a baby – these are scarce in most places. Nurseries are unlikely to be able to tell you too far in advance when you will reach the top of the list for a place, so the chances of this being at just the time you want to start work are slim if you are only on one long list.

Once you have chosen your nursery, it is worth getting in touch with them every now and then to see how the waiting list is going and whether you are likely to get the place you want. Once you have been allocated a place, it is just as important to keep in touch to discuss settling in sessions with your child and so on, even if you are many months away from needing the place.

I have heard of day nurseries allocating more places than they actually have and assuming that some people will drop out. The people they assume are no longer interested in the places are those they have had no contact with. This is obviously disastrous if you arrange to start work knowing your place is arranged and finding a week before hand that it isn't. Apparently there is not considered to be a legal contract involved in the offer of a place, so there is no recourse to law. This is not usually a problem, so don't panic, but do keep in touch with the nursery.

State nursery schools and classes may also have waiting lists, but your position on these is unlikely to be a deciding factor when places are allocated. These nurseries have to have admissions policies and these will indicate any priority given to children with special needs or social deprivation, the priority given to a catchment area and to children with siblings at the school. If someone arriving at the last minute meets more of the criteria than you do, then they will get priority no matter how long you have been on a list. However, putting yourself on the list does indicate your interest and means the school may feel the need to keep you up to date on any changes and send you information such as any inspection reports that are made.

In Scotland, you must apply through the local authority if you want a place for a four-year old to be fully or part-funded by the Pre-school Year Grant. However, it still makes sense to talk to your chosen nursery as well.

There is no appeal procedure if you do not get offered the place you want for your child. This applies throughout Great Britain.

Choosing a Childminder

The list of childminders you receive from the social services department may be simply a list of names, addresses and contact numbers or may show you which have vacancies, the hours they are prepared to offer and other details, such as whether they smoke. However, this information depends on what the childminder has told the authority, and how recently. A childminder listed as having a full-time vacancy for an under-four, may have since decided only to offer after-school care two-days a week – not uncommon.

The points to establish over the telephone are generally practical ones. It is very unlikely a childminder will have any written information about the service on offer. The first thing to establish is whether she has a suitable vacancy (whatever it says on the council list), then your questions will depend largely on your list of priorities. Do you want the childminder to take your child to nursery or pre-school sessions, in which case is she able and willing to do so; can she supply your child with a special diet if necessary; does anyone in the house smoke; does she have pets if your child is allergic, and so on.

Once you have established a list of childminders who meet your essential requirements, then you need to arrange visits. You might not bring your child on a first visit but it is important that he or she meets the minder before either you or she decide whether an arrangement will work, and you should expect to make more than one visit before an agreement is made. If the minder would be caring for children other than your own, try and arrange to visit during a normal day, even if you have to take the day off work. Different minders are more or less happy with this arrangement. The visit is bound to take longer but you will learn a lot about how the minder deals with the children in her care. The reason minders may prefer to see you in the evening is because they know children will almost certainly play up when they are trying to talk to you. A seasoned hand tells me that, although visits are very welcome when the children are all there, she knows that a first-time parent with a small baby is likely to find the normal behaviour of a two or three-year old off-putting. Seeing how they deal with this situation is very useful, but don't expect total calm or quiet. If you have to make your first visit in the evening, make sure you schedule a second one during the daytime with your child.

It is worth having a list of questions written down and going through these with the childminder once she has had the chance to tell you about her approach. Normally, when you meet people in their own homes the occasion is social, and you are looking for a childminder you feel comfortable with and can relate to. In these circumstances, it may feel awkward to ask questions that in a social situation would be intrusive. Having a written list to refer to helps you make the situation more formal, for example, you're not personally questioning the minder's obvious ability, but since the question of training is on your list, you have to ask it.

QUESTIONS TO ASK Ask about her general approach before you get on to your written list. You could ask about a typical day/week. That way, you will establish *her* priorities and see how much thought she gives to planning for the children. Questions will depend on your own priorities but will probably include:

- what children the minder has of her own and what other children are minded;

- how she combines their needs;

- does she have a regular routine;

- whether she takes them out on visits or outings and, if so, whether she would ask your permission first;

- how she handles transport (including safety aspects such as car seats), costs and so on;

- what sort of outings might they go on. (You will want to know that they are appropriate to the age of your child.) If the child is to be taken out in the car, the minder should have business cover on her insurance. Check that she does;

- approach to discipline.

Talk about:

- potty training, if the age of your child makes this relevant – minders have varying attitudes;

(see page 115)

- whether she has any training (for possible qualifications see p 115). You could expect at least an up-to-date first-aid certificate, which she should show you;

- whether she is prepared to give medicines;

- whether she may be able to look after a child with a minor illness and, if so, under what circumstances;

- whether she has an arrangement with any other minders in the area to provide cover if she is ill (if so, who are they);

- fees;

- hours and whether she would offer occasional overtime, possibly at short notice;

- do you still pay during the childminder's holiday and if she is ill. (Expect to do so, but you will want to know how many weeks a year she will take as holiday, and how much notice you would get.)

- What are you expected to supply? Food, nappies, money for outings, etc?

- If the minder supplies meals, what sort of things do they have? Do the children eat regular snacks and, if so, what?

If you have been given the childminder's number by a friend, ask to see her registration certificate. If her name came from the council's list you can be sure she is registered anyway.

Ask to see a copy of the childminder's last social services inspection report. These vary in their usefulness, just as inspectors vary in their thoroughness, so don't assume the council has done all your safety checking for you.

Ask if she has any references to show you.

(see page 59)

If you both decided to go ahead with an arrangement, ask if she would provide a written contract for you to sign (see p 59 for what this should include). If you do want to go ahead and she doesn't feel confident about writing a contract, you can always do this yourself, but it is important to have one.

Does she provide settling-in sessions? It is generally thought best to introduce your child to the new arrangement gradually, building up to a full day, if this is what is required. Expect to pay for these sessions by the hour.

OBSERVATIONS

If children are present, see how the minder handles them. I've heard of one who told the other child present to sit out of the way behind the sofa while she spoke to the visitor. That was one parent who wasn't about to become a customer. It is difficult to care for children and have an adult conversation so expect to be interrupted, but see whether the minder loses her temper or whether she can come up with any strategies to distract children.

Expect to be shown every area of the house and garden that the child is allowed into. If any areas are closed to the child, make sure the childminder knows how the child will be prevented from entering these areas.

Look for safety features such as a stair gate, if appropriate to the age, cupboard locks, medicines kept out of reach, and a fully-enclosed garden.

Expect to see the kitchen if food or even drinks are to be prepared or stored there, and look for reasonable hygiene standards.

Ask to see where the child will sleep, if appropriate.

Don't expect the whole house to be spotless or perfectly tidy. Children who are active make a mess – just make sure that this hasn't reached the level of becoming a hazard.

Ask about the toys your child would be able to play with and expect to see them. You are looking for safe, unbroken toys and an understanding of what is appropriate to his or her age. If there are older children in the house, ask how the childminder stops the smaller children playing with inappropriate toys. If the issue of toy guns is important to you, ask about the childminder's policy.

Finally, it is important to remember that the success of any childminding arrangement will depend primarily on the relationship between yourself and the childminder. You will not be there when your child is with the minder. You can lay down the law about every aspect of your child's day, but you are dependent on the minder to carry out your wishes and you will generally have only her word that she has done so. To make it work, you will have to feel able to discuss every aspect of your child's care and talk about anything you are unhappy about. She in turn, should feel free to discuss everything openly with you, expecting you to understand how your child fits into a bigger picture. If your general views on child-rearing do not fit with the minder's there is no point taking things further.

A key aspect of using a childminder is that your child experiences a home and family situation, rather than an institution, and families are based on give and take. If you don't want your child to snack, but the other children do, for example, just saying he or she is not allowed to doesn't solve the problem when he or she watches the other children eating. Instead, you may want to supply him or her with some fruit or a healthy snack as a compromise. If this is the attitude you bring towards the relationship, you are likely to be more confident that your wishes are practical and will be carried out.

Recruiting a Nanny

At present there is no state register of nannies. The government committee considering childcare turned down requests for a national register in 1998, despite the case of British nanny, Louise Woodward, who was convicted of the manslaughter of the baby in her care. (It seems in any case that she may have been in America as an au pair rather than a nanny.)

Parents who want to employ a nanny and are not blessed with a personal recommendation are therefore left with two options – advertising or using a nanny agency. (Unless they want to take on a prestigious Norland nanny in which case they can access the college's own registry – see p 102.)

(see page 102)

An agency can cost anything from a one-off fee of about £160 to 10% of the nanny's first year's gross wages, depending on where you live, what the agency will do for the money, and what they think they can get away with. If you are using an agency, they should put you in contact with nannies they have already interviewed and whose references they have seen. (Some nanny agencies belong to the Federation of Recruitment and Employment Services see p 247 for address.) If you are not using an agency, the process of advertising, gaining replies and interviewing nannies, along with the prospect of a nanny having to give existing employers notice, means you need to start the process of recruitment well in advance of the date you need a nanny to start. You should be looking at around three months.

(see page 247)

Whether you are doing it all yourself or using an agency, the first thing to do is to refer to your list of priorities and draw up a job description. This is simply what it says – a description of the duties you would want the nanny to perform. Think about your child's day, the sort of activities and routine you would like for them, including meals, sleep, educational, recreational and social activities and whether you want the nanny to launder and clean for the child. Think carefully about the social side of his or her care. If your child is to be cared for on his or her own, do you want him or her to attend a toddler group, or pre-school sessions? Are you happy for the nanny to visit other nannies with children and have them visit your home? Do you want the nanny to take your child out in the car? Will you provide a car or do you want her to use hers? Does your child have any special needs? Will she have to cater for a special diet? Do you mind if the nanny smokes?

What about your own needs? What hours do you need covered? Do you want the nanny to be willing to work overtime? Do you consider training or experience or both vital? How much are your prepared to pay? Do you want a trial period at a lower rate with an incentive to stay on if you're both happy? (See p 62 to work out how much it will cost you for the nanny to keep this amount. Remember other costs such as supplying a car, outings, pre-school sessions, and so on as required.) If your nanny is to live in, what arrangements are you offering her?

If you are trying to recruit for a nanny share, it is essential that the two families agree on exactly what they will want the nanny to do and be at this point. If you want a mother's help or nanny/housekeeper you will need to add all her domestic tasks to your job description.

Despite the lack of registration, there is one check you can ask your nanny to carry out which should reveal any previous convictions. This is courtesy of the Data Protection Act, which was really designed to protect the rights of people whose names are held on computer. By law, any organisation that holds information about you on computer has to provide you with a copy of the information it holds on request. Because police records are all held on computer, anyone can fill in a form, pay a fee (£10 in 1998), and receive a letter back confirming there are no convictions registered against him or her or if there are any, what these are.

You can ask your nanny to supply the results of this search. However, the results will also reveal any 'spent' convictions. These are convictions for crimes that have been punished some time ago, and are considered, in a legal sense, no longer to exist. These do not have to be revealed if someone comes to court for any other offence, or have to be revealed to potential employers. You are therefore asking for information which, legitimately, the nanny may not wish to show you. The best way to overcome this is to discuss it with the individual concerned.

Please note that new data protection legislation is currently being considered by Parliament, which means the law may change during 1999. If this makes it illegal for employers to insist on a police check, new means of obtaining this information may be introduced at the same time. If you are in any doubt, contact your local police headquarters for the latest information.

The checking procedure is not foolproof either. There are various forms of identity allowed, such as a driving licence. If convictions were acquired when the applicant was using a different name (because of marriage, for example) and doesn't declare this other name, then these convictions will not show up. This is what happened in the case of Helen Stacey, the Norfolk childminder who killed the baby in her care. Norfolk Social Services are now insisting on birth and marriage certificates before they run their check but, as only the nanny can make this police check, you cannot insist this is the evidence of identity she shows the police.

The government is considering a new system after 2000 to provide better information for employers taking on staff to deal with all vulnerable people, including children, but it remains to be seen whether this information will be available to individual employers such as parents.

At present, all you can do is make all your checks as thorough as possible and remember that the notorious cases you read about in the press are notorious because they are extremely rare.

DIY – advertising

Draw up your advertisement according to your job description. If you feel you are able to offer a particularly attractive package, you may wish to include some details in the advertisement. If you will only consider a nanny who is trained or experienced or both, say so. *The Lady* is a traditional magazine for nanny recruitment advertisements, and *Nursery World* is another. Or you could advertise in your local newspaper's jobs section, or even all three. You can get up-to-date information on deadlines for submitting your advert, sizes and prices at: *Nursery World*, tel: 0171 837 3130; *The Lady*, tel: 0171 379 4717 (9.15 a.m. to 4.45 p.m.).

This is an example of a typical national advertisement, but make sure your advert is tailored to meet your needs:

> **LEICESTER** Daily nanny for sole charge of 3-yr old and 8-week baby. Mon – Fri 7.30 a.m. – 7 p.m. Must be qualified. Min. 2-yrs experience. Non-smoker, driver. £160 p.w. clear + 5-weeks paid holiday. Older child at nursery p/t. Interest in early education helpful.
>
> Tel _____ *or* Send details of qualifications and experience to: (Box No.)

If you are happy to spend a lot of time talking over the telephone and interviewing in order to firm up your ideas on the kind of person you want, then make your advertisement fairly general. If you have a totally clear idea of the sort of person and qualifications you want, and don't want to waste time on people who do not fit the bill, then be very precise.

Most national adverts give a telephone number but that means you taking calls when the applicant chooses to ring and you are straight into telephone interviewing. If you want written applications it is wise to use a box number rather than your own address as you are telling the public that children live there. (*Nursery World* has removed the names of children from an advert in the past for this reason.) The magazine or newspaper will explain how this operates and the cost. It is preferable in many ways to receive written applications first but if you are in an area where demand for nannies is high, you may find nannies only reply to adverts with telephone numbers.

When you have your replies, you may be able to get rid of some straight away. In some cases, your applicants may not meet your basic stated requirements and, if you have plenty to choose from, you may be able to choose only the best to speak to initially. Don't reply to the others until you have done so though, as 'plenty to choose from' may seem a bit thin after a round of telephone conversations.

Depending on the quality and quantity of replies, you may want to ask supplementary questions before making a short-list for interview. Write down your questions based on your job description and take notes of the answers as you speak to the applicants. If you find awkward silences are created while you make notes, just explain that you are taking notes because you have quite a few people to speak to. When you have found out all you want to know, thank the applicant for her time and tell her you will get back to her when you have made a short-list. That way, you get a chance to see how they all compare before you are committed to spending a considerable amount of time interviewing them in person.

If you are advertising a live-in post nationally, you may get applicants from across the country. You will need to decide whether you are prepared to pay interview expenses.

Draw up a schedule for interviews, bearing in mind, that nannies already in work will be restricted on the times they can attend. Allow plenty of time for each interview, including thinking time between each. An hour-and-a-half is reasonable. The easiest way to complete your schedule is if you can invite applicants over the telephone. They should be able to tell you right away if they can make the date or arrange a different time. You need to ask them to bring their references and certificates of any qualifications. Providing this interview doesn't eliminate them, you will also want to see them with your child. If your applicants are coming from some distance, it makes sense to incorporate this in one visit, which means you will have to allocate a lot longer for each of them.

THE INTERVIEW

You will need to interview the applicants even if they have already been interviewed by a nanny agency, or if the nanny has been recommended by a friend. Decide where in the house the interview is going to take place. The more relaxed the applicants, the more you are likely to find out about them, but you need to be somewhere you can have your list of questions and can easily take notes. Sitting side on to someone, is less threatening than directly opposite her across a table.

Prepare a list of questions from your job description and your list of priorities, but make sure you ask plenty of open questions (those that cannot simply be answered by yes or no) and allow the applicant the chance to tell you her approach and priorities. Make sure you find out exactly the extent of her previous experience – has she had sole care of the children she has been responsible for, was she responsible for cooking for them and how long have her previous positions lasted.

However much you instantly 'take to' someone, a nanny who is easy to get on with but has left every other job after a few weeks, or whose qualifications or experience are suspect is unlikely to be the most suitable. It is essential that you can communicate with your nanny, but it is important not to decide too much on first impressions. It would be a good idea to ask her to carry out a task she would be doing if she was your nanny – plan a week's menus, describe a day of activities suitable for your child. If you want anything in writing, make sure you give her somewhere suitable to sit, and disappear for a while to allow her to think in peace. That way you will have a concrete example of a piece of work that you can compare with other applicants. If you ask about activities, make sure you ask the applicant, at a different point in the interview, to tell you about a day she spent with her former charges, so you can see whether her ideas about child development are out of a book rather than something she puts into practice.

It is also useful to ask how she would respond to certain scenarios, such as if a child was accidentally burned. You want to know if she could think clearly in a crisis and whether her first-aid knowledge is sound.

If it is a live-in post, you will also need to discuss issues such as social activities while she is in the house and so on, and show her the accommodation on offer.

Make sure at the end of the interview that all the terms and conditions you are offering are clear to the nanny and that she has correctly understood what you would want from her if she was offered the post. Remember to look at her certificates, and write down the names and addresses/contact numbers of referees. Let her know you will be contacting them. Explain that you will want to introduce her to the child/children and will need to see the result of a police check before an appointment is finally made. Explain what this is and how to get one completed. Ask her if she is still interested in the post, now that she knows what would be involved – it will save you a lot of pointless agonising if you discover at this point that she isn't.

After the interviews, check the references of any applicants you are still considering. A chat over the telephone can tell you an enormous amount about the nanny's approach to her work. Asking about her strengths and weaknesses gives the referee the chance to give you the whole picture without feeling too disloyal to the nanny.

Ask the few at the top of your now shorter list back to see your child. You could suggest they prepare a short activity for them. Try and make this a relaxed occasion so you can all get to know each other better and give her plenty of time to get over any initial nerves.

MAKING AN APPOINTMENT

Once you have chosen your nanny and established that she still wants the job, let her know that her appointment is subject to the police check previously mentioned and ask her to apply at her local police station immediately, as it can take up to 40 days to come through. (A more usual turn round time is 14 days, but 40 days is the maximum allowed.) You will need to give her a copy of your contract to look over and then sign. This is a formal contract of employment and should include: who the contract is made between (i.e. both names and addresses), the date employment starts, terms and conditions (i.e. salary and when it will be reviewed, other perks, accommodation/meals/car provided, holidays – think about bank holidays, hours, duties, sick pay), notice on each side, disciplinary procedure (for example, oral warning, followed by written warning, followed by dismissal) and reasons for instant dismissal (for example, drug abuse, drunkenness, cruelty) – you may also want to include a period of probation during which notice can be given without special cause, i.e. simply because you are not comfortable with the arrangement. After this, you are either firing your nanny because of some malpractice or breach of contract, or making her redundant. Some employers include a confidentiality clause. You may have your own contract of employment as a useful reference to the type of things included.

Finally, as you have probably applied for jobs yourself, you will appreciate how much a reply will mean to applicants, even if it is simply a brief note to say they haven't been successful.

NORLAND NANNIES

Properly known as Norland Nurses, nannies trained by The Norland College have the reputation of more than a hundred years behind them. They are easily recognised by their uniform, which has only just been updated from brown dress, hat and white gloves to include trousers. (This was considered so radical that the news made national radio.)

Many these days go into other fields of the childcare 'industry,' but the Norland College operates a register for placing its nurses with families. The registry aims to introduce a suitable applicant to a prospective employer and will provide a standard contract if requested. The minimum salary recommended by the college is £200 gross per week for a fully-qualified Norland Nurse. (1998)

A probationary nurse will have completed two year's training, gained the Diploma in Nursery Nursing awarded by the Council for Awards in Children's Care and Education and may have achieved NVQ level 3 in childcare and education. A fully-qualified Norland Nurse will have a Norland Diploma and Badge, which is only granted after a year's satisfactory work in an approved setting.

For more information you can contact the registry on, tel: 01488 681164. And if you're worried about references, the registry will definitely require them – from you!

Section Five

Support Available

If Childcare Goes Wrong

Despite all your efforts to choose the best for your child, it is still possible to discover that what seemed the perfect arrangement is not working in practice. The first thing to consider is whether you are going to try and get it put right with the existing provider.

A NURSERY

Your problem might be with one member of staff, a practical matter to do with the running of the nursery or fears about other children's behaviour. The person to talk to is the nursery manager or head. If they feel they can resolve the problem, make sure you know what they plan to do about it, and over what timescale you should expect to see improvements.

If things don't improve or you don't feel the problem will be resolved, any period of notice will have been agreed with a private provider at the outset – although this is just the period you are expected to pay for, your child doesn't have to attend. If you feel that the nursery is not providing the service promised then you can withhold payment. You may want to think this through carefully if they are prepared to go to court over it, however. If no period was agreed you can withdraw the child immediately.

If the problem is with a private nursery and you consider it serious – the nursery is not providing a reasonable standard of care, or is putting children at risk – then take it up with the social services department. They can investigate and withdraw the nursery's registration.

If your problem is with a state nursery school or class, again take it up first with the teacher, then the head. Your child does not have to attend nursery and so can be withdrawn at any time. He or she can also transfer to another state nursery class, theoretically, but that depends on finding another one with places available. If you feel the nursery class is seriously substandard then you can take it up with the local education authority.

(see page 5)

If you take a four-year old child out of a state nursery class, you can still send him or her to a private nursery and benefit from the Nursery Education Grant. (See p 5.)

AN INDIVIDUAL CARER

An individual carer, such as a nanny or childminder, is someone who plays a large part in your child's life. You would expect, and hope, that your child will form an emotional attachment to her. If things go wrong, your first consideration will be protecting your child, but only in extreme cases, where the safety of your child is at risk, is that likely to mean removing the child from the carer immediately.

If you feel the nanny is not taking the children out enough, or abusing your phone, or the childminder is not providing the balanced diet she originally proposed, or any number of things that can cause worry or resentment, then the issue needs to be dealt with quickly and firmly.

Working parents often feel reluctant to bring up issues with their childcarers because they are afraid it will be taken out on the children in their absence. In reality, it is very unlikely that childcare professionals would do anything to harm the children in their care, but the guilt and emotion often associated in our culture with not staying at home with our children does not always allow parents to be rational. Sometimes, small issues can come to seem enormous because they are never discussed until they are allowed to break down the relationship entirely, and the child suffers because he or she is wrenched from the carer he or she has become attached to.

If your child is happy it is worth a great deal of effort to sort out any problems that arise.

With a nanny or childminder, you need to sit down calmly and try and sort out the issues with them. Be open and make sure they are open with you. It is no good if she grudgingly agrees to change when she doesn't really believe she is at fault. Either she won't change or she will resent it.

If problems are too great to be resolved this way, then your employment contract with your nanny should detail how you go about dismissing her. A probationary period should allow you to discover any such problems before you are committed to any lengthy period of notice. Arrangements for ending your contract with a childminder will also have formed part of the contract you originally signed. If the problems you are having with a childminder are serious and her actions might be detrimental to other children placed in her care, then you need to talk to her social services department. They can investigate complaints and can withdraw a minder's licence.

Help with Costs

Some pre-school care and education is free, but most is expensive. There are schemes that can provide help to some families and government proposals that offer more in the future.

FREE

(see page 5)

All state nursery schools or classes, run by the local education authority are free. (This does not apply to day nurseries run by the local authority, however.)

Any kind of nursery that accepts government funding through the Nursery Education Grant for four-year olds (see p 5) should theoretically provide at least one free place of at least two-and-a-half hours, five-times-a-week for 33 weeks of the year. Details of these places will have been agreed with the education authority and should be stated in its Early Years Development Plan.

HELP TO ALL

The Nursery Education (Pre-school Year) Grant is designed to ensure an education for all four-year olds. It originated from the last government's introduction of nursery vouchers on a pilot basis. When the voucher scheme was introduced, parents would receive the vouchers and literally take them to the nursery or playgroup of their choice. These were replaced temporarily by 'certificates of eligibility' and now by the Nursery Education Grant.

The principle remains roughly the same. Parents choose where to spend the grant. This starts the term after a child is four and is worth around £1,100 if the child is in nursery education for a full year before starting school. Parents can choose a free, state nursery place or a place in a private-sector nursery or pre-school, as long as it is approved to accept the funding. In Scotland, these places are allocated by the local authority, but parental choice should still be the major consideration. Parents only have to pay towards the place if they choose a private sector provider offering more than the two-and-a-half-hour, five-day, 33-week place covered by the grant.

(see page 5)

Approval to accept this grant is dependent on the nursery or pre-school meeting certain criteria. It has to show how it is delivering, or planning to deliver, the government's Desirable Outcomes for Children's Learning (Pre-school Curriculum Framework in Scotland) (see p 5). It has to agree to inspection to check that it is reaching an acceptable standard in delivering this curriculum – funding can be withdrawn if it does not – and it has to provide copies of any inspection report to interested parents on request.

This funding is available to all parents from the term after their children become four, regardless of their financial or other circumstances.

EMPLOYEES

Some employers do help their staff with the costs of childcare or provide subsidised nursery places. If you think yours might, ask the personnel department or your immediate boss. These subsidies, when available, can be extremely valuable.

HELP FOR CHILDREN IN NEED

For the purposes of receiving special help for your child, a 'child in need' is defined by the Children Act 1989 as being:

'unlikely to achieve or maintain, or to have the opportunity of achieving or maintaining, a reasonable standard of health or development without the provision to him of services by a local authority,

'his health or development is likely to be significantly impaired or further impaired without the provision for him of such services, or

'he is disabled.'

In this context, health means physical or mental, and development includes physical, emotional, intellectual, social or behavioural development. A child is considered disabled: 'if he is blind, deaf or dumb or suffers from mental disorder of any kind or is substantially and permanently handicapped by illness, injury or congenital deformity or such other disability as may be prescribed'.

Although there are a few clear-cut cases, such as blindness, the rest of this definition may seem rather woolly when you try to apply it to your own child. This leaves it largely up to the local authority to decide who to help and how.

Provision might include sponsored childcare, where the local authority will pay the fees for a child to spend time at a day nursery, pre-school or playgroup, or with a childminder. The reasons they may provide this help can vary from ill or disabled parents struggling to cope with their children at home, to social deprivation and emotional stress preventing single parents from providing the care their child needs.

Support workers may be provided by the local social services department to help children with a disability benefit from nursery or playgroup care. The amount of help depends on the extent of the disability. In some cases, this support may be long-term. For children with lesser disabilities, such as speech problems, or behavioural problems, a support worker may be provided short-term to help them settle into a group. The need for additional help will also depend on the nursery or pre-school's ability to provide support for children in need.

Some nursery classes also reserve places for children in need.

HELP FOR FAMILIES ON LOW INCOMES

Families receiving certain benefits can also get help with their childcare costs. To qualify, parents must be entitled to Family Credit, Disability Working Allowance, Housing Benefit or Council Tax Benefit, or would be if childcare costs of up to £60 for one child and £100 for more are taken into account.

Lone parents who work 16 hours or more a week, or couples who both work 16 hours or more qualify, as do couples where one is working 16 hours or more and the other is incapacitated. For this purpose, 'incapacitated' means in receipt of a qualifying benefit for the Disability Premium or has an invalid carriage or other vehicle provided by the Secretary of State.

Help can be claimed for children from birth but they have to be attending a nursery, play scheme or childminder registered with the local authority, an out-of-hours club run on school premises by the school or local authority (or childcare scheme run on Crown property which is exempt from registration). There is no financial help available if you use a nanny.

Costs of up to £60 can be claimed per family for one child and up to £100 for more. If the costs are variable, they are assessed on the basis of the last four weeks for children under school age, or an estimate of weekly charges if the child is just starting with a childminder or nursery.

The money is not paid directly but taken into account when the other benefits are assessed. These are assessed on the basis of money coming into the family, so the childcare costs (up to the amounts mentioned) are taken away from the income. This lower figure is then used to calculate the benefit due, meaning the claimant is entitled to more benefit.

This help with childcare costs can be claimed on the normal claim forms for each kind of benefit but timing is vital for Family Credit and disability claims. With these benefits, claims are agreed for 26 weeks at a time. *If childcare costs are not claimed at the beginning they cannot be made for the whole of the next 26 weeks.* No back-dated costs will be allowed against a future claim either. This does not apply to Housing or Council Tax Benefit where claims for childcare costs can be made at any time.

For more information about Housing and Council Tax Benefits, contact your local council. There are national helplines for the other benefits: Family Credit, tel: 01253 500050; Disability Working Allowance, tel: 01772 883300, textphone: 01772 883333.

The government has introduced a major change to the way help with childcare costs will be provided to families on low incomes from October 1999. Instead of receiving Family Credit from the Benefits Agency, parents on low incomes will be entitled to a tax credit towards the cost of childcare. This will be administered by the Inland Revenue, which is taking over responsibility for current Benefits Agency staff in order to provide the service. The scheme is being piloted with some staff at present but even those running the helpline don't know yet exactly how it will operate. Parents already receiving Family Credit, however, should be better off under the new scheme with up to £70 a week for a family with one child, and up to £105 for a family of more (up to a maximum of 70% of childcare costs).

In some rare cases, nurseries themselves may offer some reductions in fees in cases of hardship. Kindergartens belonging to the Steiner Waldorf Schools Fellowship will often help parents who want their child to attend but can't afford the full fees.

Children with Special Educational Needs

The education department of your local authority has a responsibility towards children with special educational needs and may help them benefit from a nursery education by, for example, providing advice and support to the carers/teachers involved. Additional teaching or welfare support may also be provided for a child who has been assessed and provided with a 'Statement of Special Educational Needs', in England and Wales, or a 'Record of Needs', in Scotland. If you think your child may qualify, the section below describers how these assessments are made.

There may also be groups in your area that cater either exclusively, or mainly for children with special educational needs. These are generally known as 'opportunity groups' and information should be held by the local authority.

IF YOU THINK YOUR CHILD HAS SPECIAL EDUCATIONAL NEEDS

About one in five children may have learning difficulties at some time in their school life, according to the Department for Education and Employment. Recognising these problems early means your child can start getting help as soon as possible.

The law says a child has special educational needs if he or she has learning difficulties and needs special help. This may be because of a physical disability, such as problem with sight, hearing or speech, a mental disability, emotional or behavioural problems, a problem with speaking, or a medical problem.

If you become aware of any of these problems before your child is due to start school you can get help early on from your education authority. A doctor, health visitor or social worker may also be able to help. If they think your child has special educational needs they must consult you, and tell the education authority as well as giving you information about any voluntary organisation that may be able to help.

The sort of services available for pre-school children include: teachers who visit your home; help to attend a playgroup or opportunity group; home-based learning schemes, for example, the portage project, in which a trained home visitor helps suggest activities to encourage your child to develop new skills.

If your child is over two you can ask the authority to make a 'statutory assessment' of his or her special educational needs. This is a very detailed assessment taking into account your views, the views of doctors and an educational psychologist. A child can still get help without this assessment, but if you feel the help he or she is getting is inadequate, the assessment can provide a 'statement' (or 'record', in Scotland), which will define his or her needs in black and white as well as the help he or she is entitled to.

Once they have collected all the information they feel they need, the education authority will decide whether to make this Statement of Special Educational Needs, in England and Wales, or Record of Needs, in Scotland.

This statement or record means the authority has decided that your child needs help that cannot reasonably be provided within the normal resources available, and your child may need extra funding, staff time or special equipment. It may include things like use of a wheelchair and extra help from a nursery assistant, or a special highchair and more one-to-one attention.

Parents are shown a proposed statement or record, which they can comment on before it is finally drawn up, and there is a right to appeal if you disagree with the authority on the nature of your child's needs. A statement or record is not designed to be made once and define your child's needs for life. It includes arrangements for a regular review and will be discontinued if it becomes unnecessary.

The Future

The reason for much of the confusion in the regulations that cover pre-school provision is that the two elements of care and education have traditionally been thought of as separate, with an additional separation between private and state provision. Nurseries providing day-long care, pre-schools and childminders are therefore regulated by the social services departments of local authorities. Private nursery schools are too, for some reason. However, state nursery schools and classes are regulated by the local education authority. Nurseries attached to independent schools are hardly regulated at all, unless they are in Scotland or belong to the government's Nursery Education Scheme. Requirements connected with the Nursery Education (Pre-school Year) Grant for four-year olds are on top of all the other regulations.

The government has recognised that this is confusing and may duplicate effort so it is working towards one new inspection system in the future that will avoid this split of responsibilities.

The government has also promised a national helpline for later in 1999 to tell parents where they can find out about good-quality provision locally.

Its pledge of a free nursery place for all four-year olds whose parents wanted one by September 1998 was within a hair's breadth of being met. The next one is for a place for three-year olds. Places will be introduced gradually over the three years from April 1999, with a target of places for 66% of three-year olds by 2002.

The government is also planning to train more childcarers.

Other factors that might affect this sector, however, include the introduction of a minimum wage and maximum working hours. Some childcare workers currently earn less than the proposed minimum and many work more hours.

Changes in legislation and policy may be fast, but they will probably take longer to put into practice. Meanwhile it will be up to parents to seek out the dedicated and inspired people who continue to be out there, quietly caring for and educating our next generation.

Section Six

Directory

Qualifications and What They Mean

There is a wide variety of qualifications that staff working with children might hold, some of which mean they have studied full-time over several years as well as being assessed while they gain work experience, others which mean they have attended a short course. The list below is a general guide to some you may come across. There could be others and the awarding bodies (the organisations who set the standards and hand out the qualifications) may change the content over time.

Most of the information in this list has been compiled by the Norfolk Early Years Training Consortium, made up of the County Council, local colleges and trainers and day-care providers, who have usefully indicated which qualifications they consider acceptable for which roles.

Not considered to confer 'qualified status'

BTEC (British Technical Education Council) First Diploma in Caring.

City and Guilds NCFE 3593 Certificate in Sessional Crèche Work.

GNVQ (General National Vocational Qualification) Health and Social Care.

NAMCW (National Association for Maternal and Child Welfare) – Advanced Certificate in Childcare and Education, Certificate in Nursery Management Skills and Diploma in Childcare and Education.

Open College Network – Initial Course for Crèche workers, Working Together.

Open University – Child Abuse and Neglect Open Study Pack, Understanding Health and Social Care, Working with Under 5s.

Pre-school Learning Alliance – Basic Learning Through Play, Child Development, Curriculum Planning, Introduction to Observation, Introduction to pre-school practice, Special Needs.

CHILDCARE QUALIFICATIONS

These qualifications are considered suitable for work in: day nurseries and nursery schools/classes and as a childminder; and, with appropriate experience for the more senior posts, at assistant, supervisor and management level, unless specifically stated. Most courses include work experience or require it for entry on the course.

BTEC

National Certificate in Caring Services (Nursery Nursing) Part Time (P/T), 2 yrs.

National Diploma in Caring Services (Nursery Nursing) Full Time (F/T), 2 yrs.

National Certificate in Childhood Studies (Nursery Nursing) P/T, 2 yrs.

National Diploma in Childhood Studies (Nursery Nursing) F/T, 2 yrs.

ScotVec (Scottish Vocational Qualification Council) also provides National Certificate modules in childcare that are equivalent to the BTEC National Certificate.

CACHE (Council for Awards in Childcare and Education) **Certificate in Childcare and Education** (not for supervisor or above, or LEA nursery class) F/T or P/T up to 5 yrs.

City and Guilds

324.1 Caring for Children (restrictions as above) P/T 400 hrs.

325.1 Community Care Practice (gained in childcare setting, restrictions as above) F/T, 400 hrs including work experience.

331 Family and Community Care (gained in childcare setting, restrictions as above) F/T, 2 yrs.

356 Parts 1 and 2 Practical Caring Skills (gained in childcare setting, restrictions as above) P/T.

7321 Certificate in Learning Support only suitable at assistant level and as a class-room assistant in First Schools or special needs assistant P/T, 1 yr.

Montessori Training Organisation (AMI)

Foundation Course (not for supervisor or above, or day nursery or LEA nursery school) P/T, 1 yr or distance learning.

Diploma (supervisor or above only in Montessori school, not suitable for day nursery or LEA nursery class) F/T, 1 yr including 500 hrs teaching practice.

NCFE (National Council of Further Education)

Certificate in Playgroup Practice (not for supervisor or above, or LEA nursery class) P/T, 100 hrs min. + work experience.

Advanced Certificate in Playgroup Practice, P/T, min. 80 hrs.

NNEB (National Nursery Examination Board), or NNEB Diploma (CACHE), F/T, up to 5 yrs (modular).

Nursing

Diploma of Higher Education Nursing (Child Care) (not for supervisor or above, or LEA nursery class) F/T, 3 yrs.

Enrolled Nurse General to Sick Children's Nurse (restrictions as above) 49–96 wks, depending on experience.

Modified Diploma of Higher Education (Child Care) (restrictions as above) F/T, 1 yr.

Registered Sick Children's Nurse (RSCN) (restrictions as above) F/T, 53 wks

Specialist Experience in Child Care for 2nd Level Nurses (enrolled) (restrictions as above) 6 months.

NVQ/SVQ (National/Scottish Vocational Qualification)

level 2 Child Care and Education – now known as Early Years Care and Education (not for supervisor or above, or LEA nursery class), flexible, work-based.

level 3 Child Care and Education – now known as Early Years Care and Education, flexible, work-based.

level 3 Playwork (not a qualification for childminder, day nursery, nursery school or LEA nursery class), flexible, work-based.

Pre-school Learning Alliance

Diploma in Pre-school Practice, P/T, 220 hrs + work placement, or by open learning.

Certificate in Pre-school Practice (not for supervisor or above, or LEA nursery class), P/T, 120 hrs + work experience.

Experienced Playleaders' Course (recognised if completed with the foundation course below) P/T, 1 yr.

PPA (Pre-school Playgroups Association) **Foundation Course** (pre-1993) (restrictions as above, but suitable for childminder and day nursery only when working with three to five-year olds), P/T, 1 yr.

HIGHER-LEVEL QUALIFICATIONS

These are professional qualifications although a person's relevant experience would also be taken into account before they were deemed suitable for a particular post.

City and Guilds

325.3 Advanced Management for Care (as long as qualification achieved in a child-care setting), F/T or P/T, 1 yr, work-based.

325.2 Foundation Management for Care (as long as achieved in a childcare setting), P/T, 1 yr, work-based.

CACHE Advanced Diploma in Child Care and Education (if holder has appropriate experience), P/T, up to 5 yrs.

NNEB Certificate/Diploma in Post Qualifying Studies (restriction as above, qualification now replaced by above), P/T, 2 yrs.

BTEC Higher National Certificate Early Childhood Studies (Nursery Nursing) (restriction as above), P/T, 2 yrs.

ScotVec Higher National Certificate Working with Children (as above).

CCETSW (Central Council for Education and Training in Social Work)

Certificate of Qualification in Social Work (restriction as above) F/T, 1 yr postgraduate, or F/T, 2 yrs, or P/T.

Diploma in Social Work (restriction as above) normally F/T, 2 yrs.

Teaching qualifications – Cert. Ed., PGCE, BEd (restriction as above).

BA/BSc (Degree) **Early Childhood Studies** (restriction as above), F/T, 3 yrs, or P/T and modular.

Table Directory
Local Education Authorities

(see pages 234–241)

Local Authorities in England and Wales show all schools with an in-take of pupils from age 3. If your LEA is not shown or you require information for a child under 3 years of age please contact your LEA directly - see pages 234 to 241.

The type codes shown on the England tables represent the following school status:

C – County School,

GM – Self Governing School (Grant-maintained),

SA – Special Agreement School,

VA – Voluntary Aided School, VC – Voluntary Controlled School,

GMSS – Grant-maintained Special School,

MSS – Special School (maintained by the LEA).

Names and addresses and telephone numbers and school rolls of all schools in Scotland, as per September 1998. The School rolls are as per School Census September 1997. (At the request of the education authorities of Highland and South Ayrshire the address and telephone numbers of the education authority schools in those areas are not supplied).

WALES 187

Isle of Anglesey 187, Gwyned 188, Conwy 190, Denbighshire 191, Flintshire 192, Wrexham 193, Powys 195, Ceredigion 196, Pembrokeshire 196, Caramarthenshire 196, Swansea 197, Neath Port Talbot 199, Bridgend 200, The Vale of Glamorgan 200, Rhondda/Cynon/Taff 201, Marthyr Tydfil 203, Caerphilly 203, Blaenau Gwent 204, Torfaen 204, Monmouthshire 204, Newport 205, Cardiff 205

SCOTLAND 207

Aberdeen City 207, Aberdeenshire 208, Angus 209, Argyll and Bute 210, Clackmannanshire 210, Dumfries and Galloway 210, Dundee City 211, East Ayrshire 211, East Dunbartonshire 212, East Lothian 212, East Renfrewshire 213, City of Edinburgh 213, Eilean Siar 215, Falkirk 215, Fife 216, Glasgow City 218, Highland 221, Inverclyde 222, Midlothian 222, Moray 223, North Ayrshire 223, North Lanarkshire 224, Orkney Islands 225, Perth and Kinross 225, Renfrewshire 226, Scottish Borders 226, Shetland Islands 227, South Ayrshire 227, South Lanarkshire 227, Stirling 228, West Dunbartonshire 229, West Lothian 229

ENGLAND

School name, address and telephone number	Type	Age

INNER LONDON

201 CITY OF LONDON

	Type	Age
Sir John Cass's Foundation Primary School St James's Passage, Duke's Place, Aldgate, EC3A 5DE ☎ 0171 283 1147	VA	3–11

202 CAMDEN

	Type	Age
Argyle Junior Mixed and Infant School Tonbridge Street, WC1H 9EG ☎ 0171 837 4590	C	3–11
Beckford Primary School Dornfell Street, West Hampstead, NW6 1QL ☎ 0171 435 8646	C	3–11
Brecknock Primary School York Way, N7 9QE ☎ 0171 485 6334	C	3–11
Brookfield Primary School Chester Road, N19 5DH ☎ 0171 272 9627	C	3–11
Carlton Primary School Grafton Road, NW5 4AX ☎ 0171 485 1947	C	3–11
Christ Church CofE School Redhill Street, NW1 4BD ☎ 0171 387 7881	VA	3–11
Edith Neville Primary School Medburn Centre, 136 Chalton Street, NW1 1RX ☎ 0171 388 5625	C	3–11
Eleanor Palmer School Lupton Street, NW5 2JA ☎ 0171 485 2155	C	3–11
Fleet School Fleet Road, NW3 2NY ☎ 0171 485 2028	C	3–11
Gospel Oak Primary School Mansfield Road, NW3 2JB ☎ 0171 485 7435	C	3–11
Kentish Town CofE Primary School Islip Street, NW5 2TU ☎ 0171 485 1279	VA	3–11
Netley School 30 William Road, NW1 3EN ☎ 0171 387 6601	C	3–11
New End Primary School Streatley Place, Hampstead, NW3 1HU ☎ 0171 431 0961	C	3–11
Our Lady's RC Primary School Pratt Street, Camden, NW1 0DP ☎ 0171 485 7997	VA	3–11
Primrose Hill Primary School Princess Road, NW1 8JL ☎ 0171 722 8500	C	3–11
Rhyl Primary School Rhyl Street, NW5 3HB ☎ 0171 485 4899	C	3–11
Richard Cobden Primary School Camden Street, NW1 0LL ☎ 0171 387 5909	C	3–11
Rosary RC Primary School 238 Haverstock Hill, Hampstead, NW3 2AE ☎ 0171 794 6292	VA	3–11
St Alban's Primary School Baldwins Gardens, Holborn, EC1N 7SD ☎ 0171 242 8585	VA	3–11
St Dominic's RC Primary School Southampton Road, NW5 4JS ☎ 0171 485 5918	VA	3–11
St George The Martyr Primary School John's Mews, WC1N 2NX ☎ 0171 405 5640	VA	3–11
St Joseph's RC Primary School Macklin Street, Drury Lane, WC2B 5NA ☎ 0171 242 7712	VA	3–11
St Mary and St Pancras CofE School Polygon Road, NW1 1SR ☎ 0171 387 6117	VA	3–11
St Michael's CofE Primary School 88 Camden Street, NW1 0JA ☎ 0171 485 8965	VA	3–11

203 GREENWICH

	Type	Age
Bannockburn Junior Mixed and Infant School and Nursery Plumstead High Street, SE18 1HE ☎ 0181 854 2169	C	3–11
Boxgrove School Boxgrove Road, Abbey Wood, SE2 9JP ☎ 0181 310 1912	C	3–11
Briset Primary School Briset Road, Eltham, SE9 6HN ☎ 0181 859 3114	C	3–11
Cardwell Primary School Frances Street, Woolwich, SE18 5LP ☎ 0181 854 1051	C	3–11
Charlton Manor Primary School Hornfair Road, SE7 7BE ☎ 0181 856 6525	C	3–11
Ealdham Primary School Ealdham Square, Eltham, SE9 6BP ☎ 0181 850 5484	C	3–11
Foxfield Primary School Sandbach Place, SE18 7EX ☎ 0181 854 0816	C	3–11
Gordon School Grangehill Road, Eltham, SE9 1QG ☎ 0181 850 5486	C	3–11
Greenslade Junior Mixed Infant and Nursery School Erindale, Plumstead Common, SE18 2QQ ☎ 0181 316 6847	C	3–11
Henwick Primary School Henwick Road, Eltham, SE9 6NZ ☎ 0181 856 8627	C	3–11
Heronsgate Junior Mixed Infant and Nursery School Whinchat Road, SE28 0DW ☎ 0181 317 0809	C	3–11
Holy Family RC Primary School Tudway Road, Kidbrooke, Greenwich, SE3 9YX ☎ 0181 856 2708	VA	3–11
Hughes Fields School Watergate Street, Deptford, SE8 3HD ☎ 0181 692 4328	C	3–11

School name, address and telephone number	Type	Age
Linton Mead Primary School Central Way, Thamesmead, SE28 8DT ☎ 0181 310 1902	C	3–11
Middle Park Primary School Middle Park Avenue, Eltham, SE9 5RX ☎ 0181 850 8747	C	3–11
Morden Mount Primary School Lewisham Road, SE13 7QP ☎ 0181 692 2920	C	3–11
Mulgrave Primary School Rectory Place, SE18 5DA ☎ 0181 317 9211	C	3–11
Nightingale Junior Mixed Infant and Nursery School Bloomfield Road, Plumstead, SE18 7JJ ☎ 0181 854 6838	C	3–11
Plumcroft School Plum Lane, Plumstead, SE18 3HW ☎ 0181 854 1308	C	3–11
Rockliffe Manor Junior Infant and Nursery School Bassant Road, SE18 2NP ☎ 0181 854 4785	C	3–11
Ruxley Manor School Milverton Way, Eltham, SE9 3EY ☎ 0181 857 3560	C	3–11
St Alfege with St Peter's School Creek Road, SE10 9RB ☎ 0181 858 3613	VA	3–11
St Margaret Clitherow School Cole Close, Thamesmead, SE28 8AU ☎ 0181 310 1699	VA	3–11
St Margaret's CofE School St Margaret's Grove, Plumstead Common Road, SE18 7RL ☎ 0181 854 3924	VA	3–11
St Mary's RC School Glenure Road, Eltham, SE9 1UF ☎ 0181 850 7835	VA	3–11
St Thomas a Beckett Primary School Mottisfont Road, Abbey Wood, SE2 9LY ☎ 0181 310 5394	VA	3–11
Sherington Primary School Sherington Road, Charlton, SE7 7JP ☎ 0181 858 5497	C	3–11
Timbercroft Primary School Timbercroft Lane, Plumstead, SE18 2SG ☎ 0181 854 6915	C	3–11
Wingfield Primary School Moorehead Way, SE3 9XU ☎ 0181 856 5298	C	3–11
Wyborne Primary School Footscray Road, New Eltham, SE9 2EH ☎ 0181 850 4933	C	3–11

204 HACKNEY

School name, address and telephone number	Type	Age
Amherst Primary School Sigdon Road, Hackney, E8 1AS ☎ 0171 254 4090	C	3–11
Avigdor Primary School 63-67 Lordship Road, N16 0QJ ☎ 0181 800 8339	VA	3–11
Baden-Powell Primary School Ferron Road, E5 8DN ☎ 0181 985 6176	C	3–11
Burbage School Ivy Street, Hackney, N1 5JD ☎ 0171 739 8591	C	3–11
Daubeney Primary School Daubeney Road, Clapton, E5 0EG ☎ 0181 985 4380	C	3–11
De Beauvoir Junior Mixed and Infant School Tottenham Road, N1 4BH ☎ 0171 254 2517	C	3–11
Gayhurst Primary School Gayhurst Road, Hackney, E8 3EN ☎ 0171 254 6138	C	3–11
Grasmere Primary School 92 Albion Road, N16 9PD ☎ 0171 254 4564	C	3–11
Holmleigh Primary School Dunsmure Road, N16 5PU ☎ 0181 802 7420	C	3–11
Holy Trinity CofE Primary School Beechwood Road, E8 3DY ☎ 0171 254 1010	VA	3–11
Jubilee Primary School Filey Avenue, N16 6NR ☎ 0181 806 5446	C	3–11
Kingsmead School Kingsmead Way, E9 5PP ☎ 0181 985 5779	C	3–11
Lauriston Primary School Rutland Road, E9 7JS ☎ 0181 985 6331	C	3–11
London Fields Primary School Westgate Street, E8 3RL ☎ 0171 254 4330	C	3–11
Our Lady and St Joseph's Primary School Buckingham Road, N1 4DG ☎ 0171 254 7353	VA	3–11
Princess May Primary School Barrett's Grove, Stoke Newington, N16 8AJ ☎ 0171 254 1589	C	3–11
Rams Episcopal CofE Primary School Mehetabel Road, Hackney, E9 6DU ☎ 0181 985 2045	VA	3–11
Randal Cremer Primary School Ormsby Street, Shoreditch, E2 8JG ☎ 0171 739 8162	C	3–11
Rushmore Primary School Rushmore Road, Hackney, E5 0EY ☎ 0181 985 3175	C	3–11
Sebright Primary School Audrey Street, Goldsmiths Row, E2 8QH ☎ 0171 739 6531	C	3–11
William Patten Primary School Stoke Newington Church Street, N16 0NX ☎ 0171 254 4915	C	3–11

205 HAMMERSMITH AND FULHAM

School name, address and telephone number	Type	Age
Addison Primary School Addison Gardens, Blythe Road, W14 0DT ☎ 0171 603 5333	C	3–11
Avonmore School Avonmore Road, W14 8SH ☎ 0171 603 9750	C	3–11
Bentworth Primary School Bentworth Road, Westway, W12 7AJ ☎ 0181 743 2527	C	3–11
Fulham Primary School Halford Road, SW6 1JU ☎ 0171 385 0535	C	3–11
Holy Cross RC School Basuto Road, SW6 4BL ☎ 0171 736 1447	VA	3–11
Kenmont Primary School Valliere Road, NW10 6AL ☎ 0181 969 4497	C	3–11
Lena Gardens School Lena Gardens, W6 7PZ ☎ 0171 603 4043	C	3–11

123

School name, address and telephone number	Type	Age
Melcombe Primary School Fulham Palace Road, W6 9ER ☎ 0181 748 7411	C	3–11
Miles Coverdale Primary School Coverdale Road, Shepherds Bush, W12 8JJ ☎ 0181 743 5847	C	3–11
Old Oak Primary School Mellitus Street, W12 0AS ☎ 0181 743 7629	C	3–11
Peterborough Primary School Clancarty Road, SW6 3AA ☎ 0171 736 5863	C	3–11
St Mary's RC Junior Mixed and Infant School Masbro Road, W14 0 LT ☎ 0171 603 7717	VA	3–11
St Paul's CofE Primary School Worlidge Street, W6 9BP ☎ 0181 748 4951	VA	3–11
St Peter's CofE Junior Mixed and Infant School St Peter's Grove, Hammersmith, W6 9AY ☎ 0181 748 7756	VA	3–11

206 ISLINGTON

School name, address and telephone number	Type	Age
Ambler Primary School Blackstock Road, Finsbury Park, N4 2DR ☎ 0171 226 4708	C	3–11
Blessed Sacrament RC School Boadicea Street, Copenhagen Street, N1 0UF ☎ 0171 278 2187	VA	3–11
Charles Lamb School Popham Road, N1 8RF ☎ 0171 226 2407	C	3–11
Christ The King RC School 55 Tollington Park, N4 3QW ☎ 0171 272 5987	VA	3–11
Copenhagen Primary School Treaty Street, N1 0WF ☎ 0171 837 5597	C	3–11
Drayton Park School Arvon Road, Drayton Park, Highbury, N5 1PJ ☎ 0171 607 4142	C	3–11
Duncombe Primary School Sussex Way, Marlborough Road, Islington, N19 4JA ☎ 0171 272 5620	C	3–11
Ecclesbourne School Ecclesbourne Road, Islington, N1 3AG ☎ 0171 226 6696	C	3–11
Gillespie School Gillespie Road, N5 1LH ☎ 0171 226 6840	C	3–11
Grafton Primary School Eburne Road, Seven Sisters Road, N7 6AR ☎ 0171 272 3284	C	3–11
Hanover School Noel Road, St Peter's Street, N1 8BD ☎ 0171 226 2401	C	3–11
Hargrave Park Primary School Hargrave Park, N19 5JN ☎ 0171 272 3989	C	3–11
Highbury Quadrant School Highbury New Park, N5 2DP ☎ 0171 226 6531	C	3–11
Hungerford Primary School Hungerford Road, York Way, N7 9LF ☎ 0171 607 4787	C	3–11
Laycock School Laycock Street, Upper Street, N1 1SW ☎ 0171 226 2927	C	3–11
Moorfields School Bunhill Row, EC1Y 8RX ☎ 0171 253 2150	C	3–11
Moreland School Moreland Street, Goswell Road, EC1V 8BB ☎ 0171 253 8144	C	3–11
Pakeman School Hornsey Road, N7 6DU ☎ 0171 607 2575	C	3–11
Penton School Ritchie Street, N1 0EH ☎ 0171 837 2494	C	3–11
Ring Cross Primary School Eden Grove, Islington, N7 8EE ☎ 0171 607 5109	C	3–11
Robert Blair Primary School Brewery Road, Islington, N7 9QJ ☎ 0171 607 4115	C	3–11
St Joan of Arc RC Primary School Northolme Road, Highbury Park, N5 2UX ☎ 0171 226 3920	VA	3–11
St John Evangelist RC Primary School Duncan Street, Islington High Street, N1 8BL ☎ 0171 226 1314	VA	3–11
St John's (Upper Holloway) CofE Primary School Pemberton Gardens, Holloway Road, N19 5RR ☎ 0171 272 2780	VA	3–11
St Joseph's RC Junior Mixed and Infant School Highgate Hill, Highgate, N19 5NE ☎ 0171 272 1270	VA	3–11
St Luke's Primary School Radnor Street, EC1V 3SJ ☎ 0171 253 3880	VA	3–11
St Peter's and St Paul's RC Primary School Compton Street, Goswell Road, EC1V 0EU ☎ 0171 253 0839	VA	3–11
Thornhill Primary School Thornhill Road, N1 1HX ☎ 0171 607 4162	C	3–11
Tufnell Park Primary School Dalmeny Road, N7 0HJ ☎ 0171 607 4852	C	3–11
Vittoria Primary School Half Moon Crescent, Islington, N1 0TJ ☎ 0171 837 6063	C	3–11
William Tyndale School Sable Street, Canonbury Road, N1 2AQ ☎ 0171 226 6803	C	3–11
Winton Primary School Killick Street, Pentonville Road, N1 9AZ ☎ 0171 837 6096	C	3–11
Yerbury Primary School Foxham Road, Yerbury Road, N19 4RR ☎ 0171 272 6580	C	3–11

207 KENSINGTON AND CHELSEA

School name, address and telephone number	Type	Age
Ashburnham School 17 Blantyre Street, SW10 0DT ☎ 0171 352 5740	C	3–11
Bousfield School South Bolton Gardens, SW5 0DJ ☎ 0171 373 6544	C	3–11
Colville Primary School Lonsdale Road, Portobello Road, W11 2DF ☎ 0171 229 6540	C	3–11
Holy Trinity School Sedding Street, Sloane Square, SW1X 9DE ☎ 0171 730 5320	VA	3–11

School name, address and telephone number	Type	Age
Marlborough Primary School Draycott Avenue, entrance Sloane Avenue, SW3 3AP ☎ 0171 589 8553	C	3-11
Our Lady of Victories RC Primary School Clareville Street, SW7 5AQ ☎ 0171 373 4491	GM	3-11
Park Walk Primary School Park Walk, King's Road, Chelsea, SW10 0AY ☎ 0171 352 8700	C	3-11
St Charles' RC Primary School St Charles Square, W10 6EB ☎ 0181 969 5566	GM	3-11
St Cuthbert with St Matthias CofE School Warwick Road, Earls Court, SW5 9UE ☎ 0171 373 8225	VA	3-11
St Joseph's RC School Cadogan Street, SW3 2QT ☎ 0171 589 2438	VA	3-11
St Mary's Primary School East Row, Kensal Road, W10 5AW ☎ 0181 969 0321	VA	3-11
St Thomas's CofE Primary School Appleford Road, North Kensington, W10 5EF ☎ 0181 969 2810	VA	3-11
Thomas Jones Junior Mixed and Infant School St Mark's Road, W11 1RQ ☎ 0171 727 1423	C	3-11

208 LAMBETH

School name, address and telephone number	Type	Age
Allen Edwards Junior Mixed and Infant School Studley Road, SW4 6RP ☎ 0171 622 3985	C	3-11
Archbishop Sumners CofE Primary School Reedworth Street, Lambeth, SE11 4PH ☎ 0171 735 2781	VA	3-11
Ashby Mill Primary School Prague Place, off Lyham Road, SW2 5EB ☎	C	3-11
Ashmole Junior Mixed and Infant School Ashmole Street, SW8 1NT ☎ 0171 735 2419	C	3-11
Brockwell Primary School Tulse Hill Estate, Tulse Hill, Brixton, SW2 2JE ☎ 0181 671 2671	C	3-11
Caldecot Primary School Caldecot Road, Camberwell, SE5 9RN ☎	C	3-11
Clapham Manor Primary School Belmont Road, Clapham, SW4 0BZ ☎ 0171 622 3919	C	3-11
Durand Primary School Hackford Road, Stockwell, SW9 0RD ☎ 0171 735 8348	GM	3-11
Elm Wood Junior Mixed and Infant School Carnac Street, SE27 9RR ☎ 0181 670 1621	C	3-11
Granton Junior Mixed and Infant School Granton Road, SW16 5AN ☎ 0181 764 6414	C	3-11
Haselrigge Junior Mixed Infant and Nursery and Language Unit Haselrigge Road, SW4 7EP ☎ 0171 622 1208	C	3-11
Heathbrook Junior Mixed and Infant School St Rule Street, SW8 3EH ☎ 0171 622 4101	C	3-11
Henry Cavendish Junior Mixed and Infant School Hydethorpe Road, SW12 0JA ☎ 0181 673 3376	C	3-11
Herbert Morrison Primary School Hartington Road, SW8 2HP ☎ 0171 720 3439	C	3-11
Immanuel and St Andrew CofE Primary School Buckleigh Road, Streatham, SW16 5SL ☎ 0181 679 5005	GM	3-11
Jessop Primary School Lowden Road, SE24 0BJ ☎ 0171 274 2333	C	3-11
Johanna Primary School Lower Marsh, SE1 7RH ☎ 0171 928 5814	C	3-11
King's Acre Junior Mixed and Infant School King's Avenue, Clapham, SW4 8BQ ☎ 0171 622 7030	C	3-11
Kingswood Junior Mixed and Infant School Gipsy Road, SE27 9RD ☎ 0181 670 3576	C	3-11
Macaulay CofE Junior Mixed Infant and Nursery School Victoria Rise, SW4 0NU ☎ 0171 622 1355	VA	3-11
Mostyn Gardens Primary School Cowley Road, SW9 6HF ☎ 0171 735 4406	C	3-11
Norwood Park Junior Mixed and Infant School Gipsy Road, SE27 9TG ☎ 0181 670 1596	C	3-11
Paxton Primary School Woodland Road, SE19 1PA ☎ 0181 670 2935	C	3-11
Reay Primary School Hackford Road, SW9 0EN ☎ 0171 735 2978	GM	3-11
Richard Atkins Junior Mixed and Infant School New Park Road, SW2 4JP ☎ 0181 674 5601	C	3-11
St Andrew's RC Primary School Polworth Road, Streatham, SW16 2ET ☎ 0181 769 4980	GM	3-11
St John The Divine CofE Junior Mixed and Infant School Warham Street, Camberwell New Road, SE5 0SX ☎ 0171 735 4898	VA	3-11
St John's CofE Junior Mixed and Infant School 85 Angell Road, SW9 7HH ☎ 0171 274 4847	VA	3-11
St Stephen's CofE Junior Mixed and Infant School Dorset Road, SW8 1EJ ☎ 0171 735 1023	VA	3-11
Streatham Wells Primary School 50 Palace Road, SW2 3NJ ☎ 0181 674 3742	C	3-11
Sudbourne Primary School Hayter Road, Brixton, SW2 5AP ☎ 0171 274 7631	C	3-11
Sunnyhill Junior Mixed and Infant School Sunnyhill Road, SW16 2UW ☎ 0181 769 4785	C	3-11
Telferscot Primary School Telferscot Road, SW12 0HW ☎ 0181 673 7362	C	3-11
Vauxhall Junior Mixed and Infant School Vauxhall Street, SE11 5LG ☎ 0171 735 4535	C	3-11
Walnut Tree Walk Junior Mixed and Infant School Walnut Tree Walk, SE11 6DS ☎ 0171 735 1402	C	3-11
Wyvil Primary School Wyvil Road, SW8 2TJ ☎ 0171 622 1164	C	3-11

School name, address and telephone number	Type	Age
209 LEWISHAM		
Ashmead Primary School Ashmead Road, SE8 4DX ☎ 0181 692 6081	C	3–11
Athelney Primary School Athelney Street, SE6 3LD ☎ 0181 697 2945	C	3–11
Baring Primary School Linchmere Road, SE12 0NB ☎ 0181 857 5637	C	3–11
Brindishe Primary School Wantage Road, Lee Green, SE12 8NA ☎ 0181 318 4626	C	3–11
Brockley Primary School Brockley Road, SE4 2BT ☎ 0181 692 2762	C	3–11
Childeric Primary School Childeric Road, SE14 6DG ☎ 0181 692 3453	C	3–11
Christ Church Junior Mixed and Infant School Perry Vale, Forest Hill, SE23 2NE ☎ 0181 699 5127	VA	3–11
Cooper's Lane Primary School Pragnell Road, SE12 0LF ☎ 0181 857 7680	C	3–11
Dalmain Primary School Grove Close, Brockley Rise, SE23 1AS ☎ 0181 699 2675	C	3–11
Deptford Park Primary School Evelyn Street, SE8 5RJ ☎ 0181 692 4351	C	3–11
Downderry Primary School Downderry Road, Downham, BR1 5QP ☎ 0181 698 5768	C	3–11
Elfrida Primary School Elfrida Crescent, Bellingham, SE6 3EN ☎ 0181 698 5755	C	3–11
Eliot Bank Primary School Thorpewood Avenue, Sydenham, SE26 4BU ☎ 0181 699 0586	C	3–11
Ennersdale Primary School Leahurst Road, Lewisham, SE13 5JA ☎ 0181 852 7686	C	3–11
Fairlawn Primary School Honor Oak Road, SE23 3SB ☎ 0181 699 7948	C	3–11
Forster Park Primary School Boundfield Road, SE6 1PQ ☎ 0181 698 5686	C	3–11
Good Shepherd RC Primary School Moorside Road, Downham, BR1 5EP ☎ 0181 698 4173	VA	3–11
Gordonbrock Primary School Gordonbrock Road, SE4 1JB ☎ 0181 690 0801	C	3–11
Grinling Gibbons Primary School Clyde Street, Deptford, SE8 5LW ☎ 0181 692 4907	C	3–11
Haseltine Primary School Haseltine Road, Bell Green, Lower Sydenham, SE26 5AD ☎ 0181 778 6536	C	3–11
Hither Green Primary School Beacon Road, SE13 6EH ☎ 0181 852 7245	C	3–11
Holbeach Primary School Doggett Road, SE6 4QB ☎ 0181 690 4713	C	3–11
Holy Cross RC Primary School Culverley Road, Catford, SE6 2LD ☎ 0181 698 2675	VA	3–11
John Ball Primary School Southvale Road, Blackheath, SE3 0TP ☎ 0181 852 1601	C	3–11
John Stainer Primary School Mantle Road, Brockley, SE4 2DY ☎ 0171 639 0482	C	3–11
Kelvin Grove Primary School Kirkdale, SE26 6BB ☎ 0181 699 6300	C	3–11
Kilmorie Primary School Kilmorie Road, SE23 2SP ☎ 0181 291 1250	C	3–11
Launcelot Primary School Launcelot Road, Downham, BR1 5EA ☎ 0181 697 2304	C	3–11
Lee CofE Primary School Lee Church Street, SE13 5SG ☎ 0181 852 3151	VA	3–11
Lee Manor Primary School Leahurst Road, Lewisham, SE13 5LS ☎ 0181 852 0852	C	3–11
Lewisham Bridge Primary School Elmira Street, SE13 7BN ☎ 0181 852 5647	C	3–11
Lucas Vale Primary School Thornville Street, SE8 4QG ☎ 0181 692 4660	C	3–11
Marvels Lane Primary School Riddons Road, Grove Park, SE12 9RA ☎ 0181 857 3904	C	3–11
Merlin Primary School 72 Ballamore Road, Downham, BR1 5LW ☎ 0181 697 2804	C	3–11
Monson Primary School Hunsdon Road, SE14 5RD ☎ 0171 639 4563	C	3–11
Myatt Garden Primary School Rokeby Road, Brockley, SE4 1DF ☎ 0181 691 0611	C	3–11
Our Lady and St Philip RC Primary School 208 Sydenham Road, SE26 5SE ☎ 0181 778 4386	VA	3–11
Perrymount Primary School Sunderland Road, Forest Hill, SE23 2PX ☎ 0181 699 4522	C	3–11
Rathfern Primary School Rathfern Road, Catford, SE6 4NL ☎ 0181 690 3759	C	3–11
Rushey Green Primary School Culverley Road, Catford, SE6 2LA ☎ 0181 698 5001	C	3–11
St Mary's CofE Primary School 329 Lewisham High Street, SE13 6NX ☎ 0181 690 2613	VA	3–11
St Stephen's CofE Primary School Albyn Road, SE8 4ED ☎ 0181 692 1898	VA	3–11
Tidemill Primary School Frankham Street, SE8 4RN ☎ 0181 692 3470	C	3–11
Turnham Primary with Nursery GM School Turnham Road, Brockley, SE4 2HH ☎ 0171 639 0440	GM	3–11

School name, address and telephone number	Type	Age
210 SOUTHWARK		
Bellenden Primary School Reedham Street, Peckham, SE15 4PF ☎ 0171 732 7107	C	3–11
Bessemer Grange Primary School Dylways, SE5 8HP ☎ 0171 274 2520	C	3–11
The Cathedral School of St Saviour and St Mary Overe Redcross Way, Southwark, SE1 1TD ☎ 0171 407 2600	VA	3–11
Charles Dickens School Lant Street, SE1 1QP ☎ 0171 407 1769	C	3–11
Charlotte Sharman Primary School St George's Road, West Square, SE11 4SN ☎ 0171 735 5598	GM	3–11
Cobourg Primary School Cobourg Road, SE5 0JD ☎ 0171 703 2583	C	3–11
Crawford Primary School Crawford Road, SE5 9NF ☎ 0171 274 1046	C	3–11
Dog Kennel Hill Primary School Dog Kennel Hill, East Dulwich, SE22 8AB ☎ 0171 274 1829	C	3–11
Galleywall Primary School Galleywall Road, SE16 3PB ☎ 0171 237 3736	C	3–11
Gloucester Primary School Daniel Gardens, off Sumner Road, SE15 6ES ☎ 0171 703 3125	C	3–11
Ilderton Primary School Varcoe Road, SE16 3LA ☎ 0171 237 3980	C	3–11
Ivydale School Ivydale Road, Nunhead, SE15 3BU ☎ 0171 639 2702	C	3–11
John Donne School Woods Road, SE15 2SW ☎ 0171 639 0594	C	3–11
Keyworth Primary School Faunce Street, SE17 3TR ☎ 0171 735 1701	C	3–11
Michael Faraday Primary School Portland Street, Walworth, SE17 2HR ☎ 0171 703 5806	C	3–11
Oliver Goldsmith County Primary School Peckham Road, Camberwell, SE5 8UH ☎ 0171 703 4894	C	3–11
Peckham Park Primary School Friary Road, SE15 5UW ☎ 0171 639 6091	C	3–11
Redriff Junior Mixed Infant and Nursery School Salter Road, Rotherhithe, SE16 1LQ ☎ 0171 237 4272	C	3–11
Riverside School Janeway Street, SE16 4PS ☎ 0171 237 3227	C	3–11
Rotherhithe Primary School Rotherhithe New Road, SE16 2PL ☎ 0171 237 1586	C	3–11
St Francesca Cabrini RC GM School Forest Hill Road, Honor Oak, SE23 3LE ☎ 0181 699 8862	GM	3–11
St James The Great RC Primary School Peckham Road, SE15 5LP ☎ 0171 703 5870	VA	3–11
St Joseph's RC Junior Mixed Infant and Nursery School George Row, Bermondsey, SE16 4UP ☎ 0171 237 4267	VA	3–11
St Joseph's RC School Gomm Road, Lower Road, Rotherhithe, SE16 2TY ☎ 0171 237 4036	VA	3–11
Southwark Park Primary School 383 Southwark Park Road, SE16 2JH ☎ 0171 237 1180	C	3–11
Victory Primary School Victory Place, Rodney Road, SE17 1PT ☎ 0171 703 5722	C	3–11
211 TOWER HAMLETS		
Arnhem Wharf Primary School 1 Arnhem Place, Westferry Road, Isle of Dogs, E14 3RY ☎ 0171 515 4310	C	3–11
Bangabandhu Primary School Wessex Street, E2 0LB ☎ 0181 980 0580	C	3–11
Bigland Green Primary School Bigland Street, E1 2ND ☎ 0171 702 7088	C	3–11
Bygrove Primary School Bygrove Street, Poplar, E14 6DN ☎ 0171 538 4925	C	3–11
Canon Barnett School Gunthorpe Street, Aldgate, E1 7RQ ☎ 0171 247 9023	C	3–11
Chisenhale Primary School Chisenhale Road, Bow, E3 5QY ☎ 0181 980 2584	C	3–11
Christchurch CofE School 47a Brick Lane, Spitalfields, E1 6PU ☎ 0171 247 0792	VA	3–11
The Clara Grant Primary School Knapp Road, Bow, E3 4BU ☎ 0171 987 4564	C	3–11
Columbia Primary School Columbia Road, E2 7RG ☎ 0171 739 3835	C	3–11
English Martyrs' RC School St Mark Street, E1 8DJ ☎ 0171 709 0182	VA	3–11
Globe Primary School Gawber Street, Bethnal Green, E2 0JH ☎ 0181 980 1738	C	3–11
Halley Primary School Halley Street, E14 7SS ☎ 0171 265 8061	C	3–11
Harbinger School Cahir Street, E14 3QP ☎ 0171 987 1924	C	3–11
Hermitage School Vaughan Way, E1 9PT ☎ 0171 702 1037	C	3–11
Holy Family RC Primary School Wades Place, E14 0DE ☎ 0171 987 3066	VA	3–11
Manorfield School Wyvis Street, E14 6QD ☎ 0171 987 1623	C	3–11
Marner School Devas Street, E3 3LL ☎ 0171 987 2938	C	3–11
Mowlem Junior Mixed and Infant School Mowlem Street, Bishops Way, Bethnal Green, E2 9HE ☎ 0181 257 3050	C	3–11

School name, address and telephone number	Type	Age
Our Lady RC School Copenhagen Place, E14 7DA ☎ 0171 987 1798	VA	3–11
St Anne's RC Junior Mixed Infant and Nursery School Underwood Road, E1 5AW ☎ 0171 247 6327	VA	3–11
St Edmund's RC School 297 Westferry Road, E14 3RS ☎ 0171 987 2546	VA	3–11
St John's CofE School Peel Grove, Bethnal Green, E2 9LR ☎ 0181 980 1142	VA	3–11
St Luke's CofE Isle of Dogs Primary School Saunders Ness Road, E14 3EB ☎ 0171 987 1753	VA	3–11
St Matthias's CofE Primary School Bacon Street, Bethnal Green, E2 6DY ☎ 0171 739 8058	VA	3–11
St Paul's (Whitechapel) CofE Primary School Wellclose Square, E1 8HY ☎ 0171 480 6581	VA	3–11
Shapla Primary School Wellclose Square, E1 8HY ☎ 0171 480 5829	C	3–11
Smithy Street School Smithy Street, E1 3BW ☎ 0171 702 7971	C	3–11
Stewart Headlam Primary School Tapp Street, E1 5RE ☎ 0171 247 1201	C	3–11

212 WANDSWORTH

School name, address and telephone number	Type	Age
Albemarle Primary School Princes Way, SW19 6JP ☎ 0181 788 3170	GM	3–11
Alderbrook School Oldridge Road, Balham, SW12 8PP ☎ 0181 673 4913	C	3–11
Allfarthing Primary School St Ann's Crescent, Wandsworth, SW18 2LR ☎ 0181 874 1301	C	3–11
The Alton School Danebury Avenue, Roehampton, SW15 4PD ☎ 0181 876 8482	C	3–11
Beatrix Potter School Magdalen Road, Earlsfield, SW18 3ER ☎ 0181 874 1482	C	3–11
Belleville School Belleville Road, Battersea, SW11 6PR ☎ 0171 228 6727	C	3–11
Bolingbroke Primary School Westbridge Road, Battersea, SW11 3NE ☎ 0171 228 1293	C	3–11
Broadwater Primary School Broadwater Road, Garratt Lane, SW17 0DZ ☎ 0181 672 3062	C	3–11
Eardley GM Primary School Cunliffe Street, Streatham, SW16 6DS ☎ 0181 769 6486	GM	3–11
Falconbrook Primary School Wye Street, Battersea, SW11 2LX ☎ 0171 228 7706	C	3–11
Fircroft School Fircroft Road, Tooting, SW17 7PP ☎ 0181 672 6258	C	3–11
Franciscan School 221 Franciscan Road, Tooting, SW17 8HQ ☎ 0181 672 3048	C	3–11
Granard Primary School Cortis Road, SW15 6XA ☎ 0181 788 3606	C	3–11
Heathmere Primary School Alton Road, Roehampton, SW15 4LJ ☎ 0181 788 9057	C	3–11
Highview Primary School Plough Road, Battersea, SW11 2AA ☎ 0171 228 1710	C	3–11
John Milton School Thessaly Road, Battersea, SW8 5AH ☎ 0171 622 2969	C	3–11
Joseph Tritton Primary School Wynter Street, York Road, SW11 2TY ☎ 0171 228 4293	C	3–11
Ravenstone Primary School Ravenstone Street, Balham High Road, SW12 9SS ☎ 0181 673 0594	C	3–11
Riversdale School 302a Merton Road, Wandsworth, SW18 5JP ☎ 0181 874 6904	C	3–11
St Anne's CofE School 208 St Ann's Hill, SW18 2RU ☎ 0181 874 1863	VA	3–11
St Boniface RC Primary School Undine Street, SW17 8PP ☎ 0181 672 5874	VA	3–11
St Faith's CofE School Alma Road, East Hill, Wandsworth, SW18 1AF ☎ 0181 874 2653	VA	3–11
St George's CofE School Corunna Road, Battersea, SW8 4JS ☎ 0171 622 1870	VA	3–11
Shaftesbury Park Primary School Ashbury Road, Battersea, SW11 5UW ☎ 0171 228 3652	C	3–11
Sheringdale School Standen Road, Southfields, SW18 5TR ☎ 0181 874 7340	C	3–11
Smallwood School Smallwood Road, Garratt Lane, SW17 0TW ☎ 0181 672 6024	C	3–11
Swaffield School St Ann's Hill, SW18 2SA ☎ 0181 874 2825	C	3–11
Trinity St Mary's CofE Primary School 6 Balham Park Road, SW12 8DR ☎ 0181 673 4166	VA	3–11
The Wandle School 330 Garratt Lane, Earlsfield, SW18 4EJ ☎ 0181 874 1484	C	3–11
Wix Primary School Wix's Lane, Clapham Common North Side, SW4 0AJ ☎ 0171 228 3055	C	3–11

213 WESTMINSTER, CITY OF

School name, address and telephone number	Type	Age
All Souls' CofE Primary School Foley Street, W1P 7LD ☎ 0171 580 4881	VA	3–11
Burdett Coutts Primary CofE School Rochester Street, SW1P 2QQ ☎ 0171 828 9527	VA	3–11
Christ Church Bentinck Primary School Cosway Street, NW1 5NS ☎ 0171 641 4135	VA	3–11
Churchill Gardens Primary School Ranelagh Road, SW1V 3EU ☎ 0171 641 5935	C	3–11

School name, address and telephone number	Type	Age
Edward Wilson Primary School Senior Street, W2 5TL ☎ 0171 289 1415	C	3–11
Essendine Primary School Essendine Road, W9 2LR ☎ 0171 286 0318	C	3–11
Gateway Primary School Capland Street, NW8 8LN ☎ 0171 723 5665	C	3–11
Millbank Primary School Erasmus Street, SW1P 4HR ☎ 0171 834 4970	C	3–11
Our Lady of Dolours RC Primary School 19 Cirencester Street, Paddington, W2 5SR ☎ 0171 286 8264	VA	3–11
Paddington Green Primary School Park Place Villas, W2 1SP ☎ 0171 641 4122	C	3–11
Queen's Park Primary School Droop Street, W10 4DQ ☎ 0181 969 1630	C	3–11
St Augustine's CofE Primary School Kilburn Park Road, NW6 5XA ☎ 0171 328 0221	VA	3–11
St Barnabas's CofE School St Barnabas Street, Pimlico, SW1W 8PF ☎ 0171 730 0159	VA	3–11
St Clement Dane's CofE Primary School Drury Lane, WC2B 5SU ☎ 0171 836 3787	VA	3–11
St Edward's RC Primary School Lisson Grove, NW1 6LH ☎ 0171 723 5911	VA	3–11
St Joseph's RC Primary School Lanark Road, Sutherland Avenue, Maida Vale, W9 1DF ☎ 0171 286 3518	VA	3–11
St Mary Magdalene CofE Primary School Rowington Close, Warwick Estate, Paddington, W2 5TF ☎ 0171 641 4388	VA	3–11
St Mary of the Angels RC School Shrewsbury Road, Bayswater, W2 5PR ☎ 0171 229 7665	VA	3–11
St Matthew's CofE Primary School 16-18 Old Pye Street, SW1P 2DG ☎ 0171 222 5170	VA	3–11
St Peter's Eaton Square CofE Primary School Lower Belgrave Street, SW1W 0NL ☎ 0171 641 4230	VA	3–11
St Stephen's CofE Primary School 91 Westbourne Park Road, W2 5QH ☎ 0171 229 5493	VA	3–11
St Vincent de Paul School Morpeth Terrace, SW1P 1EP ☎ 0171 828 8834	VA	3–11
Wilberforce Primary School Beethoven Street, W10 4LB ☎ 0171 641 5865	C	3–11

OUTER LONDON

301 BARKING AND DAGENHAM

School name, address and telephone number	Type	Age
Beam Primary School Oval Road North, RM10 9ED ☎ 0181 270 4700	C	3–11
Becontree Primary School Stevens Road, RM8 2QR ☎ 0181 270 4900	C	3–11
Five Elms Primary School Wood Lane, RM9 5TB ☎ 0181 270 4909	C	3–11
Godwin Primary School Finnymore Road, RM9 6JH ☎ 0181 270 4150	C	3–11
Henry Green Primary School Green Lane, RM8 1UR ☎ 0181 270 4466	C	3–11
John Perry Primary School Charles Road, RM10 8UR ☎ 0181 270 4622	C	3–11
Marsh Green Primary School South Close, RM10 9NJ ☎ 0181 592 3705	C	3–11
Monteagle Primary School Burnham Road, RM9 4RB ☎ 0181 270 4613	C	3–11
Parsloes Primary School Spurling Road, RM9 5RH ☎ 0181 592 7861	C	3–11
Richard Alibon Primary School Alibon Road, RM10 8DF ☎ 0181 270 4706	C	3–11
Roding Primary School Hewett Road, RM8 2XS ☎ 0181 592 1304	C	3–11
St Joseph's RC Primary School Connor Road, RM9 5UL ☎ 0181 592 3523	VA	3–11
St Joseph's RC Primary School The Broadway, IG11 7AR ☎ 0181 594 4020	VA	3–11
St Margarets CofE Primary School 15-19 North Street, IG11 8AS ☎ 0181 594 4003	VA	3–11
St Peter's RC Primary School Goresbrook Road, RM9 6UU ☎ 0181 592 6473	VA	3–11
The St Teresa RC Primary School Bowes Road, RM8 2XJ ☎ 0181 270 4757	VA	3–11
Thomas Arnold Primary School Rowdowns Road, RM9 6NH ☎ 0181 270 4588	C	3–11

302 BARNET

School name, address and telephone number	Type	Age
All Saints' CofE Junior Mixed and Infant School 116 Oakleigh Road North, Whetstone, N20 9EZ ☎ 0181 445 2951	VA	3–11
Barnet Hill Junior Mixed Infant and Nursery School Mays Lane, EN5 2DY ☎ 0181 449 8750	C	3–11
Barnfield Primary School Silkstream Road, HA8 0DA ☎ 0181 952 6026	C	3–11
Bell Lane Junior Mixed Infant and Nursery School Bell Lane, Hendon, NW4 2AS ☎ 0181 203 3115	C	3–11
Blessed Dominic RC Junior Mixed and Infant School Lanacre Avenue, Grahame Park, NW9 5FN ☎ 0181 205 3790	VA	3–11
Brunswick Park Primary School Osidge Lane, Southgate, N14 5DU ☎ 0181 368 3468	C	3–11

School name, address and telephone number	Type	Age
Childs Hill Junior Mixed and Infant School Dersingham Road, Cricklewood, NW2 1SL ☎ 0181 452 4531	C	3–11
Colindale Junior Mixed and Infant School 30 Poolsford Road, Colindale, NW9 6HP ☎ 0181 205 8706	C	3–11
Coppetts Wood Junior Mixed and Infant School Coppetts Road, Friern Barnet, N10 1JS ☎ 0181 883 0248	C	3–11
Goldbeaters Junior Mixed and Infant School Thirleby Road, HA8 0HA ☎ 0181 959 6033	C	3–11
Hollickwood Junior Mixed and Infant School Sydney Road, Muswell Hill, N10 2NL ☎ 0181 883 6880	C	3–11
Holly Park Junior Mixed and Infant School Bellevue Road, Friern Barnet, N11 3HG ☎ 0181 368 1434	C	3–11
Holy Trinity CofE Junior Mixed and Infant School Market Place, East Finchley, N2 8DD ☎ 0181 883 1824	VA	3–11
The Hyde Junior Mixed and Infant School The Hyde, NW9 6LE ☎ 0181 205 8707	C	3–11
Manorside Junior Mixed and Infant School Squires Lane, Church End, Finchley, N3 2AB ☎ 0181 346 4847	C	3–11
Menorah Foundation Primary School Abbots Road, Burnt Oak, HA8 0QS ☎ 0181 208 0644	GM	3–11
Northside Junior Mixed and Infant School 2 Albert Street, North Finchley, N12 8JP ☎ 0181 445 4730	C	3–11
Our Lady of Lourdes RC Junior Mixed and Infant School Bow Lane, Finchley, N12 0JP ☎ 0181 346 1681	VA	3–11
Parkfield Junior Mixed and Infant School St David's Place, Park Road, Hendon, NW4 3UB ☎ 0181 202 0454	C	3–11
St Agnes's RC Junior Mixed and Infant School Thorverton Road, Cricklewood, NW2 1RG ☎ 0181 452 4565	VA	3–11
St Catherine's RC Junior Mixed and Infant School Vale Drive, EN5 2ED ☎ 0181 440 4946	VA	3–11
St John's CofE Junior Mixed and Infant School Crescent Road, Friern Barnet, N11 3LB ☎ 0181 368 1154	VA	3–11
St Mary's CofE Junior Mixed and Infant School Dollis Park, Finchley, N3 1BT ☎ 0181 343 0866	VA	3–11
St Paul's CofE Primary School The Avenue, Friern Barnet, N11 1NF ☎ 0181 368 4839	VA	3–11
Summerside Junior Mixed and Infant School Crossway, Finchley, N12 0QU ☎ 0181 445 1192	C	3–11
Sunnyfields Junior Mixed and Infant School Hatchcroft, off Greyhound Hill, Hendon, NW4 4JH ☎ 0181 203 3113	C	3–11
Tudor Junior Mixed and Infant School Queen's Road, Finchley, N3 2AG ☎ 0181 346 6010	C	3–11
Whitings Hill Junior Mixed and Infant School Whitings Road, EN5 2QY ☎ 0181 449 7635	C	3–11

303 BEXLEY

School name, address and telephone number	Type	Age
Birkbeck Primary School Alma Road, DA14 4ED ☎ 0181 300 4161	C	3–11
Bursted Wood Primary School Swanbridge Road, DA7 5BS ☎ 0181 304 9960	C	3–11
Danson Primary School Danson Lane, DA16 2BH ☎ 0181 303 1858	C	3–11
Lesney Park Primary School Lesney Park Road, DA8 3DG ☎ 01322 333780	C	3–11
Lessness Heath Primary School Erith Road, DA17 6HB ☎ 01322 433290	C	3–11
Parkway Primary School Alsike Road, DA18 4DP ☎ 0181 310 0176	C	3–11
Pelham Primary School Pelham Road, DA7 4HL ☎ 0181 303 6556	C	3–11
Royal Park Primary School Riverside Road, DA14 4PX ☎ 0181 300 7646	C	3–11
Sherwood Park Primary School Sherwood Park Avenue, DA15 9JQ ☎ 0181 303 6300	C	3–11
Sidcup Hill Primary School Oxford Road, DA14 6LW ☎ 0181 300 4878	C	3–11

304 BRENT

School name, address and telephone number	Type	Age
Anson Primary School Anson Road, NW2 4AB ☎ 0181 452 8552	C	3–11
Barham Primary School Danethorpe Road, HA0 4RQ ☎ 0181 902 3706	C	3–11
Braintcroft Primary School Warren Road, NW2 7LL ☎ 0181 452 6109	C	3–11
Brentfield Primary School and Nursery, 41-43 Meadow Garth, NW10 0SL ☎ 0181 965 5326	C	3–11
Christ Church Brondesbury CofE School Clarence Road, Willesden Lane, Kilburn, NW6 7TE ☎ 0171 624 4967	VA	3–11
Fryent Primary School Church Lane, Kingsbury, NW9 8JD ☎ 0181 205 4047	C	3–11
Gladstone Park Primary School Sherrick Green Road, NW10 1LB ☎ 0181 452 1350	C	3–11
Harlesden Primary School Acton Lane, NW10 8UT ☎ 0181 965 7445	C	3–11
John Keble CofE Junior Mixed and Infant School Crownhill Road, NW10 4DR ☎ 0181 965 5072	VA	3–11
Kensal Rise Primary School Harvist Road, NW6 6HJ ☎ 0181 969 3846	C	3–11
Newfield Primary School Longstone Avenue, Willesden, NW10 3UD ☎ 0181 961 1566	C	3–11
Oliver Goldsmith Primary School Coniston Gardens, Kingsbury, NW9 0BD ☎ 0181 205 6038	C	3–11

School name, address and telephone number	Type	Age
Our Lady of Lourdes School Wesley Road, NW10 8PP ☎ 0181 961 5037	VA	3–11
Preston Park Primary School College Road, HA9 8RJ ☎ 0181 904 3602	C	3–11
St Andrew and St Francis Junior and Infant School Belton Road, NW2 5PE ☎ 0181 459 1636	VA	3–11
St Joseph's RC GM Primary School Goodson Road, Willesden, NW10 9LS ☎ 0181 965 5651	GM	3–11
St Mary's CofE Junior and Infant School Garnet Road, NW10 9JA ☎ 0181 451 0363	VA	3–11
Stonebridge Primary School Shakespeare Avenue, NW10 8NG ☎ 0181 965 6965	C	3–11
Uxendon Manor Primary School Vista Way, Kenton, HA3 0SH ☎ 0181 907 5019	C	3–11

306 CROYDON

School name, address and telephone number	Type	Age
Downsview Junior and Infant School and Nursery Biggin Way, Upper Norwood, SE19 3XE ☎ 0181 764 4611	C	3–11
Fairchildes Primary School Fairchildes Avenue, New Addington, CR9 0AA ☎ 01689 842268	C	3–11
Gonville Primary School Gonville Road, CR7 6DL ☎ 0181 684 4006	C	3–11
Good Shepherd RC Primary School Dunley Drive, New Addington, CR0 0RG ☎ 01689 843341	VA	3–11
Heavers Farm Primary School 58 Dinsdale Gardens, SE25 6LT ☎ 0181 653 5434	C	3–11
Monks Orchard Primary School The Glade, Shirley, CR0 7UF ☎ 0181 654 2570	C	3–11
Norbury Manor Primary School Abingdon Road, Norbury, SW16 5QR ☎ 0181 679 3835	C	3–11
Roke Primary School 51 Little Roke Road, CR8 5NF ☎ 0181 660 2714	C	3–11
St James The Great RC Primary School and Nursery Windsor Road, CR7 8HJ ☎ 0181 771 3424	GM	3–11
Tollgate Junior Mixed and Infant School Malling Close, Stockbury Road, CR0 7YD ☎ 0181 656 3720	C	3–11
Wattenden Junior and Infant School Old Lodge Lane, CR8 4AZ ☎ 0181 660 1325	C	3–11

307 EALING

School name, address and telephone number	Type	Age
Blair Peach Primary School Beaconsfield Road, UB1 1DR ☎ 0181 571 9947	C	3–11
Brentside Primary School Kennedy Road, Hanwell, W7 1LJ ☎ 0181 813 2580	C	3–11
Clifton Primary School Clifton Road, UB2 5QP ☎ 0181 574 5712	C	3–11
Coston Primary School Oldfield Lane South, UB6 9JU ☎ 0181 578 1515	C	3–11
Dairy Meadow Primary School Swift Road, UB2 4RP ☎ 0181 571 7925	C	3–11
Derwentwater Primary School Shakespeare Road, Acton, W3 6SA ☎ 0181 992 5710	C	3–11
Downe Manor Primary School Down Way, UB5 6NW ☎ 0181 845 1155	C	3–11
Drayton Green Primary School Drayton Grove, West Ealing, W13 0LA ☎ 0181 997 2307	C	3–11
Durdans Park Primary School King George's Drive, off Lady Margaret Road, UB1 2PQ ☎ 0181 575 1477	C	3–11
East Acton Primary School East Acton Lane, Acton, W3 7HA ☎ 0181 740 8929	C	3–11
Edward Betham CofE Primary School Oldfield Lane South, UB6 9JU ☎ 0181 578 8928	VA	3–11
Fielding Primary School Wyndham Road, Ealing, W13 9TE ☎ 0181 567 9524	C	3–11
Gifford Primary School Greenhill Gardens, UB5 6BU ☎ 0181 845 4661	C	3–11
Greenwood Primary School Wood End Way, UB5 4QG ☎ 0181 864 7265	C	3–11
Hambrough Primary School South Road, UB1 1SF ☎ 0181 574 2002	C	3–11
Hathaway Primary School Hathaway Gardens, Ealing, W13 0DH ☎ 0181 998 2479	C	3–11
Havelock Primary School Havelock Road, UB2 4PA ☎ 0181 571 7204	C	3–11
Hobbayne Primary School Greenford Avenue, Hanwell, W7 1HA ☎ 0181 567 6271	C	3–11
Horsenden Primary School Horsenden Lane North, UB6 0PB ☎ 0181 422 5985	C	3–11
John Perryn Primary School Long Drive, East Acton, W3 7PD ☎ 0181 743 5648	C	3–11
Lady Margaret Primary School Lady Margaret Road, UB1 2NH ☎ 0181 575 8584	C	3–11
Little Ealing Primary School Weymouth Avenue, Ealing, W5 4EA ☎ 0181 567 2135	C	3–11
Mayfield Primary School High Lane, Hanwell, W7 3RT ☎ 0181 575 9885	C	3–11
Montpelier Primary School Helena Road, Ealing, W5 2RA ☎ 0181 997 5855	C	3–11
Mount Carmel RC Primary School Little Ealing Lane, Ealing, W5 4EA ☎ 0181 567 4646	VA	3–11
North Ealing Primary School Pitshanger Lane, Ealing, W5 1RP ☎ 0181 997 2653	C	3–11

School name, address and telephone number	Type	Age
Northolt Primary School Compton Crescent, UB5 5LE ☎ 0181 842 2369	C	3–11
Oaklands Primary School Oaklands Road, Hanwell, W7 2DP ☎ 0181 567 5243	C	3–11
Oldfields Primary School Oldfield Lane North, UB6 8PR ☎ 0181 578 2507	C	3–11
Perivale Primary School Federal Road, Perivale, UB6 7AF ☎ 0181 997 0619	C	3–11
Ravenor Primary School Rosedene Avenue, UB6 9SB ☎ 0181 578 1654	C	3–11
St Gregory's RC Primary School Woodfield Road, Ealing, W5 1SL ☎ 0181 997 7550	VA	3–11
St John Fisher RC Primary School Thirlmere Avenue, Perivale, UB6 8EF ☎ 0181 998 4426	VA	3–11
St John's Primary School Felix Road, West Ealing, W13 0NY ☎ 0181 567 6251	C	3–11
St Joseph's RC Primary School York Avenue, Hanwell, W7 3HU ☎ 0181 567 6293	VA	3–11
St Mark's Primary School Lower Boston Road, Hanwell, W7 2NR ☎ 0181 567 6292	C	3–11
Selborne Primary School Conway Crescent, Perivale, UB6 8JD ☎ 0181 997 1947	C	3–11
Southfield Primary School Southfield Road, Bedford Park, W4 1BD ☎ 0181 994 6173	C	3–11
Stanhope Primary School Mansell Road, UB6 9EG ☎ 0181 575 9989	C	3–11
Three Bridges Primary School Melbury Avenue, Norwood Green, UB2 4HT ☎ 0181 571 1491	C	3–11
Tudor Primary School Tudor Road, UB1 1NX ☎ 0181 571 4818	C	3–11
Vicar's Green County Primary School Lily Gardens, Alperton, HA0 1DP ☎ 0181 997 6734	C	3–11
Viking Primary School Radcliffe Way, Yeading Lane, UB5 6HW ☎ 0181 845 3186	C	3–11
West Acton Primary School Noel Road, Acton, W3 0JL ☎ 0181 992 3144	C	3–11
West Twyford Primary School Twyford Abbey Road, NW10 7DN ☎ 0181 965 6858	C	3–11
Willow Tree Primary School Arnold Road, UB5 5EF ☎ 0181 845 4181	C	3–11
Wolf Fields Primary School Norwood Road, Norwood Green, UB2 4JS ☎ 0181 843 9901	C	3–11

308 ENFIELD

School name, address and telephone number	Type	Age
Alma Primary School Alma Road, Ponders End, EN3 4UQ ☎ 0181 804 3302	C	3–11
Bush Hill Park Primary School Main Avenue, EN1 1DS ☎ 0181 366 0521	C	3–11
Churchfield Primary School Latymer Road, Edmonton, N9 9PL ☎ 0181 807 2458	C	3–11
Cuckoo Hall Primary School Cuckoo Hall Lane, Edmonton, N9 8DR ☎ 0181 804 4126	C	3–11
De Bohun Primary School Green Road, N14 4AD ☎ 0181 449 4402	C	3–11
Eastfield Primary School Eastfield Road, EN3 5UX ☎ 0181 804 5013	C	3–11
Fleecefield Primary School Brettenham Road, N18 2ES ☎ 0181 807 7899	C	3–11
Galliard Primary School Galliard Road, N9 7PE ☎ 0181 804 1818	C	3–11
Garfield Primary School Springfield Road, N11 1RR ☎ 0181 368 4500	C	3–11
Honilands Primary School Lovell Road, EN1 4RE ☎ 01992 718396	C	3–11
Houndsfield Primary School Ripon Road, N9 7RE ☎ 0181 804 4938	C	3–11
Latymer All Saints CofE Primary School 41 Hydethorpe Avenue, Edmonton, N9 9RS ☎ 0181 807 2679	VA	3–11
Prince of Wales Primary School Salisbury Road, EN3 6HG ☎ 01992 762840	C	3–11
Raynham Primary School Raynham Avenue, N18 2JQ ☎ 0181 807 4726	C	3–11
St Andrew's CofE Primary School 116 Churchbury Lane, EN1 3UL ☎ 0181 363 5003	VA	3–11
St Mary's RC Primary School Durants Road, Ponders End, EN3 7DE ☎ 0181 804 2396	VA	3–11
Southbury Primary School Swansea Road, EN3 4JG ☎ 0181 804 1710	C	3–11
Suffolks Primary School Brick Lane, EN1 3PU ☎ 0181 804 1534	C	3–11
Wilbury Primary School Wilbury Way, Edmonton, N18 1DE ☎ 0181 807 8297	C	3–11
The Wolfson Hillel Primary School 154 Chase Road, Southgate, N14 4LG ☎ 0181 882 6487	VA	3–11
Worcesters Primary School Goat Lane, EN1 4UF ☎ 0181 363 7860	C	3–11

309 HARINGEY

School name, address and telephone number	Type	Age
Alexandra JMI Primary School Western Road, N22 6UH ☎ 0181 888 9771	C	3–11
Broadwater Farm JMI Primary School Moira Close, N17 6HZ ☎ 0181 808 0247	C	3–11

School name, address and telephone number	Type	Age
Crowland JMI Primary School Crowland Road, N15 6UX ☎ 0181 800 4553	C	3–11
Devonshire Hill JMI Primary School Weir Hall Road, N17 8LB ☎ 0181 808 2053	C	3–11
The Green CE JMI Primary School Somerset Road, N17 9EJ ☎ 0181 808 2588	VA	3–11
Highgate JMI Primary School Storey Road, North Hill, Highgate, N6 4ED ☎ 0181 340 7023	C	3–11
Nightingale JMI Primary School Bounds Green Road, Wood Green, N22 4ES ☎ 0181 888 3736	C	3–11
St Aidan's JMI Primary School Albany Road, Stroud Green, N4 4RR ☎ 0181 340 2352	VC	3–11
St Ann's CE JMI Primary School Avenue Road, N15 5JG ☎ 0181 800 2781	VA	3–11
Stamford Hill JMI Primary School Berkeley Road, N15 6HD ☎ 0181 800 2898	C	3–11
Tiverton JMI Primary School Pulford Road, N15 6SP ☎ 0181 800 3779	C	3–11
Welbourne JMI Primary School High Cross Road, Tottenham, N17 9PB ☎ 0181 808 0427	C	3–11

310 HARROW

School name, address and telephone number	Type	Age
Aylward First and Middle School Pangbourne Drive, HA7 4RE ☎ 0181 958 9202	C	3–12
Little Stanmore First Middle and Nursery School St David's Drive, HA8 6JH ☎ 0181 952 3272	C	3–12
Newton Farm First and Middle School Ravenswood Crescent, South Harrow, HA2 9JU ☎ 0181 864 8081	C	3–12
Norbury First and Middle School Welldon Crescent, HA1 1QQ ☎ 0181 863 8769	C	3–12
Whitefriars First and Middle School Whitefriars Avenue, Wealdstone, HA3 5RQ ☎ 0181 427 2080	C	3–12

311 HAVERING

School name, address and telephone number	Type	Age
Broadford Primary School Faringdon Avenue, Harold Hill, RM3 8JS ☎ 01708 342880	C	3–11
Edwin Lambert Junior Mixed and Infant School Malvern Road, RM11 1BQ ☎ 01708 743704	C	3–11
Gobions Junior Mixed and Infant School Havering Road North, RM1 4TS ☎ 01708 745011	C	3–11
Hacton Junior Mixed and Infant School Chepstow Avenue, RM12 6BT ☎ 01708 443991	C	3–11
Newtons Primary School Lowen Road, RM13 8QR ☎ 01708 558613	C	3–11
Pinewood Primary School Thistledene Avenue, Collier Row, RM5 2TX ☎ 01708 743000	C	3–11
Pyrgo Priory Junior Mixed and Infant School Settle Road, Harold Hill, RM3 9RT ☎ 01708 342165	C	3–11
Rainham Village Primary School Upminster Road South, RM13 9AA ☎ 01708 552482	C	3–11
St Edward's CofE Primary School Havering Drive, RM1 4BT ☎ 01708 745971	VA	3–11

312 HILLINGDON

School name, address and telephone number	Type	Age
Highfield County Primary School Charville Lane West, Hillingdon, UB10 0DB ☎ 01895 230843	C	3–11
Longmead Primary School Laurel Lane, UB7 7TX ☎ 01895 442356	C	3–11
Ruislip Gardens Primary School Stafford Road, HA4 6PD ☎ 01895 632895	C	3–11
William Byrd Primary School Victoria Lane, Harlington, UB3 5EW ☎ 0181 759 9688	C	3–11

313 HOUNSLOW

School name, address and telephone number	Type	Age
The Andrew Ewing Primary School Westbrook Road, Heston, TW5 0NB ☎ 0181 570 9942	C	3–11
Beavers Community Primary School Arundel Road, TW4 6HR ☎ 0181 570 9347	C	3–11
Belmont Primary School Belmont Road, Chiswick, W4 5UL ☎ 0181 994 7677	C	3–11
Berkeley Primary School Cranford Lane, Heston, TW5 9HQ ☎ 0181 570 5700	C	3–11
The Blue School North Street, TW7 6RQ ☎ 0181 560 6721	VA	3–11
Cavendish Junior Infant and Nursery School Edensor Road, Chiswick, W4 2RG ☎ 0181 994 6835	C	3–11
Edward Pauling Primary School Redford Close, Bedfont Road, TW13 4TQ ☎ 0181 831 0841	C	3–11
Grove Park Primary School Nightingale Close, Chiswick, W4 3JN ☎ 0181 994 7405	C	3–11
Grove Road Primary School Cromwell Road, TW3 3QQ ☎ 0181 570 6132	C	3–11
Hogarth Primary School Duke Road, Chiswick, W4 2JR ☎ 0181 994 4782	C	3–11
Hounslow Town Primary School Pears Road, TW3 1SR ☎ 0181 570 1747	C	3–11
Isleworth Town Junior Infant and Nursery School Twickenham Road, TW7 6AB ☎ 0181 560 5701	C	3–11

School name, address and telephone number	Type	Age
Ivybridge Primary School Summerwood Road, Mogden Lane, TW7 7QB ☎ 0181 891 2727	C	3–11
Lionel Primary School and Speech and Language Centre Lionel Road, TW8 9QT ☎ 0181 560 5323	C	3–11
Marlborough Junior Infant and Nursery School London Road, TW7 5AW ☎ 0181 560 3978	C	3–11
Oriel Junior Infant and Nursery School Hounslow Road, Hanworth, TW13 6QQ ☎ 0181 894 9395	C	3–11
Our Lady and St John RC Junior and Infant School Boston Park Road, TW8 9JF ☎ 0181 560 7477	VA	3–11
St Lawrence RC Junior Infant and Nursery School Victoria Road, TW13 4FF ☎ 0181 890 3878	VA	3–11
St Mary's RC Junior and Infant School Duke Road, Chiswick, W4 2DF ☎ 0181 994 5606	VA	3–11
St Mary's RC Primary School South Street, TW7 6DL ☎ 0181 560 7166	VA	3–11
St Michael and St Martin RC Junior Infant and Nursery School Belgrave Road, TW4 7AG ☎ 0181 572 9658	VA	3–11
St Paul CofE School (Junior Infant and Nursery) St Paul's Road, TW8 0PN ☎ 0181 560 3297	VA	3–11
The Smallberry Green Primary School Turnpike Way, TW7 5BF ☎ 0181 580 2070	C	3–11
Spring Grove Junior and Infant School Star Road, TW7 4HB ☎ 0181 560 0965	C	3–11
Wellington Primary School Sutton Lane, TW3 4LB ☎ 0181 570 6130	C	3–11
Worple Primary School Queen's Terrace, TW7 7DB ☎ 0181 3218100	C	3–11

314 KINGSTON UPON THAMES

School name, address and telephone number	Type	Age
Grand Avenue Primary and Nursery School Grand Avenue, KT5 9HU ☎ 0181 399 5344	C	3–11
Green Lane Primary School Green Lane, KT4 8AS ☎ 0181 337 6976	C	3–11
King Athelstan Primary School Villiers Road, KT1 3AR ☎ 0181 546 8210	C	3–11
Knollmead Primary School Knollmead, Tolworth, KT5 9QP ☎ 0181 337 3778	C	3–11
Lovelace Primary School Mansfield Road, KT9 2RN ☎ 0181 397 3845	C	3–11
The Mount Primary School Dickerage Lane, KT3 3RZ ☎ 0181 942 5154	C	3–11
St Agatha's RC Primary School St Agatha's Drive, KT2 5TY ☎ 0181 546 3879	VA	3–11
St John's CofE Primary School Portland Road, KT1 2SG ☎ 0181 546 7179	VA	3–11
St Joseph's RC Primary School The Fairfield, KT1 2UP ☎ 0181 546 7178	VA	3–11
St Luke's CofE Primary School Acre Road, KT2 6EN ☎ 0181 546 0902	GM	3–11
St Mary's CofE Primary School Church Lane, KT9 2DH ☎ 0181 397 9597	VA	3–11

315 MERTON

School name, address and telephone number	Type	Age
St Catherine's RC Middle School Grand Drive, West Wimbledon, SW20 9NA ☎ 0181 540 4385	SA	1–9
St Thomas of Canterbury Middle School Commonside East, CR4 1YG ☎ 0181 648 0869	VA	1–9

316 NEWHAM

School name, address and telephone number	Type	Age
Brampton Primary School Masterman Road, East Ham, E6 3LB ☎ 0181 472 0830	C	3–11
Central Park Primary School Central Park Road, E6 3DW ☎ 0181 472 5588	C	3–11
Earlham Primary School Earlham Grove, Forest Gate, E7 9AW ☎ 0181 534 6127	C	3–11
Ellen Wilkinson Primary School Tollgate Road, E6 4UP ☎ 0171 511 9414	C	3–11
Essex Primary School Sheridan Road, Manor Park, E12 6QX ☎ 0181 472 0322	C	3–11
Gainsborough Primary School Gainsborough Road, E15 3AF ☎ 0171 476 3533	C	3–11
Hartley Primary School Hartley Avenue, East Ham, E6 1NT ☎ 0181 472 0855	C	3–11
Keir Hardie Primary School Edwin Street, E16 1PZ ☎ 0171 476 1284	C	3–11
Maryland Primary School Gurney Road, E15 1SL ☎ 0181 534 8135	C	3–11
New City Primary School New City Road, Plaistow, E13 9PY ☎ 0181 472 2743	C	3–11
Salisbury Primary School Romford Road, E12 5AF ☎ 0181 478 6059	C	3–11
Scott Wilkie Primary School Hoskins Close, E16 3HD ☎ 0171 474 4138	C	3–11
Southern Road Primary School Southern Road, E13 9JD ☎ 0181 471 9048	C	3–11
Storey Primary School Woodman Street, E16 2LS ☎ 0171 476 2595	C	3–11
Upton Cross Primary School Churston Avenue, Plaistow, E13 0RJ ☎ 0181 552 1081	C	3–11
William Davies Primary School Stafford Road, E7 8NL ☎ 0181 472 3864	C	3–11

School name, address and telephone number	Type	Age
317 REDBRIDGE		
Barley Lane Primary School Huxley Drive, Chadwell Heath, RM6 4RJ ☏ 0181 590 8474	C	3–11
Downshall Primary School Meads Lane, Seven Kings, IG3 8UG ☏ 0181 590 2157	C	3–11
Fullwood Primary School 21-24 Burford Close, off Hatley Avenue, Barkingside, IG6 1ER ☏ 0181 551 3288	C	3–11
Gilbert Colvin Primary and Nursery School Strafford Avenue, Clayhall, IG5 0TL ☏ 0181 550 4630	C	3–11
Glade Primary School Atherton Road, Clayhall, IG5 0PF ☏ 0181 550 5376	C	3–11
John Bramston Primary School Newcastle Avenue, New North Road, Hainault, IG6 3EE ☏ 0181 500 4640	C	3–11
Newbury Park Primary School Perryman's Farm Road, Barkingside, IG2 7LB ☏ 0181 554 6343	C	3–11
Roding Primary School Roding Lane North, Woodford Bridge, IG8 8NP ☏ 0181 504 3706	C	3–11
St Augustine's Primary School Cranbrook Road, Gants Hill, IG2 6RG ☏ 0181 554 1919	VA	3–11
Snaresbrook Primary School Meadow Walk, South Woodford, E18 2EN ☏ 0181 989 9975	C	3–11
Wanstead Church School Church Path, Wanstead, E11 2SS ☏ 0181 989 6001	VA	3–11
Wells Primary School Barclay Oval, IG8 0PP ☏ 0181 504 5937	C	3–11
318 RICHMOND UPON THAMES		
Collis Junior Mixed and Infant School Fairfax Road, TW11 9BS ☏ 0181 977 1458	C	3–11
Darell Primary School Darell Road, TW9 4LQ ☏ 0181 876 6721	C	3–11
Holy Trinity CofE Primary School Carrington Road, TW10 5AA ☏ 0181 940 2730	VA	3–11
Lowther Primary School with Nursery Stillingfleet Road, Barnes, SW13 9AE ☏ 0181 748 3984	C	3–11
Meadlands Primary School with Nursery Broughton Avenue, Ham, TW10 7TS ☏ 0181 940 9207	C	3–11
The Russell Junior Mixed and Infant School Petersham Road, Petersham, TW10 7AH ☏ 0181 940 1446	C	3–11
St James RC Junior and Infant School Stanley Road, TW2 5NP ☏ 0181 898 4670	VA	3–11
319 SUTTON		
Abbey Primary School Glastonbury Road, SM4 6NZ ☏ 0181 770 6770	C	3–11
All Saints Benhilton CofE Primary School All Saints' Road, SM1 3DA ☏ 0181 644 6492	VA	3–11
All Saints' (Carshalton) CofE School Rotherfield Road, SM5 3DW ☏ 0181 401 0075	GM	3–11
Amy Johnson Primary School Mollison Drive, Roundshaw, SM6 9JN ☏ 0181 669 3978	C	3–11
Bandon Hill Primary School Sandy Lane South, SM6 9QU ☏ 0181 647 5377	C	3–11
Barrow Hedges Primary School Harbury Road, SM5 4LA ☏ 0181 643 4428	C	3–11
Beddington Park Primary School Derry Road, Beddington Lane, Beddington, CR0 4UA ☏ 0181 688 1390	C	3–11
Cheam Fields Primary School Stoughton Avenue, SM3 8PW ☏ 0181 644 9055	C	3–11
Devonshire Primary School Devonshire Avenue, SM2 5JL ☏ 0181 643 1174	C	3–11
Dorchester Primary School Dorchester Road, KT4 8PG ☏ 0181 330 1144	C	3–11
Foresters Primary School Redford Avenue, SM6 9DP ☏ 0181 669 6910	C	3–11
Green Wrythe Primary School Green Wrythe Lane, SM5 1JP ☏ 0181 648 4989	C	3–11
High View Primary School The Chase, SM6 8JT ☏ 0181 688 3563	C	3–11
Manor Park Primary School Greyhound Road, SM1 4AW ☏ 0181 642 0144	C	3–11
Muschamp County Primary School Muschamp Road, SM5 2SE ☏ 0181 669 2514	C	3–11
Nonsuch Primary School Chadacre Road, Stoneleigh, KT17 2HQ ☏ 0181 393 9209	C	3–11
Ridge Primary School Ridge Road, SM3 9LY ☏ 0181 644 8616	C	3–11
St Cecilia's Catholic School London Road, SM3 9DL ☏ 0181 337 4566	VA	3–11
St Dunstan's Cheam CofE Primary School Anne Boleyn's Walk, SM3 8DF ☏ 0181 642 5463	VA	3–11
The Avenue Primary School Avenue Road, Belmont, SM2 6JE ☏ 0181 642 5138	C	3–11
Westbourne Primary School Anton Crescent, Collingwood Road, SM1 2NT ☏ 0181 644 8453	C	3–11

School name, address and telephone number	Type	Age
320 WALTHAM FOREST		
George Tomlinson Primary School Harrington Road, Leytonstone, E11 4QN ☎ 0181 539 3577	C	3–11
Longshaw Primary School Longshaw Road, Chingford, E4 6LH ☎ 0181 529 5693	C	3–11
Mission Grove Primary School Buxton Road, Walthamstow, E17 7EJ ☎ 0181 520 3487	C	3–11
South Grove Primary School Ringwood Road, E17 8PW ☎ 0181 521 6000	C	3–11
Thomas Gamuel Primary School Colchester Road, Walthamstow, E17 8LG ☎ 0181 520 7031	C	3–11
Thorpe Hall Primary School Hale End Road, E17 4DP ☎ 0181 527 4062	C	3–11
Wellington Primary School Wellington Avenue, E4 6RE ☎ 0181 559 4278	C	3–11
Yardley Primary School Hawkwood Crescent, E4 7PH ☎ 0181 529 3671	C	3–11
NORTHERN		
841 DARLINGTON		
Mount Pleasant Primary School Newton Lane, DL3 9HE ☎ 01325 380756	C	3–11
Rise Carr Primary School Eldon Street, DL3 0NS ☎ 01325 250700	C	3–11
St Bede's RC Primary School Kingsway, Thompson Street East, DL1 3ES ☎ 01325 466411	VA	3–11
Springfield Primary School Salters Lane South, DL1 2PW ☎ 01325 380745	C	3–11
840 DURHAM		
Barrington CofE Primary School Westcroft, Stanhope, DL13 2NU ☎ 01388 528218	VC	3–11
Beamish Primary School Co-operative Villas, Beamish, DH9 0QN ☎ 0191 370 0181	C	3–11
Benfieldside Primary School Moorlands, Blackhill, DH8 0JX ☎ 01207 591369	C	3–11
Blackhall Colliery Primary School Middle Street, Blackhall Colliery, TS27 4NA ☎ 0191 586 4049	C	3–11
Blessed John Duckett RC Primary School Smith Street, Tow Law, DL13 4AU ☎ 01388 731082	VA	3–11
Broom Cottages Primary School Broom Cottages, DL17 8AN ☎ 01740 651363	C	3–11
Burnopfield Primary School Front Street, Burnopfield, NE16 6PT ☎ 01207 270397	C	3–11
Cockfield Primary School Cockfield, DL13 5EN ☎ 01388 718263	C	3–11
Consett Moorside Primary School Chester Road, Moorside, DH8 8EQ ☎ 01207 509724	C	3–11
Durham Gilesgate Primary School Kepier Crescent, Gilesgate, DH1 1PH ☎ 0191 384 7284	C	3–11
Edmondsley Primary School Edmondsley, DH7 6DU ☎ 0191 371 0443	C	3–11
Esh Winning Primary School The Wynds, Esh Winning, DH7 9BE ☎ 0191 373 4701	C	3–11
Framwellgate Moor Primary School Newton Drive, Framwellgate Moor, DH1 5BG ☎ 0191 386 5400	C	3–11
The Grove Primary School Oakfield Lane, The Grove, DH8 8AP ☎ 01207 502938	C	3–11
Hesleden Primary School Hesleden, TS27 4PT ☎ 01429 836376	C	3–11
Howletch Lane Primary School Pennine Drive, SR8 2NQ ☎ 0191 586 2765	C	3–11
Langley Park Primary School Langley Park, DH7 9XN ☎ 0191 373 1398	C	3–11
Laurel Avenue Primary School Laurel Avenue, Sherburn Road Estate, Gilesgate Moor, DH1 2EY ☎ 0191 386 8416	C	3–11
Ludworth Primary School Moor Crescent, Ludworth, DH6 1LZ ☎ 01429 820207	C	3–11
Middleton-in-Teesdale Primary School Middleton-in-Teesdale, DL12 0TG ☎ 01833 40382	C	3–11
Montalbo Primary School Fairfield Road, DL12 8TN ☎ 01833 637718	C	3–11
New Brancepeth Primary School New Brancepeth, DH7 7EU ☎ 0191 373 0736	C	3–11
Oakley Cross Primary School and Nursery Lomond Walk, West Auckland, DL14 9UD ☎ 01388 833186	C	3–11
Our Lady of The Rosary Primary School Westway, SR8 1DE ☎ 0191 586 2264	VA	3–11
Peases West Primary School Billy Row, DL15 9SZ ☎ 01388 762380	C	3–11
Pelton Roseberry Primary School and Nursery Unit Pelton, DH2 1NP ☎ 0191 370 0182	C	3–11
St Benet's RC Primary School St Benet's Way, Ouston, DH2 1QX ☎ 0191 410 5857	VA	3–11
St Cuthbert's RC Primary School Church Hill, DL15 9DN ☎ 01388 762889	VA	3–11
St Hild's CofE Primary School Renny's Lane, Gilesgate, DH1 2HZ ☎ 0191 384 7451	VA	3–11

School name, address and telephone number	Type	Age
St John's CofE Primary School Jubilee Road, DL4 2EQ ☎ 01388 773476	VA	3–11
St Wilfrid's RC Primary School Murphy Crescent, DL14 6QH ☎ 01388 603451	VA	3–11
Stanley Burnside Primary School Mendip Terrace, South Stanley, DH9 6QP ☎ 01207 234020	C	3–11
Stephenson Way Primary School Stephenson Way, DL5 7DD ☎ 01325 300324	C	3–11
Sugar Hill Primary School Sheraton Road, DL5 5NU ☎ 01325 300334	C	3–11
Thornley Primary School Cooper's Terrace, Thornley, DH6 3DZ ☎ 01429 820280	C	3–11
Timothy Hackworth Primary School Byerley Road, DL4 1HN ☎ 01388 772959	C	3–11
West Cornforth Primary School High Street, West Cornforth, DL17 9HP ☎ 01740 654315	C	3–11
Wheatley Hill Primary School Wheatley Hill, DH6 3RQ ☎ 01429 820594	C	3–11
Willington County Primary School Chapel Street, Willington, DL15 0EQ ☎ 01388 746414	C	3–11

390 GATESHEAD

School name, address and telephone number	Type	Age
Barley Mow Primary School Pembroke Avenue, Barley Mow, DH3 2DJ ☎ 0191 410 2758	C	3–11
Bede Community Primary School Old Fold Road, NE10 0DJ ☎ 0191 477 3893	C	3–11
Birtley East Primary School Highfield, Birtley, DH3 1QQ ☎ 0191 410 2551	C	3–11
Brandling Primary School Mulberry Street, Felling, NE10 0JB ☎ 0191 469 3218	C	3–11
Brighton Avenue Primary School Brighton Road, NE8 1XS ☎ 0191 421 8080	C	3–11
Caedmon Primary School Whitehall Road, NE8 4LH ☎ 0191 477 3382	C	3–11
Carr Hill Primary School Carr Hill Road, NE9 5NB ☎ 0191 477 1203	C	3–11
Colegate Primary School Colegate West, Leam Lane Estate, NE10 9AH ☎ 0191 420 6626	C	3–11
The Drive Primary School The Drive, Felling, NE10 0PY ☎ 0191 421 0390	C	3–11
Falla Park Primary School Falla Park Road, Felling, NE10 9HP ☎ 0191 469 5528	C	3–11
Fell Dyke Primary School Springwell Road, NE9 7AA ☎ 0191 487 5097	C	3–11
Fellside Primary School Fellside Road, Whickham, NE16 5AY ☎ 0191 488 7486	C	3–11
Front Street Primary School Front Street, Whickham, NE16 4AD ☎ 0191 420 0520	C	3–11
Glynwood Primary School Glynwood Gardens, NE9 5SY ☎ 0191 421 0301	C	3–11
Greenside Primary School Rockwood Hill Road, Greenside, NE40 4AY ☎ 0191 413 2186	C	3–11
High Spen Primary School Hugar Road, High Spen, NE39 2BQ ☎ 01207 542373	C	3–11
Highfield Primary School Highfield Road, NE39 2LX ☎ 01207 542086	C	3–11
Kelvin Grove Primary School Kelvin Grove, NE8 4UN ☎ 0191 477 4186	C	3–11
Larkspur Primary School Beacon Lough East, NE9 6SS ☎ 0191 487 5628	C	3–11
Lindisfarne Primary School Lindisfarne Drive, NE8 3LB ☎ 0191 477 5395	C	3–11
Lingey House Primary School Millford, Leam Lane Estate, Felling, NE10 8DN ☎ 0191 469 2324	C	3–11
Lobley Hill Primary School Rothbury Gardens, Lobley Hill, NE11 0AT ☎ 0191 421 0314	C	3–11
Pelaw St Alban's Primary School Rothbury Avenue, Pelaw, NE10 0QY ☎ 0191 469 3251	VA	3–11
Roman Road Primary School Leam Lane Estate, Felling, NE10 8SA ☎ 0191 469 2780	C	3–11
St Oswald's RC Primary School Easington Avenue, Wrekenton, NE9 7LH ☎ 0191 487 8641	VA	3–11
St Wilfrid's RC Primary School Carville Street, Old Fold, NE10 0EP ☎ 0191 477 1909	VA	3–11
South Street Primary School Cramer Street, NE8 4BB ☎ 0191 477 3993	C	3–11
Stella RC Primary School Stella Lane, NE21 4NE ☎ 0191 414 3116	VA	3–11
Tyne View Primary School Rose Street, NE8 2LS ☎ 0191 477 4805	C	3–11
Wardley County Primary School Keir Hardie Avenue, Wardley, NE10 8TX ☎ 0191 469 3012	C	3–11
Windmill Hills Primary School Chester Place, NE8 1QB ☎ 0191 477 2568	C	3–11
Windy Nook Primary School Albion Street, NE10 9BD ☎ 0191 469 4954	C	3–11

School name, address and telephone number	Type	Age
805 HARTLEPOOL		
Barnard Grove Primary School Barnard Grove, TS24 9SD ☎ 01429 273532	C	3–11
Brougham Primary School Brougham Terrace, TS24 8EY ☎ 01429 273663	C	3–11
Clavering Primary School Clavering Road, TS27 3PN ☎ 01429 264037	C	3–11
Eldon Grove Primary School Eldon Grove, TS26 9LY ☎ 01429 273895	C	3–11
Elwick CofE Primary School Elwick, TS27 3EG ☎ 01429 274904	VC	3–11
Fens Primary School Mowbray Road, TS25 2LY ☎ 01429 870405	C	3–11
Golden Flatts Primary School Seaton Lane, TS25 1HN ☎ 01429 274711	C	3–11
Grange Primary School Owton Manor Lane, TS25 3PU ☎ 01429 272007	C	3–11
Greatham CofE Primary School Egerton Terrace, Greatham, TS25 2EU ☎ 01429 870254	VC	3–11
Hart Primary School Hart Village, TS27 3AP ☎ 01429 273283	C	3–11
Jesmond Road Primary School Percy Street, TS26 0HR ☎ 01429 274672	C	3–11
Kingsley Primary School Taybrooke Avenue, TS25 5JR ☎ 01429 273102	C	3–11
Lynnfield Primary School Grosvenor Street, TS26 8RL ☎ 01429 275122	C	3–11
Owton Manor Primary School Eskdale Road, TS25 4BT ☎ 01429 272255	C	3–11
Rift House Primary School Masefield Road, TS25 4JY ☎ 01429 275239	C	3–11
Rossmere Primary School Catcote Road, TS25 3JL ☎ 01429 274608	C	3–11
Sacred Heart RC Primary School Hart Lane, TS26 8NL ☎ 01429 272684	VA	3–11
St Aidan's CofE Memorial Primary School Loyalty Road, TS25 5BA ☎ 01429 273695	VA	3–11
St Begas RC Primary School Thorpe Street, TS24 0DX ☎ 01429 267768	VA	3–11
St Cuthbert's RC Primary School Stratford Road, TS25 5AJ ☎ 01429 275040	VA	3–11
St Helen's Primary School Durham Street, TS24 0HG ☎ 01429 267038	C	3–11
St John Vianney RC Primary School King Oswy Drive, TS24 9PA ☎ 01429 273273	VA	3–11
St Joseph's RC Primary School Musgrave Street, TS24 7HT ☎ 01429 272747	VA	3–11
St Teresa's RC Primary School Callander Road, TS25 3BG ☎ 01429 274936	VA	3–11
Stranton Primary School Southburn Terrace, TS25 1SQ ☎ 01429 275595	C	3–11
Throston Primary School Flint Walk, TS26 0TJ ☎ 01429 269052	C	3–11
Ward Jackson Primary School Clark Street, TS24 7LE ☎ 01429 275076	C	3–11
West Park Primary School Coniscliffe Road, TS26 0BU ☎ 01429 261172	C	3–11
West View Primary School Davison Drive, TS24 9BP ☎ 01429 267466	C	3–11
806 MIDDLESBROUGH		
Acklam Whin Primary School Carlbury Avenue, Acklam, TS5 8SQ ☎ 01642 813938	C	3–11
Archibald Primary School Ayresome Green Lane, TS5 4DY ☎ 01642 818473	C	3–11
The Avenue Primary School The Avenue, Nunthorpe, TS7 0AG ☎ 01642 318510	C	3–11
Brambles Primary School Kedward Avenue, Brambles Farm, TS3 9DB ☎ 01642 210704	C	3–11
Breckon Hill Primary School Breckon Hill Road, TS4 2DS ☎ 01642 243044	C	3–11
Captain Cook Primary School Stokesley Road, Marton, TS7 8DU ☎ 01642 315254	C	3–11
Easterside Primary School Erith Grove, Easterside, TS4 3RG ☎ 01642 315717	C	3–11
Green Lane Primary School Green Lane, TS5 7RU ☎ 01642 819949	C	3–11
Hemlington Hall Primary School Briscoe Way, Hemlington, TS8 9SJ ☎ 01642 591171	C	3–11
Lingfield Primary School Buxton Avenue, Marton, TS7 8LP ☎ 01642 319918	C	3–11
Marton Manor Primary School The Derby, Marton Manor, TS7 8RH ☎ 01642 311731	C	3–11
Newport Primary School St Paul's Road, TS1 5NQ ☎ 01642 861911	C	3–11
North Ormesby Primary School James Street, TS3 6LB ☎ 01642 247985	C	3–11
Pallister Park Primary School Gribdale Road, Pallister Park, TS3 8PW ☎ 01642 242174	C	3–11
Park End Primary School Overdale Road, TS3 0AA ☎ 01642 314309	C	3–11

School name, address and telephone number	Type	Age
Sacred Heart RC Primary School Ayresome Street, TS1 4NP ☎ 01642 816083	VA	3–11
St Alphonsus RC Primary School Cadogan Street, North Ormesby, TS3 6PX ☎ 01642 243400	VA	3–11
St Augustine's RC Primary School Gunnergate Lane, Coulby Newham, TS8 0TE ☎ 01642 599001	VA	3–11
St Bernadette's RC Primary School Cookgate, Nunthorpe, TS7 0PZ ☎ 01642 310198	VA	3–11
St Clare's RC Primary School Trimdon Avenue, TS5 8RZ ☎ 01642 815412	VA	3–11
St Edward's RC Primary School Eastbourne Road, TS5 6QS ☎ 01642 819507	VA	3–11
St Pius X RC Primary School Amersham Road, Park End, TS3 7HD ☎ 01642 314453	VA	3–11
St Thomas More RC Primary School Erith Grove, Easterside, TS4 3QH ☎ 01642 317350	VA	3–11
Sunnyside Primary School Manor Farm Way, Coulby Newham, TS8 0RJ ☎ 01642 596422	C	3–11
Thorntree Primary School The Greenway, Thorntree, TS3 9NH ☎ 01642 242309	C	3–11
Viewley Hill Primary School Andover Way, Hemlington, TS8 9HL ☎ 01642 591053	C	3–11

391 NEWCASTLE UPON TYNE

School name, address and telephone number	Type	Age
Benton Park Primary School Corchester Walk, NE7 7SS ☎ 0191 266 5122	C	3–11
Byker Primary School Commercial Road, Byker, NE6 2AT ☎ 0191 265 6906	C	3–11
Canning Street Primary School Wellfield Road, NE4 8PA ☎ 0191 273 5465	C	3–11
Chillingham Road Primary School Ninth Avenue, NE6 5XL ☎ 0191 265 5940	C	3–11
Christ Church CofE Primary School Shieldfield Green, NE2 1XA ☎ 0191 232 8054	VA	3–11
Delaval Community Primary School Axwell Park View, Scotswood, NE15 6NR ☎ 0191 274 5290	C	3–11
Denton Road Primary School Bankside Road, NE15 6AJ ☎ 0191 274 1181	C	3–11
English Martyrs' RC Primary School Netherby Drive, Fenham, NE5 2RT ☎ 0191 274 7463	VA	3–11
Hilton Primary School Hilton Avenue, NE5 3RN ☎ 0191 286 9297	C	3–11
Hotspur Primary School Mowbray Street, NE6 5PA ☎ 0191 276 2762	C	3–11
Kenton Bar Primary School Ryal Walk, NE3 3YF ☎ 0191 286 0536	C	3–11
Kingston Park Primary School Cranleigh Avenue, Kingston Park, NE3 2HB ☎ 0191 214 0363	C	3–11
Montagu Primary School Moorview Crescent, NE5 3HN ☎ 0191 286 9658	C	3–11
Moorside Community Primary School Beaconsfield Street, NE4 5AW ☎ 0191 272 0239	C	3–11
Mountfield Primary School Kirkwood Drive, North Kenton, NE3 3AT ☎ 0191 285 3793	C	3–11
North Fawdon Primary School Brotherlee Road, NE3 2SL ☎ 0191 285 1350	C	3–11
Our Lady and St Anne's School Summerhill Terrace, NE4 6EB ☎ 0191 232 5496	VA	3–11
Ravenswood Primary School Ravenswood Road, Heaton, NE6 5TU ☎ 0191 265 9599	C	3–11
St Alban's Primary School Westbourne Avenue, NE6 4HQ ☎ 0191 262 5552	VA	3–11
St Anthony's CofE Primary School Pottery Bank, Walker, NE6 3SU ☎ 0191 265 5109	VA	3–11
St Catherine's RC Primary School Greystoke Gardens, NE2 1PS ☎ 0191 232 6803	VA	3–11
St Cuthbert's RC Primary School Balmain Road, North Kenton, NE3 3QR ☎ 0191 286 0129	VA	3–11
St Joseph's RC Primary School Armstrong Road, Benwell, NE15 6JB ☎ 0191 273 9063	VA	3–11
St Lawrence's RC Primary School Headlam Street, Byker, NE6 2JX ☎ 0191 265 9881	VA	3–11
St Michael's RC Primary School Clumber Street, Elswick, NE4 7RD ☎ 0191 273 9383	VA	3–11
St Paul's CofE Primary School Victoria Street, NE4 7JU ☎ 0191 273 3667	VA	3–11
South Benwell Primary School Teindland Close, NE4 8HE ☎ 0191 273 5293	C	3–11
Stocksfield Avenue Primary School St Cuthbert's Road, Fenham, NE5 2DQ ☎ 0191 274 8434	C	3–11
Thomas Walling Primary School Lindfield Avenue, Blakelaw, NE5 3PL ☎ 0191 286 0333	C	3–11
Tyneview Primary School Winslow Place, Walker, NE6 3QP ☎ 0191 262 6227	C	3–11
Welbeck Primary School Flodden Street, Walker, NE6 2QL ☎ 0191 265 0353	C	3–11
West Walker Primary School Church Street, Walker, NE6 3XB ☎ 0191 262 4130	C	3–11
Westgate Hill Primary School Westgate Road, NE4 6NY ☎ 0191 273 5742	C	3–11
Wharrier Street Primary School Wharrier Street, Walker, NE6 3EY ☎ 0191 265 5743	C	3–11
Wyndham Primary School Wyndsail Place, NE3 4QP ☎ 0191 285 3895	C	3–11

School name, address and telephone number	Type	Age
392 NORTH TYNESIDE		
Balliol Primary School Chesters Avenue, Longbenton, NE12 8QP ☎ 0191 200 7471	C	3–11
Burradon County Primary School Front Street, Burradon, NE23 7NG ☎ 0191 200 8345	C	3–11
Collingwood Primary School Oswin Terrace, NE29 7JQ ☎ 0191 200 5038	C	3–11
Fordley Community Primary School Dudley Drive, Fordley, NE23 7AL ☎ 0191 200 8030	C	3–11
Forest Hall Primary School Delaval Road, Forest Hall, NE12 9BA ☎ 0191 200 8341	C	3–11
Goathland Primary School Goathland Avenue, Longbenton, NE12 8LH ☎ 0191 200 7427	C	3–11
Greenfields Community Primary School Taylor Avenue, Wideopen, NE13 6NB ☎ 0191 200 7919	C	3–11
Hazlewood Community Primary School Canterbury Way, Wideopen, NE13 6JJ ☎ 0191 200 7911	C	3–11
Holy Cross RC Primary School Coniston Road, NE28 0EP ☎ 0191 200 7357	VA	3–11
Ivy Road Primary School Ivy Road, Forest Hall, NE12 9AP ☎ 0191 200 8346	C	3–11
King Edward Primary School Preston Avenue, NE30 2BD ☎ 0191 200 6337	C	3–11
Meadow Well Primary School Wantage Avenue, NE29 7BE ☎ 0191 200 5037	C	3–11
New York Primary School Lanark Close, NE29 8DP ☎ 0191 200 6338	C	3–11
Percy Main Primary School Nelson Terrace, NE29 6JA ☎ 0191 200 6343	C	3–11
St Bartholomew's CofE Primary School Front Street, Longbenton, NE12 8AE ☎ 0191 200 7466	VA	3–11
St Bernadette's RC Primary School Rising Sun Cottages, NE28 9JW ☎ 0191 200 7363	VA	3–11
St Columba's RC Primary School Station Road, NE28 8EN ☎ 0191 200 7235	VA	3–11
St Cuthbert's RC Primary School Lovaine Place, NE29 0BU ☎ 0191 200 5620	VA	3–11
St Joseph's RC Primary School Wallsend Road, Chirton, NE29 7BT ☎ 0191 200 5077	VA	3–11
St Mary's RC Primary School Farringdon Road, Cullercoats, NE30 3EY ☎ 0191 200 8812	VA	3–11
St Stephen's RC Primary School Bardsey Place, Longbenton, NE12 8NU ☎ 0191 200 7425	VA	3–11
Wallsend CofE Primary School North Terrace, NE28 6PY ☎ 0191 200 7248	VA	3–11
Waterville Primary School Waterville Road, NE29 6SL ☎ 0191 200 6351	C	3–11
Whitehouse Primary School Whitehouse Lane, NE29 8PE ☎ 0191 200 6346	C	3–11
807 REDCAR AND CLEVELAND		
Attlee Road Primary School Attlee Road, Grangetown, TS6 7NA ☎ 01642 453187	C	3–11
Badger Hill Primary School Marston Road, Kilton Lane, Brotton, TS12 2XR ☎ 01287 676289	C	3–11
Bankfields Primary School Mansfield Road, Eston, TS6 0RZ ☎ 01642 453157	C	3–11
Belmont Primary School Lauderdale Drive, Hunters Hill, TS14 7BS ☎ 01287 635332	C	3–11
Coatham CofE Primary School Coatham Road, TS10 1QY ☎ 01642 486291	VC	3–11
Dormanstown Primary School South Avenue, Dormanstown, TS10 5LY ☎ 01642 483696	C	3–11
Galley Hill Primary School Campion Drive, Hutton Meadows, TS14 8DW ☎ 01287 635540	C	3–11
Grangetown Primary School St George's Road, Grangetown, TS6 7JA ☎ 01642 455278	C	3–11
Green Gates Primary School Kielder Close, TS10 4HS ☎ 01642 485463	C	3–11
Hummersea Primary School Westfield Way, Loftus, TS13 4XD ☎ 01287 641781	C	3–11
Ings Farm Primary School Stirling Road, TS10 2JR ☎ 01642 485369	C	3–11
John Emmerson Batty Primary School Walnut Grove, TS10 3PG ☎ 01642 483697	C	3–11
Lingdale Primary School Davison Street, Lingdale, TS12 3DU ☎ 01287 651723	C	3–11
New Marske County Primary School Birkdale Road, New Marske, TS11 8BN ☎ 01642 486392	C	3–11
Normanby Primary School Flatts Lane, Normanby, TS6 0NP ☎ 01642 469529	C	3–11
Nunthorpe Primary School Swan's Corner, Guisborough Road, Nunthorpe, TS7 0LA ☎ 01642 315508	C	3–11
Overfields Primary School Allendale Road, Ormesby, TS7 9LF ☎ 01642 314548	C	3–11
Riverdale Primary School Hambleton Avenue, TS10 4HH ☎ 01642 471298	C	3–11
St Bede's RC Primary School Redcar Road, Marske-by-Sea, TS11 6AE ☎ 01642 485217	VA	3–11
St Gabriel's RC Primary School Allendale Road, Ormesby, TS7 9LF ☎ 01642 315538	VA	3–11

School name, address and telephone number	Type	Age
St Joseph's RC Primary School Rosecroft Lane, Loftus, TS13 4PZ ☎ 01287 640613	VA	3-11
St Paulinus RC Primary School The Avenue, TS14 8DN ☎ 01287 637978	VA	3-11
St Peter's CofE Primary School Marshall Drive, Brotton, TS12 2UW ☎ 01287 676210	VC	3-11
Saltburn Primary School Marske Road, TS12 1QA ☎ 01287 622447	C	3-11
Westgarth Primary School Redcar Road, Marske-by-the-Sea, TS11 6AE ☎ 01642 485560	C	3-11
Whale Hill Primary School Sandsend Road, Eston, TS6 8AD ☎ 01642 454339	C	3-11
Whitecliffe Primary School Kilton Lane, Carlin How, TS13 4AD ☎ 01287 640414	C	3-11
Wilton Primary School Lazenby, TS6 8DY ☎ 01642 453374	C	3-11

393 SOUTH TYNESIDE

School name, address and telephone number	Type	Age
Ashley County Primary School Temple Park Road, NE34 0QA ☎ 0191 456 4977	C	3-11
Dunn Street County Junior Mixed Infant and Nursery School Minster Parade, NE32 3QH ☎ 0191 489 8160	C	3-11
Hedworthfield Primary School Linkway, Hedworth Estate, NE32 4QF ☎ 0191 537 3373	C	3-11
Laygate County Junior Mixed and Infant School and Nursery Laygate Lane, NE33 4JJ ☎ 0191 456 2470	C	3-11
Lukes Lane County Primary School Marine Drive, Luke Lane, NE31 2AX ☎ 0191 489 4771	C	3-11
Marine Park Junior Mixed Infant and Nursery School Hatfield Square, Woodbine Estate, NE33 2RD ☎ 0191 455 4513	C	3-11
Marsden County Junior Mixed and Infant School Mill Lane, Whitburn Colliery, SR6 7HJ ☎ 0191 529 2040	C	3-11
Mortimer Primary School Mortimer Road, NE34 0RW ☎ 0191 455 4504	C	3-11
St Bede's RC Junior Mixed and Infant School Harold Street, NE32 3AJ ☎ 0191 489 8218	VA	3-11
St Mary's CofE Junior and Infant School Whitehead Street, NE33 5LZ ☎ 0191 456 3778	VA	3-11
St Oswald's RC Junior Mixed and Infant School Nash Avenue, Whiteleas, NE34 8NS ☎ 0191 536 7922	VA	3-11
Valley View County Junior Mixed and Infant School Valley View, NE32 5QT ☎ 0191 489 8358	C	3-11

808 STOCKTON ON TEES

School name, address and telephone number	Type	Age
Bowesfield Primary School Northcote Street, TS18 3JE ☎ 01642 617182	C	3-11
Crooksbarn Primary School Petrel Crescent, Crooksbarn Estate, Norton, TS20 1SN ☎ 01642 531750	C	3-11
Durham Lane Primary School Amberley Way, Eaglescliffe, TS16 0NG ☎ 01642 780726	C	3-11
Egglescliffe CofE Primary School Butts Lane, Egglescliffe, TS16 9BT ☎ 01642 782462	VC	3-11
The Glebe Primary School Pulford Road, Norton, TS20 1QY ☎ 01642 397354	C	3-11
Hardwick Primary School Elwick Close, TS19 8EZ ☎ 01642 873322	C	3-11
Hartburn Primary School Adelaide Grove, TS18 5BS ☎ 01642 580852	C	3-11
Ingleby Mill Primary School Lamb Lane, Ingleby Barwick, TS17 0QP ☎ 01642 761985	C	3-11
Junction Farm Primary School Butterfield Drive, Eaglescliffe, TS16 0EU ☎ 01642 782083	C	3-11
Mandale Mill Primary School Thorntree Road, Thornaby, TS17 8AP ☎ 01642 647010	C	3-11
Most Holy Rosary RC Primary School Rievaulx Avenue, TS23 2BS ☎ 01642 552274	VA	3-11
Pentland Primary School Pentland Avenue, TS23 2RG ☎ 01642 397361	C	3-11
Preston-on-Tees Primary School Laurel Road, Eaglescliffe, TS16 0BE ☎ 01642 780153	C	3-11
St Bede's RC Primary School Green Lane, TS19 0DW ☎ 01642 678071	VA	3-11
St Cuthbert's RC Primary School Parkfield, TS18 3SY ☎ 01642 679388	VA	3-11
St John The Evangelist RC Primary School Cowpen Lane, TS23 1LJ ☎ 01642 643400	VA	3-11
St John's CofE Primary School Dover Road, Ragworth, TS19 0JT ☎ 01642 607123	VC	3-11
St Joseph's RC Primary School Ragworth Road, Norton, TS20 1HR ☎ 01642 397356	VA	3-11
St Mary's CofE Primary School The Green, Long Newton, TS21 1DL ☎ 01642 585145	VA	3-11
St Paul's RC Primary School Wolviston Mill Lane, TS22 5LU ☎ 01642 360022	VA	3-11
Saint Peter and Saint Paul's RC Primary School Ragpath Lane, TS19 9AD ☎ 01642 678633	VA	3-11
William Cassidi CofE Primary School Stillington, TS21 1JD ☎ 01740 630270	VA	3-11
Wolviston Primary School The Green, Wolviston, TS22 5LN ☎ 01740 644374	C	3-11
Yarm County Primary School Spitalfields, TS15 9HF ☎ 01642 782731	C	3-11

School name, address and telephone number	Type	Age
394 SUNDERLAND		
Albany Village Primary School Crossgill, Albany, NE37 1UA ☎ 0191 219 3650	C	3-11
Barmston Village Primary School Barmston Centre, NE38 8JA ☎ 0191 219 3700	C	3-11
Bexhill Primary School Bexhill Road, Townend Farm, SR5 4PJ ☎ 0191 553 6916	C	3-11
Bishop Harland CofE Primary School Ramillies Road, Red House, SR5 5JA ☎ 0191 553 5520	VA	3-11
Blackfell Primary School Knoulberry, Blackfell, NE37 1HA ☎ 0191 219 3670	C	3-11
Carley Hill Primary School Emsworth Road, Carley Hill Estate, SR5 2QB ☎ 0191 553 5200	C	3-11
Castletown Primary School Grange Road, Castletown, SR5 3EQ ☎ 0191 553 5210	C	3-11
Dame Dorothy Primary School Dock Street, Monkwearmouth, SR6 0EA ☎ 0191 553 7610	C	3-11
Easington Lane Primary School South Hetton Road, Easington Lane, DH5 0LH ☎ 0191 553 6730	C	3-11
East Herrington Primary School Balmoral Terrace, East Herrington, SR3 3PR ☎ 0191 553 5986	C	3-11
East Rainton Primary School School Road, East Rainton, DH5 9RA ☎ 0191 553 6505	C	3-11
English Martyrs' RC Primary School Redcar Road, SR5 5AU ☎ 0191 553 5540	VA	3-11
Gillas Lane Primary School Seaton Avenue, DH5 8EH ☎ 0191 553 6517	C	3-11
Glebe Village Primary School Lanercost, Glebe Village, NE38 7PY ☎ 0191 219 3715	C	3-11
Grangetown Primary School Spelter Works Road, Grangetown, SR2 8PX ☎ 0191 567 0394	C	3-11
Harraton Primary School Firtree Avenue,Harraton, NE38 9BA ☎ 0191 219 3725	C	3-11
Hasting Hill Primary School Tilbury Road, SR3 4LY ☎ 0191 553 6023	C	3-11
Havelock Primary School Fordfield Road, Ford Estate, SR4 0DA ☎ 0191 553 7655	C	3-11
Hudson Road Primary School Villiers Street South, SR1 2AH ☎ 0191 553 7675	C	3-11
Hylton Castle Primary School Cramlington Road, SR5 3QL ☎ 0191 553 5574	C	3-11
John F Kennedy Primary School Station Road, Columbia, NE38 7AR ☎ 0191 219 3745	C	3-11
Lsmbton Primary School Caradoc Close, Lambton Village, NE38 0PL ☎ 0191 219 3750	C	3-11
New Penshaw Primary School Langdale Road, New Penshaw, DH4 7HY ☎ 0191 382 3076	C	3-11
Newbottle Primary School Houghton Road, Newbottle, DH4 4EE ☎ 0191 553 6566	C	3-11
Oxclose Community Primary School Brancepeth Road, Oxclose Village, NE38 0LA ☎ 0191 219 3760	C	3-11
Pallion Primary School Waverley Terrace, Pallion, SR4 6TA ☎ 0191 553 7685	C	3-11
Plains Farm Primary School Tudor Grove, SR3 1SU ☎ 0191 553 6041	C	3-11
Redby Primary School Fulwell Road, SR6 9QP ☎ 0191 548 8100	C	3-11
Richard Avenue Primary School Richard Avenue, SR4 7LQ ☎ 0191 553 6053	C	3-11
Rickleton Primary School Vigo Lane, NE38 9EZ ☎ 0191 219 3785	C	3-11
St Bede's RC Primary School BHampshire Place, Usworth, NE37 2NP ☎ 0191 219 3795	VA	3-11
St Cuthbert's RC Primary School Grindon Lane, SR4 8HP ☎ 0191 553 6080	VA	3-11
St Joseph's RC Primary School Rutland Street, SR4 6HY ☎ 0191 553 7725	VA	3-11
Seaburn Dene Primary School Torver Crescent, Seaburn Dene, SR6 8LG ☎ 0191 553 5590	C	3-11
Shiney Row Primary School Rear South View, Shiney Row, DH4 4QP ☎ 0191 385 2701	C	3-11
South Hylton Primary School Union Street, South Hylton, SR4 0LS ☎ 0191 553 6853	C	3-11
Southwick Primary and Nursery School Clarence Street, Southwick, SR5 2HD ☎ 0191 553 5500	C	3-11
Springwell Village Primary School Springwell, NE9 7RX ☎ 0191 2193790	C	3-11
Thorney Close Primary School Torquay Road, SR3 4BB ☎ 0191 553 6093	C	3-11
Town End Primary School Borodin Avenue, SR5 4NX ☎ 0191 553 6996	C	3-11
Usworth Grange Primary School Marlborough Road, Sulgrave Village, NE37 3BG ☎ 0191 219 3825	C	3-11
Washington St Joseph's RC School Village Lane, NE38 7HU ☎ 0191 219 3805	VA	3-11
Witherwack Primary School Winslow Close, SR5 5RZ ☎ 0191 553 5365	C	3-11

School name, address and telephone number	Type	Age

NORTH WEST

350 BOLTON

School name, address and telephone number	Type	Age
All Saints CofE Primary School Devon Street, Farnworth, BL4 7PY ☎ 01204 573122	VA	3-11
Blackrod Church School Vicarage Road West, Blackrod, BL6 5DE ☎ 01204 696335	VC	3-11
Bolton Parish Church CofE Primary School Kestor Street, BL2 2AN ☎ 01204 528290	VA	3-11
Brandwood County Primary School Brandwood Street, BL3 4BG ☎ 01204 62454	C	3-11
Brownlow Fold County Primary School Darley Street, BL1 3DX ☎ 01204 524592	C	3-11
Chalfont Primary School Chalfont Street, BL1 8JS ☎ 01204 24155	C	3-11
Cherry Tree County Primary School Highfield Road, Farnworth, BL4 0NS ☎ 01204 73831	C	3-11
Church Road County Primary School Captains Clough Road, BL1 5RU ☎ 01204 844691	C	3-11
Clarendon County Primary School Clarendon Street, BL3 6SF ☎ 01204 523911	C	3-11
Gaskell County Primary School Thomas Holden Street, BL1 2QG ☎ 01204 522521	C	3-11
Hardy Mill County Primary School Belmont View, Harwood, BL2 3QJ ☎ 01204 520810	C	3-11
Harwood Meadows County Primary School Orchard Gardens, Harwood, BL2 3PS ☎ 01204 388268	C	3-11
Johnson Fold County Primary School Worston Avenue, Johnson Fold, BL1 5UG ☎ 01204 842880	C	3-11
Kearsley West County Primary School Primrose Street, Kearsley, BL4 9BZ ☎ 01204 573332	C	3-11
Lever Edge County Primary School Lever Edge Lane, BL3 3HP ☎ 01204 61507	C	3-11
Masefield County Primary School Masefield Road, Little Lever, BL3 1NG ☎ 01204 578755	C	3-11
Oldhams County Primary School Selkirk Road, BL1 7BN ☎ 01204 302957	C	3-11
Oxford Grove County Primary School Oxford Grove, BL1 4JH ☎ 01204 846078	C	3-11
Roscow Fold VC Primary School Stephens Street, Breightmet, BL2 5DX ☎ 01204 526556	VC	3-11
St Andrew RC Primary School Withins Drive, BL2 5LF ☎ 01204 526219	VA	3-11
St Bede CofE Primary School Morris Green Lane, BL3 3LJ ☎ 01204 61899	VA	3-11
St Columba's RC Primary School Ripley Street, BL2 3AR ☎ 01204 301264	VA	3-11
St Ethelbert's RC Primary School Melbourne Road, BL3 5RL ☎ 01204 61625	VA	3-11
St James CofE Primary School Hillside Avenue, Farnworth, BL4 9QB ☎ 01204 572587	VC	3-11
St Mary's CofE Primary School Edale Road, BL3 4QP ☎ 01204 62406	VC	3-11
St Matthew's CofE Primary School Kentford Road, BL1 2JL ☎ 01204 526306	VC	3-11
St Michael's CofE Primary School Green Lane, BL3 2PL ☎ 01204 524740	VA	3-11
St Peter and St Paul RC Primary School Pilkington Street, BL3 6HP ☎ 01204 524991	VA	3-11
St Thomas Halliwell CofE Primary School Eskrick Street, BL1 3JB ☎ 01204 841509	VA	3-11
St William of York RC Primary School Nugent Road, BL3 3DE ☎ 01204 62348	VA	3-11

351 BURY

School name, address and telephone number	Type	Age
All Saints CofE Primary School Rufford Drive, Whitefield, M45 8PL ☎ 0161 766 4429	VC	3-11
Brandlesholme Primary School Brandlesholme Road, BL8 1HS ☎ 0161 764 5360	C	3-11
Chapelfield County Primary School Clough Street, Radcliffe, M26 1LH ☎ 0161 724 7327	C	3-11
Christ Church Ainsworth CofE Primary School Tommy Lane, Ainsworth, BL2 5SQ ☎ 01204 527484	VC	3-11
East Ward County Primary School Willow Street, BL9 7QZ ☎ 0161 764 4101	C	3-11
Elton County Primary School Alston Street, BL8 1SB ☎ 0161 764 4170	C	3-11
Fairfield Primary School Rochdale Old Road, BL9 7SD ☎ 0161 764 1559	C	3-11
Gorsefield Primary School Robertson Street, Radcliffe, M26 4DW ☎ 0161 723 5361	C	3-11
Heaton Park Primary School Cuckoo Lane, Whitefield, M45 6TE ☎ 0161 773 9554	C	3-11
Mersey Drive Primary School Mersey Drive, Whitefield, M45 8LN ☎ 0161 766 6298	C	3-11
Park View Primary School Park View Road, Prestwich, M25 1FA ☎ 0161 773 5359	C	3-11
Radcliffe Hall CofE and Methodist School Bury Street, Radcliffe, M26 2GB ☎ 0161 723 2233	VC	3-11
Ribble Drive Primary School Ribble Drive, Whitefield, M45 8TD ☎ 0161 766 6625	C	3-11

School name, address and telephone number	Type	Age
St Andrew's CofE Primary School Graves Street, Radcliffe, M26 4GE ☎ 0161 723 2426	VA	3–11
St John's CofE Primary School Athlone Avenue, BL9 5EE ☎ 0161 764 5330	VC	3–11
St Marie's RC Primary School The Mosses, Edward Street, BL9 0RZ ☎ 0161 764 3204	VA	3–11
St Mary's CofE Primary School Rectory Lane, Prestwich, M25 1BP ☎ 0161 773 3794	VA	3–11
St Mary's RC Primary School Belgrave Street, Radcliffe, M26 4DG ☎ 0161 723 4210	VA	3–11
St Michael's RC Primary School Ribble Drive, Whitefield, M45 8NJ ☎ 0161 766 6628	VA	3–11
St Peter's CofE Primary School Whitefield Road, BL9 9PW ☎ 0161 764 2017	VC	3–11
St Stephen's CofE Primary School Colville Drive, BL8 2DX ☎ 0161 764 1132	VA	3–11
Springside County Primary School Springside Road, BL9 5JB ☎ 0161 764 5337	C	3–11

906 CHESHIRE

School name, address and telephone number	Type	Age
Astmoor County School Kingshead Close, Castlefields, WA7 2JE ☎ 01928 565053	C	3–11
Bewsey Lodge County Primary School Lodge Lane, Bewsey, WA5 5AG ☎ 01925 632730	C	3–11
Brook Acre County Primary School Hilden Road, Padgate, WA2 0JP ☎ 01925 815827	C	3–11
Cambridge Road Primary School Cambridge Road, Ellesmere Port, L65 4AQ ☎ 0151 355 1735	C	3–11
Castle View County Primary School Mead Way, Halton Brook, WA7 2DZ ☎ 01928 563970	C	3–11
Colshaw County Primary School Colshaw Drive, SK9 2PZ ☎ 01625 531408	C	3–11
Dallam County Primary School Boulting Avenue, Dallam, WA5 5HG ☎ 01925 633927	C	3–11
Duddon St Peter's CofE Primary School Duddon, CW6 0EL ☎ 01829 781366	VC	3–11
Evelyn St County Primary School Evelyn Street, WA5 1BD ☎ 01925 495567	C	3–11
Fairfield CofE Primary School Fairfield Street, WA1 3AJ ☎ 01925 635143	VA	3–11
Grange County Primary School Brindley Avenue, CW7 2EG ☎ 01606 592126	C	3–11
Greenfields County Primary School Whitby's Lane, Over, CW7 2LZ ☎ 01606 593622	C	3–11
Hallwood Park County Primary School & Nursery Hallwood Park Avenue, Hallwood Park, WA7 2FL ☎ 01928 716336	C	3–11
Handforth Hall County Primary School Spath Lane, Handforth, SK9 3QN ☎ 01625 525760	C	3–11
Handley Hill County Primary School off Beeston Drive, CW7 1EW ☎ 01606 592730	C	3–11
Hartford Manor County Primary School Stones Manor Lane, Hartford, CW8 1NU ☎ 01606 76183	C	3–11
Hungerford County Primary School School Crescent, Hungerford Road, CW1 5HA ☎ 01270 582408	C	3–11
Long Lane County Primary School Clough Avenue, Longford, WA2 9PH ☎ 01925 632705	C	3–11
Manor Park Primary School Manor Park North, WA16 8DB ☎ 01565 632248	C	3–11
Marlfields County Primary School Waggs Road, CW12 4BT ☎ 01260 272555	C	3–11
Millfields County Primary School Marsh Lane, CW5 5HP ☎ 01270 625587	C	3–11
Neston St Mary's CofE Primary School Raby Park Road, Neston, L64 9SL ☎ 0151 336 2414	VC	3–11
Parklands County Primary School Little Sutton, L66 3RL ☎ 0151 339 2587	C	3–11
Prestbury CofE Primary School Bollin Grove, Prestbury, SK10 4JJ ☎ 01625 828043	VA	3–11
St Alban's RC Primary School Bewsey Road, WA5 5JS ☎ 01925 632128	VA	3–11
St Barnabas CofE Primary School Collin Street, WA5 1TG ☎ 01925 633606	VA	3–11
St Gerard's RC Primary and Nursery School Lugsdale Road, WA8 6DD ☎ 0151 424 2879	VA	3–11
St James CofE Primary School Heathfield Road, Audlem, CW3 0AL ☎ 01270 811450	VC	3–11
St James CofE Primary School Old Road, WA4 1AP ☎ 01925 634967	VA	3–11
St Mary's CofE Primary School Castlefields Avenue South, WA7 2NR ☎ 01928 565995	VA	3–11
St Mary's RC Primary and Nursery School Dane Bank Avenue, CW2 8AD ☎ 01270 68912	VA	3–11
St Theresa's RC Primary School Kipling Road, Blacon, CH1 5UU ☎ 01244 390758	VA	3–11
St Thomas's CofE Primary School Parkgate Road, Stockton Heath, WA4 2AP ☎ 01925 268722	VA	3–11
Simms Cross County Primary School Kingsway, WA8 7QS ☎ 0151 424 5031	C	3–11
Tilston Parochial CofE (Controlled) Primary School Tilston, SY14 7HA ☎ 01829 250204	VC	3–11
West Bank County Primary School Cholmondeley Street, WA8 0EL ☎ 0151 424 2799	C	3–11

School name, address and telephone number	Type	Age
Westlea County Primary School Weston Grove, Upton-by-Chester, CH2 1QJ ☎ 01244 390054	C	3–11
William Stockton County Primary School Heathfield Road, Ellesmere Port, L65 8DH ☎ 0151 355 1650	C	3–11
Wincham County Primary School Church Street, Wincham, CW9 6EP ☎ 01565 733081	C	3–11
Winsford-Over-Hall County Primary School Ludlow Close, CW7 1LX ☎ 01606 553692	C	3–11

909 CUMBRIA

School name, address and telephone number	Type	Age
Askam Village School Lots Road, LA16 7DA ☎ 01229 462814	GM	3–11
Bransty Primary School Mona Road, Bransty, CA28 6EG ☎ 01946 852652	C	3–11
Broughton Primary School Great Broughton, CA13 0YT ☎ 01900 325993	GM	3–11
Castle Park County Primary School Sedbergh Drive, LA9 6BE ☎ 01539 773 633	C	3–11
Coniston CofE Primary School Shepherd's Bridge, LA21 8AL ☎ 01539 441302	VC	3–11
Dalton St Mary's CofE Primary School Coronation Drive, LA15 8QR ☎ 01229 462729	GM	3–11
Eaglesfield Paddle CofE GM Primary School Eaglesfield, CA13 0QY ☎ 01900 325947	GM	3–11
Flimby Primary School Rye Hill Road, Flimby, CA15 8PJ ☎ 01900 812264	GM	3–11
Flookburgh CofE GM Primary School Winder Lane, Flookburgh, LA11 7LE ☎ 01539 558434	GM	3–11
Ghyllside County Primary School Gillinggate, LA9 4JB ☎ 01539 773624	C	3–11
Langwathby CofE Primary School Salkeld Road, Langwathby, CA10 1HB ☎ 01768 881295	VC	3–11
Milnthorpe Primary School Firs Road, LA7 7QF ☎ 01539 562344	C	3–11
Newbarns Primary School Rising Side, LA13 9ET ☎ 01229 894615	C	3–11
North Walney Primary School Duddon Drive, Walney, LA14 3TN ☎ 01229 471781	C	3–11
St Cuthbert's RC (Aided) Primary School Victoria Road, Botcherby, CA1 2UE ☎ 01228 607 505	VA	3–11
Warwick Bridge (GM) Primary School Warwick Bridge, CA4 8RE ☎ 01228 560390	GM	3–11

340 KNOWLSLEY

School name, address and telephone number	Type	Age
Beechwood County Primary School Hillside Avenue, Huyton, L36 8EQ ☎ 0151 489 6471	C	3–11
Brookside Primary School Cremorne Hey, Stockbridge Village, L28 3QA ☎ 0151 489 4906	C	3–11
Cherryfield Primary School Rockford Avenue, Southdene, Kirkby, L32 3YE ☎ 0151 546 4780	C	3–11
Evelyn Primary School Evelyn Avenue, L34 2SP ☎ 0151 426 6377	C	3–11
Halsnead Primary School Dragon Lane, Whiston, L35 3QX ☎ 0151 426 3459	C	3–11
Holy Family RC Primary School Arncliffe Road, Halewood, L25 9PA ☎ 0151 428 2922	VA	3–11
Huyton-with-Roby CofE (Aided) Primary School Rupert Road, Huyton, L36 9TF ☎ 0151 292 1974	VA	3–11
Kirkby CofE Primary School Hall Lane, Kirkby, L32 1TZ ☎ 0151 546 6314	VC	3–11
Knowsley Village Primary School Sugar Lane, Knowsley, L34 0ER ☎ 0151 289 5349	C	3–11
Millbrook Primary School Kirkby Row, Westvale, Kirkby, L32 0TG ☎ 0151 546 4893	C	3–11
Mosscroft Primary School Bedford Close, Huyton, L36 1XH ☎ 0151 489 6511	C	3–11
New Hutte County Primary School Lichfield Road, Halewood, L26 1TT ☎ 0151 486 3699	C	3–11
Our Lady's RC Primary School Ward Street, L34 6JJ ☎ 0151 426 5005	VA	3–11
Overdale Primary School Roughwood Drive, Northwood, Kirkby, L33 9UW ☎ 0151 546 2607	C	3–11
Park Brow Primary School Broad Lane, Southdene, Kirkby, L32 6QH ☎ 0151 546 2807	C	3–11
Park View Primary School Park View, Huyton, L36 2LL ☎ 0151 489 1829	C	3–11
Ravenscroft County Primary School Ebony Way, Tower Hill, Kirkby, L33 1XT ☎ 0151 546 3047	C	3–11
Roby Park Primary School Easton Road, Huyton, L36 4NY ☎ 0151 489 1902	C	3–11
Roseheath Primary School Leathers Lane, Halewood, L26 1XQ ☎ 0151 486 3248	C	3–11
Sacred Heart RC Primary School Westhead Avenue, Northwood, Kirkby, L33 0XN ☎ 0151 546 3597	VA	3–11
St Aidan's RC Primary School Adswood Road, Huyton, L36 7XR ☎ 0151 489 3221	VA	3–11
St Albert's RC Primary School Steers Croft, Stockbridge Village, L28 8AJ ☎ 0151 228 8789	VA	3–11
St Aloysius RC Primary School Twig Lane, Huyton-with-Roby, L36 2LF ☎ 0151 489 5083	VA	3–11
St Andrew's RC Primary School Higher Road, Halewood, L26 1TD ☎ 0151 486 3637	VA	3–11

School name, address and telephone number	Type	Age
St Columba's RC Primary School Hillside Road, Huyton, L36 8BL ☎ 0151 489 2806	VA	3–11
St Gabriel's CofE Primary School Ellis Ashton Street, Huyton, L36 6BH ☎ 0151 489 5048	VA	3–11
St Laurence's RC Primary School Leeside Avenue, Southdene, Kirkby, L32 9QX ☎ 0151 546 4733	VA	3–11
St Leo's RC Primary School Lickers Lane, Whiston, L35 3SR ☎ 0151 426 1925	VA	3–11
St Mark's RC Primary School Leathers Lane, Halewood, L26 0TT ☎ 0151 486 2236	VA	3–11
Southmead Primary School Lickers Lane, Whiston, L35 3JY ☎ 0151 426 7110	C	3–11
Willis County Primary School Milton Avenue, Whiston, L35 2XY ☎ 0151 426 4584	C	3–11

923 LANCASHIRE

School name, address and telephone number	Type	Age
Bishop Martin CofE Primary School Birkrig, WN8 9BN ☎ 01695 724730	VA	3–11
Blessed Sacrament RC Primary School Farringdon Lane, Ribbleton, PR2 6LX ☎ 01772 792572	VA	3–11
Chaucer County Primary School Chaucer Road, FY7 6QN ☎ 01253 873795	C	3–11
Christ The King RC School Bathurst Avenue, Grange Park, FY3 7RJ ☎ 01253 395985	VA	3–11
Claremont Primary School Westminster Road, FY1 2QE ☎ 01253 21703	C	3–11
Clayton Brook County Primary School Great Greens Lane, Bamber Bridge, PR5 8HL ☎ 01772 313878	C	3–11
Clough Fold County Primary School Heathgate, Birch Green, WN8 6QH ☎ 01695 720018	C	3–11
Coppull County Primary School Park Road, Coppull, PR7 5AH ☎ 01257 791237	C	3–11
Daisyfield County Primary School Clinton Street, BB1 5LB ☎ 01254 52108	C	3–11
Delph Side County Primary School Eskdale, Tanhouse 5, WN8 6ED ☎ 01695 721881	C	3–11
Edisford County School Edisford Road, BB7 2LN ☎ 01200 422239	C	3–11
English Martyrs' RC Junior and Infant School Sizer Street, PR1 7DR ☎ 01772 556092	VA	3–11
Fairlie County Primary School Fairlie, Birch Green, WN8 6RG ☎ 01695 726 154	C	3–11
Frenchwood County Primary School Frenchwood Knoll, PR1 4LE ☎ 01772 253244	C	3–11
Gisburn Road County Primary School Gisburn Road, Barnoldswick, BB18 5JX ☎ 01282 812287	C	3–11
Great Harwood County Primary School Rushton Street, Great Harwood, BB6 7JQ ☎ 01254 884549	C	3–11
Griffin Park County Primary School Cavendish Place, BB2 2PN ☎ 01254 57724	C	3–11
Hillside County Primary School Egerton, Tanhouse, WN8 6DE ☎ 01695 724860	C	3–11
Holland Moor County School Cornbrook, WN8 9AG ☎ 01695 725062	C	3–11
Holy Trinity Stacksteads CofE Primary School Booth Road, Stacksteads, OL13 0QP ☎ 01706 877025	VC	3–11
Huncoat County Primary School Lynwood Road, Huncoat, BB5 6LR ☎ 01254 233369	C	3–11
Kingsfold County Primary School Martinfield Road, Penwortham, PR1 9HJ ☎ 01772 743531	C	3–11
Leyland Seven Stars Primary School Peacock Hall Road, Leyland, PR5 3AD ☎ 01772 422503	C	3–11
Lostock Hall County Primary School Linden Drive, Lostock Hall, PR5 5AS ☎ 01772 338289	C	3–11
Moor Nook County Primary School Mitton Drive, PR2 6EN ☎ 01772 796009	C	3–11
Morecambe Bay County School Station Road, LA4 5JL ☎ 01524 414303	C	3–11
Revoe County Primary School Grasmere Road, FY1 5HP ☎ 01253 763414	C	3–11
Roe Lee Park County Primary School Emerald Avenue, BB1 9RP ☎ 01254 56297	C	3–11
Roman Road County Primary School Fishmoor Drive, Higher Croft, BB2 3UY ☎ 01254 663132	C	3–11
Sabden County Primary School Whalley Road, Sabden, BB7 9DZ ☎ 01282 771000	C	3–11
Sacred Heart RC School Brooke Street, PR6 0LB ☎ 01257 262659	VA	3–11
St Cuthbert's RC School Lightwood Avenue, FY4 2AU ☎ 01253 403232	VA	3–11
St John with St Michael School Moss Side Street, Shawforth, OL12 8JB ☎ 01706 852614	VA	3–11
St Leonard's CofE School Moor Lane, Padiham, BB12 8HT ☎ 01282 771470	VA	3–11
St Luke and St Philip CofE Primary School Hancock Street, BB2 1LZ ☎ 01254 54866	VA	3–11
St Maria Goretti RC Primary School Gamull Lane, Ribbleton, PR2 6SJ ☎ 01772 700052	VA	3–11
St Mary's RC Primary School Holcombe Drive, BB10 4BH ☎ 01282 427546	VA	3–11
St Mary's RC Primary School Tong Lane, OL13 9LJ ☎ 01706 873123	VA	3–11

School name, address and telephone number	Type	Age
St Matthew's RC Primary School Blakehall, WN8 9AZ ☎ 01695 724675	VA	3–11
St Michael with St John Primary School Swallow Drive, BB1 6LE ☎ 01254 665190	VC	3–11
St Oswald's RC Primary School Hartley Avenue, BB5 0NN ☎ 01254 234924	VA	3–11
St Stephen's CofE School South Meadow Lane, PR1 8JN ☎ 01772 556306	VC	3–11
St Thomas' CofE Primary School Newton Street, BB1 1NE ☎ 01254 54706	VC	3–11
St Wulstan's RC School Poulton Road, FY7 7JY ☎ 01253 874785	VA	3–11
Tonacliffe County Primary School Tonacliffe Road, Whitworth, OL12 8SS ☎ 01706 344609	C	3–11
West Street County Primary School West Street, BB8 0HW ☎ 01282 865840	C	3–11
Whittlefield County Primary School Tabor Street, BB12 0HL ☎ 01282 429419	C	3–11

341 LIVERPOOL

School name, address and telephone number	Type	Age
Arnot County Primary School Arnot Street, Walton-on-the-Hill, L4 4ED ☎ 0151 286 1400	C	3–11
Barlows Junior Mixed and Infant School and Nursery Barlows Lane, Fazakerley, L9 9EH ☎ 0151 525 3181	C	3–11
Beaufort Junior Mixed and Infant School Beaufort Street, L8 6RS ☎ 0151 709 3721	C	3–11
Birchfield Junior Mixed Infant and Nursery School Birchfield Road, L7 9LY ☎ 0151 228 3831	C	3–11
Colwell Junior Mixed and Infant School Colwell Road, L14 8XZ ☎ 0151 228 9599	C	3–11
Cross Farm Junior Mixed and Infant School Tothale Turn, L27 4YB ☎ 0151 487 8882	C	3–11
Croxteth County Primary School Moss Way, L11 0BP ☎ 0151 546 3140	C	3–11
Earle Primary School Earle Road, L7 6HQ ☎ 0151 733 1685	C	3–11
Gwladys Street County Primary and Nursery School Walton Lane, L4 5RW ☎ 0151 525 0843	C	3–11
Holy Name RC Junior Mixed Infant & Nursery School Moss Pits Lane, Fazakerley, L10 9LG ☎ 0151 525 3545	VA	3–11
Holy Trinity RC Junior Mixed and Infant and Nursery School Banks Road, L19 8JY ☎ 0151 427 7466	VA	3–11
Kirkdale Junior Mixed and Infant School Fonthill Road, L4 1QD ☎ 0151 922 2775	C	3–11
Knotty Ash County Primary School Thomas Lane, L14 5NX ☎ 0151 228 4222	C	3–11
Maidford Junior Mixed and Infant School Maidford Road, L14 2DU ☎ 0151 228 9234	C	3–11
Matthew Arnold Junior Mixed and Infant School Dingle Lane, L8 9UB ☎ 0151 727 2145	C	3–11
Millwood Primary School Greenway Road, Speke, L24 7RZ ☎ 0151 425 3244	C	3–11
Mother Teresa RC Primary School Titchfield Street, L5 8UT ☎ 0151 207 0911	VA	3–11
Norman Pannell Primary School Brownbill Bank, L27 7AE ☎ 0151 487 7718	C	3–11
Northcote Junior Mixed and Infant School Cavendish Drive, L9 1HW ☎ 0151 284 1919	C	3–11
Our Lady and St Swithin Junior Mixed and Infant School Parkstile Lane, Gillmoss, L11 0BQ ☎ 0151 546 3868	VA	3–11
Our Lady Immaculate RC Primary School Northumberland Terrace, Everton, L5 3QF ☎ 0151 260 8957	VA	3–11
Our Lady of Mount Carmel Junior Mixed and Infant School North Hill Street, L8 8BQ ☎ 0151 727 5336	VA	3–11
Our Lady of Reconciliation School Eldon Place, L3 6HE ☎ 0151 207 2304	VA	3–11
Parkhill Primary School Parkhill Road, L8 4TF ☎ 0151 727 1401	C	3–11
Pleasant Street Junior Mixed and Infant School Pleasant Street, L3 5TS ☎ 0151 709 3802	C	3–11
Rathbone Junior Mixed and Infant School Albany Road, L7 8RL ☎ 0151 263 1680	C	3–11
St Anne's RC Primary School Overbury Street, L7 3HJ ☎ 0151 709 1698	VA	3–11
St Bernard's RC Junior Mixed Infant and Nursery School Kingsley Road, L8 2TY ☎ 0151 709 1835	VA	3–11
St Clare's RC Junior Mixed Infant and Nursery School Garmoyle Close, L15 0DW ☎ 0151 733 4318	VA	3–11
St Gerard's RC Junior Mixed and Infant School Boundary Street, L5 2 QD ☎ 0151 298 1083	VA	3–11
St Margaret's CofE Junior Mixed and Infant School Upper Hampton Street, Princes Park, L8 1TR ☎ 0151 709 7719	VA	3–11
St Sebastian's RC Junior Mixed and Infant School Holly Road, L7 0LH ☎ 0151 260 9697	VA	3–11
Springwood Junior Mixed and Infant School Danefield Road, L19 4TL ☎ 0151 427 7759	C	3–11
Tiber County Primary School Lodge Lane, L8 0TP ☎ 0151 727 4052	C	3–11
Walton St Mary CofE Primary School Bedford Road, Walton, L4 5PU ☎ 0151 525 2498	VC	3–11
Wavertree CofE Junior Mixed and Infant School Rose Villas, Wavertree, L15 8HH ☎ 0151 733 1231	VC	3–11
Whitefield Road Junior Mixed and Infant School Boundary Lane, L6 2HZ ☎ 0151 263 5976	C	3–11

School name, address and telephone number	Type	Age
352 MANCHESTER		
Abbott Primary School Livesey Street, Collyhurst, M40 7PR ☎ 0161 834 9529	C	3–11
All Saints CofE Junior and Infant School Culcheth Lane, Newton Heath, M40 1LS ☎ 0161 681 3455	VA	3–11
All Saints County Primary School Endcott Close, West Gorton, M18 8BR ☎ 0161 223 9325	C	3–11
Baguley Hall Primary School Ackworth Drive, M23 1LB ☎ 0161 998 2090	C	3–11
Bank Meadow County Primary School Lime Bank Street, Ardwick, M12 6NS ☎ 0161 273 4669	C	3–11
Barlow Hall Primary School Darley Avenue, Chorlton-cum-Hardy, M21 7JG ☎ 0161 881 2158	C	3–11
Bishop Bilsborrow Memorial RC Primary School Princess Road, Moss Side M14 7LS ☎ 0161 226 3649	VA	3–11
Bowker Vale School Middleton Road, Crumpsall, M8 4NB ☎ 0161 740 5993	C	3–11
Burgess Primary School Monsall Road, Harpurhey, M9 5QE ☎ 0161 205 4996	C	3–11
Chevassut County Primary School Jackson Crescent, Hulme, M15 5AL ☎ 0161 226 2289	C	3–11
Clayton Brook Primary School Saunton Road, Higher Openshaw, M11 1AZ ☎ 0161 223 3549	C	3–11
CofE School of The Resurrection Pilgrim Drive, Beswick, M11 3TJ ☎ 0161 223 3163	VA	3–11
Corpus Christi RC Primary School Varley Street, Miles Platting, M40 8EE ☎ 0161 205 4833	VA	3–11
Crumpsall Lane Primary School Crumpsall, M8 6SR ☎ 0161 740 3741	C	3–11
Heald Place Primary School Rusholme, M14 7PN ☎ 0161 224 7079	C	3–11
Holy Name RC Primary School Denmark Road, M15 6JS ☎ 0161 226 6303	VA	3–11
Holy Trinity CofE Primary School Capstan Street, Blackley, M9 4DU ☎ 0161 205 1216	VC	3–11
Ladybarn Primary School Briarfield Road, Withington, M20 4SR ☎ 0161 445 4898	C	3–11
Medlock Primary School Wadeson Road, Brunswick, M13 9UJ ☎ 0161 273 1830	C	3–11
Moston Fields Primary School Brookside Road, Moston, M40 9GN ☎ 0161 681 1801	C	3–11
Mount Carmel RC Primary School Wilson Road, Blackley, M9 3BG ☎ 0161 740 4696	VA	3–11
Old Hall Drive Primary School Old Hall Drive, Gorton, M18 7FU ☎ 0161 223 2805	C	3–11
Rack House County Primary School Yarmouth Drive, Northern Moor, Wythenshawe, M23 0BT ☎ 0161 998 2544	C	3–11
Ravensbury Junior and Infant School Alpine Street, Clayton, M11 4ER ☎ 0161 223 0370	C	3–11
Sacred Heart Junior and Infant School Floatshall Road, Baguley, M23 1HP ☎ 0161 998 3419	VA	3–11
St Agnes CofE Primary School Clitheroe Road, Longsight, M13 0QU ☎ 0161 224 4680	VC	3–11
St Aidan's RC Junior and Infant School Rackhouse Road, Northern Moor, M23 0BW ☎ 0161 998 4126	VA	3–11
St Ambrose Primary School Princess Road, Chorlton-cum-Hardy, M21 7QA ☎ 0161 445 3299	VA	3–11
St Andrew's CofE Primary School Broom Avenue, Levenshulme, M19 2UH ☎ 0161 432 2731	VA	3–11
St Anne's RC Junior and Infant School Moss Bank, Crumpsall, M8 5UD ☎ 0161 740 5995	VA	3–11
St Anne's RC Primary School Carruthers Street, Ancoats, M4 7EQ ☎ 0161 273 2417	VA	3–11
St Augustine's CofE Primary School Redbrook Avenue, Monsall, M40 8PL ☎ 0161 205 2812	VC	3–11
St Brigid's RC Primary School Grey Mare Lane, Beswick, M11 3DR ☎ 0161 223 5538	VA	3–11
St Chad's RC Primary School Balmfield Street, Cheetham, M8 0SP ☎ 0161 205 6965	VA	3–11
St Chrystostom's CofE Primary School Lincoln Grove, Chorlton-on-Medlock, M13 0DX ☎ 0161 273 3621	VC	3–11
St Clement's CofE Primary School Abbey Hey Lane, Higher Openshaw, M11 1LR ☎ 0161 301 3268	VC	3–11
St Cuthbert's RC Primary School Heyscroft Road, Withington, M20 4UZ ☎ 0161 445 6079	VA	3–11
St Edmund's RC Primary School Upper Monsall Street, Miles Platting, M40 8NG ☎ 0161 205 1700	VA	3–11
St Ignatius RC Junior and Infant and Nursery School Addison Close, Chorlton-on-Medlock, M13 9JR ☎ 0161 273 5662	VA	3–11
St James CofE Primary School Stelling Street, Gorton, M18 8LW ☎ 0161 223 2423	VC	3–11
St Joseph's RC Junior and Infant School Richmond Grove, Longsight, M13 0BT ☎ 0161 224 5347	VA	3–11
St Jude's CofE Primary School Cardroom Road, Ancoats, M4 6FZ ☎ 0161 205 2846	VC	3–11
St Kentigern's Catholic GM Primary School Bethnall Drive, Fallowfield, M14 7ED ☎ 0161 224 6842	GM	3–11
St Luke's CofE Primary School Langport Avenue, Longsight, M12 4NG ☎ 0161 273 3648	VC	3–11
St Mary's CofE Junior and Infant School St Mary's Road, Moston, M40 0DF ☎ 0161 681 0407	VA	3–11
St Mary's CofE Junior and Infant School Wilcock Street, Alexandra Park, Moss Side, M16 7DA ☎ 0161 226 1773	VC	3–11

School name, address and telephone number	Type	Age
St Paul's CofE Primary School Wilmslow Road, Withington, M20 4AW ☎ 0161 445 2808	VC	3–11
St Thomas County Primary School Hazelbottom Road, Lower Crumpsall, M8 5UX ☎ 0161 205 1916	C	3–11
St Wilfrid's RC Primary School St Wilfrid's Street, Hulme, M15 5BJ ☎ 0161 226 3339	VA	3–11
St Willibrord's RC Primary School Vale Street, Clayton, M11 4WR ☎ 0161 223 9345	VA	3–11
Temple Primary School Smedley Street, Cheetham, M8 8UN ☎ 0161 205 1932	C	3–11
Victoria Avenue Primary School Blackley, M9 0RD ☎ 0161 740 2185	C	3–11
Webster Primary School Denmark Road, Greenheys, M15 6JU ☎ 0161 226 3928	C	3–11
Woodhouse Park Primary School Rossett Avenue, Lornishway, Wythenshawe, M22 0WW ☎ 0161 437 1899	C	3–11

353 OLDHAM

School name, address and telephone number	Type	Age
Alt Primary School Alt Lane, OL8 2EL ☎ 0161 624 0056	C	3–11
Beal Vale County Primary School Salts Street, Shaw, OL2 7SY ☎ 01706 847185	C	3–11
Beever Junior Infant and Nursery School Moorby Street, OL1 3QU ☎ 0161 624 3740	C	3–11
Broadfield Junior Infant and Nursery School Goddard Street, OL8 1LH ☎ 0161 665 3030	C	3–11
Corpus Christi RC Primary School Stanley Road, Chadderton, OL9 7HA ☎ 0161 652 1275	VA	3–11
Freehold Community School Sidmouth Street, OL9 7RG ☎ 0161 687 2575	C	3–11
Greenacres Junior Infant and Nursery School Dunkerley Street, OL4 2AX ☎ 0161 624 1802	C	3–11
Greenhill Community Junior Infant and Nursery School Harmony Street, OL4 1RR ☎ 0161 633 0483	C	3–11
Hey-with-Zion Primary School Rowland Way, Lees, OL4 3LQ ☎ 0161 620 3860	VC	3–11
Holy Family RC School Lime Green Road, OL8 3NG ☎ 0161 652 2400	VA	3–11
Holy Rosary RC Junior Infant and Nursery School Fir Tree Avenue, Fitton Hill, OL8 2SR ☎ 0161 624 3035	VA	3–11
Holy Trinity CofE Dobcross School Delph New Road, Dobcross, OL3 5BP ☎ 01457 872860	VC	3–11
Limehurst Junior Infant and Nursery School Lime Green Road, OL8 3NG ☎ 0161 624 1196	C	3–11
Littlemoor Primary School Littlemoor Lane, OL4 2RR ☎ 0161 624 4188	C	3–11
Lyndhurst Primary and Nursery School Lyndhurst Road, OL8 4JG ☎ 0161 624 2192	C	3–11
Mayfield Primary School Mayfield Road, Derker, OL1 4LG ☎ 0161 624 6425	C	3–11
Mills Hill Primary School Baytree Avenue, Chadderton, OL9 0NH ☎ 0161 624 1133	C	3–11
Propps Hall Junior Infant and Nursery School Propps Hall Drive, Failsworth, M35 0ND ☎ 0161 682 7994	C	3–11
Roundthorn Junior Infant and Nursery School Aspull Street, OL4 5LE ☎ 0161 624 2962	C	3–11
Sacred Heart RC Junior Infant and Nursery School Whetstone Hill Road, Derker, OL1 4NA ☎ 0161 633 1461	VA	3–11
St Anne's RC Primary School Greenacres Road, OL4 1HP ☎ 0161 624 4179	VA	3–11
St Joseph's RC Junior Infant and Nursery School Oldham Road, Shaw, OL2 8SZ ☎ 01706 847218	VA	3–11
St Martin's CofE Junior Infant and Nursery School St Martin's Road, Fitton Hill, OL8 2PY ☎ 0161 624 0053	VA	3–11
St Patrick's RC Primary and Nursery School Lee Street, OL8 1EF ☎ 0161 633 0527	VA	3–11
St Thomas Junior Infant and Nursery CofE (Aided) School Coleridge Road, Sholver, OL1 4RL ☎ 0161 624 9290	VA	3–11
Stoneleigh Primary School Vulcan Street, OL1 4LJ ☎ 0161 624 9078	C	3–11
Summervale Primary School Lee Street, OL8 1EF ☎ 0161 624 3940	C	3–11
Thorp Primary and Nursery School Westerdale Drive, Royton, OL2 5TY ☎ 0161 620 8961	C	3–11
Watersheddings Primary School Broadbent Road, OL1 4HY ☎ 0161 624 1219	C	3–11

354 ROCHDALE

School name, address and telephone number	Type	Age
All Saints CofE Primary School Maud Street, OL12 0EL ☎ 01706 640728	VA	3–11
Ashfield Valley Primary School New Barn Lane, OL11 1TA ☎ 01706 522758	C	3–11
Castleton Primary School Hillcrest Road, OL11 2QD ☎ 01706 631858	C	3–11
Harwood Park Primary School Hardfield Street, OL10 1DG ☎ 01706 369592	C	3–11
Moss Field Primary School West Starkey Street, OL10 4TA ☎ 01706 369508	C	3–11
Our Lady and St Paul Primary School Sutherland Road, Darnhill, OL10 3PD ☎ 01706 360827	VA	3–11
Queensway Primary School Hartley Lane, OL11 2LR ☎ 01706 647743	C	3–11

School name, address and telephone number	Type	Age
St John The Baptist RC Primary School Ann Street, OL11 1EZ ☎ 01706 647195	VA	3–11
St Mary's RC Primary School Wood Street, Langley, Middleton, M24 5GL ☎ 0161 643 7594	VA	3–11
Smallbridge Primary School Kentmere Avenue, Smallbridge, OL12 9EE ☎ 01706 647533	C	3–11
Smithy Bridge Primary School Bridgenorth Drive, Smithy Bridge, OL15 0DY ☎ 01706 378083	GM	3–11
Whittaker Moss Primary School off Elmsfield Avenue, Norden, OL11 5UY ☎ 01706 342342	C	3–11

342 ST HELENS

School name, address and telephone number	Type	Age
Ashurst Primary School New Glade Hill, off Chain Lane, Blackbrook, WA11 9QJ ☎ 01744 757446	C	3–11
Billinge Chapel End Primary School Carr Mill Road, Billinge, WN5 7TX ☎ 01744 608058	C	3–11
Broad Oak Community Primary School Brunswick Street, Parr, WA9 2JE ☎ 01744 736090	C	3–11
Eaves County Primary School Eaves Lane, Marshalls Cross, WA9 3UB ☎ 01744 812700	C	3–11
Grange Valley Primary School Heyes Avenue, Haydock, WA11 0XQ ☎ 01744 25543	C	3–11
Rectory CofE Primary School Rectory Road, North Ashton, Ashton-in-Makerfield, WN4 0QF ☎ 01942 727138	VA	3–11
Rivington Primary School Tennis Street North, WA10 6LF ☎ 01744 27490	C	3–11
St Austin's RC Primary School Heath Street, WA9 5NJ ☎ 01744 814172	VA	3–11
Sutton Manor Community Primary School Forest Road, Sutton Manor, WA9 4AT ☎ 01744 812601	C	3–11
Willow Tree County Primary School Leach Lane, Sutton Leach, WA9 4LZ ☎ 01744 819003	C	3–11

355 SALFORD

School name, address and telephone number	Type	Age
Alder Park Primary School Walnut Road, Winton, Eccles, M30 8LD ☎ 0161 789 3705	C	3–11
Barton Moss Primary School Trippier Road, Peel Green, Eccles, M30 7PT ☎ 0161 707 2421	C	3–11
Beech Street Primary School Beech Street, Winton, Eccles, M30 8GB ☎ 0161 789 1553	C	3–11
Brentnall County Primary School Broom Lane, Bury New Road, Higher Broughton, M7 4EW ☎ 0161 792 4317	C	3–11
Bridgewater Primary School Bridgewater Street, Little Hulton, M38 9WD ☎ 0161 790 2281	C	3–11
Broadoak Primary School Fairmount Road, Swinton, M27 0EP ☎ 0161 794 2326	C	3–11
Broadwalk Primary School Belvedere Road, M6 5AN ☎ 0161 736 6868	C	3–11
Broughton Jewish Cassel Fox Primary School Legh Road, M7 4RT ☎ 0161 792 7773	VA	3–11
Christ Church CofE Primary School Nelson Street, Patricroft, Eccles, M30 0GZ ☎ 0161 789 4531	VC	3–11
Christ The King RC Primary School Holly Avenue, Walkden, M28 3DW ☎ 0161 790 4329	VA	3–11
Clarendon Road Primary School Clarendon Road, Eccles, M30 9AA ☎ 0161 789 4469	C	3–11
Clifton Primary School Wroe Street, Clifton, Swinton, M27 6PF ☎ 0161 794 4124	C	3–11
Dukesgate Primary School Earlesdon Crescent, Little Hulton, M38 9HF ☎ 0161 799 2210	C	3–11
Fiddlers Lane Community Primary School Fiddlers Lane, Irlam, M44 6QE ☎ 0161 775 2490	C	3–11
The Friars County Primary School Cannon Street, M3 7EU ☎ 0161 832 4664	C	3–11
Godfrey Ermen CofE Memorial Primary School School Road, Eccles, M30 7BJ ☎ 0161 789 4382	VA	3–11
Grosvenor Road Primary School Parkgate Drive, Swinton, M27 5LN ☎ 0161 794 1096	C	3–11
Hilton Lane County Primary School Madam's Wood Road, Little Hulton, Worsley, M28 0JY ☎ 0161 790 4357	C	3–11
Holy Cross and All Saints Primary School Trafford Road, Eccles, M30 0JA ☎ 0161 789 4386	VA	3–11
Irlam County Primary School Liverpool Road, Irlam, M44 6NA ☎ 0161 775 2015	C	3–11
Irlam Endowed Primary School Chapel Road, Irlam, M44 6EE ☎ 0161 775 2911	VC	3–11
James Brindley Primary School Parr Fold Avenue, Walkden, Worsley, M28 7HE ☎ 0161 790 8050	C	3–11
Langworthy Road Primary School Langworthy Road, M6 5PP ☎ 0161 736 4739	C	3–11
Monton Green Primary School Pine Grove, Eccles, M30 9JP ☎ 0161 707 2287	C	3–11
Moorfield Primary School Cutnook Lane, Irlam, M44 6GX ☎ 0161 775 4772	C	3–11
Moorside Primary School Holdsworth Street, Swinton, M27 0LN ☎ 0161 794 6715	C	3–11
North Grecian Street County Primary School Grecian Street North, M7 2JR ☎ 0161 792 4598	C	3–11
North Walkden County Primary School Worsley Road North, Worsley, M28 3QD ☎ 01204 571039	C	3–11
Our Lady and Lancashire Martyrs' RC Primary School Wicheaves Crescent, Worsley, M28 0HF ☎ 0161 790 5089	VA	3–11

School name, address and telephone number	Type	Age
Peel Hall Primary School Greencourt Drive, Worsley, M38 0BZ ☎ 0161 790 4641	C	3–11
Radclyffe Primary School Phoebe Street, M5 3PH ☎ 0161 872 3970	C	3–11
St Andrew's CofE Primary School Barton Lane, Eccles, M30 0FL ☎ 0161 789 4853	VC	3–11
St Augustine's CofE Primary School 380 Bolton Road, Pendlebury, Swinton, M27 8UX ☎ 0161 794 4083	VA	3–11
St Boniface RC Primary School Yew Street, M7 2HL ☎ 0161 792 5659	VA	3–11
St Charles' RC Primary School Emlyn Street, Moorside Road, Swinton, M27 9PD ☎ 0161 794 4536	VA	3–11
St John's CofE Primary School Daisy Bank Avenue, Swinton, M27 5FU ☎ 0161 737 4622	VC	3–11
St Luke's RC Primary School Swinton Park Road, M6 7WR ☎ 0161 736 6874	VA	3–11
St Luke's with All Saints CofE School Eccles New Road, M5 2NX ☎ 0161 736 3455	VC	3–11
St Mark's CofE Primary School Aviary Road, Walkden, Worsley, M28 2WF ☎ 0161 790 3423	VA	3–11
St Mary's RC Primary School Hemming Drive, Eccles, M30 0FJ ☎ 0161 789 4532	VA	3–11
St Mary's RC Primary School Milner Street, Swinton, M27 4AS ☎ 0161 794 4028	VA	3–11
St Peter and St John RC Primary School Mount Street, M3 6LU ☎ 0161 834 4150	VA	3–11
St Peter's CofE Primary School Vicarage Road, Swinton, M27 0WA ☎ 0161 794 2616	VA	3–11
St Philip's CofE Primary School Barrow Street, M3 5LF ☎ 0161 832 6637	VA	3–11
St Philip's RC Primary School Cavendish Road, M7 4WP ☎ 0161 792 4595	VA	3–11
St Sebastian's RC Primary School Douglas Green, M6 6ET ☎ 0161 736 6875	VA	3–11
St Thomas of Canterbury RC Primary School Hadfield Street, Higher Broughton, M7 4XG ☎ 0161 792 3973	VA	3–11
Seedley Primary School Liverpool Street, M6 5GY ☎ 0161 736 3700	C	3–11
Silverdale Primary School Silverdale, Clifton, Swinton, M27 8QP ☎ 0161 794 3000	C	3–11
Summerville Primary School Summerville Road, M6 7HB ☎ 0161 736 4814	C	3–11
Wardley CofE Primary School Moss Bank Road, Wardley, Swinton, M27 9XB ☎ 0161 793 7058	VC	3–11
West Liverpool Street Primary School Liverpool Street, M5 4BJ ☎ 0161 736 4056	C	3–11
Wharton Primary School Rothwell Lane, Little Hulton, Worsley, M38 9XA ☎ 0161 790 4473	C	3–11

343 SEFTON

School name, address and telephone number	Type	Age
Beach Road Primary School Beach Road, L21 2PG ☎ 0151 928 7773	C	3–11
Birkdale Primary School Matlock Road, Birkdale, PR8 4EL ☎ 01704 567516	C	3–11
Bishop David Sheppard CE Primary School Devonshire Road, PR9 7BZ ☎ 01704 227987	VA	3–11
Christ Church CE Primary School Brookhill Road, Waterworks Street, L20 3JL ☎ 0151 922 2136	VC	3–11
Churchtown Primary School St Cuthbert's Road, Churchtown, PR9 7NN ☎ 01704 228148	C	3–11
Daleacre Primary School Dale Acre Drive, L30 2QQ ☎ 0151 924 8128	C	3–11
Davenhill Primary School Aintree Lane, L10 8LE ☎ 0151 526 1162	C	3–11
Freshfield Primary School Watchyard Lane, Formby, L37 3JY ☎ 01704 876567	C	3–11
Grange Primary School Stoneyfield, Sefton, L30 0QS ☎ 0151 924 7917	C	3–11
Great Crosby RC Primary School The Northern Road, L23 2RQ ☎ 0151 924 8661	VA	3–11
Hatton Hill Primary School Alwyn Avenue, Litherland, L21 9NZ ☎ 0151 928 7012	C	3–11
Holy Spirit RC Primary School Poulsom Drive, L30 2NR ☎ 0151 525 7497	VA	3–11
Hudson Primary School Moorhey Road, Maghull, L31 5LE ☎ 0151 526 1568	C	3–11
Linaker Primary School Sefton Street, PR8 5DB ☎ 01704 532343	C	3–11
Litherland Moss Primary School Moss Lane, L21 7NW ☎ 0151 928 4544	C	3–11
Lydiate Primary School Lambshear Lane, Lydiate, L31 2JZ ☎ 0151 526 2657	C	3–11
Netherton Moss Primary School Swifts Lane, Netherton, L30 3RU ☎ 0151 525 5026	C	3–11
Netherton Park Primary School Chester Avenue, L30 1QW ☎ 0151 284 7500	C	3–11
Northway Primary School Dodds Lane, Maghull, L31 9AA ☎ 0151 526 2565	C	3–11
Our Lady of Compassion Primary School Bull Cop, Formby, L37 8BZ ☎ 01704 877281	VA	3–11
Our Lady Queen of Peace RC Primary School Ford Close, Litherland, L21 0EP ☎ 0151 928 3676	VA	3–11

School name, address and telephone number	Type	Age
St George's RC Primary School Dennett Close, Maghull, L31 5PD ☎ 0151 526 1624	VA	3–11
St James RC Primary School Chesnut Grove, L20 4LX ☎ 0151 922 2440	VA	3–11
St Joan of Arc Primary School Hemans Street, L20 4QS ☎ 0151 922 5138	VA	3–11
St Luke's Halsall CE Primary School Cooks Road, Crosby, L23 2TB ☎ 0151 924 5142	VA	3–11
St Mary's CE Primary School Waverley Street, L20 4AP ☎ 0151 922 1562	VA	3–11
St Monica's RC Primary School Aintree Road, L20 9EB ☎ 0151 525 1245	VA	3–11
Thornton Primary School Edge Lane, Thornton, L23 4TF ☎ 0151 924 6777	C	3–11
William Gladstone CE Primary School Thomson Road, Seaforth, L21 1AW ☎ 0151 284 2840	VC	3–11
Woodvale Primary School Meadow Lane, Ainsdale, PR8 3RS ☎ 01704 578512	C	3–11

356 STOCKPORT

School name, address and telephone number	Type	Age
Arden Primary School Osborne Street, Bredbury, SK6 2EX ☎ 0161 430 2675	C	3–11
Bridge Hall Primary School Siddington Avenue, Bridge Hall, SK3 8NR ☎ 0161 480 7889	C	3–11
Cale Green Primary School Shaw Road South, Shaw Heath, SK3 8JG ☎ 0161 480 2715	C	3–11
Cheadle Primary School Ashfield Road, SK8 1BB ☎ 0161 428 5026	C	3–11
Dial Park Primary School Blackstone Road, Offerton, SK2 5NE ☎ 0161 483 1445	C	3–11
Didsbury Road Primary School Didsbury Road, Heaton Mersey, SK4 3HB ☎ 0161 432 2240	C	3–11
Doodfield Primary School Windlehurst Road, Hawk Green, Marple, SK6 7HZ ☎ 0161 427 4788	C	3–11
Hazel Grove Primary School Chapel Street, Hazel Grove, SK7 4JH ☎ 0161 483 3699	C	3–11
Ladybridge Primary School Councillor Lane, SK8 2JF ☎ 0161 428 5445	C	3–11
Ladybrook Primary School Gleneagles Close, Seal Road, Bramhall, SK7 2LT ☎ 0161 439 8444	C	3–11
Maycroft Primary School Westmorland Drive, Brinnington, SK5 8HH ☎ 0161 430 5006	C	3–11
Mersey Vale Primary School Valley Road, Heaton Mersey, SK4 2BZ ☎ 0161 442 7535	C	3–11
Outwood Primary School Outwood Road, Heald Green, SK8 3ND ☎ 0161 437 1715	C	3–11
Prospect Vale Primary School Prospect Vale, off Brown Lane, Heald Green, SK8 3RJ ☎ 0161 437 4226	C	3–11
Queen's Road Primary School Buckingham Road, Cheadle Hulme, SK8 5NA ☎ 0161 485 1453	C	3–11
Queensgate Primary School Albany Road, off Meadway, Bramhall, SK7 1NE ☎ 0161 439 3330	C	3–11
Rose Hill Primary School Elmfield Drive, Rose Hill, Marple, SK6 6DW ☎ 0161 427 1432	C	3–11
St Ambrose RC Primary School Rostrevor Road, Adswood, SK3 8LQ ☎ 0161 480 8466	VA	3–11
St Bernadette's RC Primary School Foliage Road, Brinnington, SK5 8AR ☎ 0161 430 4601	VA	3–11
St Elisabeth's Primary School St Elisabeth's Way, Bedford Street, Reddish, SK5 6BL ☎ 0161 432 5785	VC	3–11
St Mary's RC Primary School Lowry Drive, Marple Bridge, SK6 5BR ☎ 0161 427 7498	VA	3–11
St Mary's RC Primary School Roman Road, SK4 1RF ☎ 0161 480 5319	VA	3–11
St Matthew's CofE Primary School Bowdon Street, Edgeley, SK3 9EA ☎ 0161 474 7110	VC	3–11
St Simon's Catholic Primary School Bosden Avenue, Hazel Grove, SK7 4LH ☎ 0161 483 9696	VA	3–11
St Thomas' CofE Primary School Marriott Street, SK1 3PJ ☎ 0161 480 4742	VC	3–11
Tame Valley Primary School Blackberry Lane, Brinnington, SK5 8LA ☎ 0161 430 3118	C	3–11
Thorn Grove Primary School Woodstock Avenue, Cheadle Hulme, SK8 7LD ☎ 0161 485 1177	C	3–11
Torkington Primary School Torkington Road, Hazel Grove, SK7 6NR ☎ 0161 483 2188	C	3–11
Vernon Park Primary School Peak Street, SK1 2NF ☎ 0161 480 4378	C	3–11

357 TAMESIDE

School name, address and telephone number	Type	Age
Arlies Primary School and Nursery Unit Broadhill Road, SK15 1HQ ☎ 0161 338 4854	C	3–11
Arundale Primary and Nursery School John Kennedy Road, SK14 6PF ☎ 01457 762328	C	3–11
Ashton West End Primary School William Street, OL7 0BJ ☎ 0161 330 4234	C	3–11
Broadoak Primary & Nursery School Norman Road, OL6 8QG ☎ 0161 330 3105	C	3–11
Canon Burrows CofE Primary School and Nursery Unit Oldham Road, OL7 9ND ☎ 0161 330 4755	VA	3–11
Corrie Primary and Nursery School Cemetery Road, Denton, M34 6FG ☎ 0161 336 4265	C	3–11

School name, address and telephone number	Type	Age
Fairfield Road Nursery and Primary School Fairfield Road, Droylsden, M43 6AF ☎ 0161 370 3625	C	3–11
Flowery Field County Primary School Main Street, off Old Road, SK14 4SN ☎ 0161 368 1466	C	3–11
Globe Lane County Primary School Globe Lane, SK16 4UJ ☎ 0161 330 1368	C	3–11
Greenfield Primary School Greenfield Street, SK14 1AW ☎ 0161 368 1898	C	3–11
Greenside Primary School Greenside Lane, Droylsden, M43 7RA ☎ 0161 370 8496	C	3–11
Greswell Primary School Percy Road, Denton, M34 2DH ☎ 0161 336 6854	C	3–11
Hollingworth Primary and Nursery School Market Street, Hollingworth, SK14 8LP ☎ 01457 762136	C	3–11
Holy Trinity CofE Primary School Kenyon Street, OL6 7DU ☎ 0161 330 1065	VA	3–11
Hurst Knoll St James CofE (Controlled) Primary and Nursery School Ladbrooke Road, OL6 8JS ☎ 0161 330 4049	VC	3–11
Manor Green County Primary School Mancunian Road, Haughton Green, Denton, M34 7NS ☎ 0161 336 5864	C	3–11
Micklehurst All Saints CofE Primary School The Rowans, Mossley, OL5 9DR ☎ 01457 832499	VC	3–11
Millbrook Primary and Nursery School Bank Road, off Huddersfield Road, SK15 3JX ☎ 01457 834314	C	3–11
Milton St John's CofE Primary and Nursery School Mill Lane, Mossley, OL5 0BN ☎ 01457 832572	VC	3–11
Oakfield Primary Nursery and Resource Base School St Mary's Road, SK14 4EZ ☎ 0161 368 3365	C	3–11
St Anne's RC Primary and Nursery School Clarendon Road, Audenshaw, M34 5QA ☎ 0161 370 8698	VA	3–11
St Christopher's RC Primary and Nursery School St Christopher's Road, OL6 9DP ☎ 0161 330 5880	VA	3–11
St George's CofE (Aided) Primary School Church Street, SK14 1JL ☎ 0161 368 2848	VA	3–11
St James Primary and Nursery School Cheriton Close, off Underwood Road, Hattersley, SK14 3DQ ☎ 0161 368 3455	VA	3–11
St Joseph's Primary and Nursery School Curzon Street, Mossley, OL5 0HD ☎ 01457 832360	VA	3–11
St Mary's CofE Primary and Nursery School Church Street, Droylsden, M43 7BR ☎ 0161 370 3948	VA	3–11
St Paul's Primary and Nursery School Turner Lane, SK14 4AG ☎ 0161 368 2934	VA	3–11
St Peter's RC Primary and Nursery School Hough Hill Road, SK15 2HB ☎ 0161 338 3303	VA	3–11
St Raphael's RC Primary and Nursery School Huddersfield Road, Millbrook, SK15 3JL ☎ 0161 338 4095	VA	3–11
St Stephen's RC Primary School Chappell Road, Droylsden, M43 7NA ☎ 0161 370 2071	VA	3–11
West End Primary School Balmoral Drive, Denton, M34 2JX ☎ 0161 336 3409	C	3–11
Wild Bank Primary and Nursery School Demesne Drive, SK15 2PG ☎ 0161 303 7404	C	3–11
Yew Tree Primary and Community School Yew Tree Lane, SK16 5BJ ☎ 0161 338 3452	C	3–11

358 TRAFFORD

School name, address and telephone number	Type	Age
All Saints RC Primary School Cedar Road, M33 5NW ☎ 0161 973 6813	VA	3–11
Altrincham CofE Primary School Townfield Road, WA14 4DS ☎ 0161 928 7288	VA	3–11
Barton Clough Primary School Audley Avenue, Stretford, M32 9TG ☎ 0161 748 7539	C	3–11
Bollin Primary School Apsley Grove, Bowdon, WA14 3AH ☎ 0161 928 8900	C	3–11
Broadheath Primary School Sinderland Road, Broadheath, WA15 5JQ ☎ 0161 928 4748	C	3–11
Broomwood Primary School Mainwood Road, Timperley, WA15 7JU ☎ 0161 980 4968	C	3–11
Cloverlea Primary School Green Lane North, Timperley, WA15 7NQ ☎ 0161 980 8338	C	3–11
Elmridge Primary School Wilton Drive, Halebarns, WA15 0JF ☎ 0161 980 4941	C	3–11
Kingsway Primary School Kingsway Park, Davyhulme, Urmston, M41 1SP ☎ 0161 748 1867	C	3–11
Lime Tree Primary School Budworth Road, M33 2RP ☎ 0161 973 1554	C	3–11
Oakwood Primary School Daniel Adamson Avenue, Partington, Urmston, M31 4PN ☎ 0161 775 4356	C	3–11
Old Trafford County Primary School Malvern Street, Old Trafford, M16 9AD ☎ 0161 872 0577	C	3–11
Oldfield Brow Primary School Taylor Road, WA14 4LE ☎ 0161 928 2082	C	3–11
Park Road Primary School Abbey Road, M33 6HT ☎ 0161 973 1392	C	3–11
Partington Primary School Central Road, Partington, Urmston, M31 4FL ☎ 0161 775 2937	C	3–11
St Alphonsus RC Primary School Hamilton Street, off Stretford Road, Old Trafford, M16 7PT ☎ 0161 872 5239	VA	3–11
St Hilda's CofE Primary School Warwick Road South, Firswood, Stretford, M16 0EX ☎ 0161 881 5466	VA	3–11
St Hugh of Lincoln School Glastonbury Road, Stretford, M32 9PD ☎ 0161 748 6343	VA	3–11

School name, address and telephone number	Type	Age
St Matthew's CofE Primary School Poplar Road, Stretford, M32 9AN ☎ 0161 865 1284	VC	3–11
St Monica's RC Primary School Woodsend Road South, Flixton, Urmston, M41 6QB ☎ 0161 748 3353	VA	3–11
Seymour Park Primary School Northumberland Road, Old Trafford, M16 9QE ☎ 0161 872 1150	C	3–11
Springfield Primary School Springfield Road, M33 7XS ☎ 0161 973 4149	C	3–11
Tyntesfield Primary School Alma Road, M33 4HE ☎ 0161 973 4877	C	3–11
Well Green Primary School Briony Avenue, Hale, WA15 8QA ☎ 0161 980 3976	C	3–11
Willows Primary School Victoria Road, Timperley, WA15 6PP ☎ 0161 980 7685	C	3–11
Worthington Primary School Worthington Road, M33 2JJ ☎ 0161 973 3504	C	3–11

359 WIGAN

School name, address and telephone number	Type	Age
All Saints RC Primary School Hazel Grove, Golborne, WA3 3LU ☎ 01942 747655	VA	3–11
Beech Hill Primary School Netherby Road, Beech Hill, WN6 7PT ☎ 01942 243582	C	3–11
Britannia Bridge Primary School Parliament Street, Lower Ince, WN3 4JH ☎ 01942 760036	C	3–11
Castle Hill CofE Junior and Infant School Hereford Road, Hindley, WN2 4BU ☎ 01942 255578	VA	3–11
Garrett Hall Junior and Infant School Garrett Lane, Tyldesley, M29 7EY ☎ 01942 883340	C	3–11
Golborne Junior and Infant School Talbot Street, Golborne, WA3 3NN ☎ 01942 748005	C	3–11
Higher Folds County Primary School Queensway, Higher Folds, WN7 2XG ☎ 01942 769712	C	3–11
Hindley Green Junior and Infant School Thomas Street, Hindley Green, WN2 4SS ☎ 01942 255406	C	3–11
Ince Holy Family RC Junior and Infant School Wigan Street, Platt Bridge, WN2 5JF ☎ 01942 704 148	VA	3–11
Ince-in-Makerfield CofE Junior and Infant School Charles Street, Ince, WN2 2AL ☎ 01942 245218	VA	3–11
Leigh Westleigh Methodist Primary School Westleigh Lane, WN7 5NJ ☎ 01942 702967	VC	3–11
Marsh Green Junior and Infant School Kitt Green Road, Marsh Green, WN5 0QL ☎ 01942 222016	C	3–11
Meadowbank Primary School and Nursery Centre Formby Avenue, Atherton, M46 0HX ☎ 01942 874271	C	3–11
Orrell Newfold County Primary School St James' Road, Orrell, WN5 7BD ☎ 01695 622605	C	3–11
Parklee County Primary School Wardour Street, Atherton, M46 0AR ☎ 01942 874203	C	3–11
Pemberton Primary School School Way, Norley Hall, Pemberton, WN5 9TQ ☎ 01942 222625	C	3–11
R L Hughes Junior and Infant School Mayfield Street, Ashton-in-Makerfield, WN4 9QL ☎ 01942 701147	C	3–11
Sacred Heart RC Primary School Springfield Road, WN6 7RH ☎ 01942 231478	VA	3–11
St Aidan's RC Primary School Holmes House Avenue, Highfield, WN3 6EE ☎ 01942 223544	VA	3–11
St John The Baptist CofE Infant and Junior School Wigan Road, New Springs, WN2 1DH ☎ 01942 241013	VA	3–11
St Mary's CofE Junior and Infant School Newton Road, Lowton, WA3 1EW ☎ 01942 769710	VA	3–11
St Patrick's RC Junior and Infant School Hardybutts, WN1 3RZ ☎ 01942 244361	VA	3–11
St Wilfrid's CofE Primary School Rectory Lane, Standish, WN6 0XB ☎ 01257 423992	VA	3–11
St William's RC Primary School Pickup Street, Ince-in-Makerfield, Ince, WN2 2DG ☎ 01942 235782	VA	3–11
Shevington Junior and Infant School Miles Lane, Shevington, WN6 8EW ☎ 01257 252859	C	3–11
Winstanley Junior and Infant School Tanhouse Drive, Winstanley, WN3 6JP ☎ 01942 211789	C	3–11

344 WIRRAL

School name, address and telephone number	Type	Age
Bedford Drive Primary School Bedford Drive, L42 6RT ☎ 0151 645 1561	C	3–11
Bidston Village CofE Primary School Bidston Village Rd, L43 7XG ☎ 0151 652 0673	VC	3–11
Cathcart Street Primary School Cathcart Street, L41 3JY ☎ 0151 647 7349	C	3–11
Christ Church CofE (Birkenhead) School Bratton Road, L41 2UJ ☎ 0151 652 1278	VC	3–11
Church Drive Primary School Church Drive, L62 5EF ☎ 0151 645 5527	C	3–11
Cole Street Primary School Alvanley Place, L43 4XA ☎ 0151 652 4280	C	3–11
The Dell Primary School The Dell, L42 1PU ☎ 0151 645 4641	C	3–11
Devonshire Park Primary School Temple Road, L42 9JX ☎ 0151 608 9243	C	3–11
Eastway Primary School Eastway, L46 8SS ☎ 0151 677 1235	C	3–11
Egremont Primary School Church Street, L44 8AF ☎ 0151 638 5406	C	3–11

School name, address and telephone number	Type	Age
Grove Street Primary School Grove Street, L62 5BA ☎ 0151 645 2170	C	3–11
Heygarth Primary School Heygarth Road, L62 8AG ☎ 0151 327 1570	C	3–11
Holy Cross RC Primary School Challis Street, L41 7DH ☎ 0151 652 8454	VA	3–11
Kingsway Primary School Ashville Road, L44 9EF ☎ 0151 638 5195	C	3–11
Lingham Primary School Townmeadow Lane, L46 7UQ ☎ 0151 677 5381	C	3–11
Liscard Primary School Withens Lane, L45 7NQ ☎ 0151 638 3910	C	3–11
Manor Primary School Beechwood Drive, L43 7ZU ☎ 0151 677 3152	C	3–11
Mersey Park Primary School Elm Road, L42 6PA ☎ 0151 647 8197	C	3–11
Millfields Primary School Willington Avenue, L62 9EB ☎ 0151 327 1722	C	3–11
New Brighton Primary School Vaughan Road, L45 1LH ☎ 0151 639 3869	C	3–11
Our Lady of Lourdes Primary School Gardenside, L46 2RP ☎ 0151 638 5180	VA	3–11
Portland Primary School Laird Street, L41 0AB ☎ 0151 652 5124	C	3–11
Poulton Primary School Alderley Road, L44 4ES ☎ 0151 638 3307	C	3–11
Riverside Primary School Brighton Street, L44 6QW ☎ 0151 639 9787	C	3–11
Rock Ferry Primary School Ionic Street, L42 2BL ☎ 0151 645 1017	C	3–11
Sacred Heart RC Primary School Danger Lane, L46 8UG ☎ 0151 677 1091	VA	3–11
St Anne's RC Primary School Highfield South, L42 4NE ☎ 0151 645 3682	VA	3–11
St George's Primary School St George's Road, L45 3NF ☎ 0151 638 6014	C	3–11
St Joseph's RC (Wallasey) School Wheatland Lane, L44 7ED ☎ 0151 638 3919	VA	3–11
St Joseph's RC (Birkenhead) School Woodchurch Road, L43 5UT ☎ 0151 652 6781	VA	3–11
St Laurence's RC Primary School Park Street, L41 3JD ☎ 0151 647 8409	VA	3–11
St Michael and All Angels Primary School New Hey Road, L49 5LE ☎ 0151 677 4088	VA	3–11
St Paul's RC Primary School Farmfield Drive, L43 7TE ☎ 0151 652 7828	VA	3–11
St Werburgh's RC Primary School Park Grove, L41 2TD ☎ 0151 647 8404	VA	3–11
Sandbrook Primary School Stavordale Road, L46 9PS ☎ 0151 677 3231	C	3–11
Vyner Primary School Bidston Village Rd, L43 7QT ☎ 0151 652 7093	C	3–11
Well Lane Primary School Well Lane, L42 5PF ☎ 0151 645 9844	C	3–11
West Kirby Primary School Anglesey Road, L48 5EQ ☎ 0151 625 5561	C	3–11
Woodlands Primary School Hollybank Road, L41 2SY ☎ 0151 647 8406	C	3–11
Woodslee Primary School Croft Avenue, L62 2BP ☎ 0151 334 1406	C	3–11

YORKSHIRE AND HUMBERSIDE

370 BARNSLEY

School name, address and telephone number	Type	Age
"The Ellis CofE Primary School, Hemingfield" School Street, Hemingfield, S73 0PS ☎ 01226 753383	VA	3–11
Grove Street Primary School Grove Street, S71 1ES ☎ 01226 281350	C	3–11
The Hill Primary School Brunswick Street, Thurnscoe, S63 0HU ☎ 01709 892145	C	3–11
Jump Primary School Roebuck Hill, Jump, S74 0JW ☎ 01226 743041	C	3–11
Lacewood Primary School Station Road, Bolton-on-Dearne, S63 8AB ☎ 01709 893238	C	3–11
Sacred Heart RC Primary School Lockwood Road, Goldthorpe, S63 9JY ☎ 01709 892385	VA	3–11
St Dominic's RC Primary School Carlton Road, S71 2BE ☎ 01226 282085	VA	3–11
Shawlands Primary School Shaw Street, S70 6JL ☎ 01226 287177	C	3–11
Tankersley St Peter's CofE (Aided) Primary School Westwood New Road, Tankersley, S75 3DA ☎ 01226 742357	VA	3–11
Wombwell Park Street Primary School Park Street, Wombwell, S73 0HS ☎ 01226 752029	C	3–11

School name, address and telephone number	Type	Age
380 BRADFORD		
St Columba's RC Primary School Tong Street, Dudley Hill, BD4 9PY ☎ 01274 681961	VA	3–11
St Francis RC Primary School Myers Lane, BD2 4ES ☎ 01274 638520	VA	3–11
St Joseph's RC Primary School Park Lane, BD5 0RB ☎ 01274 727970	VA	3–11
St Mary's RC Primary School Jermyn Street, BD1 4EJ ☎ 01274 731691	VA	3–11
St Matthew's RC Primary School Saffron Drive, Allerton, BD15 7NE ☎ 01274 541737	VA	3–11
St Walburga's RC Primary School Victoria Park, BD18 4RL ☎ 01274 531102	VA	3–11
St William's RC Primary School Young Street, BD8 9RG ☎ 01274 545743	VA	3–11
St Winefride's RC Primary School St Paul's Avenue, Wibsey, BD6 1SR ☎ 01274 677705	VA	3–11
381 CALDERDALE		
Abbey Park Junior Infant and Nursery School Keighley Road West, Illingworth, HX2 9LJ ☎ 01422 246610	C	3–11
Ash Green Primary School Mixenden Road, Mixenden, HX2 8QD ☎ 01422 244613	C	3–11
Beech Hill Junior and Infant School Mount Pleasant Avenue, HX1 5TN ☎ 01422 345004	C	3–11
Bolton Brow Junior and Infant School Bolton Brow, HX6 2BA ☎ 01422 831031	C	3–11
Burnley Road Junior Infant and Nursery School Mytholmroyd, HX7 5DE ☎ 01422 883034	C	3–11
Carr Green Junior and Infant and Nursery School Carr Green Lane, Rastrick, HD6 3LT ☎ 01484 715969	C	3–11
Castle Hill Junior and Infant School Halifax Road, OL14 5SQ ☎ 01706 813163	C	3–11
Cliffe Hill Junior and Infant School Stoney Lane, Lightcliffe, HX3 8TW ☎ 01422 202086	C	3–11
Cornholme Junior Infant and Nursery School Greenfield Terrace, Cornholme, OL14 8PL ☎ 01706 812787	C	3–11
Cross Lane Primary School Cross Lane, HX5 0LP ☎ 01422 372614	C	3–11
Dean Field Junior and Infants' School Cousin Lane, Ovenden, HX2 8DQ ☎ 01422 360616	C	3–11
Ferney Lee Junior and Infant School Ferney Lee Road, OL14 5NR ☎ 01706 812412	C	3–11
Field Lane Junior and Infant School Burnsall Road, Rastrick, HD6 3JT ☎ 01484 713792	C	3–11
Hebden Royd CofE Junior and Infant School Church Lane, HX7 6DS ☎ 01422 842821	VA	3–11
Heptonstall Junior Infant and Nursery School Smithwell Lane, Heptonstall, HX7 7NX ☎ 01422 842533	C	3–11
Holywell Green Junior and Infant School Stainland Road, Holywell Green, HX4 9AE ☎ 01422 374369	C	3–11
Lee Mount Junior and Infant School Lee Mount Road, HX3 5EB ☎ 01422 352856	C	3–11
"Ling Bob Junior, Infant & Nursery School" Albert Road, Pellon, HX2 0QD ☎ 01422 366925	C	3–11
Luddenden Dene CofE (Controlled) Junior and Infants' School Dene View, Luddendenfoot, HX2 6PB ☎ 01422 886353	VC	3–11
Mixenden Junior and Infant School Clough Lane, Mixenden, HX2 8SN ☎ 01422 244274	C	3–11
Mount Pellon Junior and Infant School Battinson Road, HX1 4RG ☎ 01422 349618	C	3–11
New Road Junior Infant and Nursery School Sowerby New Road, HX6 1DY ☎ 01422 831351	C	3–11
Northowram Primary School Baxter Lane, Northowram, HX3 7EF ☎ 01422 202704	C	3–11
Old Earth Primary School Lower Edge Road, HX5 9PL ☎ 01422 375316	C	3–11
Parkinson Lane Junior and Infant School Parkinson Lane, HX1 3XL ☎ 01422 362227	C	3–11
"Queen's Road Junior, Infant & Nursery School" Arundel Street, HX1 4LE ☎ 01422 361953	C	3–11
Rawson Junior and Infant School Rawson Street North, Boothtown Road, HX3 6PU ☎ 01422 351291	C	3–11
St Joseph's RC Junior and Infant School Wellington Road, OL14 5HP ☎ 01706 812948	VA	3–11
St Joseph's RC Junior Infant and Nursery School Finkil Street, Hove Edge, HD6 2NT ☎ 01484 713037	VA	3–11
St Malachy's RC Junior and Infant School Furness Place, Illingworth, HX2 8JY ☎ 01422 244628	VA	3–11
Shade Junior and Infant School Knowlwood Road, Shade, OL14 7PD ☎ 01706 812913	C	3–11
Siddal Primary School Oxford Lane, Siddal, HX3 9LA ☎ 01422 354976	C	3–11
Whitehill Junior and Infant School Occupation Lane, Illingworth, HX2 9RL ☎ 01422 244471	C	3–11
Withinfields Primary School Withinfields, Southowram, HX3 9QJ ☎ 01422 363581	C	3–11

School name, address and telephone number	Type	Age
371 DONCASTER		
Auckley Junior and Infant School School Lane, Auckley, DN9 3JN ☎ 01302 770701	C	3-11
Balby Central Primary School Littlemoor Lane, Balby, DN4 0LL ☎ 01302 321914	C	3-11
Balby Waverley Primary School Douglas Road, Balby, DN4 0UB ☎ 01302 853326	C	3-11
Barnburgh Primary School Church Lane, Barnburgh, DN5 7EZ ☎ 01709 893125	C	3-11
Bawtry Mayflower Junior and Infant School Station Road, Bawtry, DN10 6PU ☎ 01302 710721	C	3-11
Bentley High Street Primary School High Street, Bentley, DN5 0AA ☎ 01302 874536	C	3-11
Carcroft Primary School Owston Road, Carcroft, DN6 8DR ☎ 01302 722353	C	3-11
Castle Hills Primary School Jossey Lane, Scawthorpe, DN5 9ED ☎ 01302 780246	C	3-11
Conisbrough Balby Street Junior and Infant School Crags Road, Denaby Main, DN12 4DX ☎ 01709 862640	C	3-11
Denaby Main Primary School School Walk, Denaby Main, DN12 4HZ ☎ 01709 863622	C	3-11
Edlington Victoria Primary School Victoria Road, Edlington, DN12 1BN ☎ 01709 862175	C	3-11
Green Top Primary School Southfield Road, Thorne, DN8 5NS ☎ 01405 813181	C	3-11
Hatfield Dunsville Primary School Broadway, Dunsville, DN7 4HX ☎ 01302 882958	C	3-11
Hatfield Woodhouse Primary School Main Street, Hatfield Woodhouse, DN7 6NH ☎ 01302 840448	C	3-11
Hayfield Lane Primary School Hayfield Lane, Finningley, DN9 3NB ☎ 01302 770427	C	3-11
Hexthorpe Primary School Urban Road, Hexthorpe, DN4 0HH ☎ 01302 852245	C	3-11
Highfields Primary School Highfields, DN6 7JE ☎ 01302 722216	C	3-11
Holy Family RC Junior and Infant School Kirton Lane, Stainforth, DN7 5BL ☎ 01302 841283	VA	3-11
Ivanhoe Junior and Infant School Old Road, Conisbrough, DN12 3LR ☎ 01709 862307	C	3-11
Kirkby Avenue Primary School Kirkby Avenue, Bentley, DN5 9TF ☎ 01302 782953	C	3-11
Kirton Lane Primary School Thorne Road, Stainforth, DN7 5BG ☎ 01302 842092	C	3-11
Moorends West Road Primary School West Road, Moorends, DN8 4LH ☎ 01405 812734	C	3-11
New Village Primary School Asquith Road, Bentley, DN5 0NU ☎ 01302 874385	C	3-11
Our Lady's RC Primary School Finkle Street, Bentley, DN5 0RP ☎ 01302 874291	VA	3-11
Plover Primary School Coniston Road, DN2 6JL ☎ 01302 361450	C	3-11
Rosedale Primary School Emley Drive, Scawsby, DN5 8RL ☎ 01302 784098	C	3-11
Sheep Dip Lane Primary School Dunscroft, DN7 4AU ☎ 01302 842464	C	3-11
St Aidan's CofE Primary School Wilberforce Road, Clay Lane, DN2 4RW ☎ 01302 323066	VA	3-11
St Joseph and St Theresa's RC Junior and Infant School Doncaster Lane, Woodlands, DN6 7QN ☎ 01302 723320	VA	3-11
St Joseph's Primary School Bevan Avenue, Rossington, DN11 0NB ☎ 01302 868098	VA	3-11
St Mary's RC Junior and Infant School Bungalow Road, Edlington, DN12 1DL ☎ 01709 863280	VA	3-11
Sunnyfields Primary School Rose Crescent, Scawthorpe, DN5 9EW ☎ 01302 780386	C	3-11
Thorne South Common Primary School Peel Castle Road, Thorne, DN8 5LZ ☎ 01405 812714	C	3-11
Tickhill St Mary's CofE (VA) Primary School St Mary's Road, Tickhill, DN11 9LZ ☎ 01302 742569	VA	3-11
Toll Bar Primary School Askern Road, Toll Bar, DN5 0QR ☎ 01302 874324	C	3-11
Tranmoor Primary School Tranmoor Lane, Armthorpe, DN3 3DB ☎ 01302 831720	C	3-11
Warmsworth Primary School Mill Lane, Warmsworth, DN4 9RG ☎ 01302 852200	C	3-11
Windhill Junior and Infant School Hollingworth Close, S64 0PQ ☎ 01709 586949	C	3-11
Woodfield Primary School Gurney Road, Balby, DN4 8LA ☎ 01302 853289	C	3-11
810 CITY OF KINGSTON UPON HULL		
Bellfield Primary School Saxby Road, HU8 9DD ☎ 01482 374490	C	3-11
Biggin Hill Primary School Biggin Avenue, Bransholme, HU7 4RL ☎ 01482 825377	C	3-11
Broadacre Primary School Wawne Road, Bransholme, HU7 5YS ☎ 01482 833033	C	3-11
Chiltern Primary School Chiltern Street, HU3 3PL ☎ 01482 327315	C	3-11
Collingwood Primary School Collingwood Street, HU3 1AW ☎ 01482 327284	C	3-11

School name, address and telephone number	Type	Age
Constable Primary School Constable Street, HU3 3DJ ☎ 01482 324202	C	3–11
Court Park Primary School Courtway Road, HU6 9TA ☎ 01482 854616	C	3–11
Craven Primary School Craven Street, HU9 2AP ☎ 01482 327626	C	3–11
The Dales Primary School Snowdon Way, North Bransholme, HU7 5DS ☎ 01482 835323	C	3–11
Danepark Primary School Danepark Road, Orchard Park Estate, HU6 9AR ☎ 01482 851101	C	3–11
Dorchester Primary School Dorchester Road, Bransholme, HU7 6AH ☎ 01482 825207	C	3–11
Longhill Primary School Shannon Road, Longhill Estate, HU8 9RW ☎ 01482 814160	C	3–11
Maybury Primary School Maybury Road, HU9 3LD ☎ 01482 701387	C	3–11
Mountbatten Primary School Wivern Road, Bilton Grange Estate, HU9 4HR ☎ 01482 375224	C	3–11
Neasden Primary School Neasden Close, Wembley Park Avenue, HU8 0QB ☎ 01482 791169	C	3–11
Oldfleet Primary School Bradford Avenue, Greatfield Estate, HU9 4NH ☎ 01482 782200	C	3–11
Paisley Primary School Paisley Street, HU3 6NJ ☎ 01482 355984	C	3–11
Pearson Primary School Leicester Street, HU3 1TB ☎ 01482 328569	C	3–11
Rokeby Park Primary School Gershwin Avenue, Anlaby Park Road North HU4 7NJ ☎ 01482 508915	C	3–11
St Oswald's and St Anne's RC Primary School Nidderdale, Sutton Park, HU7 4BS ☎ 01482 825625	VA	3–11
Southcoates Primary School Southcoates Lane, HU9 3TW ☎ 01482 701407	C	3–11
Sutton Park Primary School Marsdale, Sutton Park, HU7 4AH ☎ 01482 825502	C	3–11
Thoresby Primary School Thoresby Street, HU5 3RG ☎ 01482 342972	C	3–11
Tilbury Primary School Tilbury Road, HU4 7EN ☎ 01482 645174	C	3–11
Wheeler Primary School Wheeler Street, HU3 5QE ☎ 01482 353125	C	3–11

811 EAST RIDING OF YORKSHIRE

School name, address and telephone number	Type	Age
Aldbrough Primary School Headlands Road, Aldbrough, HU11 4RR ☎ 01964 527422	C	3–11
Beverley St Nicholas Primary School Holme Church Lane, HU17 0QP ☎ 01482 862882	C	3–11
Burton Agnes CofE Primary School Rudston Road, Burton Agnes, YO25 0NE ☎ 01262 490320	VC	3–11
Easington CofE Primary School High Street, Easington, HU12 0TS ☎ 01964 650214	VC	3–11
Garton-on-the-Wolds CofE (VC) Primary School Station Road, Garton-on-the-Wolds, YO25 0EX ☎ 01377 253110	VC	3–11
Gilberdyke County Primary School Scalby Lane, Gilberdyke, HU15 2SS ☎ 01430 440668	C	3–11
North Frodingham County Primary School North Frodingham, YO25 8LA ☎ 01262 488227	C	3–11
Parkside Primary School Western Road, DN14 6RQ ☎ 01405 763634	C	3–11
Pasture Primary School Pasture Road, DN14 6DR ☎ 01405 763969	C	3–11
Skirlaugh CofE Primary School Dorset Avenue, Skirlaugh, HU11 5EB ☎ 01964 562454	VC	3–11
Wetwang CofE (VC) Primary School Pulham Lane, Wetwang, YO25 9XT ☎ 01377 236679	VC	3–11
Wilberfoss CofE Primary School Storking Lane, Wilberfoss, YO4 5NA ☎ 01759 380327	VC	3–11
Wold Newton GM Primary School Wold Newton, YO25 0YJ ☎ 01262 470633	GM	3–11

382 KIRKLEES

School name, address and telephone number	Type	Age
Batley Parish CE (A) Junior Infant and Nursery School Stocks Lane, WF17 8PA ☎ 01924 326361	VA	3–11
Beech County Junior Infant and Nursery School Beech Avenue, Golcar, HD7 4BE ☎ 01484 222214	C	3–11
Carlinghow Princess Royal Junior Infant and Nursery School Ealand Road, Carlinghow, WF17 8HT ☎ 01924 326371	C	3–11
Cawley Lane Junior Infant and Nursery School Cawley Lane, WF16 0AN ☎ 01924 402177	C	3–11
Chickenley Community Junior Infant & Nursery School Princess Road, Chickenley, WF12 8QT ☎ 01924 325273	C	3–11
Christ Church Woodhouse CE (A) Nursery Infant and Junior School Deighton Road, Deighton, HD2 1JP ☎ 01484 226595	VA	3–11
Cowlersley Junior Infant and Nursery School Winget Avenue, Cowlersley, HD4 5UL ☎ 01484 222242	C	3–11
Crow Lane Junior Infant and Nursery School Crow Lane, Milnsbridge, HD3 4QT ☎ 01484 222224	C	3–11
Eastborough Junior Infant and Nursery School Rockley Street, WF13 1NS ☎ 01924 325285	C	3–11
Field Lane Cty Junior Infant and Nursery School Albion Street, WF17 5AH ☎ 01924 326378	C	3–11
Fieldhead Junior Infant and Nursery School Charlotte Close, Birstall, WF17 9BX ☎ 01924 326382	C	3–11

School name, address and telephone number	Type	Age
Golcar Junior Infant and Nursery School Manor Road, Golcar, HD7 4QE ☎ 01484 222220	C	3–11
Headlands CE (C) Junior Infant and Nursery School Headlands Road, WF15 6PR ☎ 01924 403437	VC	3–11
Holmfirth Junior Infant and Nursery School Cartworth Road, Holmfirth, HD7 1RG ☎ 01484 222481	C	3–11
Hopton Junior Infant and Nursery School Woodend Road, Lower Hopton, WF14 8PR ☎ 01924 493286	C	3–11
Leeside Junior Infant and Nursery School Leeds Old Road, WF16 9BB ☎ 01924 326708	C	3–11
Lepton CE (C) Junior Infant and Nursery School Station Road, Lepton, HD8 0DE ☎ 01484 603234	VC	3–11
Lepton County Junior Infant and Nursery School Rowley Lane, Lepton, HD8 0JD ☎ 01484 603060	C	3–11
Linthwaite County Junior Infant and Nursery School Chapel Hill, Linthwaite, HD7 5NJ ☎ 01484 842894	C	3–11
Littletown Junior Infant and Nursery School Bradford Road, WF15 6LP ☎ 01274 335245	C	3–11
Lowerhouses CE (C) Junior Infant and Nursery School Lowerhouses Lane, Almondbury, HD5 8JY ☎ 01484 226672	VC	3–11
Meltham Junior Infant and Nursery School Birmingham Lane, Meltham, HD7 3LH ☎ 01484 850220	C	3–11
Mill Lane Junior Infant and Nursery School Mill Lane, WF17 6EG ☎ 01924 326724	C	3–11
Millbridge Junior Infant and Nursery School Vernon Road, WF15 6HU ☎ 01924 402166	C	3–11
Moldgreen Junior Infant and Nursery School The Avenue, Moldgreen, HD5 8AE ☎ 01484 226681	C	3–11
Mount Pleasant Junior Infant and Nursery School Lockwood Road, Lockwood, HD1 3QR ☎ 01484 223198	C	3–11
Nields Junior Infant and Nursery School Nields Road, Slaithwaite, HD7 5HT ☎ 01484 842820	C	3–11
Old Bank Junior Infant and Nursery School Taylor Hall Lane, WF14 0HW ☎ 01924 496627	C	3–11
Our Lady of Lourdes RC (A) Junior Infant and Nursery School Bradley Boulevard, Sheepridge, HD2 1EA ☎ 01484 310700	VA	3–11
Overthorpe CE (C) Junior Infant and Nursery School Edge Top Road, Thornhill, WF12 0BH ☎ 01924 325300	VC	3–11
Paddock Junior Infant and Nursery School Heaton Road, Paddock, HD1 4JJ ☎ 01484 226565	C	3–11
Park Road Junior Infant and Nursery School Park Road, WF17 5LP ☎ 01924 326728	C	3–11
St Joseph's RC (A) Junior Infant and Nursery School Grosvenor Road, Dalton, HD5 9HU ☎ 01484 226860	VA	3–11
St Mary's RC (A) Junior Infant and Nursery School Upton Street, WF17 8PH ☎ 01924 326740	VA	3–11
St Patrick's RC (A) Junior Infant and Nursery School Nova Lane, Birstall, WF17 9LQ ☎ 01924 326747	VA	3–11
St Paulinus RC (A) Primary School Temple Road, WF13 3QE ☎ 01924 325330	VA	3–11
St Peter's CE (A) Junior Infant and Nursery School Fieldhead Lane, Birstall, WF17 9HN ☎ 01924 326750	VA	3–11
Spring Grove Junior Infant and Nursery School Bow Street, HD1 4BJ ☎ 01484 223917	C	3–11
Warwick Road Junior Infant and Nursery School Warwick Road, WF17 6BS ☎ 01924 325344	C	3–11

383 LEEDS

School name, address and telephone number	Type	Age
Adel Primary School Tile Lane, Adel, LS16 8DY ☎ 0113 230 1116	C	3–11
All Saint's CofE Primary School Cross Aysgarth Mount, LS9 9AD ☎ 0113 293 9440	VA	3–11
Allerton Bywater Primary School Leeds Road, Allerton Bywater, WF10 2DR ☎ 01977 554275	C	3–11
Armley Primary School Salisbury Terrace, LS12 2LY ☎ 0113 263 9216	C	3–11
Asket Hill Primary School Kentmere Approach, LS14 1JL ☎ 0113 217 9922	C	3–11
Bankside Primary School Markham Avenue, LS8 4LE ☎ 0113 262 6439	C	3–11
Beechwood Primary School Kentmere Avenue, LS14 6QB ☎ 0113 293 0250	C	3–11
Beecroft Primary School Eden Way, LS4 2TF ☎ 0113 275 6125	C	3–11
Beeston Primary School Town Street, LS11 8PN ☎ 0113 271 6978	C	3–11
Beeston St Francis of Assisi RC Primary School Lady Pit Lane, Beeston, LS11 6RX ☎ 0113 270 0978	VA	3–11
Beeston St Luke's CofE Primary School Beeston Road, LS11 8ND ☎ 0113 243 3375	VA	3–11
Bentley Primary School Bentley Lane, LS6 4AJ ☎ 0113 226 7671	C	3–11
Birchfield Primary School Birchfield Avenue, Gildersome, LS27 7HU ☎ 0113 253 3009	C	3–11
Blenheim Primary School Lofthouse Place, LS2 9EX ☎ 0113 293 0808	C	3–11
Bracken Edge Primary School Newton Road, LS7 4HE ☎ 0113 262 3335	C	3–11
Bramley Primary School Fairfield Hill, Bramley, LS13 3DP ☎ 0113 256 9762	C	3–11
Broadgate Primary School North Broadgate Lane, Horsforth, LS18 5AF ☎ 0113 258 2685	C	3–11

School name, address and telephone number	Type	Age
Brodetsky Primary School George Lyttleton Centre, Wentworth Avenue, LS17 7TN ☎ 0113 293 0578	VA	3–11
Brownhill Primary School Torre Drive, LS9 7DH ☎ 0113 248 9539	C	3–11
Brudenell Primary School Welton Place, LS6 1EW ☎ 0113 278 5168	C	3–11
Calverley Parkside Primary School Victoria Street, Calverley, LS28 5PQ ☎ 0113 257 6998	C	3–11
Carlton Primary School Carlton, WF3 3RE ☎ 0113 282 2059	C	3–11
Castleton Primary School Green Lane, LS12 1JZ ☎ 0113 263 7756	C	3–11
Chapel Allerton Primary School Harrogate Road, LS7 3PD ☎ 0113 262 4851	C	3–11
Churwell Primary School Westwoodside, Churwell Morley, LS27 9HR ☎ 0113 252 7437	C	3–11
Clapgate Primary School Cranmore Drive, LS10 4AW ☎ 0113 271 6700	C	3–11
Cobden Primary School Cobden Road, LS12 5LA ☎ 0113 263 7554	C	3–11
Colton Primary School School Lane, Colton, LS15 9AL ☎ 0113 264 7514	C	3–11
Cottingley Primary School Dulverton Grove, LS11 0HU ☎ 0113 271 6666	C	3–11
Cross Flatts Park Primary School Harlech Road, LS11 7DG ☎ 0113 271 6754	C	3–11
Cross Gates Primary School Poole Crescent, LS15 7NB ☎ 0113 264 5763	C	3–11
Crossley Street Primary School Crossley Street, LS22 6RT ☎ 01937 582227	C	3–11
East Ardsley Primary School Main Street, East Ardsley, WF3 2BA ☎ 01924 822373	C	3–11
East Garforth Primary School Aberford Road, East Garforth, LS25 2HF ☎ 0113 286 3000	C	3–11
Ebor Gardens Primary School Rigton Drive, LS9 7PY ☎ 0113 248 2750	C	3–11
Farsley Farfield Primary School Cote Lane, Farsley, LS28 5ED ☎ 0113 256 5056	C	3–11
Fieldhead Carr Primary School Naburn Approach, LS14 2EG ☎ 0113 293 0226	C	3–11
Garforth Green Lane Primary School Ribblesdale Avenue, Garforth, LS25 2JX ☎ 0113 286 5177	C	3–11
Gipton Wood Primary School Thorn Walk, LS8 3LW ☎ 0113 294 1400	C	3–11
Gledhow Primary School Lidgett Lane, LS8 1PL ☎ 0113 293 0392	C	3–11
Grange Farm Primary School Barncroft Rise, LS14 1AX ☎ 0113 293 0120	C	3–11
Greenhill Primary School Gamble Hill Drive, LS13 4JJ ☎ 0113 263 5271	C	3–11
Greenmount Primary School Lodge Lane, LS11 6BA ☎ 0113 276 0771	C	3–11
Greenwood Primary School Bismarck Drive, LS11 6UA ☎ 0113 270 9439	C	3–11
Grimesdyke Primary School Stanks Drive, LS14 5BY ☎ 0113 294 1066	C	3–11
Harehills Primary School Darfield Avenue, LS8 5DQ ☎ 0113 235 0539	C	3–11
Hawksworth Wood Primary School Cragside Walk, LS5 3QE ☎ 0113 258 3984	C	3–11
Hillcrest Primary School Cowper Street, LS7 4DR ☎ 0113 262 4080	C	3–11
Hillside Primary School Beeston Road, LS11 8ND ☎ 0113 271 7259	C	3–11
Holy Family RC Primary School Parliament Road, Armley, LS12 2LH ☎ 0113 263 9290	VA	3–11
Holy Rosary and St Anne's RC Primary School Leopold Street, LS7 4AW ☎ 0113 262 1287	VA	3–11
Hovingham Primary School Hovingham Avenue, LS8 3QY ☎ 0113 248 9537	C	3–11
Hugh Gaitskell Primary School St Anthony's Drive, Beeston, LS11 8AB ☎ 0113 271 6963	C	3–11
Hunslet Carr School Woodhouse Hill Road, Hunslet, LS10 2DN ☎ 0113 271 3804	C	3–11
Hunslet Moor Primary School Fairford Avenue, LS11 5EL ☎ 0113 271 7257	C	3–11
Ingram Road Primary School Brown Lane East, Holbeck, LS11 9LA ☎ 0113 245 6136	C	3–11
Iveson Primary School Iveson Rise, LS16 6LW ☎ 0113 225 6868	C	3–11
Kerr Mackie Primary School Gledhow Lane, LS8 1NE ☎ 0113 293 0141	C	3–11
Kippax North Junior and Infant School Brexdale Avenue, Kippax, LS25 7EJ ☎ 0113 286 9427	C	3–11
Kirkstall Valley Primary School Argie Road, LS4 2QZ ☎ 0113 275 6183	C	3–11
Langdale Primary School Holmsley Lane, Woodlesford, LS26 8RY ☎ 0113 282 6063	C	3–11
Lawns Park Primary School Chapel Lane, Old Farnley, LS12 5EX ☎ 0113 263 7364	C	3–11
Leopold Primary School Leopold Street, LS7 4AW ☎ 0113 262 9246	C	3–11
Little London Primary School Oatland Close, off Meanwood Road, LS7 1SR ☎ 0113 244 2457	C	3–11

School name, address and telephone number	Type	Age
Lower Wortley Primary School Lower Wortley Road, LS12 4PX ☎ 0113 263 9272	C	3–11
Micklefield CofE School Great North Road, Micklefield, LS25 4AQ ☎ 0113 286 8828	VC	3–11
Middleton Primary School Middleton Park Avenue, LS10 4HU ☎ 0113 271 7969	C	3–11
Middleton St Mary's CofE Primary School Moor Flatts Road, LS10 3SW ☎ 0113 271 7206	VC	3–11
Middleton St Philip's Primary School St Philip's Avenue, LS10 3SL ☎ 0113 271 6763	VA	3–11
Miles Hill Primary School Beck Hill Approach, LS7 2RF ☎ 0113 268 6366	C	3–11
Moor Allerton Hall Primary School Lidgett Lane, LS17 6QP ☎ 0113 266 3431	C	3–11
Morley Newlands Junior and Infant School Wide Lane, Morley, LS27 8PG ☎ 0113 253 3231	C	3–11
Morley Victoria Primary School Victoria Road, Morley, LS27 9NW ☎ 0113 253 5253	C	3–11
Ninelands Primary School Ninelands Lane, Garforth, LS25 1NT ☎ 0113 286 3595	C	3–11
Oakwood Primary School Thorn Walk, LS8 3LW ☎ 0113 240 2526	C	3–11
Osmondthorpe Primary School Wykebeck Avenue, LS9 0JG ☎ 0113 248 3123	C	3–11
Oulton Primary School Green Lea, Oulton, LS26 8NT ☎ 0113 282 3499	C	3–11
Our Lady of Good Counsel School Pigeon Cote Road, Seacroft, LS14 1EP ☎ 0113 293 0150	VA	3–11
Park Spring Primary School Wellstone Avenue, LS13 4EH ☎ 0113 257 6589	C	3–11
Parklands County Primary School Dufton Approach, LS14 6ED ☎ 0113 293 0282	C	3–11
Potternewton Primary School Potternewton Mount, LS7 2DR ☎ 0113 262 0021	C	3–11
Primrose Hill Junior and Infant School Primrose Hill, Stanningley, LS28 6AB ☎ 0113 257 4129	C	3–11
Primrose Lane Primary School Westwood Way, Boston Spa, LS23 6DX ☎ 01937 842667	C	3–11
Pudsey Bolton Royd Primary School Moorland Grove, LS28 8EP ☎ 01274 665806	C	3–11
Pudsey Southroyd Primary School Littlemoor Crescent, LS28 8AT ☎ 0113 257 0197	C	3–11
Pudsey Tyersal Primary School Tyersal Walk, Tyersal, BD4 8ER ☎ 01274 662363	C	3–11
Quarry Mount Primary School Pennington Street, LS6 2JP ☎ 0113 245 5803	C	3–11
Queensway Primary School Coppice Wood Avenue, Yeadon, LS19 7LF ☎ 01943 874925	C	3–11
Raynville Primary School Cross Aston Grove, LS13 2TQ ☎ 0113 257 9590	C	3–11
Richmond Hill Primary School Clark Crescent, LS9 8QF ☎ 0113 249 3771	C	3–11
Robin Hood Primary School Leeds Road, Robin Hood, WF3 3BG ☎ 0113 282 3444	C	3–11
Rosebank Primary School Burley Road, LS3 1JP ☎ 0113 243 3497	C	3–11
Rothwell Primary School Carlton Lane, Rothwell, LS26 0DJ ☎ 0113 282 2195	C	3–11
Roundhay St John's CofE (Aided) School 18 North Lane, LS8 2QJ ☎ 0113 265 8451	VA	3–11
Royal Park Primary School Queen's Road, LS6 1NY ☎ 0113 275 6123	C	3–11
Sacred Heart RC Primary School Eden Way, Argie Avenue, LS4 2TF ☎ 0113 293 6200	VA	3–11
St Augustine's RC Primary School St Wilfrid's Circus, LS8 3PF ☎ 0113 293 0350	VA	3–11
St Bartholomew's CofE Primary School Strawberry Lane, Tong Road, Armley, LS12 1SF ☎ 0113 263 9292	VC	3–11
St James CofE Primary School Hallfield Lane, LS22 6JS ☎ 01937 583379	VC	3–11
St Joseph's RC Primary School Barley Fields Road, LS22 6PR ☎ 01937 582163	VA	3–11
St Peter's CofE (Aided) Primary School Cromwell Street, LS9 7SG ☎ 0113 293 4411	VA	3–11
St Theresa's RC Primary School Barwick Road, Crossgates, LS15 8RQ ☎ 0113 293 0240	VA	3–11
Scholes (Elmet) Primary School Station Road, Scholes (Elmet), LS15 4BJ ☎ 0113 264 9149	C	3–11
Seacroft Grange Primary School Moresdale Lane, Seacroft, LS14 6JR ☎ 0113 260 5385	C	3–11
Seven Hills Primary School Appleby Way, Morley, LS27 8LA ☎ 0113 252 7194	C	3–11
Shakespeare Primary School Stoney Rock Lane, LS9 7HD ☎ 0113 248 2194	C	3–11
Stanningley Primary School Leeds and Bradford Road, Stanningley, LS28 6PE ☎ 0113 257 0899	C	3–11
Summerfield Primary School Intake Lane, LS13 1DQ ☎ 0113 256 4154	C	3–11
Swarcliffe Primary School Swarcliffe Drive, LS14 5JW ☎ 0113 293 0275	C	3–11
Swillington Primary School Church Lane, Swillington, LS26 8DX ☎ 0113 286 3220	C	3–11
Swinnow Primary School Swinnow Road, LS13 4PG ☎ 0113 256 4832	C	3–11

School name, address and telephone number	Type	Age
Talbot Primary School East Moor Road, Roundhay, LS8 1AF ☎ 0113 293 4086	C	3–11
Templenewsam Halton Primary School Pinfold Lane, LS15 7SY ☎ 0113 293 0314	C	3–11
Thorpe Junior and Infant School Dolphin Lane, Thorpe, WF3 3DG ☎ 0113 282 3022	C	3–11
Upper Wortley Primary School Ashley Road, LS12 4LF ☎ 0113 263 8431	C	3–11
Victoria Primary School Ivy Avenue, LS9 9ER ☎ 0113 248 2449	C	3–11
Weetwood Primary School Weetwood Lane, LS16 5NW ☎ 0113 275 6349	C	3–11
West End Primary School West End Lane, Horsforth, LS18 5JP ☎ 0113 258 2819	C	3–11
Westerton Primary School Westerton Road, West Ardsley, WF3 1AR ☎ 0113 253 3504	C	3–11
Westwood Primary School Bodmin Garth, LS10 4NU ☎ 0113 271 2420	C	3–11
Whingate Primary School Whingate Road, LS12 3DS ☎ 0113 263 8910	C	3–11
White Laith Primary School Naburn Drive, LS14 2BL ☎ 0113 293 0280	C	3–11
Whitebridge Primary School Neville Road, LS15 0NW ☎ 0113 264 7242	C	3–11
Whitecote Primary School Wellington Grove, Bramley, LS13 2LQ ☎ 0113 216 4800	C	3–11
Windmill Primary School Windmill Road, LS10 3HQ ☎ 0113 271 2115	C	3–11
Woodlesford Junior and Infant School Church Street, Woodlesford, LS26 8RD ☎ 0113 282 3350	C	3–11
Wykebeck Primary School Brander Street, LS9 6QH ☎ 0113 249 1525	C	3–11
Wyther Park Primary School Victoria Park Avenue, LS5 3DX ☎ 0113 278 6775	C	3–11

812 NORTH EAST LINCOLNSHIRE

School name, address and telephone number	Type	Age
Fairfield Primary School Mendip Avenue, Scartho, DN33 3AE ☎ 01472 879301	C	3–11
Great Coates Primary School Crosland Road, DN37 9EN ☎ 01472 882514	C	3–11
St Mary's RC Primary School Wellington Street, DN32 7JX ☎ 01472 357982	VA	3–11
Springfield Primary School Springwood Crescent, DN33 3HG ☎ 01472 879583	C	3–11
Weelsby Primary School Weelsby Street, DN32 7PF ☎ 01472 342554	C	3–11

813 NORTH LINCOLNSHIRE

School name, address and telephone number	Type	Age
Althorpe and Keadby School Station Road, Keadby, DN17 3BN ☎ 01724 782344	C	3–11
Crosby Primary School Frodingham Road, DN15 7NL ☎ 01724 844216	C	3–11
Crowle County Primary School Manor Road, Crowle, DN17 4ET ☎ 01724 710312	C	3–11

815 NORTH YORKSHIRE

School name, address and telephone number	Type	Age
Athelstan County Primary School Rose Avenue, New Lane, Sherburn-in-Elmet, LS25 6AY ☎ 01977 684037	C	3–11
Barlby Bridge County Primary School Thomas Street, Barlby Road, Barlby Bridge, YO8 7AA ☎ 01757 703650	C	3–11
Boroughbridge County Primary School York Road, Boroughbridge, YO5 9EB ☎ 01423 322208	C	3–11
Brotherton County Primary School Vicars Croft, Brotherton, WF11 9ES ☎ 01977 672676	C	3–11
Carnagill Primary School Leadmill Estate, DL9 3HN ☎ 01748 833622	C	3–11
Colburn County Primary School Colburn Lane, Colburn, DL9 4LS ☎ 01748 832676	C	3–11
East Whitby County Primary School Stainsacre Lane, YO22 4HU ☎ 01947 602202	C	3–11
Friarage County Primary School Longwestgate, YO11 1QB ☎ 01723 374244	C	3–11
Greystone County Primary School Quarry Moor Lane, HG4 1RW ☎ 01765 603481	C	3–11
Grove Road County Primary School Grove Road, HG1 5EP ☎ 01423 506060	C	3–11
Hawes Primary School DL8 3RQ ☎ 01969 667308	C	3–11
Hinderwell County Primary School Barrys Lane, Seamer Road, YO12 4HF ☎ 01723 373110	C	3–11
Husthwaite CofE Primary School Low Street, Husthwaite, YO6 3TA ☎ 01347 868371	VC	3–11
Le Cateau Primary School Brough Road, DL9 4ED ☎ 01748 832292	C	3–11
Leavening County Primary School Leavening, YO17 9SW ☎ 01653 658313	C	3–11
Leyburn County Primary School Wensleydale Avenue, DL8 5SD ☎ 01969 623187	C	3–11
Lythe CofE Primary School High Street, Lythe, YO21 3RT ☎ 01947 893373	VC	3–11

School name, address and telephone number	Type	Age
Richmond CofE Primary School Frances Road, DL10 4NF ☎ 01748 822104	VC	3-11
Ripon Cathedral CofE Primary School Low St Agnesgate, HG4 1NA ☎ 01765 602355	VC	3-11
Seton County Primary School Seaton Close, Staithes, TS13 5AU ☎ 01947 840257	C	3-11
Skipton Ings County Primary and Nursery School Broughton Road, BD23 1TE ☎ 01756 793159	C	3-11
Stakesby County Primary School Byland Road, YO21 1HY ☎ 01947 820231	C	3-11
Stokesley County Primary School No 5 Springfield, Stokesley, TS9 5EW ☎ 01642 711071	C	3-11
Western County Primary School Cold Bath Road, HG2 0NA ☎ 01423 502737	C	3-11
Woodfield County Primary School Woodfield Road, HG1 4HZ ☎ 01423 566494	C	3-11

372 ROTHERHAM

School name, address and telephone number	Type	Age
Aston Swallownest Junior and Infant School Rotherham Road, Swallownest, S26 4UR ☎ 0114 287 2484	C	3-11
Dinnington St Joseph's RC Junior and Infant School Lidgett Lane, Dinnington, S25 2QD ☎ 01909 550123	VA	3-11
Laughton Junior and Infant School School Road, Laughton-en-le-Morthen, S25 1YP ☎ 01909 550477	C	3-11
Maltby Redwood Junior and Infant School Redwood Drive, Maltby, S66 8DL ☎ 01709 812848	C	3-11
Rockingham Junior and Infant School Roughwood Road, Wingfield Estate, S61 4HY ☎ 01709 740266	C	3-11
Thornhill Junior and Infant School Walter Street, S60 1LL ☎ 01709 740473	C	3-11
Wath Victoria Junior and Infant School Doncaster Road, Wath-upon-Dearne, S63 7AB ☎ 01709 760103	C	3-11
Whiston Worry Goose Junior and Infant School Hall Close Avenue, Whiston, S60 4AG ☎ 01709 541878	C	3-11
Woodsetts Junior and Infant School Wellfield Crescent, Woodsetts, S81 8SB ☎ 01909 550758	C	3-11

373 SHEFFIELD

School name, address and telephone number	Type	Age
Abbeydale Primary School Glen Road, S7 1RB ☎ 0114 255 0926	C	3-11
Anns Grove Primary School Anns Road, S2 3DJ ☎ 0114 255 0398	C	3-11
Ballifield Primary School Handsworth Grange Road, S13 9HH ☎ 0114 269 7557	C	3-11
Bluestone Primary School Park Grange Drive, S2 3SF ☎ 0114 272 5645	C	3-11
Bracken Hill Primary School Bracken Road, S5 6FH ☎ 0114 242 6874	C	3-11
Brunswick Primary School Station Road, Woodhouse, S17 7RB ☎ 0114 269 5315	C	3-11
Byron Wood Primary School Earldom Road, S4 7EJ ☎ 0114 272 3624	C	3-11
Daniel Hill Primary School Daniel Hill Street, Upperthorpe, S6 3JH ☎ 0114 234 3482	C	3-11
Fox Hill Nursery Junior and Infant School Keats Road, S6 1AZ ☎ 0114 231 3469	C	3-11
Greengate Lane Primary School Greengate Lane, High Green, S35 8RY ☎ 0114 284 8322	C	3-11
Longley Primary School Raisen Hall Road, S5 7NA ☎ 0114 231 0044	C	3-11
Lowedges Primary School Lowedges Road, S8 7JG ☎ 0114 237 2196	C	3-11
Meersbrook Bank Primary School Derbyshire Lane, S8 9EH ☎ 0114 255 0491	C	3-11
Meynell Primary School Meynell Road, S5 8GN ☎ 0114 231 1425	C	3-11
Monteney Primary School Monteney Crescent, S5 9DN ☎ 0114 246 7916	C	3-11
"Netherthorpe Nursery, Infant and Junior School" Netherthorpe Street, S3 7JA ☎ 0114 272 6834	C	3-11
Prince Edward Primary School 747 City Road, S12 2AA ☎ 0114 239 7142	C	3-11
Rainbow Forge Primary School Beighton Road, Hackenthorpe, S12 4LQ ☎ 0114 248 7342	C	3-11
St Catherine's RC Junior Nursery and Infant School Firshill Crescent, S4 7BX ☎ 0114 242 1177	VA	3-11
St Mary's CofE (Aided) Primary School Cundy Street, S6 2WJ ☎ 0114 234 4461	VA	3-11
Springfield Primary School Broomspring Lane, S10 2FA ☎ 0114 272 3455	C	3-11
Stradbroke Primary School Richmond Road, S13 8LT ☎ 0114 239 9320	C	3-11
Walkley Primary School Burnaby Crescent, S6 2RZ ☎ 0114 234 0550	C	3-11
Westways Primary School Mona Avenue, S10 1LA ☎ 0114 266 2471	C	3-11
Wharncliffe Side Primary School Brightholmlee Lane, S35 0DD ☎ 0114 286 2379	C	3-11
Woodhouse West Primary School Coisley Hill, S13 7EW ☎ 0114 269 2602	C	3-11
Woodseats Primary School Chesterfield Road, S8 0SB ☎ 0114 255 4619	C	3-11
Woodthorpe Community Primary School Woodthorpe Road, S13 8DD ☎ 0114 239 9167	C	3-11

School name, address and telephone number	Type	Age
384 WAKEFIELD		
All Saints CofE (Aided) Junior and Infant School North Close, Featherstone, WF7 6BQ ☎ 01977 722600	VA	3–11
Ash Grove Junior and Infant School Ash Grove, South Elmsall, WF9 2TF ☎ 01977 642195	C	3–11
Bell Lane Junior Infant and Nursery School Bell Lane, Ackworth, WF7 7JH ☎ 01977 722230	C	3–11
Burntwood Junior and Infant School Church Top, South Kirkby, WF9 3QS ☎ 01977 723800	C	3–11
Carlton Junior and Infant School Carlton Road, South Elmsall, WF9 2QQ ☎ 01977 640674	C	3–11
English Martyrs' RC Junior and Infant School Dewsbury Road, WF2 9DD ☎ 01924 303635	VA	3–11
Fitzwilliam Junior Infant and Nursery School Second Avenue, Fitzwilliam, WF9 5BA ☎ 01977 722 235	C	3–11
Gawthorpe Junior Infant and Nursery School High Street, Gawthorpe, WF5 9QP ☎ 01924 302975	C	3–11
Half Acres Junior and Infant School Temple Street, WF10 5RE ☎ 01977 723010	C	3–11
Halfpenny Lane Junior and Infant School Halfpenny Lane, WF8 4BW ☎ 01977 722820	C	3–11
Havercroft Junior Infant and Nursery School Cow Lane, Havercroft, WF4 2BE ☎ 01226 722484	C	3–11
Heath View Primary School Irwin Crescent, Eastmoor, WF1 4QY ☎ 01924 303 655	C	3–11
Hendal Primary School Hendal Lane, Kettlethorpe, WF2 7QW ☎ 01924 303295	C	3–11
Kinsley Junior Infant and Nursery School Wakefield Road, Fitzwilliam, WF9 5AS ☎ 01977 722 245	C	3–11
Knottingley CofE (Controlled) Junior and Infant School Primrose Vale, WF11 9BT ☎ 01977 722480	VC	3–11
Mackie Hill Junior and Infant School Painthorpe Lane, Crigglestone, WF4 3HW ☎ 01924 303520	C	3–11
Mill Dam Junior Infant and Nursery School Millgate, Ackworth, WF7 7NG ☎ 01977 723110	C	3–11
Moorthorpe Primary Junior and Infant School Regent Street, Moorthorpe, WF9 2BL ☎ 01977 723860	C	3–11
Newton Hill Junior and Infant School Leeds Road, Newton Hill, WF1 2HR ☎ 01924 303680	C	3–11
Northfield Junior and Infant School Northfield Lane, South Kirkby, WF9 3LY ☎ 01977 723820	C	3–11
Outwood Ledger Lane Junior and Infant School Ledger Lane, Outwood, WF1 2PH ☎ 01924 303825	C	3–11
Pontefract St Giles (Aided) Junior and Infant School Skinner Lane, WF8 1HG ☎ 01977 722880	VA	3–11
Ryhill Junior Infant and Nursery School Chapel Street, Ryhill, WF4 2AD ☎ 01226 722530	C	3–11
St Helen's CofE Junior Infant and Nursery School Highfields Road, Hemsworth, WF9 4EG ☎ 01977 723700	VA	3–11
St Joseph's RC Junior and Infant School Newgate, WF8 4AA ☎ 01977 723555	VA	3–11
St Mary's CofE (A) Primary School Charles Street, WF1 4PE ☎ 01924 303625	VA	3–11
Sandal Magna Junior and Infants School Belle Vue Road, WF1 5LT ☎ 01924 303530	C	3–11
Sharlston Junior and Infant School Hammer Lane, Sharlston Common, WF4 1DH ☎ 01924 303 920	C	3–11
Shay Lane Junior and Infants' School Shay Lane, Crofton, WF4 1NN ☎ 01924 303910	C	3–11
Simpson's Lane Junior and Infant School Sycamore Avenue, WF11 0PL ☎ 01977 722515	C	3–11
South Hiendley Junior Infant and Nursery School George Street, South Hiendley, S72 9BY ☎ 01226 711485	C	3–11
Three Lane Ends Primary (J & I) School Methley Road, WF10 1PN ☎ 01977 723065	C	3–11
Throstle Farm Junior and Infant School Hazel Road, WF11 0PA ☎ 01977 722545	C	3–11
Upton Junior and Infant School Waggon Lane, Upton, WF9 1JS ☎ 01977 723845	C	3–11
Waterton Junior and Infants School Waterton Road, Lupset, WF2 8LZ ☎ 01924 303765	C	3–11
West End Primary Junior & Infant School Regent Street, Hemsworth, WF9 4QJ ☎ 01977 723 705	C	3–11
816 CITY OF YORK		
Fishergate Primary School Fishergate, YO1 4AP ☎ 01904 623511	C	3–11
Haxby Road Primary School 154 Haxby Road, YO3 7JN ☎ 01904 653218	C	3–11
New Earswick Undenominational Primary School Hawthorn Terrace, New Earswick, YO3 4BY ☎ 01904 768228	VA	3–11
Our Lady's RC Primary School Windsor Garth, Acomb, YO2 4QW ☎ 01904 791646	VA	3–11
St Aelred's RC Primary School Fifth Avenue, YO3 0QQ ☎ 01904 422800	VA	3–11
St Lawrence's CofE Primary School Heslington Road, YO1 5BW ☎ 01904 625131	VA	3–11

School name, address and telephone number	Type	Age

EAST MIDLANDS

831 DERBY CITY

School name, address and telephone number	Type	Age
Arboretum Primary School Corden Street, DE23 8GP ☎ 01332 291140	C	3–11
Asterdale Primary School Borrowash Road, Spondon, DE21 7PH ☎ 01332 662323	C	3–11
Becket Primary School Monk Street, DE22 3QB ☎ 01332 347595	C	3–11
Bishop Lonsdale CofE (Aided) Primary School St Albans Road, DE22 3HH ☎ 01332 344795	VA	3–11
Derwent Community Primary School St Mark's Road, DE21 6AL ☎ 01332 346222	C	3–11
Firs Estate Primary School Raven Street, DE22 3WA ☎ 01332 346230	C	3–11
Grampian Primary School Grampian Way, Sinfin, DE24 9LU ☎ 01332 765546	C	3–11
Meadow Farm Community Primary School Foyle Avenue, Chaddesden, DE21 6TZ ☎ 01332 662631	C	3–11
St Alban's RC Primary School Newstead Avenue, Chaddesden, DE21 6NU ☎ 01332 673823	VA	3–11
St Mary's RC Primary School Darley Lane, DE1 3AX ☎ 01332 347369	VA	3–11
Sinfin Primary School Sheridan Street, Sinfin, DE24 9HG ☎ 01332 760071	C	3–11
Walter Evans CofE Primary School Darley Abbey Drive, Darley Abbey, DE22 1EF ☎ 01332 557139	VA	3–11
Wilmorton Primary School London Road, DE24 8UQ ☎ 01332 571485	C	3–11

830 DERBYSHIRE

School name, address and telephone number	Type	Age
Abercrombie Primary School Victoria Street, S41 7LP ☎ 01246 232425	C	3–11
Anthony Bek Primary School Rotherham Road, Pleasley, NG19 7PG ☎ 01623 810355	C	3–11
Barrow Hill Primary School Station Road, Barrow Hill, Staveley, S43 2PG ☎ 01246 472494	C	3–11
Blackwell Primary School Primrose Hill, Blackwell, DE55 5JG ☎ 01773 811281	C	3–11
Bramley Vale Primary School York Crescent, Doe Lea, S44 5PF ☎ 01246 850289	C	3–11
Brockley Primary School Clowne Road, Shuttlewood, S44 6AF ☎ 01246 823344	C	3–11
Calow CofE VC Primary School North Road, Calow, S44 5BD ☎ 01246 274370	VC	3–11
Camms CofE (Aided) Primary School Camms Close, Castle Hill, Eckington, S21 4AU ☎ 01246 432829	VA	3–11
Christ The King RC Primary School Firs Avenue, DE55 7EN ☎ 01773 832919	VA	3–11
Coppice Primary School Roper Avenue, Marlpool, DE75 7BZ ☎ 01773 712840	C	3–11
Dallimore Primary School Dallimore Road, Kirk Hallam, DE7 4GZ ☎ 0115 932 0741	C	3–11
Draycott Primary School Hopwell Road, Draycott, DE72 3NH ☎ 01332 872261	C	3–11
Duckmanton Primary School West Crescent, Duckmanton, S44 5DH ☎ 01246 825650	C	3–11
Dunston Primary School Dunston Lane, Newbold, S41 8EY ☎ 01246 450601	C	3–11
Fairmeadows Primary School Fairfield Crescent, Newhall, DE11 0SW ☎ 01283 211019	GM	3–11
Grange Primary School Station Road, Long Eaton, NG10 2DU ☎ 0115 973 4956	C	3–11
Grassmoor Primary School North Wingfield Road, Grassmoor, S42 5EP ☎ 01246 850349	C	3–11
Hady Primary School Hady Lane, Hady, S41 0DF ☎ 01246 279254	C	3–11
Heath Primary School Slack Lane, Heath, S44 5RH ☎ 01246 850277	C	3–11
Highfield Hall Primary School Highfield Lane, S41 8AZ ☎ 01246 273534	C	3–11
Highfield Primary School Wellington Street, Long Eaton, NG10 4HR ☎ 0115 973 3568	C	3–11
Hodthorpe Primary School Queen's Road, Hodthorpe, S80 4UT ☎ 01909 720315	C	3–11
Hollingwood Primary School Lilac Street, Hollingwood, S43 2JG ☎ 01246 472417	C	3–11
Holmgate Primary School Holmgate Road, Clay Cross, S45 9QD ☎ 01246 862270	C	3–11
Inkersall Primary School Green Road, Inkersall, Staveley, S43 3SE ☎ 01246 472370	C	3–11
Ironville and Codnor Park Primary School Victoria Street, Ironville, NG16 5NB ☎ 01773 602936	C	3–11
Ladywood Primary School Oliver Road, Kirk Hallam, DE7 4NH ☎ 0115 932 0585	C	3–11
Linton Primary School Main Street, Linton, DE12 6QA ☎ 01283 760382	GM	3–11
Long Row Primary School Long Row, DE56 1DR ☎ 01773 823319	C	3–11
Longmoor Primary School Newstead Road, Long Eaton, NG10 4JG ☎ 0115 973 3368	C	3–11

School name, address and telephone number	Type	Age
Mary Swanwick Primary School Church Street North, Old Whittington, S41 9QW ☎ 01246 450597	C	3–11
Model Village Primary School Central Drive, Shirebrook, NG20 8BQ ☎ 01623 742254	C	3–11
New Bolsover Primary and Nursery School New Station Road, Bolsover, S44 6PY ☎ 01246 823240	C	3–11
New Whittington Primary School London Street, New Whittington, S43 2AQ ☎ 01246 450688	C	3–11
Norbriggs Primary School Norbriggs Road, Mastin Moor, S43 3BW ☎ 01246 473398	C	3–11
Pilsley Primary School Station Road, Pilsley, S45 8EU ☎ 01773 872378	C	3–11
Poolsbrook Primary School Cottage Close, Poolsbrook, near Staveley, S43 3LF ☎ 01246 472540	C	3–11
Renishaw Primary School Hague Lane, Renishaw, S21 3UR ☎ 01246 432366	C	3–11
St George's CofE Primary School (VA) Church Lane, New Mills, SK22 4NP ☎ 01663 743222	VA	3–11
St John's CofE Primary School Dannah Street, DE5 3BD ☎ 01773 742457	VC	3–11
St Margaret's RC Primary School Glossop Road, Gamesley, SK13 9JH ☎ 01457 855818	VA	3–11
Stonebroom Primary School High Street, Stonebroom, DE55 6JY ☎ 01773 872449	C	3–11
Temple Normanton Primary School Elm Street, Temple Normanton, S42 5DW ☎ 01246 850389	C	3–11
Tupton Primary School Queen Victoria Road, New Tupton, S42 6DY ☎ 01246 862191	C	3–11
Whaley Thorns Primary School Portland Road, Langwith, NG20 9HB ☎ 01623 742604	C	3–11
Whitfield CofE Primary School Chadwick Street, SK13 8EF ☎ 01457 852427	VC	3–11
Whitwell Primary School Southfield Lane, Whitwell, S80 4NR ☎ 01909 720251	C	3–11
William Rhodes Primary School Hunloke Avenue, Boythorpe, S40 2NR ☎ 01246 234626	C	3–11

855 LEICESTERSHIRE

Albert Village Primary School Occupation Road, Albert Village, DE11 8HA ☎ 01283 217880	C	3–11
Mountfields Lodge County Primary School Epinal Way, LE11 3GE ☎ 01509 214119	C	3–11

856 LEICESTER CITY

Alderman Richard Hallam Primary School Avebury Avenue, LE4 0FQ ☎ 0116 262 4003	C	3–11
Beaumont Lodge Primary School Astill Lodge Road, Beaumont Leys, LE4 1DT ☎ 0116 236 6925	C	3–11
Belgrave CofE Primary School Thurcaston Road, LE4 5PG ☎ 0116 266 5790	VC	3–11
Buswells Lodge Primary School Beauville Drive, Beaumont Leys, LE4 0PT ☎ 0116 235 2129	C	3–11
Charnwood Primary School Nedham Street, LE2 0HE ☎ 0116 251 6574	C	3–11
Coleman Primary School Gwendolen Road, LE5 5FS ☎ 0116 249 0109	C	3–11
Dovelands Primary School Hinckley Road, LE3 0TJ ☎ 0116 285 7716	C	3–11
Eyres Monsell Primary School Simmins Crescent, LE2 9AH ☎ 0116 277 3855	C	3–11
Forest Lodge Primary School Charnor Road, LE3 6LH ☎ 0116 287 1220	C	3–11
Fosse Primary School Balfour Street, LE3 5EA ☎ 0116 251 9261	C	3–11
Granby Primary School Granby Road, LE2 8LP ☎ 0116 283 2013	C	3–11
Hazel Primary School Hazel Street, LE2 7JN ☎ 0116 233 8411	C	3–11
Herrick County Primary School Lockerbie Avenue, LE4 7NJ ☎ 0116 266 5656	C	3–11
Holy Cross RC Primary School Stonesby Avenue, LE2 6TY ☎ 0116 283 3135	VA	3–11
Kestrels' Field Primary School Maidenwell Avenue, Hamilton, LE5 1TG ☎ 0116 246 1732	C	3–11
Knighton Fields Primary School Knighton Fields Road West, LE2 7NP ☎ 0116 233 0666	C	3–11
Marriott Primary School Marriott Road, LE2 6NS ☎ 0116 283 2433	C	3–11
Mayflower Primary School Evington Drive, LE5 5PH ☎ 0116 273 7504	C	3–11
Medway Community Primary School St Stephen's Road, Highfields, LE2 1GH ☎ 0116 254 4811	C	3–11
Mellor Primary School Clarke Street, LE4 7QN ☎ 0116 266 1377	C	3–11
Montrose Primary School Wigston Lane, Aylestone, LE2 8TN ☎ 0116 283 2328	C	3–11
Mowmacre Hill Primary School Tedworth Green, LE4 2NG ☎ 0116 235 6350	C	3–11
New Parks House Primary School New Parks Crescent, LE3 9NZ ☎ 0116 287 2414	C	3–11
Northfield House Primary School Northfield Road, LE4 9DL ☎ 0116 276 7761	C	3–11

School name, address and telephone number	Type	Age
Rowlatts Hill County Primary School Balderstone Close, off Ambassador Road, LE5 4ES ☎ 0116 276 8812	C	3–11
Rushey Mead Primary School Gipsy Lane, LE4 6RB ☎ 0116 266 1114	C	3–11
Sacred Heart RC Primary School Mere Close, off Mere Road, LE5 3HH ☎ 0116 262 4418	VA	3–11
St Joseph's RC Primary School Armadale Drive, LE5 1HF ☎ 0116 241 6197	VA	3–11
St Patrick's RC Primary School Harrison Road, LE4 6QN ☎ 0116 266 1149	VA	3–11
Shenton Primary School Dunlin Road, off Humberstone Road, LE5 3FP ☎ 0116 262 8778	C	3–11
Slater Primary School Slater Street, LE3 5AS ☎ 0116 262 4587	C	3–11
Sparkenhoe Community Primary School Saxby Street, LE2 0TD ☎ 0116 251 2686	C	3–11
Spinney Hill Primary School and Community Centre Ventnor Street, LE5 5EZ ☎ 0116 273 7047	C	3–11
Stokes Wood Primary School Blackett Avenue, LE3 9BX ☎ 0116 287 5305	C	3–11
Taylor Primary School Taylor Road, St Matthew's Estate, LE1 2JP ☎ 0116 262 4597	C	3–11
Whitehall Primary School Whitehall Road, LE5 6GJ ☎ 0116 241 3087	C	3–11
Willowbrook Primary School Roborough Green, LE5 2NA ☎ 0116 241 3756	C	3–11
Wolsey House Primary School Beaumont Leys Lane, LE4 2BB ☎ 0116 266 7566	C	3–11
Woodstock Primary School Hattern Avenue, LE4 2GZ ☎ 0116 235 5825	C	3–11
Wyvern Primary School Wyvern Avenue, LE4 7HH, 0116 266 1408	C	3–11

925 LINCOLNSHIRE

School name, address and telephone number	Type	Age
Belton Lane County Primary School Green Lane, NG31 9PP ☎ 01476 564598	C	3–11
Benjamin Adlard County Primary School Sandsfield Lane, DN21 1DB ☎ 01427 612562	C	3–11
Billinghay CofE Primary School Fen Road, Billinghay, LN4 4HU ☎ 01526 860786	VC	3–11
Carlton Road Primary School Carlton Road, PE21 8LN ☎ 01205 364674	C	3–11
Fosse Way Primary School Ash Grove, North Hykeham, LN6 8DU ☎ 01522 682020	C	3–11
Hartsholme Primary GM School Carrington Drive, LN6 0DE ☎ 01522 683705	GM	3–11
Horncastle County Primary School Bowl Alley Lane, LN9 5EH ☎ 01507 522662	C	3–11
Kirton County Primary School Station Road, Kirton, PE20 1HY ☎ 01205 722236	C	3–11
Long Sutton County Primary School Dick Turpin Way, Long Sutton, PE12 9EP ☎ 01406 363381	C	3–11
Mablethorpe Primary School High Street, LN12 1EW ☎ 01507 472472	C	3–11
Market Deeping County Primary School Willoughby Avenue, Market Deeping, PE6 8JE ☎ 01778 343654	C	3–11
Monks Abbey Primary School Monks Road, LN2 5PF ☎ 01522 527705	C	3–11
Old Leake Primary and Nursery School Old Main Road, Old Leake, PE22 9HR ☎ 01205 870425	GM	3–11
St Paul's County Primary and Nursery School Queen's Road, PE11 2JQ ☎ 01775 723326	C	3–11
Seathorne Primary School Count Alan Road, PE25 1HB ☎ 01754 764689	C	3–11
Spitalgate CofE Primary School Trent Road, NG31 7XQ ☎ 01476 563963	VC	3–11
The Winchelsea County Primary School 4A Sleaford Road, Ruskington, NG34 9BY ☎ 01526 832060	C	3–11

928 NORTHAMPTONSHIRE

School name, address and telephone number	Type	Age
St Andrew's CofE Primary School Grafton Street, NN16 9DF ☎ 01536 512581	VC	3–11
St Patrick's RC Primary School Patricks Road, NN18 9NT ☎ 01536 744447	VA	3–11
Woodford Halse CofE Primary School High Street, Woodford Halse, NN11 3RQ ☎ 01327 265900	VC	3–11

930 NOTTINGHAMSHIRE

School name, address and telephone number	Type	Age
Annesley Primary and Nursery School Forest Road, Annesley Woodhouse, NG17 9BW ☎ 01623 754221	C	3–11
Arkwright Primary School Orange Gardens, off Kirkby Gardens, Wilford Grove The Meadows, NG2 2JE ☎ 0115 953 9936	C	3–11
Beardall Street Primary and Nursery School Beardall Street, Hucknall, NG15 7JU ☎ 0115 956 8285	C	3–11
Birklands Primary School Appleton Street, Warsop, NG20 0QF ☎ 01623 842163	C	3–11
Bishop Alexander Primary School Wolsey Road, NG24 2BQ ☎ 01636 680040	C	3–11
Blessed Robert Widmerpool School Listowel Crescent, Clifton, NG11 9BH ☎ 0115 921 1875	VA	3–11
Bosworth Primary School Ainsworth Drive, The Meadows, NG2 1FX ☎ 0115 955 2050	C	3–11

School name, address and telephone number	Type	Age
Brinsley Primary School Moor Road, Brinsley, NG16 5AZ ☎ 01773 712898	C	3–11
Brooksby Primary School Greencroft, Clifton Estate, NG11 8EY ☎ 0115 974 4017	C	3–11
Bulwell St Mary's CofE Primary and Nursery School Ragdale Road, Bulwell, NG6 8GQ ☎ 0115 927 8970	VC	3–11
Burford Primary School Oxclose Lane, Arnold, NG5 6FX ☎ 0115 926 7348	C	3–11
Cantrell Primary and Nursery School Cantrell Road, Bulwell, NG6 9HJ ☎ 0115 927 8521	C	3–11
Carr Hill Primary School Tiln Lane, DN22 6SW ☎ 01777 702948	C	3–11
Church Drive Primary School Church Drive, Arnold, NG5 6LD ☎ 0115 916 0034	C	3–11
Church Vale Primary School and Nursery Laurel Avenue, Church Warsop, NG20 0TE ☎ 01623 842250	C	3–11
Coddington CofE Primary and Nursery School Brownlows Hill, Coddington, NG24 2QA ☎ 01636 702974	VC	3–11
Crompton View Primary School Crompton Road, Bilsthorpe, NG22 8PS ☎ 01623 870772	C	3–11
Dalestorth Primary School Hill Crescent, NG17 4JA ☎ 01623 554089	C	3–11
Douglas Primary and Nursery School Seely Road, off Ilkeston Road, Radford, NG7 3GR ☎ 0115 978 3557	C	3–11
Eastglade Primary and Nursery School Whitcombe Gardens, Top Valley, NG5 9ED ☎ 0115 953 6098	C	3–11
Edgewood Primary School Edgewood Drive, Hucknall, NG15 6HX ☎ 0115 963 6591	C	3–11
Edna G Olds Primary and Nursery School Church Street, Lenton, NG7 1SJ ☎ 0115 947 5100	C	3–11
Elkesley Primary and Nursery School Headland Avenue, Elkesley, DN22 8AQ ☎ 01777 838615	C	3–11
Elms Primary and Nursery School Cranmer Street, NG3 4HA ☎ 0115 960 6593	C	3–11
Firbeck Primary School Firbeck Road, Wollaton, NG8 2FB ☎ 0115 928 3312	C	3–11
Forest Fields Primary and Nursery School Bradgate Road, Forest Fields, NG7 6HJ ☎ 0115 978 3096	C	3–11
Forest Town County Primary School Clipstone Road West, Forest Town, NG19 0ED ☎ 01623 21761	C	3–11
Glade Hill Primary and Nursery School Chippenham Road, Bestwood Park Estate, NG5 5TA ☎ 0115 926 3778	C	3–11
Glapton Primary and Nursery School Glapton Lane, Clifton Estate, NG11 8EA ☎ 0115 914 0302	C	3–11
Glenbrook Primary School Wigman Road, Bilborough, NG8 4PD ☎ 0115 929 2905	C	3–11
Greenwood Primary School Sutton Middle Lane, Kirkby-in-Ashfield, NG17 8FX ☎ 01623 460664	C	3–11
Haddon Primary School Haddon Close, Westdale Lane, Carlton, NG4 4GT ☎ 0115 952 3959	C	3–11
Haggonfields Primary School Marjorie Street, Rhodesia, S80 3HP ☎ 01909 473992	C	3–11
Hawthorne Primary and Nursery School School Walk, Bestwood Village, NG6 8TL ☎ 0115 927 1544	C	3–11
Haydn Primary School Haydn Road, Sherwood, NG5 2JU ☎ 0115 960 6169	C	3–11
Heathfield Primary School Scotland Road, Basford, NG5 1JU ☎ 0115 978 3928	C	3–11
Highfield Primary and Nursery School Candleby Lane, Cotgrave, NG12 3JG ☎ 0115 989 2547	C	3–11
Hillocks Primary and Nursery School Unwin Road, NG17 4ND ☎ 01623 555370	C	3–11
Hogarth Primary School Porchester Road, NG3 6JG ☎ 0115 911 1090	C	3–11
Holly Hill Primary School off Portland Road, Selston, NG16 6AW ☎ 01773 810507	C	3–11
Holy Family RC Primary and Nursery School Netherton Road, S80 2SF ☎ 01909 473917	VA	3–11
Huntingdon County Primary School Alfred Street Central, Woodborough Road, St Ann's, NG3 4AY ☎ 0115 950 1949	C	3–11
Hyson Green St Mary's Catholic Primary School Beaconsfield Street, Hyson Green, NG7 6FL ☎ 0115 970 8514	VA	3–11
Jacksdale Primary School Main Road, Jacksdale, Selston, NG16 5JU ☎ 01773 602523	C	3–11
Jeffries Primary School Vernon Road, Kirkby-in-Ashfield, NG17 8EE ☎ 01623 752229	C	3–11
Jesse Boot Primary School Hereford Road, Bakersfield, NG3 7FL ☎ 0115 912 6550	C	3–11
John Davies Primary and Nursery School Barker Street, Huthwaite, NG17 2LH ☎ 01623 554644	C	3–11
Keyworth Primary and Nursery School Nottingham Road, Keyworth, NG12 5FB ☎ 0115 937 3109	C	3–11
King Edwin Primary School Fourth Avenue, Edwinstowe, NG21 9NS ☎ 01623 822111	C	3–11
Kirkby Woodhouse Primary School Main Road, Kirkby-in-Ashfield, NG17 9EU ☎ 01623 753178	C	3–11
Lake View Primary School Water Road, Rainworth, NG21 0DU ☎ 01623 792542	C	3–11
Lantern Lane Primary & Nursery School Lantern Lane, East Leake, LE12 6QN ☎ 01509 852367	C	3–11
Leamington Primary and Nursery School Clare Road, NG17 5BB ☎ 01623 552651	C	3–11
Lenton Primary School and Nursery Lenton Boulevard, NG7 2ET ☎ 0115 978 2215	C	3–11
Mapplewells Primary School Henning Lane, NG17 1HU ☎ 01623 553229	C	3–11

School name, address and telephone number	Type	Age
Meadows Primary School Kirkby Gardens, The Meadows, NG2 2HZ ☎ 0115 956 8294	C	3–11
Mellers Primary School Norton Street, Radford, NG7 3HJ ☎ 0115 978 5994	C	3–11
Middleton Primary School Harrow Road, Wollaton Park, NG8 1FG ☎ 0115 913 0303	C	3–11
Misterton Primary School Grove Wood Road, Misterton, DN10 4EH ☎ 01427 890284	C	3–11
Newark Barnby Road County Primary School and Nursery Cromwell Road, NG23 1RP ☎ 01636 683900	C	3–11
Newark Holy Trinity RC Primary Nursery School Boundary Road, NG24 4AU ☎ 01636 689177	VA	3–11
Old Basford Primary School Percy Street, Old Basford, NG6 0GF ☎ 0115 978 5505	C	3–11
Orchard Primary School and Nursery Chapel Street, Kirkby-in-Ashfield, NG17 8JY ☎ 01623 752416	C	3–11
Portland Primary and Nursery School Westwick Road, Bilborough, NG8 4HB ☎ 0115 928 3471	C	3–11
Priestsic Primary School Park Street, NG17 4BB ☎ 01623 557506	C	3–11
Richard Bonington Primary School Calverton Road, Arnold, NG5 8FQ ☎ 0115 956 0995	C	3–11
Robert Mellors Primary School Bonington Drive, Arnold, NG5 7EX ☎ 0115 926 2556	C	3–11
Ryton Park Primary School Memorial Avenue, S80 2BW ☎ 01909 472442	C	3–11
St Andrew's CofE Primary and Nursery School Mansfield Road, Skegby, NG17 3DW ☎ 01623 556304	VC	3–11
St Augustine's RC Primary and Nursery School Park Avenue, Mapperley Road, NG3 4JS ☎ 0115 960 4714	VA	3–11
St Edmund's CofE Primary School Church Hill Avenue, Mansfield Woodhouse, NG19 9JU ☎ 01623 22962	VC	3–11
St Edward's RC Primary School Gordon Road, St Ann's, NG3 2LG ☎ 0115 950 3340	VA	3–11
St Joseph's Primary and Nursery School Main Road, Boughton, NG22 9JE ☎ 01623 860392	VA	3–11
St Joseph's Primary and Nursery School Old Babworth Road, DN22 7BP ☎ 01777 702850	VA	3–11
St Patrick's RC Primary and Nursery School Coronation Avenue, Wilford, NG11 7AB ☎ 0115 981 5510	VA	3–11
St Patrick's RC Primary and Nursery School Ling Forest Road, NG18 3NJ ☎ 01623 27918	VA	3–11
St Philip Neri with St Bede Catholic Primary School Rosemary Street, NG19 6AA ☎ 01623 23033	VA	3–11
St Swithun's CofE Primary & Nursery School Grove Street, DN22 6LD ☎ 01777 702043	VA	3–11
Seagrave Primary School Helston Drive, Strelley Estate, NG8 6JZ ☎ 0115 927 1774	C	3–11
Snape Wood Primary School Aspen Road, Bulwell, NG6 7DS ☎ 0115 975 1476	C	3–11
Sneinton CofE Primary School Windmill Lane, Sneinton, NG2 4QB ☎ 0115 912 8995	VA	3–11
Southwold Primary and Nursery School Kennington Road, Radford, NG8 1QD ☎ 0115 928 2003	C	3–11
Stanhope Primary and Nursery School Keyworth Road, Gedling, NG4 4JD ☎ 0115 955 3440	C	3–11
Trent Bridge Primary School Green Street, Meadows, NG2 2LA ☎ 0115 956 8302	C	3–11
Walter Halls Primary School Querneby Road, Mapperley, NG3 5HS ☎ 0115 960 6669	C	3–11
Whitegate Primary School Middle Fell Way, Clifton Estate, NG11 9JQ ☎ 0115 974 4010	C	3–11
Whitemoor Primary & Nursery School Bracknell Crescent, Whitemoor Estate, NG8 5FF ☎ 0115 978 6351	C	3–11
Worksop Priory CofE Primary & Nursery School Holles Street, S80 2LJ ☎ 01909 478886	VA	3–11

857 RUTLAND

School name, address and telephone number	Type	Age
Brooke Hill County Primary School Brooke Road, LE15 6HQ ☎ 01572 724214	C	3–11
Cottesmore Primary School RAF Station, Cottesmore, LE15 7BA ☎ 01572 812278	C	3–11
Edith Weston Primary School Weston Road, Edith Weston, LE15 8HQ ☎ 01780 720025	C	3–11

932 SHROPSHIRE

School name, address and telephone number	Type	Age
Brookside County Primary School Beaconsfield, Brookside, TF3 1LG ☎ 01952 592431	C	3–11
Dawley CofE Primary School Doseley Road, Dawley, TF4 3AL ☎ 01952 270505	VA	3–11
Greenacres Primary School (GM) Rutland, off York Road, Harlescott Grange, SY1 3QG ☎ 01743 464570	GM	3–11
Oswestry County Primary School Gittin Street, SY11 1DT ☎ 01691 652446	C	3–11
Queenswood County Primary School Yates Way, Ketley Bank, TF2 0BA ☎ 01952 612317	C	3–11
St George's CofE Primary School Clun, SY7 8JQ ☎ 01588 640229	VA	3–11
Shawbury County Primary School Church Road, Shawbury, SY4 4JR ☎ 01939 250323	C	3–11
Stokesay Primary School Market Street, SY7 9NW ☎ 01588 672275	C	3–11
The Wilfred Owen County Primary School Hearne Way, Monkmoor, SY2 5SL ☎ 01743 353566	C	3–11

169

School name, address and telephone number	Type	Age

WEST MIDLANDS

330 BRIMINGHAM

School name, address and telephone number	Type	Age
Anderton Park Junior and Infant School Dennis Road, Sparkhill, B12 8BL ☎ 0121 449 1581	C	3-11
The Arden Junior and Infant School Baker Street, Sparkhill, B11 4SF ☎ 0121 772 7702	C	3-11
Aston Tower Junior and Infant School (NC) Upper Sutton Street, Aston, B6 5BE ☎ 0121 327 0339	C	3-11
Barford Junior and Infant School Barford Road, Edgbaston, B16 0EF ☎ 0121 454 3765	C	3-11
Benson Community School Benson Road, Hockley, B18 5TD ☎ 0121 554 4913	C	3-11
Birchfield Junior Infant and Nursery School Trinity Road, Aston, B6 6AJ ☎ 0121 554 0661	C	3-11
Brookfields Junior Infant & Nursery School 2 Hingeston Street, Hockley, B18 6PU ☎ 0121 554 1897	C	3-11
Calshot Primary School Calshot Road, B42 2BY ☎ 0121 357 1059	C	3-11
Chandos Junior and Infant School Vaughton Street South, Highgate, B12 0YN ☎ 0121 440 3881	C	3-11
Christ Church CofE Junior and Infant School & Nursery Class Claremont Road, Sparkbrook, B11 1LF ☎ 0121 772 5121	VC	3-11
Christ The King RC Junior and Infant School Warren Farm Road, Kingstanding, B44 0QN ☎ 0121 373 1741	VA	3-11
City Road Junior and Infant School Cavendish Road, Rotton Park, B16 0HL ☎ 0121 454 3348	C	3-11
Cotteridge Junior and Infant School Breedon Road, B30 2HT ☎ 0121 458 2865	C	3-11
Dorrington Junior and Infant School Dorrington Road, Perry Barr, B42 1QR ☎ 0121 356 5330	C	3-11
Elms Farm Primary School Dorncliffe Avenue, Sheldon, B33 0PJ ☎ 0121 743 4634	C	3-11
Erdington Hall Primary School (NC) Ryland Road, Erdington, B24 8JJ ☎ 0121 373 3122	C	3-11
Greet Junior and Infant School Percy Road, Sparkhill, B11 3ND ☎ 0121 772 1449	C	3-11
Grendon Junior and Infant School Grendon Road, Kings Heath, B14 4RB ☎ 0121 474 2460	C	3-11
Grove Primary School Dawson Road, Handsworth, B21 9HB ☎ 0121 554 4669	C	3-11
Heathfield Junior and Infant School Heathfield Road, B19 1HJ ☎ 0121 523 6474	C	3-11
Heathlands Junior and Infant School (NC) Heath Way, Castle Bromwich, B34 6NB ☎ 0121 747 2705	C	3-11
Hillstone Primary School Hillstone Road, Shard End, B34 7PY ☎ 0121 747 3573	C	3-11
Hobmoor Junior and Infant School Hobmoor Road, Yardley, B25 8TN ☎ 0121 783 3269	C	3-11
Holy Family RC Primary School (NC) Coventry Road, B10 0HT ☎ 0121 772 2670	VA	3-11
Holy Trinity CofE Primary School Havelock Road, B20 3LP ☎ 0121 356 9900	VA	3-11
Kingsland Primary School (NC) Kingsland Road, Kingstanding, B44 9PU ☎ 0121 360 7707	C	3-11
Kingsthorne Primary School Cranbourne Road, Kingstanding, B44 0BX ☎ 0121 373 3897	C	3-11
Kitwell Junior and Infant School Wychbury Road, B32 4DL ☎ 0121 476 0694	C	3-11
Leigh Junior and Infant School (NC) Leigh Road, Washwood Heath, B8 2YH ☎ 0121 327 2621	C	3-11
Ley Hill Junior and Infant (NC) School Rhayader Road, B31 1TX ☎ 0121 475 4302	C	3-11
Lozells Junior and Infant School and Nursery Wheeler Street, B19 2EJ ☎ 0121 554 1880	C	3-11
Manor Park Primary School Church Lane, B6 5UQ ☎ 0121 327 1023	GM	3-11
Mere Green Combined School Mere Green Road, B75 5BL ☎ 0121 308 1384	C	3-11
Nelson Junior and Infant School King Edward's Road, Ladywood, B1 2PJ ☎ 0121 236 2201	C	3-11
Nelson Mandela Community Primary School Colville Road, Sparkbrook, B12 8EH ☎ 0121 772 3055	C	3-11
New Hall Junior and Infant NC School Langley Hall Drive, B75 7NQ ☎ 0121 378 0481	C	3-11
Oaklands Junior and Infant School Dolphin Lane, Acocks Green, B27 7BT ☎ 0121 706 2168	C	3-11
Oratory RC Primary and Nursery School Oliver Road, Ladywood, B16 9ER ☎ 0121 454 0600	VA	3-11
Our Lady and St Rose of Lima Primary & Nursery School Gregory Avenue, Weoley Castle, B29 5DY ☎ 0121 411 2283	VA	3-11
Park Hill Junior and Infant School (NC) Alcester Road, B13 8BB ☎ 0121 449 3004	C	3-11
Redhill Junior and Infant School Redhill Road, Hay Mills, B25 8HQ ☎ 0121 772 1277	C	3-11
Regents Park Junior and Infant (NC) School Arthur Street, B10 0NJ ☎ 0121 772 6746	C	3-11
Ridpool Primary School and Nursery Hurstcroft Road, Kitts Green, B33 9RD ☎ 0121 783 3253	C	3-11
Robin Hood Junior and Infant School Pitmaston Road, Hall Green, B28 9PP ☎ 0121 733 2187	C	3-11

School name, address and telephone number	Type	Age
Rosary RC Junior Infant and Nursery School Bridge Road, Saltley, B8 3SF ☎ 0121 327 0625	VA	3–11
St Andrew's Junior Infant and Nursery School St Andrew's Road, Bordesley Village, B9 4NG ☎ 0121 772 1392	C	3–11
St Brigid's RC Junior and Infant School Frankley Beeches Road, Northfield, B31 5AB ☎ 0121 475 2364	VA	3–11
St Clare's RC Junior and Infant School Robert Road, Handsworth, B20 3RT ☎ 0121 554 3289	VA	3–11
St Clement's CofE Primary School & Nursery Class Butlin Street, B7 5NS ☎ 0121 327 1842	VC	3–11
St Cuthbert's RC Junior and Infant (NC) School Gumbleberrys Close, off Cotterills Lane, Stechford, B8 2PS ☎ 0121 783 2205	VA	3–11
St John's CofE Primary School Stratford Road, Sparkhill, B11 4EA ☎ 0121 772 1469	VA	3–11
St Paul's RC Junior and Infant School Sisefield Road, B38 9JB ☎ 0121 458 1546	VA	3–11
Severne Junior Infant and Nursery School Severne Road, Acocks Green, B27 7HR ☎ 0121 706 2743	C	3–11
Shirestone Junior Infant and Nursery School Shirestone Road, Tile Cross, B33 0DH ☎ 0121 783 4686	C	3–11
Sir Theodore Pritchett Junior and Infant School Bells Lane, B14 5RY ☎ 0121 430 5330	C	3–11
Somerville Junior and Infant School Somerville Road, B10 9EN ☎ 0121 772 0956	C	3–11
Starbank Junior and Infant School Starbank Road, Small Heath, B10 9LR ☎ 0121 772 2638	C	3–11
Stirchley Junior and Infant School Pershore Road, B30 2JL ☎ 0121 458 2989	C	3–11
Summerfield Junior and Infant School Cuthbert Road, Winson Green, B18 4AH ☎ 0121 454 2355	C	3–11
Tame Valley Primary School Chillinghome Road, B36 8QJ ☎ 0121 747 4497	C	3–11
Timberley Primary School Bradley Road, Shard End, B34 7RL ☎ 0121 747 2002	C	3–11
Tindal Junior and Infant School Tindal Street, Balsall Heath, B12 9QS ☎ 0121 440 3049	C	3–11
Tiverton Junior and Infant School Tiverton Road, B29 6BW ☎ 0121 472 0563	C	3–11
Ward End Primary School Ingleton Road, B8 2RA ☎ 0121 327 0694	C	3–11
Warren Farm Primary School Aylesbury Crescent, B44 0EW ☎ 0121 373 3885	C	3–11
Westminster Junior and Infant School Stamford Road, Handsworth, B20 3LJ ☎ 0121 554 2369	C	3–11
Whittington Oval Primary School Whittington Oval, Yardley, B33 8JG ☎ 0121 783 3248	C	3–11
Woodhouse Primary School and Nursery Unit Woodhouse Road, Quinton, B32 2DL ☎ 0121 427 1614	C	3–11
Yarnfield Primary School Yarnfield Road, Tyseley, B11 3PJ ☎ 0121 693 0362	C	3–11
Yew Tree Community Junior and Infant School (NC) Yew Tree Road, Aston, B6 6RA ☎ 0121 327 0655	C	3–11

331 COVENTRY

School name, address and telephone number	Type	Age
Alderman Harris Primary School Charter Avenue, CV4 8EN ☎ 01203 466391	C	3–11
Aldermans Green Primary School Alderman's Green Road, CV2 1PP ☎ 01203 688918	C	3–11
Allesley Primary School Antrim Close, Allesley, CV5 9FY ☎ 01203 402611	C	3–11
Broad Heath Community Primary School Broad Street, CV6 5BN ☎ 01203 689558	C	3–11
Chace Primary School Robin Hood Road, Willenhall, CV3 3AN ☎ 01203 303115	C	3–11
Clifford Bridge Primary School Coombe Park Road, Binley, CV3 2PD ☎ 01203 451720	C	3–11
Courthouse Green Primary School Bell Green Road, CV6 7GX ☎ 01203 688022	C	3–11
Frederick Bird Primary School Swan Lane, CV2 4QQ ☎ 01203 221920	C	3–11
Hearsall Community Primary School Kingston Road, CV5 6LR ☎ 01203 674625	C	3–11
Holbrook Primary School Gateside Road, CV6 6FR ☎ 01203 688947	C	3–11
Holy Family RC Primary (Aided) School Penny Park Lane, CV6 2GU ☎ 01203 333631	VA	3–11
Manor Park Primary School Ulverscroft Road, Cheylesmore, CV3 5EZ ☎ 01203 501736	C	3–11
Moseley Primary School Moseley Avenue, Coundon, CV6 1AB ☎ 01203 593572	C	3–11
Park Hill Primary School Lower Eastern Green Lane, CV5 7LR ☎ 01203 466669	C	3–11
Parkgate Primary School Parkgate Road, CV6 4GF ☎ 01203 689700	C	3–11
Potters Green Primary School Ringwood Highway, CV2 2GF ☎ 01203 613670	C	3–11
Radford Primary School Lawrence Saunders Road, Radford, CV6 1HD ☎ 01203 597234	C	3–11
Ravensdale Primary School Ravensdale Road, CV2 5GQ ☎ 01203 444966	C	3–11
St Bartholomew's CofE Primary School Bredon Avenue, CV3 2LP ☎ 01203 458960	VA	3–11

School name, address and telephone number	Type	Age
St Benedict's Primary School Leigh Street, Hillfields, CV1 5HG ☎ 01203 229486	VA	3–11
St Osburg's RC Primary and Nursery School Upper Hill Street, CV1 4AP ☎ 01203 227165	VA	3–11
St Thomas More RC Primary School Watercall Avenue, Styvechale, CV3 5AZ ☎ 01203 412619	VA	3–11
Southfields Primary School East Street, CV1 5LS ☎ 01203 226810	C	3–11
Spon Gate Primary School Upper Spon Street, CV1 3BQ ☎ 01203 226031	C	3–11
Stoke Heath Primary School Heath Crescent, CV2 4PR ☎ 01203 454741	C	3–11
Stoke Primary School Briton Road, CV2 4LF ☎ 01203 451724	C	3–11
Templars Primary School Templar Avenue, Tile Hill, CV4 9DA ☎ 01203 466337	C	3–11
Walsgrave CofE Primary School School House Lane, CV2 2BA ☎ 01203 612161	VC	3–11
Whitmore Park Primary School Halford Lane, CV6 2HG ☎ 01203 332945	C	3–11
Willenhall Wood Primary School St James Lane, Willenhall Wood, CV3 3DB ☎ 01203 303691	C	3–11
Wyken Croft Primary School Wyken Croft, Wyken, CV2 3AA ☎ 01203 613932	C	3–11

332 DUDLEY

School name, address and telephone number	Type	Age
Ashwood Park Primary School Bells Lane, Wordsley, DY8 5DJ ☎ 01384 818545	C	3–11
Beauty Bank Primary School Forge Road, DY8 1XF ☎ 01384 818780	C	3–11
Belle Vue Primary School Lawnswood Road, Wordsley, DY8 5BZ ☎ 01384 818615	C	3–11
Blowers Green Primary School Blowers Green Road, DY2 8UZ ☎ 01384 818490	C	3–11
Bramford Primary School Park Road, Woodsetton, DY1 4JH ☎ 01384 818915	C	3–11
Brierley Hill Primary School Mill Street, DY5 2TD ☎ 01384 816980	C	3–11
Brockmoor Primary School Belle Isle, Brockmoor, DY5 3UZ ☎ 01384 816635	C	3–11
Bromley Primary School Bromley, Pensnett, DY5 4PJ ☎ 01384 816865	C	3–11
Caslon Primary School Beeches View Avenue, B63 2ES ☎ 01384 818875	C	3–11
Christ Church CofE Primary School Church Road, Coseley, WV14 8YD ☎ 01384 818375	VC	3–11
Colley Lane Primary School Colley Lane, B63 2TN ☎ 01384 816765	C	3–11
Dawley Brook Primary School Dubarry Avenue, Valley Fields, DY6 9BP ☎ 01384 818770	C	3–11
Dudley Wood Primary School Dudley Wood Road, DY2 0DB ☎ 01384 818690	C	3–11
Foxyards Primary School Foxyards Road, DY4 8BH ☎ 01384 818740	C	3–11
Gig Mill Primary School The Broadway, Norton, DY8 3HL ☎ 01384 818600	C	3–11
Glynne Primary School Cot Lane, DY6 9TH ☎ 01384 816960	C	3–11
Halesowen CofE Primary School High Street, B63 3BB ☎ 01384 818885	VA	3–11
Hawbush Primary School Hawbush Road, DY5 3NH ☎ 01384 816930	C	3–11
Hob Green Primary School Hob Green Road, Pedmore Fields, DY9 9EX ☎ 01384 816730	C	3–11
Holt Farm Primary School Holt Road, B62 9HG ☎ 01384 818865	C	3–11
Huntingtree Primary School Bournes Hill, Hasbury Estate, B63 4DZ ☎ 01384 818650	C	3–11
Jesson's CofE Primary School (Aided) School Street, DY1 2AQ ☎ 01384 816825	VA	3–11
Kate's Hill Primary School Peel Street, Kate's Hill, DY2 7HP ☎ 01384 818700	C	3–11
Milking Bank Primary School Aintree Way, Milking Bank, DY1 2SL ☎ 01384 816695	C	3–11
Mount Pleasant Primary School Mount Pleasant, Quarry Bank, DY5 2YN ☎ 01384 816910	C	3–11
Netherbrook Primary School Chester Road, Netherton, DY2 9RZ ☎ 01384 818415	C	3–11
Netherton CofE Primary School Highbridge Road, Netherton, DY2 0HU ☎ 01384 816895	VC	3–11
Olive Hill Primary School Springfield Road, B62 8JZ ☎ 01384 818855	C	3–11
Priory Primary School Cedar Road, Priory Estate, DY1 4HN ☎ 01384 816845	C	3–11
Quarry Bank Primary School High Street, Quarry Bank, DY5 2AD ☎ 01384 818750	C	3–11
Queen Victoria Primary School Bilston Street, Sedgley, DY3 1JB ☎ 01384 812545	C	3–11
Red Hall Primary School Zoar Street, Lower Gornal, DY3 2PA ☎ 01384 813850	C	3–11
Rufford Primary School Bredon Avenue, DY9 7NR ☎ 01384 818975	C	3–11

School name, address and telephone number	Type	Age
St Joseph's RC Primary School Hillcrest Road, DY2 7PW ☎ 01384 818925	VA	3–11
St Mark's CofE Primary School High Street, Pensnett, DY5 4DZ ☎ 01384 818935	VC	3–11
Sledmere Primary School School Drive, off Buffery Road, DY2 8EH ☎ 01384 818425	C	3–11
Tenterfields Primary School Tenterfields, B63 3LH ☎ 01384 818560	C	3–11
Wollescote Primary School Drummond Road, Wollescote, DY9 8YA ☎ 01384 818500	C	3–11
Wrens Nest Primary School Foxglove Road, Wrens Nest Estate, DY1 3NQ ☎ 01384 818515	C	3–11

918 HEREFORD AND WORCESTER

School name, address and telephone number	Type	Age
Broadlands Primary School Prospect Walk, Tupsley, HR1 1NZ ☎ 01432 266772	C	3–11
Dines Green Primary School Tudor Way, WR2 5QH ☎ 01905 423228	C	3–11
Elbury Mount Primary School Fairfield Close, WR4 9TX ☎ 01905 25261	C	3–11
Gorse Hill Primary School Hollymount Road, WR4 9SG ☎ 01905 23159	C	3–11
Great Malvern Primary School Pickersleigh Road, WR14 2BY ☎ 01684 574219	C	3–11
Kington Primary School HR5 3AL ☎ 01544 230363	C	3–11
Lord Scudamore Primary School Friar Street, HR4 0AS ☎ 01432 273951	C	3–11
Meadow Green Primary School Meadow Road, Wythall, B47 6EQ ☎ 01564 823495	C	3–11
Poolbrook Primary School Bluebell Close, Poolbrook, WR14 3QR ☎ 01905 575179	C	3–11
St Clement's CofE Primary School Henwick Road, WR2 5NS ☎ 01905 423861	VA	3–11
Somers Park Primary School Somers Park Avenue, WR14 1SE ☎ 01684 572949	C	3–11
Stanley Road Primary School Stanley Road, WR5 1BD ☎ 01905 355043	C	3–11
Weobley Primary School Weobley, HR4 8QL ☎ 01544 318273	C	3–11
Withington Primary School Withington, HR1 3QE ☎ 01432 850289	C	3–11

333 SANDWELL

School name, address and telephone number	Type	Age
Bearwood Junior and Infant School Bearwood Road, B66 4HB ☎ 0121 434 4499	C	3–11
Blackheath Primary School Powke Lane, B65 0AB ☎ 0121 559 1033	C	3–11
Brandhall County Primary School Edinburgh Road, B68 0ST ☎ 0121 422 5336	C	3–11
Brickhouse Junior and Infant School Dudhill Road, B65 8HS ☎ 0121 559 1629	C	3–11
The Cape Primary School Cape Hill, B66 4SH ☎ 0121 558 1667	C	3–11
Charlemont Junior and Infant School Willett Road, B71 3DL ☎ 0121 588 2230	C	3–11
Christ Church CofE (Aided) Primary School Albert Street, B69 4DE ☎ 0121 552 3625	VA	3–11
Hargate Junior and Infant School Hargate Lane, B71 1PG ☎ 0121 553 4178	C	3–11
Holy Name RC Junior and Infant School Cross Lane, Great Barr, B43 6LN ☎ 0121 357 3216	VA	3–11
Holy Trinity CofE Junior and Infant School Trinity Road South, B70 6NF ☎ 0121 553 1573	VC	3–11
Holyhead Primary School Holyhead Road, WS10 7PZ ☎ 0121 556 0114	C	3–11
Joseph Turner Junior and Infant School Powis Avenue, DY4 0RN ☎ 0121 557 8733	C	3–11
Langley Primary School Titford Road, B69 4QB ☎ 0121 552 1744	C	3–11
Leasowes Primary School Nine Leasowes, B66 1JA ☎ 0121 558 1650	C	3–11
Lodge Primary School Oak Lane, B70 8PN ☎ 0121 553 2389	C	3–11
Old Hill Junior and Infant School Lawrence Lane, B64 6DR ☎ 01384 569213	C	3–11
Old Park Primary School Old Park Road, WS10 9LX ☎ 0121 526 2669	C	3–11
Park Hill Primary School Coronation Road, WS10 0TJ ☎ 0121 556 2188	C	3–11
Princes End Primary School Tibbington Terrace, DY4 9QJ ☎ 0121 557 1773	C	3–11
Rounds Green Primary School Brades Road, B69 2DP ☎ 0121 552 1910	C	3–11
Rowley Hall Primary School Windsor Road, B65 9HU ☎ 0121 559 1400	C	3–11
Ryders Green Primary School Claypit Lane, B70 9UJ ☎ 0121 553 0658	C	3–11
Sacred Heart RC Junior and Infant School Victoria Road, DY4 8SW ☎ 0121 557 1511	VA	3–11
St Gregory's RC Junior and Infant School Park Road, B67 5HX ☎ 0121 429 4609	VA	3–11

173

School name, address and telephone number	Type	Age
St Margaret's CofE Junior Infant and Nursery School Birmingham Road, Great Barr, B43 7AP ☎ 0121 357 2758	VA	3–11
St Martin's CofE Junior and Infant School Lower Church Lane, DY4 7PG ☎ 0121 557 1543	VC	3–11
St Mary's RC Primary School Manor House Road, WS10 9PN ☎ 0121 505 3595	VA	3–11
St Matthew's CofE Junior and Infant School Windmill Lane, B66 3LX ☎ 0121 558 1651	VA	3–11
St Paul's CofE Primary School Robert Road, DY4 9BH ☎ 0121 557 2573	VC	3–11
"St Philip's RC Junior, Infant & Nursery School" Messenger Road, B66 3DU ☎ 0121 558 1643	VA	3–11
Temple Meadow Junior and Infant School Wrights Lane, B64 6RH ☎ 01384 569021	C	3–11
Tividale Hall Junior and Infant School Regent Road, Tividale, B69 1TR ☎ 01384 254865	C	3–11
Tividale Primary School Dudley Road West, Tividale, B69 2HT ☎ 0121 557 1765	C	3–11
Wednesbury Oak Primary School Greenacre Road, DY4 0AR ☎ 0121 556 3387	C	3–11

334 SOLIHULL

School name, address and telephone number	Type	Age
Alcott Hall Junior and Infant School Lime Grove, Chelmsley Wood, B37 7PY ☎ 0121 770 4349	C	3–11
Balsall Common Primary School Balsall Street East, Balsall Common, CV7 7FS ☎ 01676 532254	C	3–11
Bentley Heath CofE Primary School Widney Close, Bentley Heath, B93 9AS ☎ 01564 772132	VC	3–11
Bosworth Wood Junior Infant School Auckland Drive, Chelmsley Wood, B36 0DD ☎ 0121 748 1318	C	3–11
Burtons Farm Primary School Kingfisher Drive, Chelmsley Wood, B36 0SZ ☎ 0121 770 4088	C	3–11
Cheswick Green Junior and Infant School Cheswick Way, Shirley, B90 4HG ☎ 01564 703336	C	3–11
Coleshill Heath Primary School Marlene Croft, Chelmsey Wood, B37 7JT ☎ 0121 770 4340	C	3–11
George Fentham Endowed Junior and Infant School Fentham Road, Hampton-in-Arden, B92 0AY ☎ 01675 442800	VA	3–11
Green Lanes Primary School Tamar Drive, Chelmsley Wood, B36 0SY ☎ 0121 748 2360	C	3–11
Greswold Junior and Infant School Buryfield Road, B91 2AZ ☎ 0121 705 4738	C	3–11
Hatchford (GM) Primary School Yorklea Croft, Chelmsley Wood, B37 5EG ☎ 0121 770 4050	GM	3–11
Monkspath Primary School Farmhouse Way, Shirley, B90 4EH ☎ 0121 705 2686	C	3–11
Peterbrook Primary School High Street, Solihull Lodge, Shirley, B90 1HR ☎ 0121 430 2545	C	3–11
St Anne's RC Primary School Nineacres Drive, Chelmsley Wood, B37 5DD ☎ 0121 770 3878	VA	3–11
St Anthony's RC Junior Infant and Nursery School Fordbridge Road, Kingshurst, B37 6LW ☎ 0121 770 3168	VA	3–11
St John The Baptist Junior Infant and Nursery School Arran Way, Smiths Wood, B36 0QE ☎ 0121 770 1892	VA	3–11
St Mary and St Margaret's CofE (Aided) Junior and Infant School Southfield Avenue, Castle Bromwich, B36 9AX ☎ 0121 747 2025	VA	3–11
Tidbury Green Junior and Infant School Dickens Heath Road, Tidbury Green, B90 1QW ☎ 01564 823189	C	3–11
Ulverley Junior and Infant School Rodney Road, B92 8RZ ☎ 0121 742 3251	C	3–11
Windy Arbor Junior and Infant School Woodlands Way, Chelmsley Wood, B37 6RN ☎ 0121 770 4964	C	3–11
Yorkswood Primary School Kingshurst Way, Kingshurst, B37 6DF ☎ 0121 770 3144	C	3–11

860 STAFFORDSHIRE

School name, address and telephone number	Type	Age
Birds Bush Primary School Birds Bush Road, Belgrave, B77 2NE ☎ 01827 285751	C	3–11
Castlechurch Primary School Tennyson Road, ST17 9SY ☎ 01785 258032	C	3–11
Chadsmead Primary School Friday Acre, WS13 7HJ ☎ 01543 510600	C	3–11
Cheadle Primary School The Avenue, Cheadle, ST10 1EN ☎ 01538 753227	C	3–11
Chesterton Primary School Brittain Avenue, Chesterton, ST5 7NT ☎ 01782 561255	C	3–11
Churchfields Primary School School Street, Chesterton, ST5 7HY ☎ 01782 562049	C	3–11
Dumolo's County Primary School Hawksworth, Glascote Heath, B77 2HH ☎ 01827 475020	C	3–11
Flash Ley County Primary School Hawksmoor Road, ST17 9DR ☎ 01785 356642	C	3–11
The Grove Primary School Highfields Grove, ST17 9RF ☎ 01785 251098	C	3–11
Hayes Meadow Primary School Spode Avenue, Handsacre, WS15 4EU ☎ 01543 490616	C	3–11
Heathcote County Primary School The Drive, Alsagers Bank, ST7 8BB ☎ 01782 720406	C	3–11
Holly Grove Primary School Holly Grove Lane, WS7 8LU ☎ 01543 278620	C	3–11

School name, address and telephone number	Type	Age
Holy Trinity (Controlled) Primary School Wetmore Road, DE14 1SN ☎ 01283 239495	VC	3–11
Huntington Primary School Stafford Road, Huntington, WS12 4PD ☎ 01543 502115	C	3–11
The Jerome Primary School Hussey Road, Norton Canes, WS11 3NT ☎ 01543 278595	C	3–11
The John Bamford School Crabtree Way, Etching Hill, WS15 2PA ☎ 01889 585022	C	3–11
Landywood Primary School Holly Lane, Landywood, Great Wyrley, WS6 6AQ ☎ 01922 857020	C	3–11
Norton Canes Primary School School Road, Norton Canes, WS11 3SQ ☎ 01543 279402	C	3–11
St Giles' and St George's CofE (C) Primary School Barracks Road, ST5 1SL ☎ 01782 616891	VC	3–11
St Mary's RC (A) Primary School Hunter Road, WS11 3AE ☎ 01543 503471	VA	3–11
St Mary's RC Primary School Cruso Street, ST13 8BW ☎ 01538 382403	VA	3–11
Silverdale County Primary School The Racecourse, Silverdale, ST5 6PB ☎ 01782 624264	C	3–11
Springhill County Primary School Moss Bank Avenue, Chasetown, WS7 8UN ☎ 01543 510460	C	3–11
Tillington Manor Primary School Young Avenue, ST16 1PW ☎ 01785 255245	C	3–11
Waterhouses CofE Primary School Waterfall Lane, Waterhouses, ST10 3HT ☎ 01538 308356	VC	3–11
Westfield Primary School Ounsdale Road, Wombourne, WV5 8BH ☎ 01902 892143	C	3–11

861 STOKE ON TRENT

School name, address and telephone number	Type	Age
Ash Green Primary School The Lea, Trentham, ST4 8BX ☎ 01782 658977	C	3–11
Bentilee Primary School Beverley Drive, Ubberley, ST2 0QD ☎ 01782 312614	C	3–11
Blurton Primary School Poplar Drive, Blurton, ST3 3AZ ☎ 01782 319507	C	3–11
Brookhouse Green Primary School Wellfield Road, Bucknall, ST2 0DP ☎ 01782 281122	C	3–11
Cauldon Primary School Cauldon Road, Shelton, ST4 2DZ ☎ 01782 235711	C	3–11
Eaton Park Primary School Arbourfield Drive, Bucknall, ST2 9PF ☎ 01782 234760	C	3–11
Florence Primary School Lilleshall Street, Longton, ST3 4NH ☎ 01782 313533	C	3–11
Forest Park County Primary School Woodall Street, Waterloo Road, Cobridge, ST1 5ED ☎ 01782 234979	C	3–11
Hanley St Luke's CofE Aided Primary School Wellington Road, Hanley, ST1 3QH ☎ 01782 234390	VA	3–11
Hill Top Primary School Greenhead Street, Burslem, ST6 4AF ☎ 01782 234969	C	3–11
Hollywall Primary School Burnaby Road, Sandyford, Tunstall, ST6 5PT ☎ 01782 235 055	C	3–11
Mill Hill Primary School Sunnyside Avenue, Tunstall, ST6 6ED ☎ 01782 234466	C	3–11
New Ford Primary School Brownley Road, Smallthorne, ST6 1PY ☎ 01782 234605	C	3–11
North Primary School North Road, Cobridge, ST6 2BP ☎ 01782 235070	C	3–11
Norton Primary School Norton Lane, Norton-in-the-Moors, ST6 8BZ ☎ 01782 234792	C	3–11
Oakhill Primary School Rookery Lane, Oakhill, ST4 5NS ☎ 01782 235238	C	3–11
Our Lady and Benedict RC Primary School Abbey Lane, Abbey Hulton, ST2 8AU ☎ 01782 234646	VA	3–11
Packmoor County Primary School Carr Street, Packmoor, ST7 4SP ☎ 01782 234544	C	3–11
Pinewood Primary School Pinewood Crescent, Meir, ST3 6HZ ☎ 01782 318145	C	3–11
Queen's Primary School Brocksford Street, Fenton, ST4 3HA ☎ 01782 233440	C	3–11
St George and St Martin's RC (A) Primary School Boulton Street, Birches Head, ST1 2NQ ☎ 01782 219977	VA	3–11
St Maria Goretti Primary School Aylesbury Road, Bucknall, ST2 0LY ☎ 01782 234737	VA	3–11
St Peter's RC (A) Primary School Waterloo Road, Cobridge, ST6 3HL ☎ 01782 235040	VA	3–11
St Teresa's RC Primary School Stone Road, Trent Vale, ST4 6SP ☎ 01782 235005	VA	3–11
St Wilfrid's RC (Aided) Primary School Queen's Avenue, Tunstall, ST6 6EE ☎ 01782 838496	VA	3–11
Smallthorne Primary School Regina Street, Smallthorne, ST6 1PW ☎ 01782 235265	C	3–11
Sneyd Green Primary School Sneyd Street, Burslem, ST6 2NS ☎ 01782 234460	C	3–11
Summerbank Central Primary School Summerbank Road, Tunstall, ST6 5HA ☎ 01782 837765	C	3–11
Sutherland Primary School Beaconsfield Drive, Blurton, ST3 3DY ☎ 01782 313977	C	3–11
Trent Vale CofE (Aided) Primary School Newcastle Road, Trent Vale, ST4 6NS ☎ 01782 234989	VA	3–11
Whitfield Valley Primary School Oxford Road, Fegg Hayes, ST6 6TD ☎ 01782 837299	C	3–11

School name, address and telephone number	Type	Age
335 WALSALL		
Abbey Junior Mixed and Infant School Glastonbury Crescent, Mossley Estate, Bloxwich, WS3 2RP ☎ 01922 710753	C	3–11
Birchills CofE Primary Community School Farringdon Street, WS2 8UH ☎ 01922 721063	VC	3–11
Blackwood School Blackwood Road, Streetly, B74 3PH ☎ 0121 353 1876	C	3–11
Busill Jones County Primary School Ashley Road, Bloxwich, WS3 2QF ☎ 01922 710700	C	3–11
Butts Primary School Butts Road, WS4 2AH ☎ 01922 721073	C	3–11
Caldmore Primary School Carless Street, WS1 3RH ☎ 01922 721359	C	3–11
Clothier Street Primary School Harry Perks Street, WV13 1BN ☎ 01902 368764	C	3–11
County Bridge Junior Mixed and Infant School Anson Road, Bentley, WS2 0DH ☎ 01922 720718	C	3–11
Green Rock Junior Mixed and Infant School Mersey Road, Blakenall, WS3 1NP ☎ 01922 710164	C	3–11
Greenfield Primary School Coalheath Lane, Shelfield, WS4 1PL ☎ 01922 682234	C	3–11
Harden Primary School Goldsmith Road, Harden, WS3 1DL ☎ 01922 710182	C	3–11
King Charles Primary School Wilkes Avenue, Bentley, WS2 0JN ☎ 01922 721368	C	3–11
Kings Hill Junior Mixed and Infant School Old Park Road, WS10 9JG ☎ 0121 568 6301	C	3–11
Lakeside Junior Mixed and Infant School Noose Crescent, off Noose Lane, WV13 3AN ☎ 01902 366485	C	3–11
Leamore Junior Mixed and Infant School Bloxwich Road, Leamore, WS3 2BB ☎ 01922 710514	C	3–11
Lindens Junior Mixed and Infant School Hundred Acre Road, Streetly, B74 2BB ☎ 0121 353 9273	C	3–11
Little London Junior Mixed and Infant School Stafford Street, WV13 2PG ☎ 01902 368859	C	3–11
Lodge Farm Junior Mixed and Infant School Pineneedle Croft, WV12 4BU ☎ 01902 368587	C	3–11
Lower Farm Junior Mixed and Infant School Bakewell Close, Bloxwich, WS3 3QH ☎ 01922 710479	C	3–11
Manor Primary School GM Briar Avenue, Streetly, B74 3HX ☎ 0121 353 1738	GM	3–11
Meadow View Primary School Frampton Way, Great Barr, B43 7UJ ☎ 0121 366 6182	C	3–11
Millfield Primary School Catshill Road, Brownhills, WS8 6BN ☎ 01543 452513	C	3–11
Old Church CofE (Controlled) School School Street, Darlaston, WS10 8DL ☎ 0121 568 6329	VC	3–11
Pelsall Village Junior Mixed and Infant School Old Town Lane, Pelsall, WS3 4NJ ☎ 01922 682073	C	3–11
Pheasey Park Farm Primary School Wimperis Way, Great Barr, B43 7LH ☎ 0121 366 6183	GM	3–11
Pool Hayes Junior Mixed and Infant School Bridgnorth Grove, WV12 4RX ☎ 01902 368144	C	3–11
Redhouse Junior Mixed and Infant School Gorsey Way, Aldridge, WS9 0EQ ☎ 01922 743840	C	3–11
Rushall Junior Mixed and Infant School Pelsall Lane, Rushall, WS4 1NQ ☎ 01922 682300	C	3–11
Ryders Hayes Junior Mixed and Infant School Gilpin Crescent, Pelsall, WS3 4HX ☎ 01922 683008	C	3–11
St Anne's RC Junior Mixed and Infant School Blackwood Road, Streetly, B74 3PL ☎ 0121 353 5114	VA	3–11
St Bernadette's RC Junior Mixed and Infant School Narrow Lane, Brownhills, WS8 6HX ☎ 01543 452921	VA	3–11
St Francis RC Primary School Mill Road, Shelfield, WS4 1RH ☎ 01922 682583	VA	3–11
St John's CofE Junior Mixed and Infant School Brook Lane, Walsall Wood, WS9 9NA ☎ 01543 452197	VC	3–11
St Mary's RC Primary School Jesson Road, WS1 3AY ☎ 01922 720711	VA	3–11
Salisbury Primary School Salisbury Street, Darlaston, WS10 8BQ ☎ 0121 568 6779	C	3–11
Woodlands Junior Mixed and Infant School Bloxwich Road North, Short Heath, WV12 5PR ☎ 01922 710613	C	3–11
937 WARWICKSHIRE		
Keresley Newland Primary School Grove Lane, Keresley End, CV7 8JZ ☎ 01203 332434	C	3–11
Park Lane Primary School Park Lane, CV10 8NL ☎ 01203 382924	C	3–11
St Mary's RC Primary School and Nursery Daventry Road, Southam, CV33 0PP ☎ 01926 812512	VA	3–11
Welford-on-Avon Primary School Headland Road, Welford-on-Avon, CV37 8ER ☎ 01789 750214	C	3–11
Wembrook Primary School Avenue Road, CV11 4LU ☎ 01203 382961	C	3–11
Wood End Primary School Wood Street, Wood End, CV9 2QL ☎ 01827 872237	C	3–11

School name, address and telephone number	Type	Age
336 WOLVERHAMPTON		
All Saints CofE Junior and Infant School All Saints Road, WV2 1EL ☎ 01902 352340	VC	3-11
Bilston CofE Junior and Infant School Albany Crescent, WV14 0HU ☎ 01902 353886	VC	3-11
Bingley Junior and Infant School Aston Street, Penn Fields, WV3 0HY ☎ 01902 312193	C	3-11
Brickkiln Junior and Infant School Great Brickkiln Street, WV3 0PR ☎ 01902 312172	C	3-11
Castlecroft Junior and Infant School Windmill Crescent, Castlecroft, WV3 8HS ☎ 01902 761654	C	3-11
Claregate Junior and Infant School Chester Avenue, Tettenhall, WV6 9JU ☎ 01902 558575	C	3-11
Corpus Christi RC Junior and Infant School Ashmore Avenue, Ashmore Park, Wednesfield, WV11 2LT ☎ 01902 305976	VA	3-11
Danesmore Park Junior and Infant School Russell Close, Wednesfield, WV11 2LA ☎ 01902 558551	C	3-11
Dunstall Hill Junior and Infant School Dunstall Avenue, WV6 0NH ☎ 01902 312173	C	3-11
Ettingshall Junior and Infant School Herbert Street, WV14 0NF ☎ 01902 353946	C	3-11
The Giffard RC Junior and Infant School Hordern Close, Hordern Road, Newbridge, WV6 0HR ☎ 01902 752145	VA	3-11
Goldthorn Park Junior and Infant School Ward Road, Penn, WV4 5ET ☎ 01902 342814	C	3-11
Graiseley Junior and Infant School Graiseley Hill, WV2 4NE ☎ 01902 312175	C	3-11
Grove Junior and Infant School Caledonia Road, Parkfields, WV2 1HZ ☎ 01902 352353	C	3-11
Hill Avenue Junior and Infant School Hill Avenue, Lanesfield, WV4 6PY ☎ 01902 880396	C	3-11
Holy Trinity RC Junior and Infant School Fraser Street, WV14 7PD ☎ 01902 353942	VA	3-11
Lanesfield Junior and Infant School Newman Avenue, Lanesfield, WV4 6BZ ☎ 01902 353884	C	3-11
Long Knowle Junior and Infant School Blackwood Avenue, Wednesfield, WV11 1EB ☎ 01902 305978	C	3-11
Long Ley Junior and Infant School Long Ley, Heath Town, WV10 0HG ☎ 01902 352355	C	3-11
Loxdale Junior and Infant School Chapel Street, WV14 0PH ☎ 01902 558570	C	3-11
Merridale Junior and Infant School Aspen Way, WV3 0UP ☎ 01902 312176	C	3-11
Moat House Junior and Infant School Moat House Lane East, Wednesfield, WV11 3DB ☎ 01902 731809	C	3-11
Oxley Junior and Infant School Ripon Road, Bushbury Lane, WV10 9TR ☎ 01902 312177	C	3-11
Perry Hall Junior and Infant School Colman Avenue, Wednesfield, WV11 3RT ☎ 01902 366831	C	3-11
St Alban's CofE Junior and Infant School St Albans Close, Ashmore Park, Wednesfield, WV11 2PF ☎ 01902 305947	VC	3-11
St Anthony's RC Junior and Infant School Stafford Road, Fordhouses, WV10 6NW ☎ 01902 397623	VA	3-11
St Bartholomew's CofE Junior and Infant School Sedgley Road, Penn, WV4 5LG ☎ 01902 341542	VC	3-11
St Martin's CofE Junior and Infant School Wallace Road, Bradley, WV14 8BS ☎ 01902 353966	VC	3-11
St Mary's RC Junior and Infant School Cannock Road, Fallings Park, WV10 8PG ☎ 01902 305982	VA	3-11
St Michael's RC Junior and Infant School Telford Gardens, Merry Hill, WV3 7LE ☎ 01902 334766	VA	3-11
St Patrick's RC Junior and Infant School Graiseley Lane, Wednesfield, WV11 1PG ☎ 01902 305949	VA	3-11
St Stephen's CofE Junior and Infant School Woden Road, Heath Town, WV10 0BB ☎ 01902 352371	VC	3-11
Spring Vale Junior and Infant School Kenilworth Crescent, Parkfield, WV4 6SD ☎ 01902 334040	C	3-11
Stowlawn Junior and Infant School Green Park Avenue, Stowlawn, WV14 6EH ☎ 01902 353890	C	3-11
Underhill Junior and Infant School Greenacres Avenue, Underhill Estate, WV10 8NZ ☎ 01902 558556	C	3-11
Villiers Junior and Infant School Prouds Lane, WV14 6PR ☎ 01902 353967	C	3-11
Warstones Junior and Infant School Warstones Road, Penn, WV4 4LU ☎ 01902 653333	C	3-11
Wednesfield Village Junior and Infant School Lichfield Road, Wednesfield, WV11 1TN ☎ 01902 305975	C	3-11
West Park Junior and Infant School Devon Road, Whitmore Reans, WV1 4BE ☎ 01902 558238	C	3-11
Wilkinson Junior and Infant School Walter Road, Bradley, WV14 8UR ☎ 01902 353892	C	3-11
Woden Junior and Infant School Springfield Road, Springfields, WV10 0LH ☎ 01902 352359	C	3-11
Wodensfield Junior and Infant School Woden Avenue, Wednesfield, WV11 1PW ☎ 01902 305955	C	3-11
Wood End Junior and Infant School Wood End Road, Wednesfield, WV11 1YQ ☎ 01902 305984	C	3-11
Woodthorne Junior and Infant School Woodthorne Road South, Tettenhall, WV6 8XL ☎ 01902 757968	C	3-11

School name, address and telephone number	Type	Age

EASTERN

825 BUCKINGHAMSHIRE

	Type	Age
Bell Lane County Combined School Bell Lane, Little Chalfont, HP6 6PF ☎ 01494 764521	C	3–12
Claytons Combined School Wendover Road, SL8 5NS ☎ 01628 525277	C	3–12
Francis Edmonds County Combined School Edmonds Road, Lane End, HP14 3EU ☎ 01494 881169	C	3–12
Haydon Abbey School Weedon Road, HP19 3NS ☎ 01296 482278	C	3–12
Highworth County Combined School Highworth Close, HP13 7PH ☎ 01494 525534	C	3–12
Robertswood County Combined School Denham Lane, Chalfont St Peter, SL9 0EW ☎ 01753 888327	C	3–12
St Peter's CofE Combined School Minniecroft Road, Burnham, SL1 7DE ☎ 01628 602295	VC	3–11

905 CAMBRIDGESHIRE

	Type	Age
Abbotsmede Primary School Kingsley Road, PE1 5JS ☎ 01733 566 847	C	3–11
Colville Primary School Colville Road, Cherry Hinton, CB1 4EJ ☎ 01223 576246	C	3–11
King's Hedges County Primary School Northfield Avenue, CB4 2LG ☎ 01223 518330	C	3–11
Queen Edith County Primary School Godwin Way, CB1 4QP ☎ 01223 712200	C	3–11
St Andrew's CofE Primary School Sand Street, Soham, CB7 5AA ☎ 01353 720345	VC	3–11
Thorpe County Primary School Atherstone Avenue, PE3 9UG ☎ 01733 264340	C	3–11

915 ESSEX

	Type	Age
Blenheim County Primary School School Way, Blenheim Chase, SS9 4HX ☎ 01702 74684	C	3–11
Bonnygate County Primary School Arisdale Avenue, RM15 5BA ☎ 01708 853316	C	3–11
Broadfields County Primary School Freshwaters, CM20 3QA ☎ 01279 454688	C	3–11
Canewdon Endowed Primary School and Nursery Anchor Lane, Canewdon, SS4 3PA ☎ 01702 258238	VC	3–11
Chase Lane Primary School Chase Lane, Dovercourt, CO12 4NB ☎ 01255 502416	GM	3–11
Dilkes County Primary School Garron Lane, RM15 5JQ ☎ 01708 852128	C	3–11
Doggetts County Primary School The Boulevard, SS4 1QF ☎ 01702 546237	C	3–11
The Downs County Primary School and Nursery The Hides, CM20 3RB ☎ 01279 445538	C	3–11
Fairways County Primary School The Fairway, SS9 4QW ☎ 01702 525693	C	3–11
The Frobisher County Primary School Frobisher Drive, Jaywick, CO15 2QH ☎ 01255 427073	C	3–11
Harwich County Primary School and Nursery 66 Main Road, CO12 3LP ☎ 01255 503819	C	3–11
Henham and Ugley County Primary School Henham, CM22 6BP ☎ 01279 850213	C	3–11
The Hereward County Primary School Colebrook Lane, IG10 2LS ☎ 0181 508 6465	C	3–11
Holy Cross RC Primary School Daiglen Drive, RM15 5RP ☎ 01708 853000	VA	3–11
Jack Lobley County Primary School Leicester Road, RM18 7AX ☎ 01375 859100	C	3–11
Katherines Primary School Brookside, CM19 5NJ ☎ 01279 421495	GM	3–11
Laindon Park County Primary School Church Hill, Laindon, SS15 5SE ☎ 01268 544808	C	3–11
Lansdowne County Primary School Alexandra Road, RM18 7BH ☎ 01375 844184	C	3–11
Lexden County Primary School Trafalgar Road, OCO3 5AS ☎ 01206 573519	C	3–11
Lubbins Park County Primary School May Avenue, SS8 7HF ☎ 01268 697181	C	3–11
Maunds Wood County Primary School Parnall Road, CM18 7NG ☎ 01279 436284	C	3–11
Melbourne Park County Primary School Melbourne Avenue, CM1 2DX ☎ 01245 354605	C	3–11
Milton Hall GM Primary School Salisbury Avenue, SS0 7AU ☎ 01702 330758	GM	3–11
North County Primary School John Harper Street, CO1 1RP ☎ 01206 574225	C	3–11
Pear Tree Mead County Primary and Nursery School Trotters Road, CM18 7DA ☎ 01279 424815	C	3–11
Prince Avenue Primary School Hornby Avenue, SS0 0LG ☎ 01702 343604	GM	3–11
Purfleet County Primary School Tank Hill Road, RM19 1TA ☎ 01708 865038	C	3–11

School name, address and telephone number	Type	Age
Ravenscroft County Primary School Nayland Drive, CO16 8TZ ☎ 01255 424328	C	3–11
Rayne County Primary and Nursery School Capel Road, Rayne, CM7 5BZ ☎ 01376 324959	C	3–11
Rochford Primary GM School 6 Ashingdon Road, SS4 1NJ ☎ 01702 544342	GM	3–11
Ryedene County Primary School Ryedene, off Clover Way, Vange, SS16 4SY ☎ 01268 559291	C	3–11
St Mary's RC Primary School Calcutta Road, RM18 7QH ☎ 01375 843254	VA	3–11
Shaw County Primary School Avon Green, RM15 5QJ ☎ 01708 852367	C	3–11
Somers Heath County Primary School Stifford Road, RM15 5LX ☎ 01708 853397	C	3–11
Temple Sutton County Primary School Eastern Avenue, SS2 4BA ☎ 01702 468582	C	3–11
The Thomas Willingale GM School The Broadway, IG10 3SR ☎ 0181 508 7287	GM	3–11
Vange County Primary School & Nursery London Road, Vange, SS16 4QA ☎ 01268 552160	C	3–11
West Thurrock County Primary School The Rookery, London Road, West Thurrock, RM20 3HX ☎ 01708 866743	C	3–11
The Westborough Primary School Macdonald Avenue, SS0 9BS ☎ 01702 349249	GM	3–11
Woodside County Primary School Grangewood Avenue, Little Thurrock, RM16 2GJ ☎ 01375 372513	C	3–11

919 HERTFORDSHIRE

School name, address and telephone number	Type	Age
Abbots Langley Junior Mixed and Infant School Parsonage Close, WD5 0BQ ☎ 01923 263174	C	3–11
All Saints CofE Primary School and Nursery Parsonage Lane, CM23 5BE ☎ 01279 836006	VA	3–11
Applecroft School Applecroft Road, AL8 6JZ ☎ 01707 323758	C	3–11
Ashwell Junior Mixed and Infant School Silver Street, Ashwell, SG7 5QL ☎ 01462 742297	C	3–11
Aycliffe Drive Junior Mixed and Infant School Aycliffe Drive, HP2 6LJ ☎ 01442 267850	C	3–11
Bedmond Junior Mixed and Infant School Meadow Way, Bedmond, WD5 0RD ☎ 01923 262825	C	3–11
Bengeo County Primary School The Avenue, Bengeo, SG14 3DX ☎ 01992 582765	C	3–11
Christ Church VA Junior Mixed and Infant School New Road, SG12 7BT ☎ 01920 462158	VA	3–11
Cranborne Primary School Laurel Fields, Mutton Lane, EN6 3AD ☎ 01707 652714	C	3–11
Cuffley Primary School Theobalds Road, Cuffley, EN6 4HN ☎ 01707 874677	GM	3–11
Fairfields Junior Mixed and Infant School Rosedale Way, Cheshunt, EN7 6JG ☎ 01992 633195	C	3–11
Five Oaks Primary and Nursery School Travellers Lane, AL10 8TQ ☎ 01707 264712	C	3–11
Gade Valley Junior Mixed Infant and Nursery School Gadebridge Road, HP1 3DT ☎ 01442 391 324	C	3–11
Grove Road Primary School Grove Road, HP23 5PD ☎ 01442 822056	C	3–11
Harvey Road Primary School Harvey Road, Croxley Green, WD3 3BN ☎ 01923 773801	C	3–11
High Wych Junior Mixed and Infant School High Wych, CM21 0JB ☎ 01279 722109	VC	3–11
Highover Junior Mixed and Infant School Cambridge Road, SG4 0JP ☎ 01462 432954	C	3–11
Hillmead Junior Mixed and Infant School and Nursery Heath Row, CM23 5DN ☎ 01279 656876	C	3–11
Holdbrook Junior Mixed and Infant and Nursery School Longcroft Drive, EN8 7QG ☎ 01992 716789	C	3–11
Hollybush Primary School Fordwich Rise, SG14 2DF ☎ 01992 581454	C	3–11
The Holy Family RC Junior Mixed and Infant School Crookhams, AL7 1PG ☎ 01707 327419	VA	3–11
How Wood Junior Mixed and Infant School Spooners Drive, Park Street, AL2 2HU ☎ 01727 872586	C	3–11
Lannock Junior Mixed and Infant School Whiteway, SG6 2PP ☎ 01462 672805	C	3–11
Leavesden Green Junior Mixed Infant and Nursery School High Road, Leavesden, WD2 7AU ☎ 01923 674143	C	3–11
Ley Park Junior Mixed Infant and Nursery Unit Cozens Lane East, EN10 6QA ☎ 01992 444320	C	3–11
The Leys Primary School Ripon Road, SG1 4QZ ☎ 01438 314148	C	3–11
Little Furze Junior Mixed and Infant School Gosforth Lane, WD1 6RE ☎ 0181 428 1950	C	3–11
Little Reddings Primary and Nursery School Harcourt Road, Bushey, WD2 3PR ☎ 0181 950 5388	GM	3–11
Longlands Primary School and Nursery Nunsbury Drive, Turnford, EN10 6AG ☎ 01992 460072	C	3–11
"Lordship Farm Junior Mixed, Infant & Nursery School" Fouracres, Manor Park Estate, SG6 3UF ☎ 01462 673594	C	3–11
Manor Fields Junior Mixed and Infant School Penningtons, CM23 4LE ☎ 01279 757193	C	3–11
Martindale Junior Mixed Infant and Nursery School Boxted Road, Warners End, HP1 2QS ☎ 01442 256407	C	3–11

179

School name, address and telephone number	Type	Age
Meriden Primary School Harvest End, WD2 4TB ☎ 01923 676380	C	3–11
Micklem Junior Mixed and Infant School Boxted Road, HP1 2QH ☎ 01442 252166	C	3–11
Mill Mead Primary School Port Vale, SG14 3AA ☎ 01992 582776	C	3–11
Morgans Junior Mixed and Infant School Morgans Road, SG13 8DR ☎ 01992 582162	C	3–11
Moss Bury Junior Mixed and Infant School Webb Rise, SG1 5PA ☎ 01438 314724	C	3–11
Nash Mills CofE Junior Mixed and Infant School Belswains Lane, Nash Mills, HP3 9XB ☎ 01442 252972	VA	3–11
New Briars Junior Mixed and Infant School Briars Lane, AL10 8ES ☎ 01707 263158	C	3–11
Orchard Junior Mixed Infant and Nursery School Gammons Lane, WD2 5JW ☎ 01923 672280	C	3–11
Panshanger Junior Mixed and Infant School Daniells, AL7 1QY ☎ 01707 328846	C	3–11
Park Street CofE JMI and Nursery School Branch Road, Park Street, AL2 2LX ☎ 01727 872158	VA	3–11
Priors Wood Junior Mixed and Infant School Cozens Road, SG12 7HZ ☎ 01920 464135	C	3–11
Purwell Junior Mixed and Infant School Fairfield Way, SG4 0PU ☎ 01462 432950	C	3–11
Reddings Junior Mixed and Infant School Bennetts End Road, HP3 8DX ☎ 01442 255314	C	3–11
Richard Whittington Junior Mixed and Infant School Thornbera Gardens, CM23 3NP ☎ 01279 657778	C	3–11
Roundwood Junior Mixed Infant and Nursery School Roundwood Park, AL5 3AD ☎ 01582 460756	C	3–11
The Russell School Brushwood Drive, Chorleywood, WD3 5RR ☎ 01923 284272	C	3–11
The Ryde Junior Mixed Infant & Nursery School Pleasant Rise, AL9 5DR ☎ 01707 267333	C	3–11
St Andrew's CofE Junior Mixed and Infant School Tower Hill, SG10 6DL ☎ 01279 842626	VA	3–11
St Andrew's Junior Mixed and Infant School Stanstead Abbotts, SG12 8EZ ☎ 01920 870097	VC	3–11
St Anthony's RC Junior Mixed and Infant School Croxley View, WD1 8BW ☎ 01923 226987	VA	3–11
St Catherine's Junior Mixed and Infant School Park Road, SG12 0AW ☎ 01920 462653	VC	3–11
St Dominic RC Primary School Southdown Road, AL5 1PF ☎ 01582 760047	VA	3–11
St John's CofE (Aided) Junior Mixed Infant and Nursery School Hertford Road, Digswell, AL6 0BX ☎ 01438 714283	VA	3–11
St John's RC Junior Mixed and Infant School Providence Way, SG7 6TT ☎ 01462 892478	VA	3–11
St Joseph's Catholic Primary School Great Hadham Road, CM23 2NL ☎ 01279 652576	VA	3–11
St Joseph's RC Junior Mixed and Infant School North Road, SG14 2BY ☎ 01992 583148	VA	3–11
St Joseph's RC Junior Mixed Infant School and Nursery Ainsdale Road, South Oxhey, WD1 6DW ☎ 0181 428 5371	VA	3–11
St Mary's CofE Junior Mixed Infant and Nursery School Stockers Farm Road, WD3 1NY ☎ 01923 776529	VA	3–11
St Michael's CofE Primary School Apton Road, CM23 3SN ☎ 01279 652607	VA	3–11
St Nicholas School St Nicholas Close, Elstree, WD6 3EW ☎ 0181 953 3015	VA	3–11
St Peter's Junior Mixed Infant and Nursery School Cottonmill Lane, AL1 1HL ☎ 01727 853075	C	3–11
St Teresa's RC Junior Mixed and Infant School Brook Road, WD6 5HL ☎ 0181 953 3753	VA	3–11
Shenley Junior Mixed Infant and Nursery School London Road, Shenley, WD7 9DX ☎ 01923 855864	C	3–11
Sheredes Primary School Benford Road, EN11 8LL ☎ 01992 465154	C	3–11
Springmead Junior Mixed and Infant School Hillyfields, AL7 2HB ☎ 01707 331508	C	3–11
Templewood Junior Mixed and Infant School Pentley Park, AL8 7SD ☎ 01707 324251	C	3–11
Weston Junior Mixed and Infant School Maiden Street, Weston, SG4 7AG ☎ 01462 790317	VC	3–11
Wheatcroft Junior Mixed and Infant School Stanstead Road, SG13 7HQ ☎ 01992 587899	C	3–11
Wormley Junior Mixed and Infant School St Laurence Drive, EN10 6LH ☎ 01992 465516	VC	3–11
Yorke Mead Junior Mixed and Infant School Dulwich Way, Croxley Green, WD3 3PX ☎ 01923 778420	C	3–11

821 LUTON

Beech Hill Community Primary School Dunstable Road, LU4 8BW ☎ 01582 429 403	C	3–11

School name, address and telephone number	Type	Age
826 MILTON KEYNES		
New Bradwell Combined School Bounty Street, New Bradwell, MK13 0BQ ☎ 01908 312244	C	3-12
St Monica's RC Combined School Currier Drive, Neath Hill, MK14 6HB ☎ 01908 606966	VA	3-12
926 NORFOLK		
Clackclose Primary School Nursery Road, PE38 9PF ☎ 01366 383824	C	3-11
St Edmund's Community Primary School Kilhams Way, PE30 2HU ☎ 01553 772018	C	3-11
Sheringham County Primary School Cooper Road, off Holway Road, NR26 8UH ☎ 01263 823848	C	3-11
Thorpe Hillside Avenue County Primary School Hillside Avenue, Thorpe St Andrew, NR7 0QW ☎ 01603 433453	C	3-11
Wells-next-the-Sea Primary and Nursery School Polka Road, NR23 1JG ☎ 01328 710320	C	3-11
935 SUFFOLK		
Hadleigh Primary School Station Road, Hadleigh, IP7 5HQ ☎ 01473 822161	C	3-11
Hillside School Belstead Avenue, IP2 8NU ☎ 01473 601402	C	3-11
Langer County Primary School Langer Road, IP11 8HL ☎ 01394 283065	C	3-11
Morland County Primary School Morland Road, IP3 0LH ☎ 01473 727646	C	3-11
Murrayfield Primary School Nacton Road, IP3 9JL ☎ 01473 728564	C	3-11
Priory Heath Primary School Lindbergh Road, IP3 9QU ☎ 01473 728565	C	3-11
Woodbridge County Primary School New Street, IP12 1DT ☎ 01394 382516	C	3-11
SOUTH WEST		
800 BATH AND NORTH EAST SOMERSET		
Keynsham County Primary School Kelston Road, Keynsham, BS31 2JH ☎ 0117 986 2039	C	3-11
The Midsomer Norton Primary School High Street, Midsomer Norton, BA3 2DR ☎ 01761 412289	C	3-11
St Andrew's CofE VA Primary School Northampton Street, Julian Road, BA1 2SN ☎ 01225 310135	VA	3-11
801 CITY OF BRISTOL		
Ashton Gate Primary School Ashton Gate Road, BS3 1SZ ☎ 0117 966 3600	C	3-11
Avonmouth CofE Primary School Catherine Street, Avonmouth, BS11 9LG ☎ 0117 982 3595	VC	3-11
Badocks Wood Primary School Doncaster Road, Southmead, BS10 5PU ☎ 0117 950 4800	C	3-11
Bank Leaze Primary School Corbet Close, Lawrence Weston, BS11 0SN ☎ 0117 982 2759	C	3-11
Begbrook Primary School Begbrook Drive, Stapleton, BS16 1HG ☎ 0117 965 5445	C	3-11
Bishop Road Primary School Bishop Road, Bishopston, BS7 8LS ☎ 0117 924 7131	C	3-11
Blaise Primary and Nursery School Clavell Road, Henbury, BS10 7EJ ☎ 0117 950 2222	C	3-11
Burnbush Primary School Whittock Road, Stockwood, BS14 8DQ ☎ 01275 832961	C	3-11
Fair Furlong Primary School Vowell Close, Withywood, BS13 9HX ☎ 0117 964 2222	C	3-11
Four Acres Primary School Four Acres, Withywood, BS13 8RB ☎ 0117 987 2474	C	3-11
Gay Elms Primary School Withywood Road, Withywood, BS13 9AX ☎ 0117 964 1155	C	3-11
Headley Park Primary School Headley Lane, BS13 7QB ☎ 0117 964 6353	C	3-11
Hotwells Primary School Hope Chapel Hill, BS8 4ND ☎ 0117 927 6787	C	3-11
May Park Primary School Coombe Road, Eastville, BS5 6LD ☎ 0117 951 0106	C	3-11
Millpond Primary School Baptist Street, Baptist Mills, BS5 0YR ☎ 0117 939 3378	C	3-11
Parson Street Primary School Bedminster Road, Bedminster, BS3 5NR ☎ 0117 966 3679	C	3-11
St Anne's Park Primary School Lichfield Road, St Anne's, BS4 4BJ ☎ 0117 977 5736	C	3-11
St Barnabas CofE VC Primary School Albany Road, Montpelier, BS6 5LQ ☎ 0117 955 3178	VC	3-11
St George CofE Primary School Queen's Parade, Brandon Hill, BS1 5XJ ☎ 0117 926 0191	VC	3-11

School name, address and telephone number	Type	Age
St Mary Redcliffe CofE Primary School Windmill Close, Windmill Hill, BS3 4DP ☎ 0117 966 4875	VC	3–11
South Street Primary School South Street, Bedminster, BS3 3AU ☎ 0117 966 3060	C	3–11
Southville Primary School Merrywood Road, Southville, BS3 1EB ☎ 0117 940 6211	C	3–11
Teyfant Community School Teyfant Road, Hartcliffe, BS13 0RG ☎ 0117 964 4011	C	3–11

837 BOURNEMOUTH

Christ The King Primary School Durdells Avenue, Kinson, BH11 9EH ☎ 01202 574277	VA	3–11
Elmrise Primary School Holloway Avenue, BH11 9JN ☎ 01202 574211	C	3–11
Heathlands Primary School Springwater Road, BH11 8HB ☎ 01202 574452	C	3–11
Townsend Primary and Nursery School Jewell Road, Townsend, BH8 0LT ☎ 01202 302121	C	3–11

908 CORNWALL

The Bishops VA CofE Primary School Treninnick Hill, TR7 2SR ☎ 01637 876317	VA	3–11
King Charles VC CofE Primary School Western Terrace, TR11 4EP ☎ 01326 313607	VC	3–11
Lanner County Primary School Lanmoor Estate, Lanner, TR16 6AZ ☎ 01209 216346	C	3–11
Pondhu County Primary School Penwinnick Road, PL25 5DS ☎ 01726 74550	C	3–11
Porthleven County Primary School Torleven Road, Porthleven, TR13 9BX ☎ 01326 562249	C	3–11
Roskear County Primary School Roskear, TR14 8DJ ☎ 01209 714241	C	3–11
St Dennis County Primary School Carne Hill, St Dennis, PL26 8AY ☎ 01726 822546	C	3–11
St Stephen Churchtown Junior and Infant School Creakavose, St Stephen, PL26 7PY ☎ 01726 822568	C	3–11
Sandy Hill County Primary School Sandy Hill, PL25 3AT ☎ 01726 75858	C	3–11
Tregolls County Primary School Chellew Road, TR1 1LH ☎ 01872 274020	C	3–11
Troon County Primary School New Road, Troon, TR14 9ES ☎ 01209 714289	C	3–11
Wadebridge County Primary School Gonvena Hill, PL27 6BL ☎ 01208 814560	C	3–11

911 DEVON

Appledore County Primary School and Nursery Richmond Road, Appledore, EX39 1PF ☎ 01237 474365	C	3–11
Ashleigh CofE Primary School Bevan Road, EX32 8LJ ☎ 01271 345149	VC	3–11
Barne Barton Primary School Poole Park Road, St Budeaux, PL5 1JH ☎ 01752 365321	C	3–11
Beaford Primary School Beaford, EX19 8LJ ☎ 01805 603263	C	3–11
Bradley Barton Primary School Ogwell Mill Road, Bradley Valley, TQ12 1PR ☎ 01626 360276	C	3–11
Bull Point Primary School Foulston Avenue, Bull Point, PL5 1HL ☎ 01752 365297	C	3–11
Combe Mead Primary School Lazenby Road, Wilcombe, EX16 4AL ☎ 01884 253025	C	3–11
Curledge Street Primary School Curledge Street, TQ4 5BA ☎ 01803 557726	C	3–11
Dartington CofE Primary School and Nursery Shinners Bridge, Dartington, TQ9 6JD ☎ 01803 863934	VC	3–11
Dartmouth Primary School Milton Lane, TQ6 9HW ☎ 01803 833521	C	3–11
Decoy Primary School Deer Park Road, TQ12 1DH ☎ 01626 353282	C	3–11
East-the-Water Primary School Mines Road, EX39 4BZ ☎ 01237 475178	C	3–11
Eggbuckland Vale Primary School Charfield Drive, Eggbuckland, PL6 5PS ☎ 01752 703656	C	3–11
Forches Cross Primary School Forches Avenue, EX32 8EF ☎ 01271 343 214	C	3–11
Ford Primary School Cambridge Road, Ford, PL2 1PU ☎ 01752 567661	C	3–11
Fremington Primary School Beechfield Road, Fremington, EX31 3DD ☎ 01271 373979	C	3–11
Heathcoat Primary School Broad Lane, EX16 5HE ☎ 01884 252445	C	3–11
High Street Primary School High Street, Stonehouse, PL1 3SJ ☎ 01752 225649	C	3–11
Higher Brixham Primary School Chestnut Drive, TQ5 0EQ ☎ 01803 857242	C	3–11
Highweek Primary School Coronation Road, TQ12 1TX ☎ 01626 365550	C	3–11
Holsworthy CofE Primary School North Road, EX22 6HB ☎ 01409 253700	VC	3–11
Honiton Primary School Clapper Lane, EX14 8QF ☎ 01404 42264	C	3–11
Horwood and Newton Tracey Primary School Lovacott, EX31 3PU ☎ 01271 858373	C	3–11

School name, address and telephone number	Type	Age
Langtree Primary School Langtree, EX38 8NF ☎ 01805 601354	C	3–11
Littleham CofE Primary School Littledown Close, Littleham, EX8 2QY ☎ 01395 266535	VC	3–11
Littletown Primary School Honiton Bottom Road, EX14 8EG ☎ 01404 42835	C	3–11
Marlborough Primary School Morice Square, Devonport, PL1 4NJ ☎ 01752 567681	C	3–11
Marpool Primary School Moorfield Road, EX8 3QW ☎ 01395 263961	C	3–11
Morice Town Primary School Charlotte Street, Devonport, PL2 1RJ ☎ 01752 567609	C	3–11
Mount Street Primary School Mount Street, Greenbank, PL4 8NZ ☎ 01752 205091	C	3–11
Mount Wise Primary School James Street, Devonport, PL1 4LA ☎ 01752 567602	C	3–11
North Prospect Primary School Cookworthy Road, North Prospect, PL2 2JS ☎ 01752 567664	C	3–11
Okehampton Primary School Glendale Road, EX20 1JB ☎ 01837 52866	C	3–11
Oldway Primary School Higher Polsham Road, TQ3 2SY ☎ 01803 557190	C	3–11
St Peter's CofE Primary School Rendle Street, PL1 1TP ☎ 01752 667724	VA	3–11
St Sidwell's CofE Combined School York Road, EX4 6PG ☎ 01392 55551	VA	3–12
Sherwell Valley Primary School Hawkins Avenue, TQ2 6ES ☎ 01803 613296	C	3–11
Southway Primary School Bampfylde Way, Southway, PL6 6SR ☎ 01752 706360	C	3–11
Tavistock Primary School Plymouth Road, PL19 8BX ☎ 01822 616044	C	3–11
Tidcombe Primary School Marina Way, EX16 4BP ☎ 01884 252973	C	3–11
Two Moors Primary School Cowleymoor Road, EX16 6HH ☎ 01884 253006	C	3–11
Warberry CofE Primary School Cedars Road, TQ1 1SB ☎ 01803 292642	VC	3–11
Watcombe Primary School Moor Lane, TQ2 8NU ☎ 01803 327419	C	3–11
West and East Putford Primary School West Putford, EX22 7UT ☎ 01409 241371	C	3–11
West Park Primary School Wanstead Grove, PL5 2LY ☎ 01752 771475	C	3–11
Weston Mill Primary School Camel's Head, PL2 2ED ☎ 01752 365250	C	3–11
Yeo Valley Primary School Derby Road, EX32 7BT ☎ 01271 375429	C	3–11

916 GLOUCESTERSHIRE

Severnbanks Primary School Naas Lane, GL15 5AU ☎ 01594 842789	GM	3–11
Whaddon Primary School Clyde Crescent, GL52 5QH ☎ 01242 515775	C	3–11

802 NORTH SOMERSET

Oldmixon Primary School Monkton Avenue, BS24 9DA ☎ 01934 812879	C	3–11

933 SOMERSET

Archbishop Cranmer Community Primary School Cranmer Road, TA1 1XU ☎ 01823 272553	VC	3–11
Bishop Henderson VC CofE Primary School Farley Dell, Coleford, BA3 5PN ☎ 01373 812557	VC	3–11
St Joseph's RC Primary and Nursery School Oxford Street, TA8 1LG ☎ 01278 784641	VA	3–11
Woolavington Primary School Higher Road, Woolavington, TA7 8DP ☎ 01278 683267	C	3–11

803 SOUTH GLOUCESTERSHIRE

Beacon Rise County Primary School Hanham Road, Kingswood, BS15 2NU ☎ 0117 967 3700	C	3–11
Blackhorse Primary School Beaufort Road, Downend, BS16 6UH ☎ 0117 956 0722	C	3–11
Gillingstool Primary School Gillingstool, Thornbury, BS35 2EG ☎ 01454 850063	C	3–11
Parkwall County Primary School Earlstone Crescent, Cadbury Heath, BS30 8AA ☎ 0117 967 4476	C	3–11
St John's Mead CofE Primary School Hounds Road, Chipping Sodbury, BS37 6EE ☎ 01454 866501	VC	3–11

866 SWINDON

Salt Way County Primary School Pearl Road, Middleleaze, SN5 9TD ☎ 01793 881065	C	3–11
Seven Fields Junior and Infant School Leigh Road, Penhill, SN2 5DE ☎ 01793 723833	C	3–11

School name, address and telephone number	Type	Age
865 WILTSHIRE		
Bulford CofE School John French Way, Bulford Village, SP4 9HP ☎ 01980 632309	VC	3–11
Kiwi County Primary School Hubert Hamilton Road, Bulford Camp, SP4 9JY ☎ 01980 632364	C	3–11
Zouch Primary School (GM) Wavell Road, SP9 7JS ☎ 01980 842293	GM	3–11

SOUTH EAST

	Type	Age
903 BERKSHIRE		
Basildon CofE Primary School Beckfords Lane, Upper Basildon, RG8 8PD ☎ 01491 671445	VC	3–11
Broadmoor County Primary School Lower Broadmoor Road, RG45 7HD ☎ 01344 772034	C	3–11
Castleview Combined School Woodstock Avenue, SL3 7LJ ☎ 01753 810615	GM	3–12
Christ The King RC Primary School Lulworth Road, RG2 8LX ☎ 0118 987 3819	VA	3–11
Coley Park Primary School Wensley Road, RG1 6DU ☎ 0118 957 1712	C	3–11
Coley Primary School Wolseley Street, RG1 6AZ ☎ 0118 957 4656	C	3–11
E P Collier Primary School Ross Road, RG1 8DZ ☎ 0118 957 2352	C	3–11
Ellington Primary School Cookham Road, SL6 7JA ☎ 01628 621741	C	3–11
Fir Tree Primary School Fir Tree Lane, RG14 2RA ☎ 01635 42129	C	3–11
Fox Hill Primary School Pond Moor Road, RG12 7JZ ☎ 01344 421809	C	3–11
Foxborough Primary School Common Road, Langley, SL3 8TX ☎ 01753 546376	C	3–11
Harmans Water Primary School Wellington Drive, Harmans Water, RG12 9NE ☎ 01344 420797	C	3–11
Holy Family RC School High Street, Langley, SL3 8NF ☎ 01753 541442	GM	3–12
Holyport CofE Primary and Nursery School Stroud Farm Road, Holyport, SL6 2LP ☎ 01628 627743	VC	3–11
Katesgrove Primary School Dorothy Street, RG1 2NL ☎ 0118 957 4678	C	3–11
Lambourn CofE Primary School Greenways, Lambourn, RG17 7LJ ☎ 01488 71479	VC	3–11
Larchfield County Primary School Bargeman Road, SL6 2SG ☎ 01628 622522	C	3–11
Lynch Hill Combined School Garrard Road, SL2 2HX ☎ 01753 524170	GM	3–12
Manor Primary School 110 Ashampstead Road, RG30 3LJ ☎ 0118 957 5194	C	3–11
Meadow Vale Primary School Moordale Avenue, RG42 1SY ☎ 01344 421046	C	3–11
New Scotland Hill Primary School Grampian Road, GU47 8NQ ☎ 01344 772184	C	3–11
New Town Primary School School Terrace, RG1 3LS ☎ 0118 926 1946	C	3–11
Oxford Road Primary School 146 Oxford Road, RG1 7PJ ☎ 0118 957 3148	C	3–11
Pangbourne Primary School Kennedy Drive, Pangbourne, RG8 7LB ☎ 0118 984 2315	C	3–11
Priory School Orchard Avenue, SL1 6HE ☎ 01628 604767	GM	3–11
Ranikhet County Primary School Spey Road, Tilehurst, RG30 4ED ☎ 0118 942 2733	C	3–11
Ryvers School Trelawney Avenue, SL3 7TS ☎ 01753 544474	GM	3–11
St John's CofE Primary School Orts Road, RG1 3JN ☎ 0118 966 3439	VA	3–11
Springfield Primary School Barton Road, Tilehurst, RG31 5NJ ☎ 0118 942 1797	C	3–11
Woodlands Park County Primary School Heywood Avenue, Woodlands Park, SL6 3JB ☎ 01628 822350	C	3–11
846 BRIGHTON AND HOVE		
Bevendean Primary School Heath Hill Avenue, Lower Bevendean, BN2 4JP ☎ 01273 681292	C	3–11
Fairlight Primary School St Leonards Road, BN2 3AJ ☎ 01273 601270	C	3–11
Middle Street Primary School Middle Street, BN1 1AL ☎ 01273 323184	C	3–11
Queen's Park County Primary School Park Street, BN2 2BN ☎ 01273 686822	C	3–11
St Mark's CofE Primary School Manor Road, BN2 5EA ☎ 01273 605588	VA	3–11
St Mary Magdalen RC Primary School Spring Street, BN1 3EF ☎ 01273 327533	VA	3–11
St Paul's CofE Primary School and Nursery St Nicholas Road, BN1 3LP ☎ 01273 721001	VA	3–11
Westdene Primary School Bankside, Westdene, BN1 5GN ☎ 01273 551900	C	3–11

School name, address and telephone number	Type	Age

845 EAST SUSSEX

Bourne County Primary School Melbourne Road, BN22 8BD ☎ 01323 724729	C	3-11
Castledown Primary School Priory Road, TN34 3QT ☎ 01424 444046	C	3-11
Christchurch CofE Primary School Woodland Vale Road, TN37 6JJ ☎ 01424 422953	VA	3-11
Churchwood Primary School Church-in-the-Wood Lane, TN38 9PB ☎ 01424 852326	C	3-11
Elphinstone Primary School Parker Road, TN34 2DE ☎ 01424 425670	C	3-11
Marshlands Primary School Marshfoot Lane, BN27 2PH ☎ 01323 841420	C	3-11
Red Lake Primary School Rye Road, TN35 5DB ☎ 01424 422979	C	3-11
Robsack Wood County Primary School Whatlington Way, TN38 9TE ☎ 01424 853521	C	3-11
Shinewater County Primary School Milfoil Drive, Langney, BN23 8ED ☎ 01323 762129	C	3-11
Sidley County Primary School Buxton Drive, TN39 4BD ☎ 01424 213611	C	3-11
Willingdon Trees Primary School Magnolia Drive, BN22 0SS ☎ 01323 501251	C	3-11

850 HAMPSHIRE

St Bede CofE Primary School Gordon Road, SO23 7DD ☎ 01962 852463	VC	3-11

922 KENT

Aylesham County Primary School Attlee Avenue, Aylesham, CT3 3BS ☎ 01304 840392	C	3-11
Bishops Down County Primary School Rydal Drive, Culverden Down, TN4 9SU ☎ 01892 520114	C	3-11
Cecil Road County Primary School Cecil Road, DA11 7BT ☎ 01474 534544	C	3-11
George Spurgen County Primary School TC Unit and Nursery Sidney Street, CT19 6HG ☎ 01303 251583	C	3-11
Holy Trinity CofE Primary School Trinity Road, DA12 2PG ☎ 01474 534746	GM	3-11
Lawn County Primary School High Street, Northfleet, DA11 9HB ☎ 01474 365303	C	3-11
Linden Grove Primary School Stanhope Road, TN23 5RN ☎ 01233 622242	C	3-11
New Road Primary School Bryant Street, ME4 5QN ☎ 01634 843084	C	3-11
Northcourt Primary School Dickens Road, DA12 2JY ☎ 01474 352199	C	3-11
Northdown County Primary School Tenterden Way, Northdown, CT9 3RE ☎ 01843 226077	C	3-11
Oak Trees Primary School Oaktree Avenue, ME15 9AX ☎ 01622 755960	C	3-11
St Mary's CofE (Aided) Primary School St Mary's Road, BR8 7BU ☎ 01322 665212	VA	3-11
Sherwood Park County Primary School Friar's Way, TN2 3UA ☎ 01892 520562	C	3-11
Temple Hill County Primary and Nursery School St Edmund's Road, Temple Hill, DA1 5ND ☎ 01322 224600	C	3-11
Wayfield Primary School and Nursery Unit Wayfield Road, ME5 0HH ☎ 01634 843544	C	3-11
Wrotham Road County Primary School Gravesend, Wrotham Road, DA11 0QF ☎ 01474 534540	C	3-11

931 OXFORDSHIRE

Berinsfield County Primary School Wimblestraw Road, Berinsfield, OX10 7LZ ☎ 01865 340420	C	3-11
Edith Moorhouse County Primary School Lawton Avenue, OX18 3HP ☎ 01993 842372	C	3-11
Eynsham School Beech Road, Eynsham, OX8 1LJ ☎ 01865 881294	C	3-11
Grimsbury St Leonard's CofE Primary School Overthorpe Road, OX16 8SB ☎ 01295 262507	VC	3-11
John Blandy School Laurel Drive, Southmoor, OX13 5DJ ☎ 01865 820422	VC	3-11
St Mary's CofE (Controlled) Primary School Southam Road, OX16 7EG ☎ 01295 263026	VC	3-11
St Swithun's CofE Primary School Grundy Crescent, Kennington, OX1 5PS ☎ 01865 739608	VC	3-11
Southwold County Primary School Holm Way, OX6 9UU ☎ 01869 324061	C	3-11
Stanford-in-the-Vale Primary School High Street, Stanford-in-the-Vale, SN7 8LH ☎ 01367 710474	VC	3-11
West Witney Primary School Edington Road, OX8 5FZ ☎ 01993 706249	C	3-11
William Morris Primary School Bretch Hill, OX16 0UZ ☎ 01295 258224	C	3-11
Witney County Primary School Hailey Road, OX8 5HL ☎ 01993 702388	C	3-11
Woodstock CofE Primary School Shipton Road, OX20 1LL ☎ 01993 812209	VC	3-11
Wychwood CofE Primary School Milton Road, Shipton-upon-Wychwood, OX7 6BD ☎ 01993 830059	VC	3-11

School name, address and telephone number	Type	Age
851 PORTSMOUTH		
Paulsgrove Primary School Cheltenham Road, Paulsgrove, PO6 3PL ☎ 01705 375302	C	3–11
Portsdown Primary School Sundridge Close, Wymering, Cosham, PO6 3JL ☎ 01705 378991	C	3–11
St George's Beneficial CofE (C) Primary School Hanover Street, Portsea, PO1 3BN ☎ 01705 822886	VC	3–11
St John's RC Primary School and Nursery Cottage View, Landport, PO1 1PX ☎ 01705 821055	VA	3–11
Somers Park Primary School Somers Road, PO5 4LS ☎ 01705 824828	C	3–11
852 SOUTHAMPTON		
Northam Primary School Kent Street, Northam, SO14 5SP ☎ 01703 225934	C	3–11
St Mary's CofE (C) Primary School Ascupart Street, SO14 1LU ☎ 01703 223930	VC	3–11
Shirley Warren Primary School Warren Crescent, SO16 6AY ☎ 01703 773975	C	3–11
936 SURREY		
Ash Grange County Primary School Ash Church Road, Ash, GU12 6LX ☎ 01252 328589	C	3–11
Broadmere County Primary School Devonshire Avenue, Sheerwater, GU21 5QE ☎ 01932 343747	C	3–11
Chandlers Field Primary School High Street, KT8 2LX ☎ 0181 224 4731	C	3–11
Cuddington Croft Primary School West Drive, Cheam, SM2 7NA ☎ 0181 642 4325	C	3–11
Epsom County Primary School Pound Lane, KT19 8SD ☎ 01372 720608	C	3–11
Furzefield Primary School Delabole Road, Merstham, RH1 3PA ☎ 01737 642842	C	3–11
Hale County Primary School Upper Hale, GU9 0LR ☎ 01252 716729	C	3–11
Hillcroft County Primary School Chaldon Road, CR3 5PG ☎ 01883 342606	C	3–11
Hurst Park County Primary School Hurst Road, KT8 1QW ☎ 0181 979 1709	C	3–11
Kenyngton Manor Primary School Bryony Way, off Beechwood Avenue, TW16 7QL ☎ 01932 783778	C	3–11
Lakeside County Primary School Alphington Avenue, Frimley, GU16 5LL ☎ 01276 24055	C	3–11
Lingfield Primary School Vicarage Road, RH7 6HA ☎ 01342 832626	C	3–11
Marden Lodge Primary School Croydon Road, CR3 6QE ☎ 01883 343014	C	3–11
Merland Rise Primary School St Leonards Road, KT18 5RJ ☎ 01737 354313	C	3–11
Monument Hill Primary School Alpha Road, Maybury, GU22 8HA ☎ 01483 769302	C	3–11
Mytchett County Primary School Hamesmoor Road, Mytchett, GU16 6JB ☎ 01252 544009	C	3–11
Riverview CofE Primary School Riverview Road, West Ewell, KT19 0JP ☎ 0181 337 1245	VC	3–11
St Catherine's Bletchingley Village School & Language Unit Coneybury, Bletchingley, RH1 4PP ☎ 01883 743337	C	3–11
St Charles Borromeo RC School Portmore Way, KT13 8JD ☎ 01932 842617	VA	3–11
St John's County Primary School Victoria Road, Knaphill, GU21 2AS ☎ 01483 476450	C	3–11
St Mark's CofE Primary School Franklyn Road, GU7 2LD ☎ 01483 422924	VA	3–11
St Matthew's CofE (Aided) Primary School Linkfield Lane, RH1 1JF ☎ 01737 762080	VA	3–11
Sythwood County Primary School Sythwood, Horsell, GU21 3AX ☎ 01483 770063	C	3–11
Thorpe Lea Primary School Huntingfield Way, Thorpe Lea, TW20 8DY ☎ 01784 456398	C	3–11
Town Farm Primary School St Mary's Crescent, Stanwell, TW19 7HU ☎ 01784 254380	C	3–11
Westborough County Primary School Southway, GU2 6DA ☎ 01483 575073	C	3–11
Westwood Park County Primary School Southway, GU2 6DT ☎ 01483 504713	C	3–11
938 WEST SUSSEX		
St James' County School St James Road, PO19 4HR ☎ 01243 783939	C	3–11

660 ISLE OF ANGLESEY/SIR YNYS MON

Y Parch Thomas Ellis Ffordd Treseifion, Caergybi, Ynys Mon LL65 1LD ☎ 01407 762387

Yr Ysgol Gymuned Moelfre Moelfre, Ynys Mon, LL72 8HA ☎ 01248 410546

Ysgol Corn Hir Llangefni, Ynys Mon, LL77 7JB ☎ 01248 722558

Ysgol Cylch Y Garn Llanrhuddlad Llanrhuddlad, Caergybi, Ynys Mon, LL65 4HT ☎ 01407 730432

Ysgol Ffrwd Win Llanfaethlu, Caergybi, Ynys Mon, LL65 4YW ☎ 01407 730448

Ysgol Goronwy Owen Benllech, Ynys Mon, LL74 8SG ☎ 01248 852667

Ysgol Gymuned Bodffordd Bodffordd, Llangefni, Ynys Mon, LL77 7LZ ☎ 01248 723384

Ysgol Gymuned Bodorgan Bodorgan ,Ynys Mon, LL62 5AB ☎ 01407 840386

Ysgol Gymuned Bryngwran Bryngwran ,Caergybi, Ynys Mon, LL65 3PP ☎ 01407 720400

Ysgol Gymuned Dwyran Dwyran ,Llanfairpwllgwyngyll, Ynys Mon, LL61 6AQ ☎ 01248, 430447

Ysgol Gymuned Garreglefn Garreglefn, Amlwch, Ynys Mon, LL68 0PH ☎ 01407 710508

Ysgol Gymuned Llanfechell Llanfechell, Amlwch, Ynys Mon, LL68 0SA ☎ 01407 710512

Ysgol Gymuned Pentraeth Pentraeth, Ynys Mon, LL75 8UP ☎ 01248 450315

Ysgol Gymuned Rhosybol Rhosybol, Amlwch, Ynys Mon, LL68 9AP ☎ 01407 830484

Ysgol Gymuned Y Dyffryn Y Fali Dyffryn, Ynys Mon, LL65 3EU ☎ 01407 740518

Ysgol Gynradd Aberffraw Aberffraw, Ty Croes, Ynys Mon, LL63 5EJ ☎ 01407 840471

Ysgol Gynradd Amlwch Amlwch, nys Mon, LL68 9DY ☎ 01407 830414

Ysgol Gynradd Beaumaris Maeshyfryd, Beaumaris, Ynys Mon, LL58 8HL ☎ 01248 810451

Ysgol Gynradd Bodedern Bodedern, Caergybi, Ynys Mon, LL65 3TL ☎ 01407 740201

Ysgol Gynradd Brynsiencyn Brynsiencyn, Llanfairpwll, Ynys Mon, LL61 6HZ ☎ 01248 430457

Ysgol Gynradd Cemaes Cemaes, Ynys Mon, LL67 0LB ☎ 01407 710225

Ysgol Gynradd Esceifiog Y Gaerwen, Ynys Mon, LL60 6DD ☎ 01248 421669

Ysgol Gynradd Kingsland Caergybi, Ynys Mon, LL65 2TH ☎ 01407 763295

Ysgol Gynradd Llanbedrgoch Llanbedrgoch, Ynys Mon, LL76 8SX ☎ 01248 450291

Ysgol Gynradd Llanddeusant Llanddeusant, Caergybi, Ynys Mon, LL65 4AD ☎ 01407 730467

Ysgol Gynradd Llanddona Llanddona, Beaumaris, Ynys Mon, LL58 8TS ☎ 01248 810371

Ysgol Gynradd Llandegfan Llandegfan, Porthaethwy, Ynys Mon, LL59 5UW ☎ 01248 713431

Ysgol Gynradd Llandrygarn Llandrygarn, Ty'n Lon P.O., Caergybi, LL65 3AJ ☎ 01407 720438

Ysgol Gynradd Llanfachraeth Llanfachraeth, Caergybi, LL65 4UY ☎ 01407 740610

Ysgol Gynradd Llangoed Llangoed, Beaumaris, Ynys Mon, LL58 8SA ☎ 01248 490680

Ysgol Gynradd Niwbwrch Niwbwrch, Llanfairpwll, Ynys Mon, LL61 6TE ☎ 01248 440651

Ysgol Gynradd Pencarnisiog Pencarnisiog, Ty Croes, Ynys Mon, LL63 5RY ☎ 01407 810622

Ysgol Gynradd Rhosneigr Rhosneigr, Ynys Mon, LL64 5XA ☎ 01407 810571

Ysgol Gynradd Santes Gwenfaen Rhoscolyn, Caergybi, Ynys Mon, LL65 2DX ☎ 01407 860264

Ysgol Gynradd Y Parc Newry Fields, Caergybi, Ynys Mon, LL65 1LA ☎ 01407 763156

Ysgol Gynradd Y Talwrn Talwrn, Llangefni, Ynys Mon, LL77 7TG ☎ 01248 723363

Ysgol Henblas Llangristiolus, Bodorgan, Ynys Mon, LL62 5DN ☎ 01248 723944

Ysgol Llaingoch South Stack Road, Holyhead, Ynys Mon, LL65 1LD ☎ 01407 762938

Ysgol Llanerch Y Medd Llanerch Y Medd, Ynys Mon, LL71 8DP ☎ 01248 470466

Ysgol Llanfairpwllgwyngyll Llanfairpwll, Ynys Mon, LL61 5TX ☎ 01248 714478

Ysgol Llanfawr Caergybi, Ynys Mon, LL65 2DS ☎ 01407 762552

Ysgol Llangaffo Llangaffo, Gaerwen, Ynys Mon, LL60 6LT ☎ 01248 440666

Ysgol Morswyn Caergybi, Ynys Mon, LL65 2TH ☎ 01407 762233

School name, address and telephone number

Ysgol Parc Y Bont Llanedwen, Llanfairpwll, Ynys Mon, LL61 6EQ ☎ 01248 714460

Ysgol Penysarn Penysarn, Ynys Mon, LL69 9AZ ☎ 01407 830678

Ysgol Santes Fair, St Mary' s R.C. School Longford Road, Holyhead, Anglesey, LL65 1TR ☎ 01407 763176

Ysgol Ty Mawr Capel Coch, Llangefni, Ynys Mon, LL77 7UT ☎ 01248 470397

Ysgol Y Borth Porthaethwy, Ynys Mon, LL59 5HS ☎ 01248 713000

Ysgol Y Ffridd Gwalchmai, Caergybi, Ynys Mon, LL65 4SG ☎ 01407 720477

Ysgol Y Graig Llangefni, Ynys Mon, LL77 7JA ☎ 01248 723092

661 GWYNED

Y.G. Abergynolwyn Abergynolwyn Tywyn, Gwynedd, LL36 9YP ☎ 01654 782257

Y.G. Llanaelhaearn Llanaelhaearn Caernarfon, Gwynedd, LL54 5AL ☎ 01758 750263

Y.G. Llawrybetws Glanrafon Corwen, Gwynedd, LL21 0BA ☎ 01490 460467

Y.G. Llwyngwril Llwyngwril Gwynedd, LL37 2QA ☎ 01341 250530

Y.G. Rhostryfan Rhostryfan Caernarfon, Gwynedd, LL54 7LR ☎ 01286 830727

Y.G. Rhydyclafdy Rhydyclafdy, Pwllheli, Gwynedd, LL53 7YW ☎ 01758 740632

Y.G. Y Groeslon Groeslon, Caernarfon, Gwynedd, LL54 7DT ☎ 01286 830111

Ysgol Abercaseg Bethesda, Bangor, Gwynedd, LL57 3BE ☎ 01248 600194

Ysgol Baladeulyn Nantlle, Caernarfon, Gwynedd, LL54 6BT ☎ 01286 880884

Ysgol Beuno Sant Y Bala Heol y Castell, Bala, LL23 7UU ☎ 01678 520710

Ysgol Bodfeurig Tregarth, Gwynedd, LL57 4RH ☎ 01248 600760

Ysgol Borthygest Porthmadog, Gwynedd, LL49 9UF ☎ 01766 513285

Ysgol Bro Cynfal Ffestiniog, Blaenau Ffestiniog, Gwynedd, LL41 4NF ☎ 01766 762668

Ysgol Bro Hedd Wyn Trawsfynydd, Blaenau Ffestiniog, Gwynedd, LL41 4SE ☎ 01766 540247

Ysgol Bro Lleu Penygroes, Caernarfon, Gwynedd, LL54 6RE ☎ 01286 880883

Ysgol Bro Plennydd Y Ffor, Pwllheli, Gwynedd, LL53 6UP ☎ 01766 810625

Ysgol Bro Tegid Y Bala, Gwynedd, LL23 7BN ☎ 01678 520278

Ysgol Bro Tryweryn Frongoch, Bala, Gwynedd, LL23 7NT ☎ 01678 520740

Ysgol Bronyfoel Y Fron, Caernarfon, Gwynedd, LL54 7BB ☎ 01286 880882

Ysgol Cefn Coch Penrhyndeudraeth, Gwynedd, LL48 6AE ☎ 01766 770291

Ysgol Crud Y Werin Aberdaron, Pwllheli, Gwynedd, LL53 9BP ☎ 01758 760205

Ysgol Cymerau Ffordd Mela, Pwllheli, Gwynedd, LL53 5NU ☎ 01758 612001

Ysgol Dinas Mawddwy Dinas Mawddwy, Machynlleth, Gwynedd, SY20 9LN ☎ 01650 531321

Ysgol Dolbadarn Llanberis, Gwynedd, LL55 4SH ☎ 01286 870711

Ysgol Dyffryn Ardudwy Dyffryn Ardudwy, Gwynedd, LL44 2EP ☎ 01341 247294

Ysgol Edmwnd Prys Gellilydan, Blaenau Ffestiniog, Gwynedd, LL41 4DY ☎ 01766 590348

Ysgol Eifion Wyn Porthmadog, Gwynedd, LL49 9NU ☎ 01766 513286

Ysgol Ein Harglwyddes Caernarfon Road, Bangor, Gwynedd, LL57 2UT ☎ 01248 352463

Ysgol Ffridd Y Llyn Cefnddwysarn, Bala, Gwynedd, LL23 7HE ☎ 01678 530373

Ysgol Foel Gron Mynytho, Pwllheli, Gwynedd, LL53 7RN ☎ 01758 740567

Ysgol Garndolbenmaen Garndolbenmaen, Gwynedd, LL51 9SZ ☎ 01766 750626

Ysgol Glancegin Maesgeirchen, Bangor, Gwynedd, LL57 1ST ☎ 01248 353097

Ysgol Gwaun Gynfi Deiniolen, Gwynedd, LL55 3LT ☎ 01286 870687

Ysgol Gymuned Penisarwaun Penisarwaen, Caernarfon, Gwynedd, LL55 3BW ☎ 01286 870879

Ysgol Gynradd Abererch Abererch, Pwllheli, Gwynedd, LL53 6YU ☎ 01758 613441

Ysgol Gynradd Abersoch Pwllheli, Gwynedd, LL53 7EA ☎ 01758 712764

Ysgol Gynradd Beddgelert Beddgelert, Gwynedd, LL55 4UY ☎ 01766 890307

Ysgol Gynradd Bethel Caernarfon, Gwynedd, LL55 1AX ☎ 01248 670663

School name, address and telephone number

Ysgol Gynradd Bontnewydd Bontnewydd, Caernarfon, Gwynedd, LL55 2UF ☎ 01286 673880

Ysgol Gynradd Brithdir Brithdir, Dolgellau, Gwynedd, LL40 2RH ☎ 01341 423035

Ysgol Gynradd Bryncrug Bryncrug, Tywyn, Gwynedd, LL36 9PR ☎ 01654 710931

Ysgol Gynradd Cae Top Hill Street, Bangor, Gwynedd, LL57 2HA ☎ 01248 352325

Ysgol Gynradd Chwilog Chwilog, Pwllheli, Gwynedd, LL53 6PS ☎ 01766 810627

Ysgol Gynradd Corris Corris, Machynlleth, Powys, SY20 9TQ ☎ 01654 761622

Ysgol Gynradd Croesor Croesor, Penrhyndeudraeth, Gwynedd, LL48 6SR ☎ 01766 770603

Ysgol Gynradd Cwm-y-Glo Cwm-y-Glo, Caernarfon, Gwynedd, LL55 4DE ☎ 01286 870860

Ysgol Gynradd Edern Ffordd y Rhos, Edern, Pwllheli, LL53 8YW ☎ 01758 720272

Ysgol Gynradd Felinwnda Llanwnda, Caernarfon, Gwynedd, LL54 5UG ☎ 01286 830017

Ysgol Gynradd Hirael Orme Road, Bangor, Gwynedd, LL57 1BA ☎ 01248 352182

Ysgol Gynradd Llanbedr Llanbedr, Gwynedd, LL45 2NW ☎ 01341 241422

Ysgol Gynradd Llandwrog Llandwrog, Caernarfon, Gwynedd, LL54 5ST ☎ 01286 830223

Ysgol Gynradd Llanegryn Llanegryn, Tywyn, Gwynedd, LL36 9SS ☎ 01654 710051

Ysgol Gynradd Llanelltyd Llanelltyd, Dolgellau, Gwynedd, LL40 2TA ☎ 01341 423156

Ysgol Gynradd Llanllechid Llanllechid, Bangor, Gwynedd, LL57 3EH ☎ 01248 600600

Ysgol Gynradd Llanrug Caernarfon, Gwynedd, LL55 4AL ☎ 01286 674905

Ysgol Gynradd Maesincla Maesincla Caernarfon, Gwynedd, LL55 1DF ☎ 01286 673787

Ysgol Gynradd Nebo Nebo, Caernarfon, Gwynedd, LL54 6EE ☎ 01286 881273

Ysgol Gynradd Nefyn Ffordd Dewi Sant, Nefyn, Pwllheli, LL53 6EA ☎ 01758 720765

Ysgol Gynradd Pennal Pennal, Machynlleth, Gwynedd, SY20 9JT ☎ 01654 791225

Ysgol Gynradd Rhiwlas Rhiwlas, Bangor, Gwynedd, LL57 4EH ☎ 01248 352483

Ysgol Gynradd Rhosgadfan Rhosgadfan, Caernarfon, Gwynedd, LL54 7EU ☎ 01286 830160

Ysgol Gynradd Talsarnau Talsarnau, Gwynedd, LL47 6TA ☎ 01766 770768

Ysgol Gynradd Talysarn Talysarn, Caernarfon, Gwynedd, LL54 6RH ☎ 01286 880885

Ysgol Gynradd Tanygrisiau Blaenau Ffestiniog, Gwynedd, LL41 3SU ☎ 01766 830795

Ysgol Gynradd Tudweiliog Tudweiliog, Pwllheli, Gwynedd, LL53 8ND ☎ 01758 770669

Ysgol Gynradd Y Felinheli Felinheli, Gwynedd, LL56 4JS ☎ 01248 670748

Ysgol Gynradd Y Ganllwyd Ganllwyd, Dolgellau, Gwynedd, LL40 2TG ☎ 01341 440219

Ysgol Gynradd Y Parc Parc, Bala, Gwynedd, LL23 7BN ☎ 01678 540286

Ysgol Ieuan Gwynedd Rhydymain, Dolgellau, Gwynedd, LL40 2YW ☎ 01341 450636

Ysgol Llanbedrog Llanbedrog, Pwllheli, Gwynedd, LL53 7NU ☎ 01758 740631

Ysgol Llandygai Llandygai, Bangor, Gwynedd, LL57 4HU ☎ 01248 352163

Ysgol Llangybi Llangybi, Pwllheli, Gwynedd, LL53 6DQ ☎ 01766 810564

Ysgol Llanllyfni Llanllyfni, Caernarfon, Gwynedd, LL54 6SH ☎ 01286 880729

Ysgol Llanystumdwy Llanystumdwy, Criccieth, Gwynedd, LL52 0SP ☎ 01766 522961

Ysgol Llidiardau Rhoshirwaen, Pwllheli, Gwynedd, LL53 8LB ☎ 01758 760319

Ysgol Machreth Llanfachreth, Dolgellau, Gwynedd, LL40 2DY ☎ 01341 423036

Ysgol Maenofferen Blaenau Ffestiniog, Gwynedd, LL41 3DL ☎ 01766 831256

Ysgol Morfa Nefyn Morfa Nefyn, Pwllheli, Gwynedd, LL53 6AR ☎ 01758 720870

Ysgol O.M. Edwards Llanuwchllyn, Bala, Gwynedd, LL23 7UB ☎ 01678 540242

Ysgol Pentreuchaf Pentreuchaf, Pwllheli, Gwynedd, LL53 8DZ ☎ 01758 750600

Ysgol Penybryn Tywyn, Gwynedd, LL36 9EF ☎ 01654 710237

Ysgol Pont Y Gof Botwnnog, Pwllheli, Gwynedd, LL53 8RA ☎ 01758 730318

Ysgol Santes Helen Twtil, Caernarfon, Gwynedd, LL55 1PF ☎ 01286 674856

Ysgol Sarn Bach Sarn Bach, Pwllheli, Gwynedd, LL53 7LF ☎ 01758 712714

Ysgol Tanycastell Harlech, Gwynedd, LL46 2SW ☎ 01766 780454

School name, address and telephone number

Ysgol Treferthyr Criccieth, Gwynedd, LL52 0DS ☎ 01766 522300

Ysgol Tregarth Tregarth, Bangor, Gwynedd, LL57 4PG ☎ 01248 600735

Ysgol Waunfawr Waunfawr, Caernarfon, Gwynedd, LL55 4LJ ☎ 01286 650451

Ysgol Y Clogau Bontddu, Dolgellau, Gwynedd, LL40 2UA ☎ 01341 430658

Ysgol Y Faenol Penrhosgarnedd, Bangor, Gwynedd, LL57 2NN ☎ 01248 352162

Ysgol Y Friog Friog, Fairbourne, Gwynedd, LL38 2RQ ☎ 01341 250521

Ysgol Y Garreg Llanfrothen, Penrhyndeudraeth, Gwynedd, LL48 6LJ ☎ 01766 770727

Ysgol Y Gelli Ffordd Bethel, Caernarfon, Gwynedd, LL55 1DU ☎ 01286 674847

Ysgol Y Gorlan Tremadog, Porthmadog, Gwynedd, LL49 9NU ☎ 01766 512773

Ysgol Y Manod Blaenau Ffestiniog, Gwynedd, LL41 3AF ☎ 01766 830272

Ysgol Y Traeth Abermaw, Gwynedd, LL42 1HH ☎ 01341 280479

Ysgol Yr Eifl Trefor, Caernarfon, Gwynedd, LL54 5LU ☎ 01286 660523

Ysgol Yr Hendre Caernarfon, Gwynedd, LL55 2LY ☎ 01286 674332

662 CONWY

Betws Yn Rhos Primary School Betws Yn Rhos, Abergele, LL22 8AP ☎ 01492 680603

Blessed William Davies Bodnant Crescent, Llandudno, Conwy, LL30 1LL ☎ 01492 875930

Conwy Road Infants School Conway Road, Colwyn Bay, Conwy, LL28 5NA ☎ 01492 530876

Douglas Road Infants School Douglas Road, Colwyn Bay, LL29 7PE ☎ 01492 532865

Llandrillo Yn Rhos Primary School Elwy Road, Llandrillo Yn Rhos, Colwyn Bay, LL28 4LX ☎ 01492 549648

Llannefydd School Llannefydd, Denbigh, LL16 5EA ☎ 01745 540228

Mochdre Infants C.P. School Station Road, Mochdre, Conwy, LL28 5EF ☎ 01492 540194

Penmaenrhos Infants School Craig Road, Old Colwyn, Colwyn Bay, LL29 9HN ☎ 01492 515083

St George Controlled Primary School Primrose Hill, St George, Abergele, LL22 9BU ☎ 01745 833213

St Joseph's R.C. Primary School Brackley Avenue, Colwyn Bay, LL29 7UU ☎ 01492 532394

Ysgol Babanod Gyffin Maes-Y-Llan, Conwy, LL32 8NB ☎ 01492 592859

Ysgol Betws-y-Coed Bro Gethin, Betws-Y-Coed, Conwy, LL24 0BP ☎ 01690 710581

Ysgol Bod Alaw Abergele Road, Colwyn Bay, LL29 7ST ☎ 01492 530420

Ysgol Bodafon Ffordd Bodafon, Llandudno, Conwy, LL30 3BA ☎ 01492 547996

Ysgol Bodlondeb Ffordd Bangor, Conwy, LL32 8NU ☎ 01492 593857

Ysgol Bro Aled Llansannan Llansannan, Dinbych, Conwy, LL16 5HN ☎ 01745 870660

Ysgol Bro Cernyw Llangernyw, Abergele, Conwy, LL22 8PP ☎ 01745 860238

Ysgol Bro Gwydir Heol Watling, Llanrwst, LL26 0EY ☎ 01492 640342

Ysgol Capel Garmon Capel Garmon, Llanrwst, Conwy, LL26 0RL ☎ 01690 710287

Ysgol Capelulo Ffordd Treforris, Dwygyfylchi, Penmaenmawr, LL34 6RA ☎ 01492 622693

Ysgol Craig Y Don Clarence Drive, Craig Y Don, Llandudno, LL30 1TD ☎ 01492 878906

Ysgol Deganwy Park Drive, Deganwy, Conwy, LL31 9YB ☎ 01492 581285

Ysgol Dinmael Dinmael, Corwen, Conwy, LL21 0PP ☎ 01492 460240

Ysgol Eglwys Bach Eglwysbach, Bae Colwyn, Conwy, LL28 5UD ☎ 01492 650463

Ysgol Ffordd Dyffryn Ffordd Dyffryn, Llandudno, Conwy, LL30 2LZ ☎ 01492 878907

Ysgol Glan Conwy Ffordd Top Llan, Glan Conwy, Conwy, LL28 5ST ☎ 01492, 580421

Ysgol Glan Gele Ffordd y Morfa, Abergele, Conwy, LL22 7NU ☎ 01745 823584

Ysgol Glan Morfa Ffordd y Morfa, Abergele, Conwy, LL22 7NU ☎ 01745 832922

Ysgol Glanwydden Ffordd Derwen, Bae Penrhyn, Llandudno, LL30 3LB ☎ 01492, 540798

Ysgol Gynradd Dolwyddelan Dolwyddelan, , LL25 0SZ ☎ 01690 750293

Ysgol Gynradd Llysfaen Dolwen Road, Llysfaen, Colwyn Bay, LL29 8SS ☎ 01492 517326

Ysgol Gynradd Ro Wen Ffordd Pont Wgan, Ro Wen, Conwy, LL32 8TS ☎ 01492 650643

School name, address and telephone number

Ysgol Gynradd Tal-Y-Bont Ffordd Conwy, Tal Y Bont, Ger Conwy, LL32 8QF ☎ 01492 660377

Ysgol Llanddoged Llanddoged, Llanrwst, Conwy, LL26 0BJ ☎ 01492 640363

Ysgol Llanddulas Controlled Minffordd Road, Llanddulas, Abergele, LL22 8EW ☎ 01492 516865

Ysgol Llanfair Talhaiarn Llanfair Talhaiarn, Abergele, Conwy, LL22 8SE ☎ 01745 720242

Ysgol Llangelynnin Henryd, Conwy, LL32 8YB ☎ 01492 592898

Ysgol Maelgwn Broad Street, Cyffordd, Llandudno, LL31 9HG ☎ 01492 584631

Ysgol Morfa Rhiannedd Ffordd Cwm, Llandudno, Conwy, LL30 1EG ☎ 01492 875464

Ysgol Nant Y Coed Rhondfa Ronald, Cyffordd, Llandudno, LL31 9EU ☎ 01492 581900

Ysgol Pencae Ffordd Graiglwyd, Penmaenmawr, LL34 6YG ☎ 01492 622219

Ysgol Penmachno Penmachno, Betws-Y-Coed, Conwy, LL24 0PT ☎ 01690 760394

Ysgol T. Gwynn Jones Llanelian Road, Old Colwyn, Colwyn Bay, LL29 9AU ☎ 01492 516594

Ysgol Trefriw Ffordd Llanrwst, Trefriw, Llanrwst, LL27 0PX ☎ 01492 640747

Ysgol Tudno Trinity Avenue, Llandudno, LL30 2SJ ☎ 01492 875252

Ysgol Y Foryd Morfa Avenue, Foryd, Conwy, LL18 5LE ☎ 01745 351892

Ysgol Y Plas Llanelian, Old Colwyn, Conwy, LL29 8YY ☎ 01492 680601

Ysgol Yr Wyddfid Llwynon Road, Great Orme, Llandudno, LL30 2QF ☎ 01492 878297

Ysgol Ysbyty Ifan Ysbyty Ifan, Betws Y Coed, Conwy, LL24 9NY ☎ 01690 770645

DENBIGHSHIRE/SIR DDINBYCH

Betws Gwerfil Goch School Betws Gwerfil Goch, Corwen, Denbighshire, LL21 9PY ☎ 01490 460315

Bodfari C.P. School Bodfari, Denbighshire, LL16 4DA ☎ 01745 710329

Bodnant Infants School Marine Road, Prestatyn, Denbighshire, LL19 7HA ☎ 01745 852783

Borthyn V.C. Primary School Denbigh Road, Ruthin, Denbighshire, LL15 1NT ☎ 01824 702727

Bryn Hedydd C.P. School Spruce Avenue, Tynewydd Road, Rhyl, LL18 2RH ☎ 01745 351676

Christchurch C.P. School Ernest Street, Rhyl, Denbighshire, LL18 2DS ☎ 01745 353982

Clocaenog C.P. School Clocaenog, Ruthin, Denbighshire, LL15 2AY ☎ 01824 750636

Froncysyllte C.P. School Woodlands Road, Froncysyllte, Llangollen, LL20 7SA ☎ 01691 773310

Garth C.P. School Trevor, Llangollen, Denbighshire, LL20 7UY ☎ 01978 820582

Gellifor C.P. School Gellifor, Ruthin, Denbighshire, LL15 1SG ☎ 01824 790387

Gwaenynog Infants C.P. School Ffordd Ysgubor, Denbigh, LL16 3RU ☎ 01745 812660

Llanbedr C.I.W. Controlled School Llanbedr, Ruthin, Denbighshire, LL15 1SU ☎ 01824 702927

Llandrillo C.P. School Llandrillo, Corwen, Denbighshire, LL21 0SR ☎ 01490 440300

Llantysilio C.I.W. Controlled School Llantysilio, Llangollen, Denbighshire, LL20 8BT ☎ 01978 860551

Nantglyn C.P. School Nantglyn, Denbigh, LL16 5PL ☎ 01745 550235

Rhewl C.P. School Rhewl, Ruthin, Denbighshire, LL15 2TU ☎ 01824 703296

Rhos Street C.P. School Rhos Street, Ruthin, Denbighshire, LL15 1DY ☎ 01824 702565

St Asaph V.P. Infants Upper Denbigh Road, St Asaph, Denbighshire, LL17 0RL ☎ 01745 583416

St Winefrides R.C. School Heol Esgob, St Asaph, Denbighshire, LL17 0PN ☎ 01745 583329

Twm O'r Nant Ffordd Rhyl, Dinbych, LL16 3DP ☎ 01745 812261

Yr Ysgol Gynradd Sirol Glyndyfrdwy, Corwen, Denbighshire, LL21 9HH ☎ 01490 430214

Ysgol Bro Cinmeirch Llanrhaedr Y.C., Dinbych, Sir Ddinbych, LL16 4NL ☎ 01745 890347

Ysgol Bro Famau - Graianrhyd Unit Ysgol Bro Famau, Graianrhyd, Nr. Llanarmon-Yn-Ial, CH7 4DQ ☎ 01824 780201

Ysgol Bro Famau - Llanarmon Unit Ysgol Bro Famau, Eryrys Road, Llanarmon-Yn-Ial, CH7 4QX ☎ 01824 780722

Ysgol Bro Famau - Llanferres Unit Ty'n Lan, Llanferres, Denbighshire, CH7 5SP ☎ 01824 810242

Ysgol Bryn Clwyd Llandyrnog, Sir Ddinbych, LL16 4EY ☎ 01559 790324

Ysgol Bryn Collen Llangollen Pengwern, Llangollen, Denbighshire, LL20 8AR ☎ 01978 861125

Ysgol Caer Drewyn Clawadd Poncen, Corwen, Denbighshire, LL21 9RT ☎ 01490 412418

School name, address and telephone number

Ysgol Cefn Meir Groesffordd Marli, Cefn Meiriadog, Abergele, LL22 9DS ☎ 01745 582224

Ysgol Cyffylliog Cyffylliog, Ruthin, Sir Ddinbych, LL15 2DL ☎ 01824 710274

Ysgol Dewi Sant Ffordd Rhuddlan, Rhyl, Denbighshire, LL18 2RE ☎ 01745 351355

Ysgol Dyffryn Ial Allt Yr Efail, Llandegla, Wrecsam, LL11 3AW ☎ 01490 450241

Ysgol Emmanuel Victoria Road, Rhyl, Denbighshire, LL18 2EG ☎ 01745 353447

Ysgol Gynradd Carrog Carrog, Nr Corwen, Denbighshire, LL21 9AW ☎ 01490 430262

Ysgol Gynradd Gwyddelwern Gwyddelwern, Corwen, Sir Ddinbych, LL21 9DF ☎ 01490 412332

Ysgol Gynradd Henllan Ffordd Dinbych, Henllan, Dinbych, LL16 5AW ☎ 01745 812959

Ysgol Gynradd Pentrecelyn Pentrecelyn, Ruthun, Sir Ddinbych, LL15 2HE ☎ 01978 790288

Ysgol Hiraddug Thomas Avenue, Dyserth, Rhyl, LL18 6AN ☎ 01745 570467

Ysgol Llywelyn Trellewelyn Road, Rhyl, Denbighshire, LL18 4EU ☎ 01745 353392

Ysgol Maes Hyfryd Cynwyd, Corwen, Sir Ddinbych, LL21 0LG ☎ 01490 412500

Ysgol Mair R.C. School St Margaret's Drive, Rhyl, Denbighshire, LL18 2HY ☎ 01745 350762

Ysgol Melyd Ffordd Pennant, Meliden, Prestatyn, LL19 8PE ☎ 01745 852782

Ysgol Pen Barras Stryd Y Rhos, Ruthun, Sir Ddinbych, LL15 1DY ☎ 01824 704129

Ysgol Penmorfa Dawson Drive, Prestatyn, Denbighshire, LL19 8SY ☎ 01745 852757

Ysgol Reoledig Llanfair D.C. Llanfair Dyffryn Clwyd, Ruthin, Denbighshire, LL15 2RU ☎ 01824 703169

Ysgol Reoledig Pantpastynog Prion, Denbighshire, LL16 4SG ☎ 01745 890331

Ysgol Trefnant Henllan Road, Trefnant, Nr. Denbigh, LL16 5UF ☎ 01745 730276

Ysgol Tremeirchion Tremeirchion, Llanelwg, St Asaph, LL17 0UN ☎ 01745 710328

Ysgol Y Castell C.P. Hylas Lane, Rhuddlan, Denbighshire, LL18 5AG ☎ 01745 590545

Ysgol Y Faenol John's Drive, Bodelwyddan, Nr. Rhyl, LL18 5TG ☎ 01745 583370

Ysgol Y Llys Rhodfa'r Tywysog, Prestatyn, Denbighshire, LL19 8RW ☎ 01745 853019

Ysgol Y Parc Infants Ruthin Road, Denbigh, LL16 3ER ☎ 01745 812989

664 FLINTSHIRE/SIR Y FFLINT

Abermorddu C.P. School Cymau Road, Caergwrle, Nr. Wrexham, LL12 9DH ☎ 01978 760647

Broughton Infants School Broughton Hall Road, Broughton, Nr.Chester, CH4 0QQ ☎ 01244 533752

Bryn Deva C.P. School Linden Avenue, Connah's Quay, Flintshire, CH5 4SN ☎ 01244 830080

Brynford C.P. School Brynford, Holywell, Flintshire, CH8 8AD ☎ 01352 713184

Cornist Park C.P. School Cornist Drive, Flintshire, CH6 5HJ ☎ 01352 735657

Dee Road Infants School Dee Road, Connah's Quay, Deeside, CH5 4NY ☎ 01244 812983

Drury C.P. School Beech Road, Drury, Buckley, CH7 3EG ☎ 01244 543005

Ewloe Green C.P. School Old Mold Road, Ewloe, Deeside, CH5 3AU ☎ 01244 532569

Golftyn C.P. School York Road, Connah's Quay, Deeside, CH5 4XA ☎ 01244 830569

Greenfield C.P. School School Lane, Greenfield, Holywell, CH8 7HR ☎ 01352 711497

Gwernymynydd C.P. School Godre'r Coed, Gwernymynydd, Mold, CH7 4DT ☎ 01352 756756

Gwynedd C.P. School Prince Of Wales Avenue, Flint, Flintshire, CH6 5NF ☎ 01352 732365

Hawarden C.P. Infants Cross Tree Lane, Hawarden, Deeside, CH5 3PY ☎ 01244 532311

Lixwm C.P. School Ffordd Gledlom, Lixwm, Holywell, CH8 8NF ☎ 01352 780455

Llanfynydd C.P. School Llanfynydd, Wrexham, Flintshire, LL11 5HG ☎ 01978 760351

Merllyn C.P. School Foel Gron, Bagillt, Flintshire, CH6 6BB ☎ 01352 733366

Nannerch Primary School Nannerch Village, Nr Mold, Flintshire, CH7 5RD ☎ 01352 741377

Nercwys Primary School Village Road, Nercwys, Mold, CH7 4EW ☎ 01352 752654

Northop Hall C.P. School Llys Ben, Northop Hall, Nr.Mold, CH7 6HS ☎ 01244 815980

Penarlag C.P. School Carlines Avenue, Carlines Park, Ewloe, CH5 3RQ ☎ 01244 533867

Perth Y Terfyn Infants School Halkyn Road, Holywell, Flintshire, CH8 7TZ ☎ 01352 711417

School name, address and telephone number

Rhes-Y-Cae Controlled Rhes-y-cae, Nr Holywell, Flintshire, CH8 8JQ ☎ 01352 780473

Saltney Ferry C.P. School Saltney Ferry Road, Saltney Ferry, Chester, CH4 0BL ☎ 01244 680302

Saltney Wood Memorial C.P. School Off Boundary Lane, Saltney, Chester, CH4 8SE ☎ 01244 671807

Sandycroft C.P. School Leaches Lane, Mancot, Deeside, CH5 2EH ☎ 01244 532083

Sealand C.P. School Farm Road, Sealand, Deeside, CH5 2HH ☎ 01244 830089

Shotton Infants School Plymouth Street, Shotton, Deeside, CH5 1JD ☎ 01244 812806

St Anthony's R.C. Primary High Street, Saltney, Flintshire, CH4 8SF ☎ 01244 680480

St David's R.C. School St David's Lane, Mold, Flintshire, CH7 1LH ☎ 01352 752651

St Mary's R.C. Primary School Ffordd Llewelyn, Pen Goch, Flintshire, CH6 5JZ ☎ 01352 733231

St Winefredes R.C. School Whitford Street, Holywell, Flintshire, CH8 7NJ ☎ 01352 713182

Sychdyn C.P. School Vownog Road, Sychdyn, Mold, CH7 6ED ☎ 01352 753654

Trelawnyd V.P. London Road, Rhyl, Trelawnyd, LL18 6DL ☎ 01745 570171

Ven Edward Morgan R.C. Primary Caernavon Close, Shotton, Deeside, CH5 1EB ☎ 01244 830408

Wepre C.P. School Connah's Quay, Deeside, Flintshire, CH5 4NE ☎ 01244 830104

West Lea Infants Tabernacle Street, Buckley, Flintshire, CH7 2JT ☎ 01745 543207

Ysgol Bro Carmel Carmel Road, Carmel, Holywell, CH8 8NU ☎ 01352 712234

Ysgol Bryn Coch C.P. Victoria Road, Mold, Flintshire, CH7 1EN ☎ 01352 752975

Ysgol Bryn Garth Ffynnongroew, Holywell, Flintshire, CH8 9HJ ☎ 01745 560435

Ysgol Bryn Gwalia C.P. Clayton Road, Mold, Flintshire, CH7 1SU ☎ 01352 752659

Ysgol Bryn Pennant C.P. Ffordd Pennant, Mostyn, Nr. Holywell, CH8 9NU ☎ 01745 560274

Ysgol Croes Atti Chester Road, Sir Y Fflint, CH6 5DU ☎ 01352 733335

Ysgol Derwenfa Queen Street, Leeswood, Nr. Mold, CH7 4RQ ☎ 01352 770477

Ysgol Estyn C.P. Hawarden Road, Hope, Nr. Wrexham, LL12 9NL ☎ 01978 760501

Ysgol Glan Aber C.P. Boot End, Bagillt, Flintshire, CH6 6LW ☎ 01452 711995

Ysgol Glanrafon Lon Bryn Coch, Yr Wyddgrug, Sir Y Fflint, CH7 1PA ☎ 01352 700384

Ysgol Gronant Nant Y Gro, Gronant, Nr. Prestatyn, LL19 9YP ☎ 01745 856119

Ysgol Gwenffrwdd Stryd Chwitffordd, Treffynnon, Sir Y Fflint, CH8 7NJ ☎ 01352 713158

Ysgol Gymraeg Mornant Picton Road, "Picton, Penyffordd", Treffynnon, CH8 9JQ ☎ 01745 560433

Ysgol Gynradd Trelogan Berthengam, Treffynnon, Sir Y Fflint, CH8 9BN ☎ 01745 560432

Ysgol Maes Edwin School Lane, Flint Mountain, Nr. Flint, CH6 5QR ☎ 01352 761331

Ysgol Parc Y Llan Ffordd Y Llan, Treuddyn, Mold, CH7 4LN ☎ 01352 770304

Ysgol Rhos Helyg Rhosesmor, Mold, Flintshire, CH7 6PJ ☎ 01352 780265

Ysgol Terrig Ffordd y Llan, Treuddyn, Yr Wyddgrug, CH7 4LN ☎ 01352 770235

Ysgol Y Ddol Rhydymwyn, Mold, Flintshire, CH7 5HW ☎ 01352 741357

Ysgol Y Foel Ffordd Y Llan, Cilcain, Mold, CH7 5NW ☎ 01352 740197

"Ysgol Y Llan, Whitford V.P." Whitford, Holywell, Flintshire, CH8 9AN ☎ 01745 560431

Ysgol Yr Esgob Pen Y Cefn Road, Caerwys, Mold, CH7 5AD ☎ 01352 720287

665 WREXHAM/WRECSAM

Acton Park C.P. Infants School Box Lane, Wrexham, LL12 8BT ☎ 01978 266344

All Saints Primary Gresford School Hill, Gresford, Wrexham, LL12 8RW ☎ 01978 852342

Barker's Lane C.P. School Barker's Lane, Wrexham, LL13 9TP ☎ 01978 357754

Black Lane C.P. School Long Lane, Pentre Broughton, Wrexham, LL11 6BT ☎ 01978 757959

Borderbrook School Talwrn Green, Malpas, Willington, SY14 7LR ☎ 01948 830676

Borras Park C.P. Infants School Borras Park Road, Wrexham, LL12 7TH ☎ 01978 352106

Brynteg County School Maesteg, Brynteg, Wrexham, LL11 6NB ☎ 01978 756398

Bwlchgwyn C.P. School Brymbo Road, Bwlchgwyn, Wrexham, LL11 5UD ☎ 01978 757743

School name, address and telephone number

Cefn Mawr Infants School Plas Kynaston Lane, Cefn Mawr, Wrexham, LL14 3PY ☎ 01978 822388

Cefn Mawr Primary School Plas Kynaston Lane, Cefn Mawr, Wrexham, LL14 3PY ☎ 01978 820719

Chirk Infants School Chapel Lane, Chirk, Wrexham, LL14 5NF ☎ 01691 773497

Deiniol C.P. School The Ridgeway, Marchwiel, Wrexham, LL13 0SB ☎ 01978 353760

Eyton Primary School Bangor Road, Eyton, Wrexham, LL13 0YD ☎ 01978 823392

Gwenfro Infants C.P. School Queensway, Wrexham, LL13 8UW ☎ 01978 354947

Hafod Y Wern Infants C.P. School Deva Way, Queens Park, Wrexham, LL13 9HD ☎ 01978 354264

Hanmer Primary School Whitchurch, Shropshire, SY13 3DG ☎ 01948 830238

Johnstown Infants School Melyd Avenue, Johnstown, Wrexham, LL14 2SW ☎ 01978 841666

Madras Primary School Penley, Wrexham, LL13 0LU ☎ 01978 710419

Minera Primary School Hall Road, Minera, Wrexham, LL11 3YE ☎ 01978 757742

New Broughton Infants School School Lane, New Broughton, Wrexham, LL11 6SF ☎ 01978 757583

Park C.P. Infants School School Road, Llay, Wrexham, LL12 0TR ☎ 01978 852414

Penycae Infants School Copperas Hill, Penycae, Wrexham, LL14 2SD ☎ 01978 841175

Penygelli Infants School Heol Maelor, Coedpoeth, Nr. Wrexham, LL11 3LS ☎ 01978 757209

Rhosddu Primary School Price's Lane, Wrexham, LL11 2NB ☎ 01978 266831

Rhostyllen C.P. School School Street, Rhostyllen, Wrexham, LL14 4AN ☎ 01978 352357

Rhosymedre Infants C.P. School Parc Road, Acrefair, Wrexham, LL14 3EG ☎ 01978 821409

St Anne's R.C. Primary Prince Charles Road, Wrexham, LL13 9ND ☎ 01978 261623

St Mary's Aided Primary School Ael y Bryn, Brymbo, Wrexham, LL11 5DA ☎ 01978 758340

St Mary's C.I.W. Aided School Lane, Overton On Dee, Wrexham, LL13 0ES ☎ 01978 710370

St Mary's Primary (Ruabon) Park Street, Ruabon, Wrexham, LL14 6LE ☎ 01978 820979

St Mary's R.C. Primary School Lea Road, Wrexham, LL13 7NA ☎ 01978 352406

St Paul's Primary School Bowling Bank, Isycoed, Wrexham, LL13 9RL ☎ 01978 661556

St Peter's Primary School Chapel Lane, Rossett, Wrexham, LL12 0EE ☎ 01244 570594

Tanyfron C.P. School Tanyfron Road, Tanyfron, Wrexham, LL11 5SA ☎ 01978 758118

The Rofft C.P. School Wynnstay Lane, Marford, Wrexham, LL12 8LA ☎ 01978 853116

Wat's Dyke C.P. School Garden Village, Wrexham, LL11 2TE ☎ 01978 355731

Ysgol Acrefair C.P. Acrefair, Wrexham, LL14 3SH ☎ 01978 820616

Ysgol Bodhyfryd Range Road, Wrexham, LL13 7DA ☎ 01978 351168

Ysgol Bryn Golau Sunnyview, Off First Avenue, Gwersyllt, LL11 4HS ☎ 01978 758574

Ysgol Bryn Tabor Heol Maelor, Coedpoeth, Wrecsam, LL11 3RU ☎ 01978 757893

Ysgol Hooson Pentredwr, Rhos, Wrexham, LL14 1DD ☎ 01437 840889

Ysgol Llanarmon Dyffryn Ceiriog Llanarmon Dyffryn Ceiriog, Llangollen, Wrexham, LL20 7LF ☎ 01691 718437

Ysgol Maes Y Llan C.P. Maes y Llan Lane, Ruabon, Wrexham, LL16 6AE ☎ 01978 820991

Ysgol Min-Y-Ddol Lon Plas Kynmaston, Cefn Mawr, Wrexham, LL14 3PA ☎ 01978 820903

Ysgol Plas Coch C.P. Ffordd Stansty, Plas Coch, Wrexham, LL11 2BU ☎ 01978 311198

Ysgol Sant Dunawd Sandown Road, Bangor-On-Dee, Wrexham, LL13 0JA ☎ 01978 780757

Ysgol Y Gaer Dodds Lane, Ffordd Bryn Y Cabanau, Hightown, LL11 4NT ☎ 01978 720722

Ysgol Y Ponciau C.P. School Lane, Ponciau, Wrexham, LL14 1RP ☎ 01437 840569

Ysgol Yn Rhos Llwynenion Road, Maesenion, Rhos, LL14 1DD ☎ 01978 840688

Ysgol-Y-Wern Hill Street, Rhos, Llanerch Ru Goe, LL14 1LN ☎ 01437 840603

School name, address and telephone number

666 POWYS

Archdeacon Griffiths C.I.W. Primary School, Llyswen, Brecon, Powys, LD3 0YB ☎ 01874 754334

Arddleen C.P. School Arddleen, Llanymynech, Powys, SY22 6RT ☎ 01938 590445

Ardwyn Nursery & Infant School Redbank, Welshpool, Powys, SY21 7PW ☎ 01938 552005

Beguildy C.I.W. School Beguildy, Nr. Knighton, Powys, LD7 1YE ☎ 01547 510645

Berriew C.P. School Berriew, Welshpool, Powys, SY21 8BA ☎ 01686 640312

Builth Wells C.P. School Park Road, Builth Wells, Powys, LD2 3BA ☎ 01982 553600

Caersws C.P. School Maesawelon, Caersws, Powys, SY17 5HG ☎ 01686 688458

Carreghofa C.P. School Llanymynech, Powys, SY22 6PA ☎ 01691 830396

Crickhowell C.P. School Oakfield Drive, Crickhowell, Powys, NP8 1DH ☎ 01873 810300

Cwmdu C.I.W. School Cwmdu, Crickhowell, Powys, NP8 1RU ☎ 01874 730358

Forden C.I.W. School Forden, Welshpool, Powys, SY21 8NE ☎ 01938 580334

Glasbury C.I.W.(A) School Glasbury-On-Wye, Hereford, Powys, HR3 5NU ☎ 01497 847364

Guilsfield C.P. School Guilsfield, Nr Welshpool, Powys, SY21 9ND ☎ 01938 553979

Gungrog C.I.W. Infant School Gungrog Road, Welshpool, Powys, SY21 7EJ ☎ 01938 553223

Hafren C.P. School Park Lane, Newtown, Powys, SY16 1EG ☎ 01686 626143

Irfon Valley C.P. School Garth, Llangammarch Wells, Powys, LD4 4AT ☎ 01591 620281

Knighton C.I.W. School Ludlow Road, Knighton, Powys, LD7 1HP ☎ 01547 528691

Ladywell Green Nurs. & Inf. School Newtown, Powys, SY16 1EG ☎ 01686 626303

Llanbedr C.I.W. (Aided) Llanbedr, Crickhowell, Powys, NP8 1SR ☎ 01873 810619

Llanbister C.P. School Llanbister, Llandrindod Wells, Powys, LD1 6TN ☎ 01597 840258

Llanbrynmair C.P. School Llanbrynmair, Powys, SY19 7AB ☎ 01650 521339

Llandrindod Wells C.P. School Cefnllys Lane, Llandrindod Wells, Powys, LD1 5WA ☎ 01597 822297

Llanelwedd C.I.W. School Llanelwedd, Builth Wells, Powys, LD2 3TY ☎ 01982 552616

Llanfaes C.P. School Bailihelig Road, Llanfaes, Brecon, LD3 8EB ☎ 01874 623326

Llangattock C.I.W. School Llangattock, Crickhowell, Powys, NP8 1PH ☎ 01873 810608

Llangedwyn Primary School Llangedwyn, Oswestry, Powys, SY10 9LD ☎ 01691 780264

Llangorse V.P. School Llangorse, Brecon, Powys, LD3 7UB ☎ 01874 658633

Llangynidr C.P. School Church Close, Llangynidr, Crickhowell, NP8 1NY ☎ 01874 730681

Llanidloes C.P. School Llangurig Road, Llanidloes, Powys, SY18 6EX ☎ 01686 412603

Maesyrhandir C.P. School Plantation Lane, Newtown, Powys, SY16 1LQ ☎ 01686 626337

Montgomery C.I.W. School Church Bank, Montgomery, Powys, SY15 6QA ☎ 01686 668387

Mount Street C.P. Infants Rhosferig Road, Brecon, Powys, LD3 7NG ☎ 01874 623038

Oldford Nursery & Infant School Oldford Lane, Welshpool, Powys, SY21 7TE ☎ 01938 552781

Penycae C.P. School Brecon Road, Penycae, Swansea, SA9 1FA ☎ 01639 730608

Penygloddfa C.P. School School Lane, Newtown, Powys, SY16 2HD ☎ 01686 626715

Presteigne C.P. School Slough Road, Presteigne, Powys, LD8 2NH ☎ 01544 267422

Priory C.I.W. School Pendre Close, Brecon, Powys, LD3 9EU ☎ 01874 623549

Rhayader C.I.W. School Bryntirion, Rhayader, Powys, LD6 5LT ☎ 01597 810288

St Joseph's R.C. (A) School Silver Street, Llanfaes, Brecon, LD3 8BL ☎ 01874 624488

St Mary`s R.C. (A) School Milford Road, Newtown, Powys, SY16 2EH ☎ 01686 625582

St. Michael's C.I.W. School Kerry, Newtown, Powys, SY16 4NU ☎ 01686 670208

Trecastle C.P. School Trecastle, Brecon, Powys, LD3 8UN ☎ 01874 636489

Treowen C.P. School Treowen, Newtown, Powys, SY16 1NJ ☎ 01686 627569

Ysgol Dolafon Dol Y Coed Road, Llanwrtyd Wells, Powys, LD5 4TB ☎ 01591 610326

Ysgol Gynradd Llanfyllin Llanfyllin, Powys, SY22 5BJ ☎ 01691 648207

Ysgol Thomas Stephens Pontneathvaughan, Neath, SA11 5UW, 01639 720348

Ysgol Y Bannau Orchard Street, Llanfaes, Aberhonddu, LD3 8AW, 01874 622207

School name, address and telephone number

667 CEREDIGION/SIR CEREDIGION

Ffynnon Bedr C.P. School Heol Y Bryn, Llanbedr Pont Steffan, Ceredigion, SA48 7EF ☎ 01570 422461

Plascrug C.P. School Plascrug Avenue, Aberystwyth, Ceredigion, SY23 1HL ☎ 01970 612286

Y.G. Rhydypennau Bow Street, Aberystwyth, Ceredigion, SY24 5AD ☎ 01970 828608

Ysgol Cenarth Cenarth, Newcastle Emlyn, Carmarthenshire, SA38 9JP ☎ 01239 710060

Ysgol Gymraeg Aberystwyth Plascrug Avenue, Aberystwyth, Ceredigion, SY23 1HL ☎ 01970 617613

Ysgol Gynradd Aberaeron Gerddi Wellington, Aberaeron, Ceredigion, SA46 0BQ ☎ 01545 570313

Ysgol Llwyn-Yn-Eos Penparcau, Aberystwyth, Ceredigion, SY23 1SH ☎ 01970 617011

Ysgol Y Dderi Llangybi, Lampeter, Ceredigion, SA48 8NG ☎ 01570 493424

668 PEMBROKESHIRE/SIR BENFRO

Albion Square C.P. Infant School Bush Street, Pembroke Dock, Pembrokeshire, SA72 6XF ☎ 01646 684490

Johnston C.P. School Cranham Park, Johnston, Haverfordwest, SA62 3PU ☎ 01437 890280

Letterston V.C. School St David's Road, Letterston, Haverfordwest, SA62 5SL ☎ 01348 840248

Manorbier V.C.P. School Station Road, Manorbier, Tenby, SA70 7SN ☎ 01834 871228

Mary Immaculate V.R.C. School Merlins Terrace, Haverfordwest, Pembrokeshire, SA61 1PH ☎ 01437 762324

Mount Airey C.P. Augustine Way, Haverfordwest, Pembrokeshire, SA61 1PA ☎ 01437 756376

Neyland C.P. Infant & Nursery Charles Street, Neyland, Milford Haven, SA73 1SA ☎ 01646 600882

Prendergast Infants & Nursery Stokes Avenue, Prendergast, Haverfordwest, SA61 2RB ☎ 01437 765379

Saundersfoot C.P. School Francis Lane, Saundersfoot, Pembrokeshire, SA69 9HB ☎ 01834 812819

St David's C.P. School Quickwell, St David's, Haverfordwest, SA62 6PD ☎ 01437 720590

St Mary's V.R.C. School Britannia Road, Bufferland, Pembroke Dock, SA72 6PD ☎ 01646 682879

St Teilos V.R.C. School Greenhill Road, Tenby, Pembrokeshire, SA70 7LJ ☎ 01834 843995

Stackpole V.C.P. School Stackpole, Pembroke, Pembrokeshire, SA71 5DB ☎ 01646 672234

Tenby Infants V.C. School Heywood Lane, Tenby, Pembrokeshire, SA70 8BN ☎ 01834 843241

The Meads C.P. Infant & Nursery School Priory Road, Milford Haven, Pembrokeshire, SA73 2EE ☎ 01646 693861

The Mount C.P. Infant & Nursery Off Steynton Road, Milford Haven, Pembrokeshire, SA73 1BS ☎ 01646 694154

Ysgol Glan Cleddau Off Portfield, Haverfordwest, Pembrokeshire, SA61 1BS ☎ 01437 769859

Ysgol Gynradd Sirol Wdig Hill Street, Wdig, Sir Benfro, SA64 0ET ☎ 01348 872503

Ysgol Y Babanod A Meithinfa Abergwaun Sladeway, Fishguard, Pembrokeshire, SA65 9NY ☎ 01348 873644

669 CARAMARTHENSHIRE/SIR GAERFYRDDIN

Bigyn County Primary Bigyn Park Terrace, Bigyn, Llanelli, SA15 1DH ☎ 01554 771817

Brynamman C.P. Infants School Cwmgarw Road, Brynamman, Ammanford, SA18 1BU ☎ 01269 822583

Copperworks Infant & Nursery School Neville Street, Llanelli, Carmarthenshire, SA15 2RS ☎ 01554 758837

Cross Hands C.P. School Carmanthen Road, Cross Hands, Llanelli, SA14 6SU ☎ 01269 842764

Dafen Primary School Lon-Yr-Ysgol, Dafen, Llanelli, SA14 8LL ☎ 01554 773290

Halfway C.P. School Havard Road, Llanelli, Carmarthenshire, SA14 8SA ☎ 01554 758601

Johnstown C.P. School Salen Road, Johnstown, Carmarthen, SA31 3HS ☎ 01267 236653

Llandeilo C.P. School 20 Rhosmaen Street, Llandeilo, Carmarthenshire, SA19 6LU ☎ 01558 822498

Llandybie C.P. School Llandybie, Ammanford, Carmarthenshire, SA18 3JB ☎ 01269 850243

Llangain C.P. School Llangain, Carmarthenshire, SA33 5AE ☎ 01267 241478

Llangunnor C.P. School Penymorfa Lane, Pensarn, Llangunnor, SA31 2NN ☎ 01267 237841

Model C.I.W. School College Road, Carmarthen, Carmarthenshire, SA31 3EQ ☎ 01267 234386

Morfa Infants & Nursery School New Street, Morfa, Llanelli, SA15 2BR ☎ 01554 72945

Myrddin C.P. School Heol Disgwylfa, Carmarthen, Carmarthenshire, SA31 1TE ☎ 01267 232626

Penygaer Primary School Bryndulais Avenue, Llanelli, Carmarthenshire, SA14 8ER ☎ 01554 750900

School name, address and telephone number

Richmond Park Primary School Priory Street, Carmarthen, Carmarthenshire, SA31 1HF ☎ 01267 238298

St Mary's R.C. Primary Union Street, Carmarthen, Carmarthenshire, SA31 3DE ☎ 01267 234297

St Mary's R.C. Primary School Havard Road, Llanelli, Carmarthenshire, SA14 8SD ☎ 01554 759178

Stebonheath C.P. School Marble Hall Road, Llanelli, Carmarthenshire, SA15 1NB ☎ 01554 758603

Trimsaran C.P. School Heol Llanelli, Trimsaran, Kidwelly, SA17 4AG ☎ 01554 810670

Y.G. Nantgaredig Heol Yr Osaf, Nantgaredig, Sir Gaerfyrddin, SA32 7LG ☎ 01267 290444

Ysgol Gruffydd Jones Heol Yr Osaf, San Cler, Sir Gaerfyrddin, SA33 4BT ☎ 01994 230589

Ysgol Gymraeg Brynsierfel Cefncaeau, Llwynhendy, Llanelli, SA14 9HD ☎ 01554 758582

Ysgol Gymraeg Dewi Sant Rhodfa Bryndulais, Llanelli, Carmarthenshire, SA14 8RS ☎ 01554 750081

Ysgol Gymraeg Gwenllian Cydweli, Sir Gaerfyrddin, SA17 4UT ☎ 01554 890523

Ysgol Gynradd Bancffosfelen Heol Bancffosfelen, Pontyberem, Llanelli, SA15 5DR ☎ 01269 870272

Ysgol Gynradd Llanarthne Llanarthne, Caerfyrddin, Sir Gaerfyrddin, SA32 8HJ ☎ 01558 668570

Ysgol Gynradd Ystradowen Berrington Villas, Cwmllynfell, Abertawe, SA9 2YN ☎ 01639 830341

Ysgol Teilo Sant Stryd Rhosmaen, Llandeilo, Sir Gaerfyrddin, SA19 6LU ☎ 01558 823489

Ysgol Y Castell Priory Street, Kidwelly, Carmarthenshire, SA17 4TR ☎ 01554 890762

Ysgol Y Dderwen Heol Spurrell, Caerfyrddin, Sir Gaerfyrddin, SA31 1TG ☎ 01267 235598

Ysgol Yr Ynys Ynys Las, Llwynhendy, Llanelli, SA14 9BT ☎ 01554 776168

670 SWANSEA/ABERTAWE

Arfryn Primary School Heol Frank, Penlan, Swansea, SA5 7AH ☎ 01792 584441

Birchgrove Infants School Heol Nant Bran, Birchgrove, Swansea, SA7 9LS ☎ 01792 813524

Bishopston Primary School Bishopston Road, Bishopston, Swansea, SA3 3EN ☎ 01792 232754

Blaenymaes Primary School Broughton Avenue, Blaenymaes, Swansea, SA5 5LW ☎ 01792 583366

Brynhyfryd Infants School Llangyfelach Road, Brynhyfryd, Swansea, SA5 9LN ☎ 01792 650129

Brynmill Primary School Trafalgar Place, Brynmill, Swansea, SA2 0BU ☎ 01792 463019

Cadle Primary School Middle Road, Fforestfach, Swansea, SA5 5DU ☎ 01792 584498

Casllwchwr Primary School Castle Street, Loughor, Swansea, SA4 6TU ☎ 01792 892420

Christchurch C.I.W. School Rodney Street, Swansea, SA1 3US ☎ 01792 654832

Cila C.P. School 577 Gower Road, Upper Killay, Swansea, SA2 7DR ☎ 01792 202775

Clase Infant School Rheidol Avenue, Clase, Swansea, SA6 7JX ☎ 01792 781747

Clwyd Primary School Eppynt Road, Penlan, Swansea, SA5 7AZ ☎ 01792 588673

Clydach Infant School Sybil Street, Clydach, SA6 5EU ☎ 01792 843356

Craigcefnparc C.P. School Craigcefnparc, Clydach, Swansea, SA6 5TE ☎ 01792 843225

Craigfelen Primary School Woodside Crescent, Craig Felen, Clydach, SA6 5DP ☎ 01792 843278

Crwys C.P. School Chapel Road, Three Crosses, Nr Swansea, SA4 3PU ☎ 01792 872473

Cwm Primary School Jersey Road, Bonymaen, Swansea, SA1 7DL ☎ 01792 774519

Cwmbwrla Primary School Middle Road, Cwmbwrla, Swansea, SA5 8HQ ☎ 01792 652350

Cwmglas Primary School Colwyn Avenue, Winchwen, Swansea, SA1 7EN ☎ 01792 771693

Cwmrhydyceirw Primary School Maes y Gwernen Road, Morriston, Swansea, SA6 6LL ☎ 01792 771524

Danygraig Primary School Ysgol Street, Port Tennant, Swansea, SA1 8LE ☎ 01792 650946

Dunvant Infant School Dunvant Road, Dunvant, Swansea, SA2 7SN ☎ 01792 207336

Garnswllt C.P. School Heol-Y-Mynydd, Garnswllt, Ammanford, SA18 2SE ☎ 01269 592748

Gendros Primary School Armine Road, Gendros, Swansea, SA5 8DB ☎ 01792 586570

Glais Primary School School Road, Glais, Swansea, SA7 9EY ☎ 01792 842627

Glyncollen Primary School Heol Dolfain, Ynysforgan, Swansea, SA6 6QF ☎ 01792 791727

Gors Infants School Gors Avenue, Cockett, Swansea, SA1 6SF ☎ 01792 579529

Gorseinon Infants School High Street, Gorseinon, Swansea, SA4 2BN ☎ 01792 892739

Graig Infants School Tanylan Terrace, Morriston, Swansea, SA6 7DU ☎ 01792 772800

Grange Primary School West Cross Avenue, West Cross, Swansea, SA3 5TS ☎ 01792 404766

School name, address and telephone number

Gwyrosydd Infants School Parkhill Terrace, Treboeth, Swansea, SA5 7DJ ☎ 01792 798673

Hafod Primary School Odo Street, Hafod, Swansea, SA1 2LT ☎ 01792 461356

Hendrefoilan Primary School Dunvant Road, Dunvant, Swansea, SA2 7LF ☎ 01792 290223

Knelston Primary School Reynoldston, Gower, SA3 1AR ☎ 01792 390071

Llanforlais Primary School School Lane, Llanforlais, Swansea, SA4 3TL ☎ 01792 850201

Llangyfelach C.P. School Pengors Road, Llangyfelach, Swansea, SA5 7JE ☎ 01792 771497

Llanrhidian Primary School Llanrhidian, Swansea, SA3 1EH ☎ 01792 390181

Manselton Primary School Manor Road, Manselton, Swansea, SA5 9PA ☎ 01792 652977

Mayals C.P. School Fairwood Road, West Cross, Swansea, SA3 5JP ☎ 01792 402755

Mayhill Infants School Creidiol Road, Mayhill, Swansea, SA1 6TX ☎ 01792 650274

Morriston Primary School Neath Road, Morriston, Swansea, SA6 8EP ☎ 01792 781811

Newton C.P. School Slade Road, Newton, Swansea, SA3 4UE ☎ 01792 369826

Oystermouth Primary School Newton Road, Mumbles, Swansea, SA3 4BE ☎ 01792 369233

Parkland Primary School Sketty Park, Sketty, Swansea, SA2 8NG ☎ 01792 205462

Pen Y Fro Primary Priors Crescent, Dunvant, Swansea, SA2 7UF ☎ 01792 203728

Penclawdd Primary School Park Road, Penclawdd, Swansea, SA4 3FH ☎ 01792 850239

Pengelli Primary School Station Road, Grovesend, Swansea, SA4 4GY ☎ 01792 892736

Penllergaer Primary School Pontardulais Road, Penllergaer, Swansea, SA4 1AY ☎ 01792 892354

Pennard Primary School Pennard Road, Pennard, Swansea, SA3 2AD ☎ 01792 233343

Pentrechwyth Primary School Bonymaen Road, Pentrechwyth, Swansea, SA1 7AP ☎ 01792 653186

Pentrepoeth Infant School School Road, Morriston, Swansea, SA6 6HZ ☎ 01792 771831

Penyrheol Primary School Frampton Road, Gorseinon, Swansea, SA4 4LY ☎ 01792 892337

Plasmarl C.P. School Britannia Road, Plasmarl, Swansea, SA6 8LH ☎ 01792 798210

Pontarddulais Primary School Upper James Street, Pontarddulais, Swansea, SA4 1JD ☎ 01792 882383

Pontlliw C.P. School Clordir Road, Pontlliw, Pontarddulais, SA4 1EY ☎ 01792 882553

Pontybrenin Primary School Glyn Rhosyn, Kingsbridge, Gorseinon, SA4 6HX ☎ 01792 891151

Portmead Primary School Cheriton Crescent, Portmead, Swansea, SA5 5LA ☎ 01792 583549

St David's R.C. Primary School West Cross Avenue, West Cross, Swansea, SA3 5TS ☎ 01792 404581

St Helen's Primary School Vincent Street, Swansea, SA1 3TY ☎ 01792 655763

St Illtyd's R.C. Primary Jersey Road, Bonymaen, Swansea, SA1 7DG ☎ 01792 462104

St Joseph's Cathedral Infant School Caepistyll Street, Grennhill, Swansea, SA3 2EB ☎ 01792 653609

St Joseph's R.C. Primary School Pontardawe Road, Clydach, Swansea, SA6 5NX ☎ 01792 842494

Talycopa Primary School Heol Hafdy, Llansamlet, Swansea, SA7 9RZ ☎ 01792 793660

Terrace Road C.P. School Terrace Road, Mount Pleasant, Swansea, SA1 6JD ☎ 01792 654257

Trallwn Primary School Glanywern Road, Trallwn, Swansea, SA7 9UJ ☎ 01792 792478

Tre Uchaf C.P. School Heol Cae Ty Newydd, Ty Newydd, Upper Loughor, SA4 6QB ☎ 01792 893682

Tregwyr Infant School Talbot Street, Gowerton, SA4 3DB ☎ 01792 873484

Waun Wen Primary School Lion Street, Waun Wen, Swansea, SA1 2BZ ☎ 01792 651010

Waunarlwydd Primary School Brithwen Road, Waunarlwydd, Swansea, SA5 4QS ☎ 01792 872431

Whitestone C.P. School Off Rushwind Close, West Cross, Swansea, SA3 5RF ☎ 01792 404113

Y.G. Bryn-Y-Mor Heol St Alban, Brynmill, Abertawe, SA2 0BP ☎ 01792 466354

Ynystawe C.P. School Clydach Road, Ynystawe, Swansea, SA6 5AY ☎ 01792 842628

Ysgol Gymraeg Pontybrenin Loughor Road, Knightsbridge, Gorseinon, SA4 6AU ☎ 01792 894210

Ysgol Gynradd Felindre Heol Myddfai, Felindre, Abertawe, SA5 7ND ☎ 01792 771182

Ysgol Gynradd Gymraeg Bryniago Lower James Street, Pontarddulais, SA4 1HY ☎ 01792 882012

Ysgol Gynradd Gymraeg Lonlas Walters Road, Llansamlet, Abertawe, SA7 9RW ☎ 01792 771160

Ysgol Gynradd Gymraeg Tirdeunaw Heol Ddu, Treboeth, Abertawe, SA5 7HB ☎ 01792 774612

Ysgol Login Fach Roseland Road, Waunarlwydd, Abertawe, SA5 4ST ☎ 01792 874399

School name, address and telephone number

671 NEATH PORT TALBOT/CASTELL-NEDD PORT TALBOT

Abergwynfi Infant School Park Lane, Blaengwynfi, Nr Port Talbot, SA13 3UL ☎ 01639 850316

Ald. Davies' C.I.W. School St David's Street, Neath, SA11 3AA ☎ 01639 642863

Alltwen County Primary School Alltwen Hill, Pontardawe, Swansea, SA8 3AB ☎ 01792 863275

Baglan Primary School Elmwood Road, Baglan, Port Talbot, SA12 8TF ☎ 01639 813112

Blaenbaglan Primary School Maes-Ty-Canol, Baglan, Port Talbot, SA12 8YF ☎ 01639 812451

Blaendulais Primary School Seven Sisters, Nr Neath, SA10 9AA ☎ 01639 700261

Blaengwrach C.P. School Cwmgwrach, Nr Neath, SA11 5PS ☎ 01639 720342

Blaenhonddan C.P. School Tyn Yr Haul, Bryncoch, Nr Neath, SA10 7PE ☎ 01639 644366

Bryn Primary School Old Neath Road, Bryn, Port Talbot, SA13 2RS ☎ 01639 896486

Bryncoch C.I.W. School Furzeland Drive, Nr Neath, SA10 7TT ☎ 01639 643359

Catwg Primary School Main Road, Cadoxton, Nr Neath, SA10 8BL ☎ 01639 642731

Central Infant School Theodore Road, Port Talbot, SA13 1SP ☎ 01639 882866

Cilffriw Primary School Penscynor, Cilfrew, Neath, SA10 8LW ☎ 01639 630816

Clun Primary School Clyne, Neath, SA11 4BW ☎ 01639 710260

Coedffranc Infant School Stanley Road, Skeween, Nr Neath, SA10 6LP ☎ 01792 813504

Creunant Primary School School Road, Crynant, Neath, SA10 8NS ☎ 01639 750224

Croeserw Primary School Croeserw, Port Talbot, SA13 3PL ☎ 01639 850265

Crymlyn Primary School School Road, Jersey Marine, Neath, SA10 6JJ ☎ 01792 812285

Crynallt Infant School Cimla, Nr Neath, SA11 3AZ ☎ 01639 635256

Cwm Nedd Primary School New Street, Glynneath, Nr Neath, SA11 5AA ☎ 01639 720220

Cwmafan Infant School Ty'r Owen Row, Cwmafan, Port Talbot, SA12 9BB ☎ 01639 896119

Cwmllynfell C.P. School Heol-Y-Bryn, Cwmllynfell, Swansea, SA9 2FL ☎ 01639 830630

Cymer Afan Primary School Margam Street, Cymmer, Port Talbot, SA13 3EL ☎ 01639 850885

Dyffryn Afan School Dyffryn Rhondda, Port Talbot, SA13 3HF ☎ 01639 850342

Eastern Primary School Incline Row, Taibach, Port Talbot, SA13 1TT ☎ 01639 882819

Glan-Y-Mor C.P. School Severn Crescent, Port Talbot, SA12 6TA ☎ 01639 882817

Glyn Primary School Lower Brynamman, Ammanford, SA18 1SU ☎ 01269 822333

Glyncorrwg Primary School Bridge Street, Glyncorrwg, Nr Port Talbot, SA13 3BB ☎ 01639 850323

Gnoll Primary School Wellfield Avenue, Neath, SA11 1AQ ☎ 01639 642938

Godrergraig Primary School Graig Road, Godrergraig, SA9 2NY ☎ 01639 843116

Groes Primary School Bertha Road, Margam, Port Talbot, SA13 2AW ☎ 01639 886541

Hen Gwrt Primary School Llansawel Crescent, Briton Ferry, Neath, SA11 2UN ☎ 01639 812229

Llangiwg Primary School Brecon Road, Pontardawe, SA8 4PJ ☎ 01792 863274

Llansawel C.P. School Vernon Place, Briton Ferry, Neath, SA11 2JJ ☎ 01639 813224

Maesmarchog Primary School Main Road, Dyffryn Cellwen, Nr Neath, SA10 9LB ☎ 01639 700228

Melin County Infant School Herbert Road, Neath, SA11 2ED ☎ 01639 643218

Neath Abbey Infants New Road, Neath Abbey, Nr Neath, SA10 7NG ☎ 01792 812227

Pontrhydyfen Primary School School Road, Oakwood, Pontrhydyfen, SA12 9SB ☎ 01639 896055

Rhiwfawr Primary School Rhiw Road, Rhiwfawr, Swansea, SA9 2RF ☎ 01639 830651

Rhos C.P. School Neath Road, Rhos, Swansea, SA8 3EB ☎ 01792 862177

Rhydyfro Primary School Commercial Road, Rhydyfro, Pontardawe, SA8 4SS ☎ 01792 865680

Sandfields Primary School Lilian Street, Port Talbot, SA12 6AX ☎ 01639 882355

St Joseph's Infant School Water Street, Port Talbot, SA12 6LE ☎ 01639 882579

St Josephs R.C.Primary School Cook Rees Avenue, Westernmoor, Neath, SA11 1UR ☎ 01639 635099

St Therese's R.C. School Southdown Road, Sandfields, Port Talbot, SA12 7HL ☎ 01639 882797

Tairgwaith Primary School Tairgwaith, Ammanford, SA18 1UT ☎ 01269 823258

School name, address and telephone number

Tirmorfa Primary School Marine Drive, Port Talbot, SA12 7NN ☎ 01639 884019

Tonmawr Primary School Tonmawr Road, Tonmawr, Nr Port Talbot, SA12 9UW ☎ 01639 642219

Tonna Primary/Comm. School School Road, Tonnau, Nr Neath, SA11 3EZ ☎ 01639 637062

Traethmelyn Primary School Southdown View, Sandfields Estate, Port Talbot, SA12 7AH ☎ 01639 882317

Trebannws Primary School Swansea Road, Pontardawe, Swansea, SA8 4BL ☎ 01792 863272

Tywyn Primary School Channel View, Sandfields, Port Talbot, SA12 6JF ☎ 01639 882313

Waunceirch C.P. School Caewern, Neath, SA10 7RW ☎ 01639 636084

Y Wern Primary School Clare Road, Ystalyfera, SA9 2AJ ☎ 01639 842242

Y.G.G. Blaendulais Pen Y Banc, Blaendulais, Castell Nedd, SA10 9AA ☎ 01639 700342

Y.G.G. Gwaun Cae Gurwen New Road, Gwauncaegurwen, Ammanford, SA18 1UN ☎ 01269 822238

Ynysfach Comm. Primary School Resolven, Nr Neath, SA11 4AB ☎ 01639 710238

Ynysmaerdy C.P. School Neath Road, Briton Ferry, Neath, SA11 2BQ ☎ 01639 813132

Ysgol G.G. Pontardawe Stryd Thomas, Pontardawe, Abertawe, SA8 4AD ☎ 01792 862136

Ysgol G.G. Cwmnedd New Street, Glynneath, Nr Neath, SA11 5AA ☎ 01639 720530

Ysgol Gymraeg Castell Nedd Heol Woodland, Castell-Nedd, SA11 3BW ☎ 01639 637701

Ysgol Gymraeg Rhosafan Marine Drive, Port Talbot, SA12 7NN ☎ 01639 896338

Ysgol Gynradd Cwmgors Heol-Y-Gors, Rhydaman, Gwauncaegurwen, SA18 1RF ☎ 01269 822306

672 BRIDGEND/PEN-Y-BONT AR OGWR

Aber Infants School Fern Street, Ogmore Vale, Bridgend, CF32 7AP ☎ 01656 840269

Afon-Y-Felin Primary School Heol y Parc, North Cornelly, Bridgend, CF33 4PA ☎ 01656 740627

Archdeacon John Lewis C.I.W. Primary School, Brackla Way, Brackla, CF31 2JS ☎ 01656 767502

Blaengarw Primary School Station Street, Blaengarw, Pontycymer, CF32 8BA ☎ 01656 870353

Bryntirion Infants School Bryngolau, Bryntirion, Bridgend, CF31 4DD ☎ 01656 766227

Cefn Cribwr Primary School Cefn Road, Cefn Cribbwr, Bridgend, CF32 0AW ☎ 01656 740293

Cefn Glas Infant School St Winifred's Road, Bridgend, CF31 4PL ☎ 01656 766229

Mynydd Cynffig Infants Commercial Street, Kenfig Hill, Bridgend, CF33 6DN ☎ 01656 740330

Oldcastle Infants School South Street, Bridgend, CF31 3ED ☎ 01656 766230

Pandy'r Betws Infant School Bettws, Bridgend, CF32 8TB ☎ 01656 720468

Porthcawl Primary School Meadow Lane, Ogwr, Porthcawl, CF36 5EY ☎ 01656 784228

Tondu Primary School Meadow Street, Aberkenfig, Bridgend, CF32 9BE ☎ 01656 722447

Ysgol G.G. Cwm Garw Hillview, Ponytcymmer, Bridgend, CF32 8LU ☎ 01656 870306

673 THE VALE OF GLAMORGAN/BRO MORGANNWG

Albert C.P. School Albert Road, Penarth, CF6 1BX ☎ 01222 707682

All Saints C.I.W. Primary School Plas Cleddau (Off Severn Road), Cwm Talwg, Barry, CF62 7FG ☎ 01446 745726

Colcot Primary School Florence Avenue, Barry, Vale of Glamorgan, CF62 9XH ☎ 01446 735719

Dinas Powys Infants Cardiff Road, Dinas Powys, Vale of Glamorgan, CF64 4JU ☎ 01222 512151

Eagleswell Infant & Nursery School Eagleswell Road, Llantwit Major, CF61 2UE ☎ 01446 796844

Gibbonsdown Infant & Nursery School Amroth Court, Caldy Close, Gibbonsdown, CF6 3DU ☎ 01446 744606

Gladstone Primary School Gladstone Road, Barry, CF6 6NA ☎ 01446 735321

High Street Primary School St Paul's Avenue, Barry, Vale of Glamorgan, CF62 8HT ☎ 01446 734553

Jenner Park Primary Hannah Street, Barry, Vale of Glamorgan, CF6 7DG ☎ 01446 735587

Palmerston Primary School Pen-y-Bryn, Cadoxton, Barry, CF6 8QH ☎ 01446 747393

St Athan Infant School Rock Road, St Athan, Nr. Barry, CF6 9PG ☎ 01446 751480

St Helen's R.C. Infant & Nursery School Maes-Y-Cwm Street, Barry, Vale of Glamorgan, CF63 4EH ☎ 01446 732834

Ysgol Pen Y Garth 1 heol Tircoch, Penarth, CF62 2QN ☎ 01222 700262

Ysgol Sant Baruc St Paul's Avenue, Barry, CF62 8HT ☎ 01446 735595

School name, address and telephone number

674 RHONDDA, CYNON, TAFF/RHONDDA, CYNON, TAF

Abercynon Infants School Ynysmeurig Road, Abercynon, Mountain Ash, CF45 4SU ☎ 01443 740393

Aberdare Town C.I.W. Primary Wind Street, Aberdare, "Rhondda, Cynon, Taff", CF44 7HF ☎ 01685 871520

Aberllechau Primary School Victoria Terrace, Wattstown, Porth, CF39 0PF ☎ 01443 730264

Abertaf Primary School Greenfield Terrace, Abercynon, Mountain Ash, CF45 4TS ☎ 01443 740265

Alaw Primary School Egypt Street, Trealaw, Tonypandy, CF40 2UU ☎ 01443 432350

Blaenclydach Infants School East Street, Blaenclydach, Tonypandy, CF40 2RX ☎ 01443 433332

Blaengwawr Primary School Gwawr Street, Aberaman, Aberdare, CF44 6YP ☎ 01685 871064

Blaenllechau Infant School Mountain Row, Blaenllechau, Rhondda, CF43 4PA ☎ 01443 730262

Blaenrhondda Primary School Brook Street, Blaenrhondda, Treorchy, CF42 5SB ☎ 01443 771432

Blaenycwm Primary School Hendrewen Road, Blaencwm, "Treherbert, Treorchy", CF42 5DR ☎ 01443 771431

Bodringallt Primary School Bodringallt Terrace, Ystrad, Pentre, CF41 7QE ☎ 01443 422100

Caegarw Primary School Troed Y Rhiw Road, Caegarw, Mountain Ash, CF45 4BH ☎ 01443 473730

Capcoch Primary School School Street, Abercwmboi, Aberdare, CF44 6AD ☎ 01443 472746

Caradog Primary School Clifton Street, Aberdare, CF44 7PB ☎ 01685 874715

Carnetown Primary School Salisbury Road, Carnetown, Abercynon, CF45 4NU ☎ 01443 740492

Cefn Primary School Greenfield Avenue, Glyncoch, Pontypridd, CF37 3BD ☎ 01443 486826

Cilfynydd Primary School Ann Street, Cilfynydd, Pontypridd, CF37, 4EN ☎ 01443 486827

Coedpenmaen County Primary School Coedpenmaen Close, Pontypridd, "Rhondda, Cynon, Taff", CF37 4LE ☎ 01443 486828

Coedylan Primary School Tyfica Road, Pontypridd, CF37 2DB ☎ 01443 486829

Comin Infants School Hirwaun Road, Trecynon, Aberdare, CF44 8LU ☎ 01685 874026

Craig-Yr-Eos Infants School Bishop Street, Penygraig, Tonypandy, CF40 1PQ ☎ 01443 433263

Craig-Yr-Hesg Primary School Cefn Lane, Glyncoch, Pontypridd, CF37 3BP ☎ 01443 486830

Cwmaman Infants School Fforchaman Road, Cwmaman, Aberdare, CF44 6NS ☎ 01685 875862

Cwmbach C.I.W. Primary School Tirfounder Road, Cwmbach, Aberdare, CF44 0AT ☎ 01685 873336

Cwmclydach Infants School Wern Street, Clydach Vale, Tonypandy, CF40 2BQ ☎ 01443 434370

Cwmdar County Primary School The Square, Cwmdare, Aberdare, CF44 8UA ☎ 01685 871198

Cwmlai Primary School Penygarreg Road, Tonyrefail, Porth, CF39 8AS ☎ 01443 670356

Cymmer Infants School Graigwen Road, Cymmer, Porth, CF39, 9HA ☎ 01443 682481

Cynon Infants School Aberdare Road, Mountain Ash, "Rhondda, Cynon, Taff", CF45 3PT ☎ 01443 474597

Darran Park Primary School Brook Street, Ferndale, "Rhondda, Cynon, Taff", CF43 4LE

Darrenlas Primary School Kingcraft Street, Darrenlas, Mountain Ash, CF45 3LT ☎ 01443 473291

Dunraven Primary School Blaenycwm Terrace, Tynewydd, Treherbert, CF42 5ND ☎ 01443 771434

Ferndale Infants School North Road, Ferndale, "Rhondda, Cynon, Taff", CF43 4PS ☎ 01443 755858

Gelli Primary School Ystrad Road, Ystrad, Pentre, CF41 7PX ☎ 01443 435311

Gilfach Goch Infants School High Street, Gilfach Goch, Porth, CF39 8SH ☎ 01443 672531

Glanffrwd Infant School Buarth y Capel, Ynysybwl, Pontypridd, CF37 3PE ☎ 01443 791424

Glantaf Infant School Powys Place, Rhydyfelin, Pontypridd, CF37 5PG ☎ 01443 486832

Glenboi Primary School Abercwmboi Isaf Road, Glenboi, Mountain Ash, CF45 3DW ☎ 01443 473747

Graig-Y-Wion Primary School Albert Road, Graig, Pontypridd, CF37 1LA ☎ 01443 486833

Gwaunmeisgyn Infants School Woodland Road, Beddau, Pontypridd, CF38 2DH ☎ 01443 203175

Hafod Primary School Wayne Street, Trehafod, Pontypridd, CF37 2NL ☎ 01443 682234

Hawthorn PrimarySchool School Lane, Hawthorn, Pontypridd, CF37 5AL ☎ 01443 841230

Hendrefadog Infants School Tylorstown, Ferndale, CF43 3DT ☎ 01443 730576

Hendreforgan Infants School Hendreforgan, Gilfach Goch, Porth, CF39 8UH ☎ 01443 672394

Heol-Y-Celyn Primary School Holly Street, Rhydyfelin, Pontypridd, CF37 5DB ☎ 01443 486834

Llanhari Primary School Aelfryn, Llanharry, Pontyclun, CF72 9LQ ☎ 01443 237832

School name, address and telephone number

Llanilltud Faerdref Primary St Illtyd's Road, Church Road, Pontypridd, CF38 1DB ☎ 01443 204626

Llwyncelyn Infants School Heather Way, Llwyncelyn, Porth, CF39 9TL ☎ 01443 684321

Llwyncrwn Primary School Llwyn-Crwn Road, Beddau, Pontypridd, CF38 2BE ☎ 01443 203557

Llwynypia Primary School School Terrace, Llwynypia, Tonypandy, CF40 2HL ☎ 01443 432354

Maerdy Infants School School Street, Maerdy, Ferndale, CF43 4DN ☎ 01443 755238

Maes-Y-Coed Primary School Lanwern Road, Maes-Y-Coed, Pontypridd, CF37 1EQ ☎ 01443 486835

Miskin Primary School York Street, Miskin, Mountain Ash, CF45 3BG ☎ 01443 476426

Nantgarw Infants School Quarry Street, Nantgarw, CF4 7SY ☎ 01443 841232

Newtown Primary School Mary Street, Newtown, Mountain Ash, CF45 4HH ☎ 01443 473398

Oaklands Primary School Maes Y Deri, The Oaklands, Aberaman, CF44 6AJ ☎ 01685 882577

Our Ladys R.C. Primary School Miskin Road, Miskin, Mountain Ash, CF45 3UA ☎ 01443 472230

Parc Primary School Tallis Street, Cwmparc, Treorchy, CF42 6LY ☎ 01443 776601

Parclewis Primary School Broadway, Pontypridd, CF37 1BE ☎ 01443 486836

Penderyn Primary School Pontpren, Penderyn, Aberdare, CF44 9JW ☎ 01685 811259

Pengeulan Primary School Penrhiwceiber Road, Miskin, Mountain Ash, CF45 3UW ☎ 01443 473365

Penrhiwceibr Infants School Church Street, Penrhiwceiber, Mountain Ash, CF45 3YD ☎ 01443 473487

Penrhiwfer Infants School Ardwyn Terrace, Penrhiwfer Penygraig, Tonypandy, CF40 1SF ☎ 01443 437707

Penrhys Infant School Penrhys, Tylorstown, Ferndale, CF43 3PL ☎ 01443 730146

Pentre Primary School Upper Alma Place, Pentre, CF41 DG ☎ 01443 435435

Penygraig Infants School Hendrecafn Road, Penygraig, Tonypandy, CF40 1LJ ☎ 01443 432236

Penyrenglyn Infant School Charles Street, Treherbert, Treorchy, CF42 5HF ☎ 01443 773540

Penywaun Infants School Coed Glas, Penywaun, Aberdare, CF44 9DR ☎ 01685 811959

Perthcelyn Infants Glamorgan Street, Perthcelyn, Mountain Ash, CF45 3RJ ☎ 01443 473296

Pontygwaith Primary School Graig Street, Pontygwaith, Ferndale, CF43 3LY ☎ 01443 730471

Porth Infants School Mary Street, Porth, CF39 9UH ☎ 01443 682261

Rhigos Primary School Heol y Graig, Rhigos, Aberdare, CF44 9YY ☎ 01685 811253

Rhiwgarn Infant School Waun Wen, Trebanog, Porth, CF39 9LX ☎ 01443 682811

St Gabriel & Raphael R.C.P. School Grovefield Terrace, Penygraig, Rhondda, CF40 1HL ☎ 01443 433094

St Margaret's R.C. Primary School Elizabeth Street, Aberdare, "Rhondda, Cynon, Taff", CF44 7LN ☎ 01685 876072

Ton Infants School School Street, Ton Pentre, "Rhondda, Cynon, Taff", CF41 7LS ☎ 01443 435438

Tonypandy Primary School Primrose Street, Tonypandy, CF40 1BQ ☎ 01443 433006

Trallwng Infants School Bonvilston Road, Trallwn, Pontypridd, CF37 4RD ☎ 01443 486842

Trealaw Primary School Miskin Road, Trealaw, Tonypandy, CF40 2QW ☎ 01443 432217

Tref-Y-Rhyg Primary School The Avenue, Tonyrefail, Porth, CF39 8PS ☎ 01443 670306

Trefforest Primary School Wood Road, Treforest, Pontypridd, CF37 1RJ ☎ 01443 486843

Treherbert Infants Stuart Street, Treorchy, Rhondda, CF42 5PR ☎ 01443 771371

Trehopcyn Primary School Plymouth Road, Hopkinstown, Pontypridd, CF37 2RH ☎ 01443 486844

Treorchy Primary School Glyncoli Road, Treorchy, Rhondda, CF42 6SA ☎ 01443 773084

Trerobart Primary School Crawshay Street, Ynysybwl, Pontypridd, CF37 3EF ☎ 01443 790233

Tylorstown Primary School Edmund Street, Tylorstown, Ferndale Rhondda, CF43 3HH ☎ 01443 730396

Williamstown Primary School Arthur Street, Williamstown, Tonypandy, CF40 1NZ ☎ 01443 432186

Y.G.G. Pont Sion Norton Heol Pont Sion Norton, Pontypridd, "Rhondda, Cynon, Taff", CF37 4ND ☎ 01443 486838

Ynysboeth Infant School Ynysboeth, Matthewstown, Mountain Ash, CF45 4YT ☎ 01443 473054

Ynyshir Infants School Gynor Place, Ynyshir, "Rhondda, Cynon, Taff", CF39 0NR ☎ 01443 682480

Ynyswen Infant School Ynyswen Road, Rhondda, Treorchy, CF42 6ED ☎ 01443 772410

Ysgol G. G. Llwyncelyn Heatherway, Llwyncelyn, Porth, CF39 9TL ☎ 01443 682491

Ysgol G.G. Aberdar Heol Caerdydd, Aberaman, Aberdar, CF44 6HJ ☎ 01685 872939

School name, address and telephone number

Ysgol G.G. Bodringallt Bryn Terrace, Ystrad, Pentre, CF41 7RX ☎ 01443 434096

Ysgol G.G. Bronllwyn Colwyn Road, Gelli, "Rhondda, Cynon, Taff", CF41 7NW ☎ 01443 435294

Ysgol G.G. Castellau Ffordd Castellau, Beddau, Pontypridd, CF38 2AA ☎ 01443 208700

Ysgol G.G. Evan James Ffordd Y Rhondda, Pontypridd, "Rhondda, Cynon, Taff", CF37 1HQ ☎ 01443 486813

Ysgol G.G. Llyn Y Forwyn Darran Terrace, Ferndale, Rhondda, CF43 4LG ☎ 01443 730278

Ysgol G.G. Tonyrefail School Street, Tonyrefail, Porth, CF39 8LE ☎ 01443 670319

Ysgol G.G. Ynyswen Clinic Road, Ynyswen, Treorci, CF42 6ED ☎ 01443 772432

Ysgol Gymraeg Abercynon Greenfield Terrace, Glancynon, Abercynon, CF45 4TH ☎ 01443 740239

675 MERTHYR TYDFIL/MERTHYR TUDFUL

Bedlinog Infants School Commercial Street, Bedlinog, Treharris, CF46 6RF ☎ 01443 710244

Brecon Road Infants School Norman Terrace, Merthyr Tydfil, CF47 8SD ☎ 01685 722934

Caedraw Primary School Caedraw Road, Merthyr Tydfil, CF47 8HA ☎ 01685 722620

Dowlais Infants School Market Street, Dowlais, Merthyr Tydfil, CF48 3HW ☎ 01685 723747

Gellideg Infants School Gellideg Estate, Merthyr Tydfil, CF48 1LG ☎ 01685 722916

Gellifaelog Primary School Penydarren, Merthyr Tydfil, CF47 9TJ ☎ 01685 723078

Graig Bedlinog Infants School Graig Terrace, Bedlinog, Treharris, CF46 6RY ☎ 01443 710229

Gwaunfarren Primary School Alexandra Avenue, Merthyr Tydfil, CF47 9AF ☎ 01685 722096

Heolgerrig Primary School Heolgerrig Road, Heolgerrig, Merthyr Tydfil, CF48 1SB ☎ 01685 722571

Pantysgallog Primary School Pant, Dowlais, Merthyr Tydfil, CF48 2AD ☎ 01685 722971

Pentrebach Infants School Dyffryn Road, Pentrebach, Merthyr Tydfil, CF48 4BJ ☎ 01443 690380

Trelewis Primary School Trelewis, Treharris, Merthyr Tydfil, CF46 6AH ☎ 01443 412324

Troedyrhiw Infant School The Square, Troedyrhiw, Merthyr Tydfil, CF48 4EB ☎ 01443 690252

Twynyrodyn Infants School Gilfach Cynon, Twynyrodyn, Merthyr Tydfil, CF47 0LW ☎ 01685 722469

Ysgol Rhyd-Y-Grug Rodericks Terrace, Mynwent Y Crynwyr, Treharris, CF46 5AW ☎ 01443 410212

Ysgol Santes Tudful Heol Y Frenhines, Twynyrodyn, Merthyr Tydfil, CF47 0HE ☎ 01685 722212

676 CAERPHILLY/CAERFFILI

Bargoed Infants School Usk Road, Bargoed, Caerphilly, CF81 8RJ ☎ 01443 875513

Blackwood Infant School Apollo Way, Blackwood, NP2 1WA ☎ 01495 224111

Brithdir Primary School School Street, Brithdir, New Tredegar, NP2 6XX ☎ 01443 875514

Cefn Fforest Infant & Nursery School Tyn-Y-Coed Crescent, Cefn Fforest, Blackwood, NP2 1JX ☎ 01443 830602

Crumlin High Level Primary School Commercial Road, Crumlin, NP1 4PX ☎ 01495 244606

Cwm Glas Infant School Pant Glas, Llanbradach, Caerphilly, CF83 3PD ☎ 01222 852515

Cwmaber County Infant School Bryngelli Terrace, Abertridwr, Caerphilly, CF8 2FF ☎ 01222 830248

Cwmcarn Primary School Newport Road, Cwmcarn Crosskeys, Caerphilly, NP1 7LZ ☎ 01495 270494

Cwmfelinfach Primary School King Street, Cwmfelinfach, Ynysddu, NP1 7HL ☎ 01495 200225

Cwmsyfiog Primary School Upper Road, Elliotstown, New Tredegar, NP2 6EA ☎ 01443 875515

Derwendeg Primary School Hengoed Road, Cefn Hengoed, Hengoed, CF82 7HP ☎ 01443 813138

Elliot Town Primary School White Rose Way, New Tredegar, NP2 6DW ☎ 01443 875517

Fleur-De-Lis Primary School School Street, Fleur-De-Lis, Blackwood, NP2 1UX ☎ 01443 830539

Gelligaer Village Infants School Glyngaer Road, Gelligaer, Hengoed, CF82 8FF ☎ 01443 875519

Gilfach Fargod Primary School Vere Street, Gilfach, Bargoed, CF81 8LB ☎ 01443 875510

Glan-Y-Nant Infants School Hanbury Street, Glanynant, Blackwood, NP2 1XP ☎ 01443 875520

Graig-Y-Rhacca Primary School Machen, Newport, NP1 8RJ ☎ 01222 852516

Hendredenny Park Primary Groeswen Drive, Hendredenny Estate, Caerphilly, CF8 2RL ☎ 01222 852520

Lansbury Park Infant School Lansbury Park, Caerphilly, CF83 1QH ☎ 01222 852522

Libanus Primary School Libanus Rd, Blackwood, Caerphilly, NP2 1EH ☎ 01495 225736

Llanfabon Infants School Bryncelyn Avenue, Nelson, Treharris, CF46 6HL ☎ 01443 450275

School name, address and telephone number

Lower Rhymney Primary School Eglwys Fan, Rhymney, Caerphilly, NP2 5QA ☎ 01685 840230

Markham Primary School Pantycefn Road, Markham, Blackwood, NP2 0QD ☎ 01495 224811

Nant Y Parc Primary School Universal Site, Westside, Senghenydd, CF8 2GL ☎ 01222 832116

Oakdale Infant School Maes y Garn Road, Oakdale, Blackwood, NP2 0NA ☎ 01495 222829

Penllwyn Infants School Fleur-De-Lys Avenue, Pontllanfraith, Blackwood, NP2 2NT ☎ 01495 223505

Phillipstown Primary School Cefn Rhychdir Road, Phillipstown, New Tredegar, NP2 6XE ☎ 01443 875522

Pontllanfraith Primary School Penmaen Road, Pontllanfraith, Blackwood, NP2 2DN ☎ 01495 222128

Pontlottyn Infants & Nursey School Waterloo Terrace, Pontlottyn, Bargoed, CF81 9RG ☎ 01685 841350

St Helen's R.C. Primary School Lansbury Park, Caerphilly, CF83 1QH ☎ 01222 852532

Tirphil Primary School Birchgrove, Tirphil, New Tredegar, NP2 1AH ☎ 01443 875527

Trinant Infant School Wesley Terrace, Trinant, Crumlin, NP1, 4LG ☎ 01495 214227

Ty Isaf Infants & Nursery School Mill Street, Risca, Caerphilly, NP1 6EF ☎ 01633 612420

Tyn Y Wern Infant School Navigation Street, Trethomas, Newport, NP1 8FR ☎ 01222 852529

Waunfawr Primary Waunfawr Road, Crosskeys, Caerphilly, NP1 7PG ☎ 01495 270269

Y.G. Cwm Gwyddon Heol Gwyddon, Abercarn, Caerphilly, NP1 5GX ☎ 01495 244267

Ystrad Mynach Infants Lewis Street, Ystrad Mynach, Hengoed, CF82 7AQ ☎ 01443 812507

677 BLAENAU GWENT

Arael Primary School Aberbeeg Road, Aberbeeg, Abertillery, NP3 2EG ☎ 01495 212176

Blaentillery Infants School Bridge Terrace, Cwmtillery, Abertillery, NP3 1LD ☎ 01495 212412

Blaina Infant School High Street, Blaina, Blaenau Gwent, NP3 3BN ☎ 01495 290232

Brynhyfryd Primary School Upper Court Terrace, Llanhilleth, Abertillery, NP3 2RH ☎ 01495 214577

Cwm Primary School Canning Street, Cwm, Ebbw Vale, NP3 6RD ☎ 01495 370437

Garn Fach Infant School Co-Operative Terrace, Nantyglo, Brynmawr, NP3 4LL ☎ 01495 310462

Garnlydan Primary School Commonwealth Road, Garnlydan, Ebbw Vale, NP3 5ER ☎ 01495 302004

Glyncoed Infant School Badminton Grove, Ebbw Vale, Blaenau Gwent, NP3 5UL ☎ 01495 302402

Sirhowy Infant School King Street, Sirhowy, Tredegar, NP2 4PA ☎ 01495 722237

Sofrydd C.P. School Sofrydd Road, Crumlin, Newbridge, NP1 5DW ☎ 01495 244003

Willowtown Infants & Nursery School Brynheulog Street, Ebbw Vale, Blaenau Gwent, NP3, 6NJ, 01495 302436

Ysgol Gymraeg Brynmawr Stryd Y Brenin, Brynmawr, Blaenau Gwent, NP3, 4RG, 01495 310735

678 TORFAEN/TOR-FAEN

Croesyceiliog North Rd Infants North Road, Croesyceiliog, Cwmbran, NP44 2LL ☎ 01633 482352

George Street C.P. School Upper George Street, Wainfelin Road, Pontypool, NP4 6BX ☎ 01495 756436

Kemys Fawr Infants School Elm Grove, Sebastopol, Pontypool, NP4 5DD ☎ 01495 763175

New Inn Infants School Hillcrest Jerusalem Lane, New Inn, Pontypool, NP4 0NG ☎ 01495 757649

Oakfield Primary School Green Willows, Oakfield, Cwmbran, NP44 3DU ☎ 01633 482838

Penygarn Infant School Penygarn Road, Penygarn, Pontypool, NP4 8JR ☎ 01495 762601

Upper Cwmbran Infants School Upper Cwmbran Road, Upper Cwmbran, Cwmbran, NP44 1SN ☎ 01633 482102

Woodlands Infants School Thornhill Road, Upper Cwmbran, Cwmbran, NP44 5UA ☎ 01633 865383

679 MONMOUTHSHIRE/SIR FYNWY

Caldicot Sandy Lane Infants School Sandy Lane, Caldicot, Newport, NP6 4NQ ☎ 01291 420677

Caldicot West End Infants School Masefield Road, Caldicot, Newport, NP6 4JY ☎ 01291 420428

Llwynu Infants School Llwynu Lane, Abergavenny, Monmouthshire, NP7 6AR ☎ 01873 853350

Magor V.A. Primary School Sycamore Terrace, Magor, Newport, NP6 3EG ☎ 01633 880327

Pembroke Infants School Fairfield Road, Bulwark, Chepstow, NP6 5JN ☎ 01291 622118

Thornwell Primary School Thornwell Road, Bulwark, Chepstow, NP6 5NT ☎ 01291 623390

Wyesham Infants School Wyesham Road, Wyesham, Monmouth, NP5 3JT ☎ 01600 712927

School name, address and telephone number

680 NEWPORT/CASNEWYDD

Alway Infant School Aberthaw Road, Newport, NP9 9QP ☎ 01633 277952

Caerleon (Lodge Hill) Infants School Roman Way, Caerleon, Newport, NP6 1DY ☎ 01633 421735

Caerleon Endowed Infant school High Street, Caerleon, Newport, NP6 1AZ ☎ 01633 421237

Cefn Wood C.P. School Ebenezer Drive, Highcross Estate, Rogerstone, NP1 9YX ☎ 01633 894591

Crindau Junior & Infant School Ailesbury Street, Newport, NP9 5ND ☎ 01633 858268

Duffryn Infant School Partridge Way, Duffryn, Newport, NP9 9WP ☎ 01633 815032

Eveswell Primary School Chepstow Road, Newport, NP9 8GX ☎ 01633 272142

Gaer Infant School Melfort Road, Newport, NP9 3FP ☎ 01633 265620

Llanmartin Primary School Waltwood Road, Llanmartin, Newport, NP6 2HB ☎ 01633 412660

Lliswerry Infant School Nash Road, Newport, NP9 0NG ☎ 01633 277018

Maesglas C.P. School Maesglas Road, Newport, NP9 3DG ☎ 01633 816047

Maindee C.P. School 108 Corporation Road, Newport, NP9 8BY ☎ 01633 263309

Malpas Court Primary School Whittle Drive, Newport, NP9 6NS ☎ 01633 855005

Milton Infants School Hendre Farm Drive, Newport, NP9 9HB ☎ 01633 273505

Pillgwenlly C.P. School Capel Crescent, Newport, NP9 2FT ☎ 01633 265268

Ringland Infant School Dunstable Road, Newport, NP9 9LU ☎ 01633 277789

Somerton Primary School Hawthorn Fosse, Newport, NP9 9AB ☎ 01633 272504

St Andrew's Infant School Milner Street, Newport, NP9 0GS ☎ 01633 257262

St Julians Infant School Beaufort Road, Newport, NP9 7PB ☎ 01633 259507

681 CARDIFF/CAERDYDD

Adamsdown Primary School System Street, Adamsdown, Cardiff, CF2 1JF ☎ 01222 493600

Albany Primary School Albany Road, Cardiff, CF2 3RR ☎ 01222 499520

Allensbank Primary School Llanishen Street, Heath, Cardiff, CF4 3QE ☎ 01222 619022

Baden Powell Primary School and Nursery Unit Muirton Road, Tremorfa, Cardiff, CF2 2SJ ☎ 01222 461894

Bryn Celyn Infant School Glyn Collen, Pentwyn, Cardiff, CF2 7ES ☎ 01222 733479

Bryn Hafod Primary School Blagdon Close, Llanrumney, Cardiff, CF3 9HF ☎ 01222 793402

Cefn Onn Primary School Llangranog Road, Llanishen, Cardiff, CF4 5BL ☎ 01222 753088

Creigiau Primary School Tregarth Court, Creigiau, Cardiff, CF4 8NN ☎ 01222 891045

Danescourt Infants & Nursery Danescourt Way, Llandaff, Cardiff, CF5 2RB ☎ 01222 552422

Gabalfa Primary School Colwill Road, Gabalfa, Cardiff, CF4 2QQ ☎ 01222 624615

Gladstone Infant &Nursery School Whitchurch Road, Cathays, Cardiff, CF4 3JL ☎ 01222 399615

Greenway Primary Llanstephan Road, Rumney, Cardiff, CF3 8JB ☎ 01222 777048

Hawthorn Infant School Hawthorn Road East, Llandaff North, Cardiff, CF4 2LR ☎ 01222 564465

Herbert Thompson Infants Plymouthwood Road, Ely, Cardiff, CF5 4XD ☎ 01222 561115

Hywel Dda Infants & Nursery Cambria Road, Ely, Cardiff, CF5 4PD ☎ 01222 591275

Kitchener Primary School Kitchener Road, Canton, Cardiff, CF1 8HT ☎ 01222 387505

Llanedeyrn Primary School Wellwood, Llanedeyrn, Cardiff, CF3 7JS ☎ 01222 736421

Meadowlane Primary School Heol Maes Eirwg, St Mellons, Cardiff, CF3 0JZ ☎ 01222 360340

Moorland Primary School Singleton Road, Splott, Cardiff, CF2 2LJ ☎ 01222 462170

Mount Stuart Primary Adelaide Street, Docks, Cardiff, CF1 6BS ☎ 01222 481188

Ninian Park Primary Virgil Street, Grangetown, Cardiff, CF1 7TF ☎ 01222 388991

Pen-Y-Bryn Primary Dunster Road, Llanrumney, Cardiff, CF3 9TP ☎ 01222 777618

Pentrebane Primary School Beechley Drive, Pentrebane, Cardiff, CF5 3SG ☎ 01222 565773

Peter Lea Primary Carter Place, Fairwater, Cardiff, CF5 3NP ☎ 01222 562034

Roath Park Primary School Penywain Road, Roath Park, Cardiff, CF2 3NB ☎ 01222 499549

School name, address and telephone number

Rumney Infants & Nursery Wentloog Road, Rumney, Cardiff, CF3 8HD ☎ 01222 791345

Severn Infants & Nursery School Severn Road, Canton, Cardiff, CF1 9DZ ☎ 01222 229638

Springwood Primary School Pennsylvania, Llanedeyrn, Cardiff, CF3 7LS ☎ 01222 735101

St Bernadette's R.C. Primary Bryn Heulog, Off Pentwyn Drive, Pentwyn, CF2 7JB ☎ 01222 733443

St David's C.I.W. Primary Bryn Celyn Road, Pentwyn, Cardiff, CF2 7ED ☎ 01222 734308

St Mary The Virgin C.I.W. Primary North Church Street, Butetown, Cardiff, CF1 5HB ☎ 01222 481608

St Peter's R.C. Primary Southey Street, Roath, Cardiff, CF2 1AP ☎ 01222 497847

St Philip Evans R.C. 134-340 Coed-Y-Gores, Llanedeyrn, Cardiff, CF3 7NX ☎ 01222 732514

Stacey Primary School Stacey Road, Roath, Cardiff, CF2 1DW ☎ 01222 499508

Tongwynlais C.P. Merthyr Road, Tongwynlais, Cardiff, CF4 7LF ☎ 01222 810383

Tredegarville C.I.W. Primary Glossop Road, Roath, Cardiff, CF2 1JT ☎ 01222 483680

Trelai C.P. School Bishopston Road, Cardiff, CF5 5DY ☎ 01222 561575

Trowbridge Infants & Nursery Glan-Y-Mor Road, Trowbridge, Rumney, CF3 8RQ ☎ 01222 791255

Willowbrook C.P. School Sandbrook Road, St Mellons, Cardiff, CF3 0ST ☎ 01222 795965

Windsor Clive Infant & Nursery Grand Avenue, Ely, Cardiff, CF5 4XH ☎ 01222 591297

Ysgol Bro Eirwg Ridgeway Road, Rumney, Cardiff, CF3 9AB ☎ 01222 777124

Ysgol Gynradd Gwaelod-Y-Garth Primary School Main Road, Gwaelodygarth, Cardiff, CF4 8HJ ☎ 01222 810489

Ysgol Pwll Coch Adjacent to Fitzalan High, Lawrenny Avenue, Cardiff, CF1 8XB

SOEID Number	School name, address and telephone number	No. of pupils in nursery class
ABERDEEN CITY		
5237521	**Abbotswell School** Faulds Gate, Aberdeen, AB12 5QX ☎ 01224 872714	40
5237726	**Ashgrove Nursery/Infant School** Gillespie Place, Aberdeen, AB25 3BE ☎ 01224 482293	71
5237823	**Ashley Road School** 45 Ashley Road, Aberdeen, AB10 6RU ☎ 01224 588732	40
5238021	**Braeside Nursery/Infant School** Braeside Place, Aberdeen, AB15 7TX ☎ 01224 313953	38
5234220	**Bucksburn School** Inverurie Road, Bucksburn, Aberdeen, AB21 9LL ☎ 01224 712862	34
5238420	**Byron Park Nursery/Infant School** Cruden Park, Northfield, Aberdeen, AB16 7JL ☎ 01224 693529	70
5238528	**Causewayend School** Causewayend, Aberdeen, AB25 3TJ ☎ 01224 636776	32
5234522	**Culter School** 22 School Road, Peterculter, Aberdeen, AB14 0RX ☎ 01224 733197	80
5234727	**Cults Primary School** Earlswells Road, Cults, Aberdeen, AB15 9RG ☎ 01224 869221	37
5246326	**Danestone Primary School** Fairview Brae, Bridge Of Don, Aberdeen, AB22 8ZN ☎ 01224 825062	38
5239125	**Donbank School** Dill Road, Tillydrone, Aberdeen, AB24 2XL ☎ 01224 483217	40
5239427	**Fernielea School** Stronsay Place, Aberdeen, AB15 6HD ☎ 01224 318533	80
5239524	**Ferryhill School** Caledonian Place, Aberdeen, AB11 6TT ☎ 01224 586755	40
5246121	**Forehill School** Jesmond Drive, Bridge Of Don, Aberdeen, AB22 8UR ☎ 01224 820904	39
5241626	**Gilcomstoun School** Skene Street, Aberdeen, AB10 1PG ☎ 01224 642722	30
5235529	**Glashieburn School** Jesmond Drive, Bridge Of Don, Aberdeen, AB22 8UR ☎ 01224 704476	40
5239621	**Greenfern Nursery/Infant School** Maidencraig Place, Aberdeen, AB16 6QN ☎ 01224 693598	40
5239729	**Hanover Street School** Beach Boulevard, Aberdeen, AB24 5HN ☎ 01224 588864	51
5237017	**Hilton Nursery School** Hilton Avenue, Aberdeen, AB24 4RE ☎ 01224 484664	76
5245923	**Kaimhill Primary School** Pitmedden Terrace, Aberdeen, AB10 7HR ☎ 01224 316356	80
5235227	**Kingswells Primary School** Kingswells Avenue, Kingswells, Aberdeen, AB15 8TG ☎ 01224 740262	38
5240328	**Kingswood Nursery/Infant School** Birkhall Parade, Aberdeen, AB16 5QT ☎ 01224 692680	38
5240425	**Kittybrewster School** Great Northern Road, Aberdeen, AB24 3QG ☎ 01224 484451	38
5246024	**Loirston School** Loirston Avenue, Cove Bay, Aberdeen, AB12 3HE ☎ 01224 897686	38
5240727	**Marchburn Nursery/Infant School** Marchburn Drive, Aberdeen, AB16 7PN ☎ 01224 695436	80
5235324	**Milltimber School** Monearn Gardens, Milltimber, Aberdeen, AB13 0DX ☎ 01224 732517	33
5241022	**Muirfield School** Mastrick Drive, Aberdeen, AB16 6UE ☎ 01224 694958	80
5234123	**Scotstown School** Scotstown Road, Bridge Of Don, Aberdeen, AB22 8HH ☎ 01224 703331	68
5241529	**Seaton School** Seaton Place East, Aberdeen, AB24 1XE ☎ 01224 483414	49
5241421	**Skene Square School** 61 Skene Square, Aberdeen, AB25 2UN ☎ 01224 630493	57
5241723	**Smithfield School** Clarke Street, Aberdeen, AB16 7XJ ☎ 01224 696952	50
5241928	**St Joseph's RC School** 1-5 Queen's Road, Aberdeen, AB15 4YL ☎ 01224 322730	55
5242029	**St Machar School** Harris Drive, Tillydrone, Aberdeen, AB24 2TF ☎ 01224 484254	33
5237114	**St Peter's Nursery School** 137 Spital, Aberdeen, AB24 3HX ☎ 01224 636150	37
5242223	**Sunnybank School** Sunnybank Road, Aberdeen, AB24 3NJ ☎ 01224 633363	46
5237319	**Torry Nursery School** Oscar Road, Torry, Aberdeen, AB11 8ER ☎ 01224 876736	79
5242428	**Tullos School** Girdleness Road, Aberdeen, AB11 8FJ ☎ 01224 876621	73
5248620	**Upper Westfield School** Braehead Way, Bridge Of Don, Aberdeen, AB22 8RR ☎ 01224 703796	99
5242525	**Victoria Road School** Victoria Road, Torry, Aberdeen, AB11 9NT ☎ 01224 876784	31
5242827	**Walker Road School** Walker Road, Aberdeen, AB11 8DL ☎ 01224 879720	40
5243122	**Woodside School** Clifton Road, Aberdeen, AB24 4EA ☎ 01224 484778	70

SOEID Number	School name, address and telephone number	No. of pupils in nursery class
INDEPENDENT		
5281628	**Aberdeen Waldorf School** Craigton Road, Cults, Aberdeen, AB15 9QD ☎ 01224 868366	18
5280737	**International School of Aberdeen** 296 North Deeside Road, Milltimber, Aberdeen, AB13 0AB ☎ 01224 735648	19
5282039	**Robert Gordon's College** Schoolhill, Aberdeen, AB10 1FE ☎ 01224 646346	42
5282136	**St Margaret's School for Girls** Aberdeen, 17 Albyn Place, Aberdeen, AB10 1RU ☎ 01224 584466	24
5282527	**The Hamilton School** 80-84 Queens Road, Aberdeen, AB15 4YE ☎ 01224 317295	167
ABERDEENSHIRE		
5212227	**Aberchirder Primary School** Smith Crescent, Aberchirder, Huntly, Aberdeenshire, AB54 7TW ☎ 01466 780241	37
5256127	**Aboyne Primary School** Aboyne, Aberdeenshire, AB34 5JN ☎ 01339 886638	43
5232422	**Alehousewells School** Bremner Way, Kemnay, Aberdeenshire, AB51 5FT ☎ 01467 642247	60
5224020	**Alford Primary School** Greystone Road, Alford, Aberdeenshire, AB33 8TY ☎ 01975 562395	38
5251524	**Arduthie School** Arduthie Road, Stonehaven, Kincardineshire, AB39 2DP ☎ 01569 762996	59
5225922	**Auchterellon Primary School** Millwood Road, Ellon, Aberdeenshire, AB41 9FA ☎ 01358 720863	106
5224225	**Balmedie School** Forsyth Road, Balmedie, Aberdeenshire, AB23 8YN ☎ 01358 742474	40
5257824	**Banchory Primary School** Arbeadie Road, Banchory, Kincardineshire, AB31 4EH ☎ 01330 823351	98
5249120	**Bervie School** Church Street, Inverbervie, Angus, DD10 0RU ☎ 01561 361312	60
5215927	**Buchanhaven School** Hope Street, Peterhead, Aberdeenshire, AB42 1HD ☎ 01779 472543	92
5218624	**Clerkhill School** Cairntrodlie, Peterhead, Aberdeenshire, AB42 2AX ☎ 01779 472473	30
5216125	**Crimond School** Logie Road, Crimond, Fraserburgh, Aberdeenshire, AB43 8QL ☎ 01346 532251	36
5232627	**Crombie School** Hays Way, Westhill, Aberdeen, AB32 6UH ☎ 01224 740900	44
5221927	**Dales Park School** Berryden Road, Peterhead, Aberdeenshire, AB42 2GD ☎ 01779 477133	26
5233224	**Elrick School** Rowan Drive, Westhill, Aberdeenshire, AB32 6QB ☎ 01224 741900	42
5216923	**Fraserburgh North School** Finlayson Street, Fraserburgh, AB43 9JR ☎ 01346 518015	34
5210119	**Fyvie/Monquhitter Nursery** c/o Fyvie School, Fyvie, Turriff, AB53 8RD ☎ 01651 891247	57
5226724	**Gordon Primary School** Huntly, Aberdeenshire, AB54 4SE ☎ 01466 792550	60
5210216	**Howe O' The Mearns Nursery** c/o Laurencekirk School, Aberdeen Road, Laurencekirk, AB30 1AJ ☎ 01561 377739	68
5231523	**Insch School** Alexander Street, Insch, Aberdeenshire, AB52 6JH ☎ 01464 820252	58
5217326	**Inverallochy School** School Street, Inverallochy, Fraserburgh, Aberdeenshire, AB43 8XZ ☎ 01346 582217	20
5232228	**Kellands School** Inverurie, Aberdeenshire, AB51 3YH ☎ 01467 620153	103
5212014	**Kingswell Nursery School** Seafield Street, Banff, AB45 1ED ☎ 01261 812215	80
5230012	**Kintore/Kinellar Nursery** 41 School Road, Kintore, Aberdeenshire, AB51 0UX ☎ 01467 632246	55
5222020	**Lochpots School** Robertson Road, Fraserburgh, AB43 9BF ☎ 01346 515751	56
5222222	**Markethill School** Baden Powell Road, Turriff, Aberdeenshire, AB53 4FA ☎ 01888 562828	60
5218721	**Meethill School** School Road, Peterhead, Aberdeenshire, AB42 2BF ☎ 01779 474920	68
5232724	**Meiklemill School** Provost Davidson Drive, Ellon, Aberdeenshire, AB41 9BQ ☎ 01358 721852	48
5227828	**Meldrum School** Commercial Road, Oldmeldrum, Aberdeenshire, AB51 0BF ☎ 01651 872283	42
5257727	**Mill O'Forest School** Woodview Place, Stonehaven, Kincardineshire, AB39 2TD ☎ 01569 763561	93
5228425	**New Machar School** 7 School Road, Newmachar, Aberdeenshire, AB21 0WB ☎ 01651 862245	36
5220424	**New Pitsligo & St John's School** School Street, New Pitsligo, Fraserburgh, Aberdeenshire, AB43 6NE ☎ 01771 653232	16
5251028	**Newtonhill School** St Michael's Road, Newtonhill, Stonehaven, Kincardineshire, AB39 3XW ☎ 01569 730597	57
5221722	**Pitfour School** Newlands Road, Mintlaw, Peterhead, AB42 5GP ☎ 01771 622855	60
5228824	**Pitmedden School** Pitmedden, Ellon, Aberdeenshire, AB41 7NY ☎ 01651 842374	58
5219027	**Port Erroll School** Braehead Drive, Cruden Bay, Aberdeenshire, AB42 0NP ☎ 01779 812622	50
5251125	**Portlethen Primary School** Cookston Road, Portlethen, Aberdeen, AB12 4PT ☎ 01224 780238	106

SOEID Number	School name, address and telephone number	No. of pupils in nursery class
5213029	**Portsoy School** Chapel Street, Portsoy, Banffshire, AB45 2RB ☎ 01261 842238	18
5216729	**St Andrew's Primary School** 113 Charlotte Street, Fraserburgh, AB43 9LS ☎ 01346 518247	64
5220920	**Strichen School** North Street, Strichen, Fraserburgh, Aberdeenshire, AB43 6SX ☎ 01771 637250	18
5257425	**Torphins School** Beltie Road, Torphins, Banchory, Kincardineshire, AB31 4JT ☎ 01339 882269	47
5210313	**Upper Deeside Nursery** c/o Tarland School, School Road, Tarland, AB34 4UU ☎ 01339 881204	39
5210410	**Upper Donside Nursery** c/o Tullynessle School, Tullynessle, Alford, AB33 8QN ☎ 01975 562365	43
5230527	**Westhill Primary School** Westhill Drive, Westhill, Aberdeenshire, AB32 6FY ☎ 01224 740225	50
5213126	**Whitehills School** Forbes Road, Whitehills, Banff, AB45 2LX ☎ 01261 861431	20
INDEPENDENT		
5282128	**Glen Morven School** Ballogie, Aboyne, Aberdeenshire, AB34 5DP ☎ 01339 886765	22

ANGUS

SOEID Number	School name, address and telephone number	No. of pupils in nursery class
5300223	**Airlie Primary School** By Kirriemuir, DD8 5NP ☎ 01575 530254	7
5320720	**Birkhill Primary School** Dronley Road, Birkhill, Dundee, DD2 5QD ☎ 01382 580524	40
5308925	**Borrowfield Primary School** Newhame Road, Montrose, DD10 9EZ ☎ 01674 673091	60
5307821	**Carlogie Primary School** Caesar Avenue, Carnoustie, DD7 6DS ☎ 01241 859484	67
5303125	**Chapelpark Primary School** Academy Street, Forfar, Angus, DD8 2HA ☎ 01307 462996	55
5302722	**Edzell Primary School** Church Street, Edzell, Brechin, DD9 7TQ ☎ 01356 648245	10
5303028	**Ferryden Primary School** Craig Crescent, Ferryden, Montrose, DD10 9RF ☎ 01674 672248	19
5303621	**Friockheim Primary School** Friockheim, By Arbroath, DD11 4XB ☎ 01241 828315	29
5300428	**Hayshead Primary School** St Abb's Road, Arbroath, DD11 5AB ☎ 01241 872453	60
5304121	**Inverarity Primary School** Inverarity, By Forfar, DD8 2JN ☎ 01307 820262	5
5300525	**Inverbrothock Primary School** East Kirkton Road, Arbroath, DD11 4HR ☎ 01241 873410	36
5304229	**Inverkeilor Primary School** Station Road, Inverkeilor, Arbroath, DD11 5RY ☎ 01241 830260	9
5301823	**Kinloch Primary School** Links Avenue, Carnoustie, DD7 7EP ☎ 01241 853567	61
5303222	**Kirkriggs Primary School** St James Road, Forfar, DD8 1LE ☎ 01307 463791	53
5300622	**Ladyloan Primary School** Millgate Loan, Arbroath, DD11 1LX ☎ 01241 875302	46
5303427	**Langlands Primary School** Glamis Road, Forfar, DD8 1JY ☎ 01307 463893	58
5304822	**Letham Primary School** 3 Braehead Road, Letham, By Forfar, DD8 2PG ☎ 01307 818284	18
5307929	**Lochside Primary School** Glenesk Avenue, Montrose, DD10 9AN ☎ 01674 672549	57
5305624	**Monikie Primary School** Craigton Road, Monikie, By Dundee, DD5 3QN ☎ 01382 370338	10
5300827	**Muirfield Primary School** School Road, Arbroath, DD11 3LU ☎ 01241 875303	29
5320828	**Murroes Primary School** Duntrune, By Dundee, DD4 0PL ☎ 01382 350202	8
5308232	**Newtyle Primary School** Dunarn Street, Newtyle, Blairgowrie, PH12 8UJ ☎ 01828 650232	10
5308127	**Northmuir Primary School** 91 Roods, Kirriemuir, DD8 4HA ☎ 01575 572184	54
5320623	**Seaview Primary School** Victoria Street, Monifieth, Tayside, DD5 4HL ☎ 01382 533401	85
5305926	**Southesk Primary School** Hill Place, Montrose, DD10 8BP ☎ 01674 673100	33
5304725	**Southmuir Primary School** Glamis Road, Kirriemuir, DD8 5BN ☎ 01575 572042	40
5306825	**Tannadice Primary School** Tannadice, By Forfar, DD8 3SH ☎ 01307 850200	16
5301025	**Timmergreens Primary School** Annesley Drive, Arbroath, DD11 2HJ ☎ 01241 874593	59
5300711	**Townhead Nursery School** St Andrew Street, Brechin, Tayside, DD9 6JJ ☎ 01356 622925	112
5301122	**Warddykes Primary School** Brechin Road, Arbroath, DD11 4AN ☎ 01241 874379	59
INDEPENDENT		
5281334	**Lathallan Preparatory School** Brotherton Castle, Johnshaven, By Montrose, DD10 0HN ☎ 01561 362220	50

SOEID Number	School name, address and telephone number	No. of pupils in nursery class
ARGYLL & BUTE		
8111812	**Campbeltown Nursery Centre** Ralston Road, Campbeltown, Argyll, PA28 6LE ☎ 01586 552397	92
8111324	**Dalintober Primary School** High Street, Campbeltown, Argyll, PA28 6HG ☎ 01586 552053	21
8102821	**Dunoon Primary School** Hillfoot Street, Dunoon, Argyll, PA23 7DR ☎ 01369 704159	27
8103127	**Easdale Primary School** Isle of Seil, By Oban, Argyll, PA34 4RF ☎ 01852 300243	13
8302928	**John Logie Baird Primary School** Winston Road, Helensburgh, G84 9EP ☎ 01436 674001	27
8300313	**Kirkmichael Nursery School** Townhead Road, Kirkmichael, Helensburgh, G84 7LY ☎ 01436 675843	114
8106827	**Newton Primary School** Isle of Islay, Argyll, PA44 7PD ☎ 01496 810374	8
8108323	**Sandbank Primary School** Sandbank, By Dunoon, Argyll, PA23 8PW ☎ 01369 706350	10
8111448	**White Gates Learning Centre** White Gates Road, Lochgilphead, PA31 8SY ☎ 01546 602583	24
INDEPENDENT		
8380139	**Lomond School** 10 Stafford Street, Helensburgh, G84 9JX ☎ 01436 672476	36
8380023	**Park Lodge School** 17 Charlotte Street, Helensburgh, G84 7EY ☎ 01436 673008	39
CLACKMANNANSHIRE		
5701929	**Abercromby Primary School** 4 School Road, Tullibody, FK10 2QA ☎ 01259 722972	58
5700825	**Alva Primary School** Brook Street, Alva, FK12 5LY ☎ 01259 760987	60
5700116	**Clackmannan Nursery School** Port Street, Clackmannan, FK10 4JS ☎ 01259 217486	75
5701023	**Coalsnaughton Primary School** Blackfaulds Street, Coalsnaughton, FK13 6JU ☎ 01259 750204	18
5703115	**Ladywell Nursery School** St Serf's Road, Tullibody, Alloa, FK10 2RD ☎ 01259 216200	93
5700213	**Sauchie Nursery School** by Holton Cottages, Sauchie, By Alloa, FK10 3NQ ☎ 01259 214752	137
5701120	**Strathdevon Primary School** Park Place, Dollar, FK14 7AA ☎ 01259 742435	29
5701821	**Tillicoultry Primary School** Fir Park, Tillicoultry, FK13 6PL ☎ 01259 750228	60
5703417	**Tower Nursery School** Scott Crescent, Alloa, FK10 1BD ☎ 01259 216748	134
DUMFRIES & GALLOWAY		
5945526	**Beattock School** Beattock, Moffat, DG10 9RB ☎ 01683 300363	15
5910323	**Belmont School** Galloway Avenue, Stranraer, DG9 7BH ☎ 01776 702952	47
5941326	**Cargenbridge School** Cargenbridge, Dumfries, DG2 8LW ☎ 01387 269046	46
5915422	**Castle Douglas Primary School** Jenny's Loaning, Castle Douglas, DG7 1JA ☎ 01556 502516	71
5916828	**Castledykes School** Castledykes Road, Kirkcudbright, DG6 4JT ☎ 01557 330363	50
5935628	**Closeburn School** Closeburn, Thornhill, Dumfriesshire, DG3 5HP ☎ 01848 331240	34
5916127	**Dalbeattie Primary School** Southwick Road, Dalbeattie, DG5 4HR ☎ 01556 610323	89
5918332	**Dalry Secondary** Dalry, Castle Douglas, DG7 3UZ ☎ 01644 430259	12
5946328	**Eastriggs School** Annan Road, Eastriggs, Annan, DG12 6PZ ☎ 01461 40301	25
5918928	**Gatehouse School** Gatehouse Of Fleet, Castle Douglas, DG7 2JX ☎ 01557 814262	28
5937329	**Georgetown School** Gillbrae Road, Dumfries, DG1 4EJ ☎ 01387 263703	88
5947022	**Gretna School** Victory Avenue, Gretna, DG16 5AG ☎ 01461 338305	58
5945127	**Hecklegirth School** Solway Street, Annan, Dumfriesshire, DG12 6HY ☎ 01461 202606	61
5946425	**Hoddom School** Langlands Road, Ecclefechan, Lockerbie, DG11 3DS ☎ 01576 300613	29
5937825	**Kelloholm School** Hyslop Street, Kelloholm, Sanquhar, DG4 6QJ ☎ 01659 67228	41
5949025	**Langholm Primary School** Thomas Telford Road, Langholm, DG13 0BL ☎ 01387 380900	49
5935822	**Laurieknowe School** Laurieknowe, Dumfries, DG2 7AJ ☎ 01387 252459	41
5936020	**Lincluden School** Priory Road, Lincluden, Dumfries, DG2 0PU ☎ 01387 252028	47
5937922	**Locharbriggs School** Wallamhill Road, Locharbriggs, Dumfries, DG1 1UW ☎ 01387 710241	61
5947820	**Lochmaben School** Lochmaben, Lockerbie, DG11 1NR ☎ 01387 810208	57
5936128	**Lochside School** Lochside Road, Dumfries, DG2 0NF ☎ 01387 720318	47

SOEID Number	School name, address and telephone number	No. of pupils in nursery class
5948827	**Lockerbie Primary School** King Edward Park, Lockerbie, DG11 2PQ ☎ 01576 203361	64
5910226	**Minnigaff School** McGregor Drive, Minnigaff, Newton Stewart, DG8 6PE ☎ 01671 402477	62
5948738	**Moffat Academy** Academy Road, Moffat, DG10 9DA ☎ 01683 220114	40
5945224	**Newington School** Hospital Road, Annan, Dumfriesshire, DG12 6LA ☎ 01461 202459	57
5936322	**Noblehill School** Annan Road, Dumfries, DG1 3HB ☎ 01387 252167	124
5902223	**Park School** Ashwood Drive, Stranraer, DG9 7NW ☎ 01776 703243	41
5902320	**Rephad School** Ladies Walk, Stranraer, DG9 8BW ☎ 01776 704195	72
5940427	**Sanquhar Primary School** Queensberry Court, Lovedale, Sanquhar, DG4 6AE ☎ 01659 50275	38
5902525	**Sheuchan School** Leswalt High Road, Stranraer, DG9 0AL ☎ 01776 702835	49
5936527	**St Ninian's School** Lochside Road, Dumfries, DG2 0EL ☎ 01387 720364	38
5936721	**St Teresa's R.C.School** Lochside Road, Dumfries, DG2 0DY ☎ 01387 255732	25
5936829	**Troqueer School** Troqueer, Dumfries, DG2 7LR ☎ 01387 252615	48
5903629	**Whithorn School** Whithorn, Newton Stewart, DG8 8PN ☎ 01988 500291	21
5902622	**Wigtown Primary School** New Road, Wigtown, DG8 9JE ☎ 01988 402300	22
INDEPENDENT		
5680239	**Cademuir International School** Crawfordton House, Moniaive, Thornhill, DG3 4HG ☎ 01848 200212	9

DUNDEE CITY

SOEID Number	School name, address and telephone number	No. of pupils in nursery class
5352622	**Newfields Primary School** Maybole Place, Dundee, DD4 0NE ☎ 01382 438522	45
5327024	**Powrie Primary School** Baluniefield Road, Dundee, DD4 8SZ ☎ 01382 436882	39
5329221	**Sidlaw View Primary School** Helmsdale Place, Dundee, DD3 0NE ☎ 01382 436458	7
5328020	**St Margarets RC Primary School** Nithsdale Avenue, Dundee, DD3 9BA ☎ 01382 436481	37
5328225	**St Mary's RC Primary School** St Mary's Lane, Lochee, Dundee, DD2 3AQ ☎ 01382 436707	35
5328527	**St Ninian's Primary School** Dochart Terrace, Menzieshill, Dundee, DD2 4HB ☎ 01382 435904	37
5328829	**St Vincent's RC Primary School** Pitkerro Road, Dundee, DD4 8EP ☎ 01382 438552	24

EAST AYRSHIRE

SOEID Number	School name, address and telephone number	No. of pupils in nursery class
8240019	**Auchinleck Nursery School** Main Street, Auchinleck, KA18 2BB ☎ 01290 421260	88
8225214	**Cairns Nursery School** Farm Road, Kilmarnock, KA3 1PH ☎ 01563 533177	128
8240116	**Catrine Nursery School** 57 Newton Street, Catrine, KA5 6RY ☎ 01290 551233	75
8241627	**Dalrymple Primary School** Hillview, Dalrymple, KA6 6PZ ☎ 01292 560368	31
8244316	**Dame Helen's Nursery School** Ayr Road, Dalmellington, KA6 7SJ ☎ 01292 550607	40
8220018	**Darvel Nursery School** 18 Ronaldcoup Road, Darvel, KA17 0JU ☎ 01560 320785	86
8240310	**Drongan Nursery School** Millmannoch Avenue, Drongan, KA6 7BY ☎ 01292 591521	64
8220115	**Galston Nursery School** Brewlands Street, Galston, KA4 8DX ☎ 01563 820360	92
8225427	**Gargieston Primary School** Dundonald Road, Kilmarnock, KA1 1UG ☎ 01563 533067	32
8221421	**Hurlford Primary School** Union Street, Hurlford, KA1 5BT ☎ 01563 525098	37
8225117	**Kilmaurs Nursery School** Sunnyside, Kilmaurs, KA3 2SA ☎ 01563 538674	56
8241929	**Mauchline Primary School** The Loan, Mauchline, KA5 6AN ☎ 01290 550306	60
8240418	**Muirkirk Nursery School** Pagan Walk, Muirkirk, KA18 3PU ☎ 01290 661474	24
8223726	**Nether Robertland Primary School** Pokelly Place, Stewarton, KA3 5PF ☎ 01560 482035	34
8241120	**Netherthird Primary School** Craigens Road, Cumnock, KA18 3AN ☎ 01290 421980	42
8240515	**New Cumnock Nursery School** 4 The Castle, New Cumnock, KA18 4AH ☎ 01290 338593	83
8225311	**Onthank Nursery School** Meiklewood Road, , Kilmarnock, KA3 2ES ☎ 01563 534660	111
8242720	**Patna Primary School** Carnshalloch Avenue, Patna, KA6 7NP ☎ 01292 531271	45
8225710	**Riccarton Nursery School** Campbell Street, Kilmarnock, KA1 4DY ☎ 01563 535633	94
8220212	**Shortlees Nursery School** Knockmarloch Drive, Kilmarnock, KA1 4QY ☎ 01563 533678	70
8222827	**St Matthew's Primary School** MacDonald Drive, Kilmarnock, KA3 7HQ ☎ 01563 533555	75

SOEID Number	School name, address and telephone number	No. of pupils in nursery class
EAST DUNBARTONSHIRE		
8340021	**Auchinairn Primary School** Beech Road, Bishopbriggs, Glasgow, G64 1NE ☎ 0141 7723753	40
8324123	**Baljaffray Primary School** Grampian Way, Bearsden, G61 4RA ☎ 0141 9423638	59
8325227	**Clober Primary School** Kirk Street, Milngavie, G62 7PN ☎ 0141 9563874	65
8324328	**Colquhoun Park Primary School** Canniesburn Road, Bearsden, G61 1HD ☎ 0141 9427552	28
8350221	**Craighead Primary School** Milton Of Campsie, By Glasgow, G65 8DL ☎ 01360 311570	58
8336229	**Gartconner Primary School** Gartshore Road, Kirkintilloch, G66 3TE ☎ 0141 7750170	54
8336628	**Hillhead Primary School** Newdyke Avenue, Kirkintilloch, G66 2DQ ☎ 0141 7762650	49
8336725	**Holy Family Primary School** Boghead Road, Kirkintilloch, G66 4AT ☎ 0141 7762585	37
8324425	**Killermont Primary School** 1 Aviemore Gardens, Bearsden, G61 2BL ☎ 0141 942 0359	55
8350329	**Lennoxtown Primary School** School Lane, Lennoxtown, Nr Glasgow, G65 7LX ☎ 01360 312352	50
8336326	**Lenzie Primary School** Kirkintilloch Road, Lenzie, G66 4LF ☎ 0141 776 1361	30
8340323	**Meadowburn Primary School** Lendale Lane, Bishopbriggs, G64 3LL ☎ 0141 7724543	38
8336113	**Meiklehill Nursery School** Highfield Road, Kirkintilloch, Glasgow, G66 2DX ☎ 0141 776 3156	107
8325022	**Milngavie Primary School** Hillhead Street, Milngavie, G62 8AG ☎ 0141 956 1564	62
8350523	**Torrance Primary School** West Road, Torrance, By Glasgow, G64 4DE ☎ 01360 622275	44
8338426	**Twechar Primary School** Main Street, Twechar, G65 9TA ☎ 01236 822280	30
8340722	**Woodhill Primary School** Kirriemuir Road, Bishopbriggs, Glasgow, G64 1DL ☎ 0141 772 1762	42
INDEPENDENT		
8380325	**Atholl Preparatory School** Mugdock Road, Milngavie, Glasgow, G62 8NP ☎ 0141 956 3758	51
8482128	**Gask House School** 28 Colston Drive, Bishopbriggs, Glasgow, G64 2AZ ☎ 0141 772 4708	79
EAST LOTHIAN		
5552621	**Aberlady Primary School** Aberlady, East Lothian, EH32 0RQ ☎ 01875 870232	11
5552729	**Athelstaneford Primary School** Athelstaneford, North Berwick, EH39 5BE ☎ 01620 880241	3
5550122	**Campie Primary School** 3 Stoneyhill Farm Road, Musselburgh, EH21 6QS ☎ 0131 665 2045	75
5553024	**Dunbar Primary School** Lammermuir Crescent, Dunbar, EH42 1DG ☎ 01368 863773	68
5553121	**East Linton Primary School** School Road, East Lothian, EH40 3AJ ☎ 01620 860216	38
5553229	**Elphinstone Primary School** Elphinstone, Tranent, East Lothian, EH33 2LX ☎ 01875 610358	11
5553326	**Gullane Primary School** Muirfield Terrace, Gullane, East Lothian, EH31 2HL ☎ 01620 843455	35
5553423	**Haddington Infant School** Victoria Road, Haddington, EH41 4DJ ☎ 01620 823271	73
5553822	**Humbie Primary School** Humbie, East Lothian, EH36 5PJ ☎ 01875 833247	14
5553725	**Innerwick Primary School** Innerwick, Dunbar, East Lothian, EH42 1SD ☎ 01368 840227	12
5556813	**Levenhall Nursery School** Moir Place, Musselburgh, EH21 8JD ☎ 0131 665 7599	101
5554020	**Longniddry Primary School** Kitchener Crescent, Longniddry, EH32 0LR ☎ 01875 853161	47
5550424	**Loretto RC Primary School** 20 Newbigging, Musselburgh, EH21 7AH ☎ 0131 665 2572	40
5554128	**Macmerry Primary School** Macmerry, Tranent, EH33 1QA ☎ 01875 610234	27
5550025	**Musselburgh Burgh Primary School** Kilwinning Street, Musselburgh, EH21 7EE ☎ 0131 6653407	43
5552311	**North Berwick Nursery School** Law Road, North Berwick, East Lothian, EH39 4PN ☎ 01620 893782	118
5554322	**Ormiston Primary School** Meadowbank, Ormiston, EH32 5LQ ☎ 01875 610382	31
5554527	**Pencaitland Primary School** The Glebe, Pencaitland, EH34 5EZ ☎ 01875 340260	37
5552419	**Prestonpans Nursery School** Kirk Street, Prestonpans, East Lothian, EH32 9DY ☎ 01875 811440	120
5554926	**Saltoun Primary School** East Saltoun, Pencaitland, EH34 5DY ☎ 01875 340318	13
5555329	**St Martin's Primary School** High Street, Tranent, East Lothian, EH33 1HJ ☎ 01875 610211	39
5555728	**Stoneyhill Primary School** Clayknowes Way, Stoneyhill, Musselburgh, EH21 6UL ☎ 0131 6653119	40
5552516	**Tranent Nursery School** Sandersons Wynd, Tranent, East Lothian, EH33 1DA ☎ 01875 610899	99

SOEID Number	School name, address and telephone number	No. of pupils in nursery class
5550629	**Wallyford Primary School** 39 Salters Road, Wallyford, EH22 2DG ☎ 0131 6652865	37
5550726	**Whitecraig Primary School** 44a Whitecraig Crescent, Whitecraig, Musselburgh, EH21 8NG ☎ 0131 6653278	31
5555620	**Yester Primary School** Walden Terrace, Gifford, EH41 4QP ☎ 01620 810435	34
INDEPENDENT		
5582520	**The Compass School** West Road, Haddington, East Lothian, EH41 3RD ☎ 01620 822642	15

EAST RENFREWSHIRE

SOEID Number	School name, address and telephone number	No. of pupils in nursery class
8600228	**Busby Primary School** Church Road, Clarkston, G76 8EB ☎ 0141 644 1866	69
8454922	**Calderwood Lodge P School** 28 Calderwood Road, Glasgow, G43 2RU ☎ 0141 637 5654	45
8620725	**Carlibar Primary School** Main Street, Barrhead, Glasgow, G78 1SW ☎ 0141 881 1254	36
8600821	**Giffnock Primary School** Academy Road, Giffnock, Glasgow, G46 6JL ☎ 0141 638 3641	56
8602115	**Glenwood Nursery School** Woodfarm Road, Glasgow, G46 7JJ ☎ 0141 638 9185	153
8602212	**Hazeldene Nursery School** 9 Rosemount Avenue, Newton Mearns, Glasgow, G77 ☎ 0141 616 3227	54
8632510	**Madras Nursery School** High Street, Neilston, G78 1HJ ☎ 0141 880 5593	126
8600929	**Netherlee Primary School** Clarkston Road, Netherlee, Glasgow, G44 3SF ☎ 0141 637 5892	90
8601526	**Thornliebank Primary School** Main Street, Thornliebank, Glasgow, G46 7RW ☎ 0141 638 3738	69
INDEPENDENT		
8680434	**Belmont House School** Sandringham Avenue, Newton Mearns, Glasgow, G77 5DU ☎ 0141 639 2922	20

EDINBURGH, CITY OF

SOEID Number	School name, address and telephone number	No. of pupils in nursery class
5519217	**Balgreen Nursery School** 175 Balgreen Road, Edinburgh, EH11 3AT ☎ 0131 3371454	65
5519314	**Calderglen Nursery School** Wester Hailes Road, Edinburgh, EH11 4NG ☎ 0131 453 5754	83
5519411	**Cameron House Nursery School** Cameron House Avenue, Edinburgh, EH16 5LF ☎ 0131 6675117	38
5519519	**Children's House Nursery School** Wauchope Terrace, Edinburgh, EH16 4NU ☎ 0131 6611401	39
5519810	**Cowgate Nursery School** 144 Cowgate, Edinburgh, EH1 1RP ☎ 0131 2257251	36
5519918	**Grassmarket Nursery School** 11/15 The Vennel, Edinburgh, EH1 2HU ☎ 0131 2296540	26
5519713	**Greengables Nursery School** 8a Niddrie House Gardens, Edinburgh, EH16 4UR ☎ 0131 6699083	70
5520010	**High School Yards Nursery School** Off Infirmary Street, Edinburgh, EH1 1LZ ☎ 0131 556 6536	29
5520118	**Hope Cottage Nursery School** Cowans Close, East Cross Causeway, Edinburgh, EH8 9HF ☎ 0131 6675795	45
5521211	**Kirkliston Nursery School** Queensferry Road, Kirkliston, EH29 9AQ ☎ 0131 3332336	80
5520215	**Liberton Nursery School** Mount Vernon Road, Edinburgh, EH16 6JQ ☎ 0131 664 3155	89
5520312	**Lochrin Nursery School** 8 West Tollcross, Edinburgh, EH3 9QN ☎ 0131 2297743	27
5522811	**Princess Elizabeth Nursery School** Clearburn Crescent, Edinburgh, EH16 5ER ☎ 0131 6670946	21
5520517	**St Leonards Nursery School** 6 West Adam Sreet, Edinburgh, EH8 9SY ☎ 0131 667 4674	96
5520614	**Stanwell Nursery School** Junction Place,Leith, Edinburgh, EH6 5JB ☎ 0131 5541309	68
5541115	**The Spinney Lane Nursery School** 13a The Spinney, Edinburgh, EH17 7LD ☎ 0131 6649102	75
5520711	**Tynecastle Nursery School** McLeod Street, Edinburgh, EH11 2NJ ☎ 0131 3375461	49
5520819	**Westfield Court Nursery School** Alexander Drive, Edinburgh, EH11 2RJ ☎ 0131 3374914	58
5520924	**Abbeyhill Primary School** Abbey Street, Edinburgh, EH7 5SJ ☎ 0131 6613054	46
5540925	**Bonaly Primary School** Bonaly Grove, Edinburgh, EH13 0QD ☎ 0131 441 7211	75
5521327	**Bonnington Primary School** Bonnington Road, Edinburgh, EH6 5NQ ☎ 0131 5541370	51
5521424	**Broomhouse Primary School** Saughton Road, Edinburgh, EH11 3RQ ☎ 0131 4433783	58
5521521	**Broughton Primary School** Broughton Road, Edinburgh, EH7 4LD ☎ 0131 5567028	72
5521629	**Brunstane Primary School** Magdalene Drive, Edinburgh, EH15 3BE ☎ 0131 6694498	40
5541220	**Buckstone Primary School** Buckstone Loan East, Edinburgh, EH10 6UY ☎ 0131 445 4545	39
5521823	**Burdiehouse Primary School** Burdiehouse Crescent, Edinburgh, EH17 8EX ☎ 0131 6642351	51
5521920	**Carrick Knowe Primary School** Lampacre Road, Edinburgh, EH12 7HU ☎ 0131 3344505	68

SOEID Number	School name, address and telephone number	No. of pupils in nursery class
5522021	**Clermiston Primary School** Parkgrove Place, Edinburgh, EH4 7NP ☎ 0131 3363361	84
5532027	**Clovenstone Primary School** 54 Clovenstone Park, Edinburgh, EH14 3EY ☎ 0131 453 4242	26
5522129	**Colinton Primary School** Redford Place, Edinburgh, EH13 0AL ☎ 0131 4411946	33
5522323	**Corstorphine Primary School** Corstorphine High Street, Edinburgh, EH12 7SY ☎ 0131 3343865	75
5522420	**Craigentinny Primary School** Loganlea Drive, Edinburgh, EH7 6LR ☎ 0131 6612749	85
5522625	**Craigmillar Primary School** Harewood Road, Edinburgh, EH16 4NT ☎ 0131 6613481	10
5522722	**Craigmuir Primary School** West Pilton Park, Edinburgh, EH4 4ET ☎ 0131 3326666	41
5522927	**Cramond Primary School** Cramond Crescent, Edinburgh, EH4 6PG ☎ 0131 3126450	36
5540127	**Curriehill Primary School** Lanark Road West, Currie, EH14 5NN ☎ 0131 4493359	74
5531527	**Dalmeny Primary School** Carlowrie Crescent, Dalmeny, South Queensferry, EH30 9TZ ☎ 0131 3311447	36
5523028	**Dalry Primary School** Dalry Road, Edinburgh, EH11 2JB ☎ 0131 3376086	51
5523125	**Davidson's Mains P.School** Corbiehill Road, Edinburgh, EH4 5DZ ☎ 0131 3361184	58
5540429	**Dean Park Primary School** Marchbank Gardens, Balerno, EH14 7ET ☎ 0131 449 4529	59
5523427	**Drumbrae Primary School** Ardshiel Avenue, Edinburgh, EH4 7HP ☎ 0131 3395071	40
5523524	**Duddingston Primary School** Duddingston Road, Edinburgh, EH15 1SW ☎ 0131 6695092	46
5523621	**Dumbryden Primary School** Dumbryden Gardens, Edinburgh, EH14 2NZ ☎ 0131 4535686	44
5531225	**East Craigs Primary School** Craigmount Brae, Edinburgh, EH12 8XF ☎ 0131 3397115	59
5523729	**Fernieside Primary School** Moredun Park Road, Edinburgh, EH17 7HL ☎ 0131 6642154	45
5541522	**Ferryhill Primary School** Groathill Road North, Edinburgh, EH4 2SQ ☎ 0131 538 7382	48
5523826	**Flora Stevenson Primary** Comely Bank, Edinburgh, EH4 1BG ☎ 0131 3321604	87
5523923	**Fort Primary School** North Fort Street, Edinburgh, EH6 4HF ☎ 0131 4677131	102
5524423	**Gracemount Primary School** Lasswade Road, Edinburgh, EH16 6UA ☎ 0131 6642331	43
5524520	**Granton Primary School** Boswall Parkway, Edinburgh, EH5 2DA ☎ 0131 5523987	60
5524822	**Gylemuir Primary School** Wester Broom Place, Edinburgh, EH12 7RT ☎ 0131 3347138	102
5525020	**Hailesland Primary School** Hailesland Place, Edinburgh, EH14 2SL ☎ 0131 4423894	42
5525128	**Hermitage Park Primary School** Hermitage Park, Edinburgh, EH6 8HD ☎ 0131 5542952	52
5525225	**Holy Cross Primary School** Craighall Road, Edinburgh, EH6 4RE ☎ 0131 5521972	46
5525322	**Hunter's Tryst Primary School** Oxgangs Green, Edinburgh, EH13 9JE ☎ 0131 4451510	124
5525721	**Inchview Primary School** West Pilton Avenue, Edinburgh, EH4 4BX ☎ 0131 3328186	31
5525829	**James Gillespie's Primary School** Whitehouse Loan, Edinburgh, EH9 1AT ☎ 0131 4471014	50
5525926	**Juniper Green Primary School** Baberton Mains Wynd, Edinburgh, EH14 3EE ☎ 0131 4422121	58
5532221	**Leith Primary School** St Andrews Place, Edinburgh, EH6 7EG ☎ 0131 5544844	25
5526124	**Leith Walk Primary School** Brunswick Road, Edinburgh, EH7 5NG ☎ 0131 5563873	31
5531829	**Liberton Primary School** Gilmerton Road, Edinburgh, EH16 5UD ☎ 0131 6642337	32
5526329	**Lismore Primary School** Bingham Avenue, Edinburgh, EH15 3HZ ☎ 0131 6694588	33
5526523	**Longstone Primary School** Redhall Grove, Edinburgh, EH14 2DU ☎ 0131 4434743	41
5526825	**Moredun Primary School** Moredunvale Place, Edinburgh, EH17 7LB ☎ 0131 6642384	21
5526922	**Muirhouse Primary School** Muirhouse Place West, Edinburgh, EH4 4PX ☎ 0131 3322793	30
5527023	**Murrayburn Primary School** Sighthill Loan, Edinburgh, EH11 4NP ☎ 0131 453 5339	33
5527120	**Newcraighall Primary School** Whitehill Street, Newcraighall, EH21 8QZ ☎ 0131 6693598	34
5527228	**Niddrie Mill Primary School** Niddrie Mains Road, Edinburgh, EH15 3HG ☎ 0131 4687025	27
5527325	**Orwell Primary School** Orwell Place, Edinburgh, EH11 2AD ☎ 0131 3376181	27
5527422	**Oxgangs Primary School** Colinton Mains Drive, Edinburgh, EH13 9AE ☎ 0131 4413649	44
5527627	**Parsons Green** Meadowfield Drive, Edinburgh, EH8 7LU ☎ 0131 6614459	38
5527724	**Peffermill Primary School** Craigmillar Castle Avenue, Edinburgh, EH16 4DH ☎ 0131 6613456	23
5527821	**Pirniehall Primary School** West Pilton Crescent, Edinburgh, EH4 4HP ☎ 0131 3325256	17

SOEID Number	School name, address and telephone number	No. of pupils in nursery class
5527929	**Prestonfield Primary School** Peffermill Road, Edinburgh, EH16 5LJ ☎ 0131 6671336	41
5518024	**Queensferry Primary School** Burgess Road, South Queensferry, EH30 9NX ☎ 0131 3311349	115
5540623	**Ratho Primary School** School Wynd, Ratho, EH28 8TT ☎ 0131 3331293	33
5528224	**Roseburn Primary School** Roseburn Street, Edinburgh, EH12 5PL ☎ 0131 3376096	47
5541727	**Royal Mile Primary School** Canongate, Edinburgh, EH8 8BZ ☎ 0131 5563347	34
5528429	**Royston Primary School** Boswall Parkway, Edinburgh, EH5 2JH ☎ 0131 5524534	48
5528623	**Sighthill Primary School** Calder Park, Edinburgh, EH11 4NF ☎ 0131 453 2464	25
5528720	**Silverknowes Primary School** Muirhouse Gardens, Edinburgh, EH4 4SX ☎ 0131 3361508	47
5528925	**South Morningside Primary School** Comiston Road, Edinburgh, EH10 5QN ☎ 0131 4475446	50
5529425	**St David's Primary School** West Pilton Place, Edinburgh, EH4 4DF ☎ 0131 3323500	29
5529522	**St Francis' Primary School** Niddrie Mains Road, Edinburgh, EH16 4DS ☎ 0131 621 6600	27
5529824	**St John Vianney Primary** Ivanhoe Crescent, Edinburgh, EH16 6AU ☎ 0131 664 1742	46
5529727	**St John's Primary School** Hamilton Terrace, Edinburgh, EH15 1NB ☎ 0131 6691363	70
5529921	**St Joseph's Primary School** Broomhouse Crescent, Edinburgh, EH11 3TD ☎ 0131 4434591	37
5530024	**St Mark's Primary School** Firrhill Crescent, Edinburgh, EH13 9EE ☎ 0131 4412948	37
5530229	**St Mary's Primary School** Links Gardens, Edinburgh, EH6 7JG ☎ 0131 5547291	76
5530326	**St Ninian's Primary School** Restalrig Road South, Edinburgh, EH7 6JA ☎ 0131 6613431	50
5530520	**St Peter's Primary School** Falcon Gardens, Edinburgh, EH10 4AP ☎ 0131 447 5742	48
5529026	**Stenhouse Primary School** 4 Saughton Mains Street, Edinburgh, EH11 3HH ☎ 0131 4431255	46
5529123	**Stockbridge Primary School** Hamilton Place, Edinburgh, EH3 5BA ☎ 0131 3326109	57
5530628	**Tollcross Primary School** Fountainbridge, Edinburgh, EH3 9QG ☎ 0131 2297828	15
5530725	**Towerbank Primary School** Figgate Bank, Edinburgh, EH15 1HX ☎ 0131 6691551	68
5540828	**Westburn Primary School** Sighthill Road, Edinburgh, EH11 4PB ☎ 0131 442 2997	32
INDEPENDENT		
5580439	**Cargilfield School** 37 Barnton Avenue West, Edinburgh, EH4 6HU ☎ 0131 336 2207	20
5580633	**The Edinburgh Academy** 42 Henderson Row, Edinburgh, EH3 5BL ☎ 0131 556 4603	64
5583535	**George Heriot's School** Lauriston Place, Edinburgh, EH3 9HE ☎ 0131 229 7263	52
5583632	**George Watson's College** 67-71 Colinton Road, Edinburgh, EH10 5EG ☎ 0131 447 7931	94
5584220	**Mary Erskine/Stewart's Melville** Ravelston, Edinburgh, EH4 3NT ☎ 0131 332 0888	119
5584124	**Regius School** 41a South Clerk Street, Edinburgh, EH8 9NZ ☎ 0131 668 2662	10
5581931	**Rudolf Steiner School of Edinburgh** 60 Spylaw Road, Edinburgh, EH10 5BR ☎ 0131 337 3410	46
5581230	**St George's School for Girls** Garscube Terrace, Edinburgh, EH12 6BG ☎ 0131 332 4575	35
EILEAN SIAR		
6231829	**Stornoway Primary School** Stornoway, Isle of Lewis, HS1 2LF ☎ 01851 703418	26
FALKIRK		
5740223	**Airth Primary School** Elphinstone Crescent, Airth, By Falkirk, FK2 8JY ☎ 01324 831265	19
5759226	**Antonine Primary School** Broomhill Road, Bonnybridge, FK4 2AT ☎ 01324 812100	29
5740320	**Avonbridge Primary School** Main Street, Avonbridge, Falkirk, FK1 2NG ☎ 01324 861247	12
5742129	**Bainsford Primary School** Waverley Street, Bainsford, Falkirk, FK2 7NW ☎ 01324 620446	40
5740428	**Bankier Primary School** Bankier Road, Banknock, Bonnybridge, FK4 1TF ☎ 01324 840206	33
5758122	**Bo'ness Primary School** Stewart Avenue, Bo'ness, EH51 9NL ☎ 01506 822588	50
5740525	**Bonnybridge Primary School** Wellpark Terrace, Bonnybridge, FK4 1LR ☎ 01324 812624	31
5741327	**Carronshore Primary School** Kincardine Road, Carronshore, By Falkirk, FK2 8AE ☎ 01324 562827	56
5742420	**Comely Park Primary School** Cow Wynd, Falkirk, FK1 1PZ ☎ 01324 621709	60
5758521	**Deanburn Primary School** Hazeldean Avenue, Bo'ness, EH51 0NS ☎ 01506 823165	40

SOEID Number	School name, address and telephone number	No. of pupils in nursery class
5740711	**Denny Nursery School** 7 Glasgow Road, Denny, FK6 6BB ☎ 01324 825966	134
5740118	**Glenfair Nursery School** Fairlie Street, Camelon, Falkirk, FK1 4NH ☎ 01324 627449	122
5758327	**Grange Primary School** Grange Loan, Bo'ness, EH51 9DX ☎ 01506 822743	38
5742625	**Hallglen Primary School** New Hallglen Road, Hallglen, By Falkirk, FK1 2RA ☎ 01324 620995	40
5745527	**Head Of Muir Primary School** Haypark Road, Denny, FK6 5JZ ☎ 01324 813578	32
5759013	**Heathrigg Nursery School** Bank Street, Slamannan, Falkirk, FK1 3EZ ☎ 01324 504570	33
5759110	**Inchlair Nursery School** Valeview, Stenhousemuir, Larbert, FK5 3BY ☎ 01324 557340	146
5741211	**Inchyra Nursery School** Tinto Drive, Grangemouth, FK3 0DZ ☎ 01324 473861	151
5758424	**Kinneil Primary School** Dean Road, Bo'ness, EH51 0DJ ☎ 01506 822451	38
5744326	**Ladeside Primary School** Carronvale Road, Larbert, FK5 3LH ☎ 01324 562503	40
5742722	**Langlees Primary School** David's Loan, Falkirk, FK2 7RG ☎ 01324 622206	36
5742927	**Laurieston Primary School** School Road, Laurieston, Falkirk, FK2 9JA ☎ 01324 626485	26
5744520	**Maddiston Primary School** Main Road, Maddiston, Falkirk, FK2 0LH ☎ 01324 712718	46
5759323	**Moray Primary School** Moray Place, Grangemouth, FK3 9DL ☎ 01324 501300	40
5740010	**Queen Street Nursery School** Queen Street, Falkirk, FK2 7AF ☎ 01324 624387	110
5744725	**Shieldhill Primary School** Main Street, Shieldhill, By Falkirk, FK1 2HA ☎ 01324 621154	37
5745721	**St Margaret's Primary School** Salmon Inn Road, Polmont, Falkirk, FK2 0XF ☎ 01324 715181	70
5745128	**Wallacestone Primary School** Braemar Gardens, Brightons, Falkirk, FK2 0JB ☎ 01324 712801	51
5745225	**Westquarter Primary School** Westquarter Avenue, Westquarter, Falkirk, FK2 9RN ☎ 01324 712719	32
5745322	**Whitecross Primary School** Avontoun Crescent, Whitecross, Linlithgow, EH49 6JN ☎ 01506 778400	14

FIFE

SOEID Number	School name, address and telephone number	No. of pupils in nursery class
5440327	**Aberdour Primary School** Hawkcraig Road, Aberdour, Burntisland, KY3 0UP ☎ 01383 860313	21
5420423	**Auchtermuchty Primary School** Blinkbonny, Back Dykes, Auchtermuchty, KY14 7AB ☎ 01337 828335	35
5401127	**Balcurvie Primary School** Balcurvie Road, Windygates, Leven, KY8 5DY ☎ 01333 350251	14
5420628	**Balmullo Primary School** Hayston Park, Balmullo, Leuchars, St Andrews, KY16 0DH ☎ 01334 870304	18
5440114	**Beanstalk Nursery School** Fergus Place, Dunfermline, KY11 4PZ ☎ 01383 720190	130
5447224	**Bellyeoman Primary School** 149 Robertson Road, Dunfermline, KY12 0XP ☎ 01383 738981	26
5440424	**Benarty Primary School** 67-69 Lochleven Road, Lochore, Lochgelly, KY5 8DA ☎ 01592 414375	34
5440521	**Blairhall Primary School** Rintoul Avenue, Blairhall, Dunfermline, KY12 9HG ☎ 01383 850269	16
5401224	**Buckhaven Primary School** College Street, Buckhaven, Leven, KY8 1JZ ☎ 01592 414555	54
5401321	**Burntisland Primary School** Ferguson Place, Burntisland, KY3 9ES ☎ 01592 872234	65
5440823	**Cairneyhill Primary School** Northbank Road, Cairneyhill, Dunfermline, KY12 8RN ☎ 01383 881104	40
5444721	**Camdean Primary School** King's Road, Rosyth, Dunfermline, KY11 2RY ☎ 01383 313388	106
5425026	**Canongate Primary School** Maynard Road, St Andrews, KY16 8RU ☎ 01334 474774	37
5403421	**Capshard Primary School** Barry Road, Kirkcaldy, KY2 6JD ☎ 01592 412355	49
5401429	**Cardenden Primary School** Carden Castle Avenue, Cardenden, Lochgelly, KY5 0EW ☎ 01592 414799	27
5401917	**Carleton Nursery School** Bighty Road, Woodside, Glenrothes, KY7 5AS ☎ 01592 415675	92
5402026	**Caskieberran Primary School** Ravenswood Drive, Glenrothes, KY6 2NZ ☎ 01592 415282	36
5421829	**Castlehill Primary School** Ceres Road, Cupar, KY15 5JT ☎ 01334 412470	104
5421020	**Cellardyke Primary School** School Road, Cellardyke, Anstruther, KY10 3HX ☎ 01333 592065	35
5421128	**Ceres Primary School** St Andrews Road, Ceres, Cupar, KY15 5NJ ☎ 01334 828327	27
5440211	**Clentry Nursery School** Keltyhill Road, Kelty, KY4 0LB ☎ 01383 830351	68
5408725	**Collydean Primary School** Magnus Drive, Glenrothes, KY7 6TR ☎ 01592 743355	71
5440920	**Cowdenbeath Primary School** 45 Broad Street, Cowdenbeath, KY4 8JP ☎ 01383 313077	48
5421322	**Crail Primary School** Backdykes, Crail, Anstruther, KY10 3UW ☎ 01333 450276	22
5441323	**Crossford Primary School** Dean Drive, Crossford, Dunfermline, KY12 8PE ☎ 01383 312383	32

SOEID Number	School name, address and telephone number	No. of pupils in nursery class
5441420	**Crossgates Primary School** 97 Dunfermline Road, Crossgates, Cowdenbeath, KY4 8AR ☎ 01383 510993	38
5441625	**Dalgety Bay Primary School** St Bridget's Brae, Dalgety Bay, Dunfermline, KY11 5LT ☎ 01383 318922	49
5401526	**Denbeath Primary School** Wall Street, Buckhaven, Leven, KY8 1JG ☎ 01592 414567	33
5447127	**Donibristle Primary School** Morlich Road, Dalgety Bay, Dunfermline, KY11 5UE ☎ 01383 823552	74
5403529	**Dunearn Primary School** Cawdor Crescent, Kirkcaldy, KY2 6LJ ☎ 01592 412360	31
5422221	**Dunino Primary School** Dunino, St Andrews, KY16 8LU ☎ 01334 880305	5
5440017	**Dunmore Nursery School** Kirkland Avenue, Ballingry, Lochgelly, KY5 8JS ☎ 01592 860284	47
5403626	**Dunnikier Primary School** Balsusney Road, Kirkcaldy, KY2 5LH ☎ 01592 412173	53
5401720	**Dysart Primary School** Normand Road, Dysart, Kirkcaldy, KY1 2XW ☎ 01592 418315	35
5401828	**East Wemyss Primary School** School Wynd, East Wemyss, Kirkcaldy, KY1 4RN ☎ 01592 414560	21
5408911	**Fair Isle Children's Centre** Fair Isle Road, Kirkcaldy, KY2 6EG ☎ 01592 412240	95
5422523	**Falkland Primary School** Pleasance, Falkland, Cupar, KY15 7AW ☎ 01337 857248	25
5427010	**Ferryport Nursery** 50 William Street, Tayport, DD6 9HQ ☎ 01382 552670	36
5441021	**Foulford Primary School** Johnston Park, Cowdenbeath, KY4 9DE ☎ 01383 313160	40
5422728	**Freuchie Primary School** Lomond Road, Freuchie, Cupar, KY15 7HF ☎ 01337 857354	15
5400112	**Gallatown Nursery** Rosslyn Street, Kirkcaldy, KY1 3AB ☎ 01592 651879	65
5443229	**Hill Of Beath Primary School** Main Street, Hill Of Beath, Cowdenbeath, KY4 8DP ☎ 01383 313100	30
5352517	**Inverkeithing Nursery** Hillend Road, Inverkeithing, KY11 1PL ☎ 01383 313374	67
5444624	**Inzievar Primary School** Station Road, Oakley, Dunfermline, KY12 9RJ ☎ 01383 850220	62
5402921	**Kennoway Primary & Community School** Langside Crescent, Kennoway, Leven, KY8 5JR ☎ 01333 350274	78
5423120	**Kettle Primary School** 6 Rumdewan, Kingskettle, Cupar, KY15 7QR ☎ 01337 830355	20
5444829	**King's Road Primary School** King's Crescent, Rosyth, Dunfermline, KY11 2RS ☎ 01383 313470	46
5403022	**Kinghorn Primary School** Baliol Street, Kinghorn, Burntisland, KY3 9UD ☎ 01592 890332	29
5403227	**Kinglassie Primary School** Main Street, Kinglassie, Lochgelly, KY5 0YE ☎ 01592 882245	25
5423422	**Kingsbarns Primary School** 8 Main Street, Kingsbarns, St Andrews, KY16 8SZ ☎ 01334 880273	3
5403820	**Kirkcaldy North Primary School** Nile Street, Kirkcaldy, KY2 5AY ☎ 01592 412250	29
5404525	**Kirkcaldy West Primary School** Milton Road, Kirkcaldy, KY1 1TL ☎ 01592 412570	65
5423724	**Ladybank Primary School** 47 Church Street, Ladybank, Cupar, KY15 7LE ☎ 01337 830406	21
5352410	**Ladybird Nursery** Stuart Road, Glenrothes, KY7 4JX ☎ 01592 415340	91
5425328	**Lawhead Primary School** Strathkinness Low Road, St Andrews, KY16 9NG ☎ 01334 475895	24
5400414	**Leslie Nursery** 2 Anderson Drive, Leslie, Glenrothes, KY6 3BY ☎ 01592 741324	35
5424127	**Leuchars Primary School** Pitlethie Road, Leuchars, St Andrews, KY16 0EZ ☎ 01334 839315	65
5443628	**Limekilns Primary School** 8 Dunfermline Road, Limekilns, Dunfermline, KY11 3JS ☎ 01383 872330	20
5444225	**Lumphinnans Primary & Community School** Main Street, Lumphinnans, Cowdenbeath, KY4 9HG ☎ 01383 313150	31
5424224	**Lundin Mill Primary School** Pitcruvie Park, Lundin Links, Leven, KY8 6HY ☎ 01333 320721	25
5442028	**Lynburn Primary School** Nith Street, Dunfermline, KY11 4LU ☎ 01383 312879	50
5405025	**Markinch Primary School** Betson Street, Markinch, Glenrothes, KY7 6AA ☎ 01592 415295	28
5442125	**McLean Primary School** Baldridgeburn, Dunfermline, KY12 9EE ☎ 01383 312390	55
5424526	**New Gilston Primary School** New Gilston, By Leven, KY8 5TF ☎ 01334 840301	6
5424429	**Newburgh Primary School** Cupar Road, Newburgh, Cupar, KY14 6HA ☎ 01337 840239	32
5424321	**Newport Primary School** Cupar Road, Newport-on-Tay, DD6 8JT ☎ 01382 542116	29
5444322	**North Queensferry Primary School** The Brae, North Queensferry, Inverkeithing, KY11 1JH ☎ 01383 412841	14
5444926	**Park Road Primary School** Park Road, Rosyth, Dunfermline, KY11 2NH ☎ 01383 313399	37
5403928	**Pathhead Primary School** Cairns Street West, Kirkcaldy, KY1 2JA ☎ 01592 418330	38
5400619	**Paxton Nursery** Selkirk Street, Methil, Leven, KY8 3LX ☎ 01333 426513	71
5408520	**Pitcoudie Primary School** 20 Iona Park, Glenrothes, KY7 6NU ☎ 01592 741220	44

217

SOEID Number	School name, address and telephone number	No. of pupils in nursery class
5442524	**Pitreavie Primary School** Pitcorthie Drive, Dunfermline, KY11 5AB ☎ 01383 312990	75
5442621	**Pittencrieff Primary School** Dewar Street, Dunfermline, KY12 8AB ☎ 01383 312935	46
5424720	**Pittenweem Primary School** James Street, Pittenweem, Anstruther, KY10 2QN ☎ 01333 592071	23
5402123	**Pitteuchar East Primary** Glamis Avenue, Glenrothes, KY7 4NU ☎ 01592 415840	69
5408121	**Pitteuchar West Primary** Inverary Avenue, Glenrothes, KY7 4QL ☎ 01592 415854	35
5402220	**Rimbleton Primary School** Bilsland Road, Glenrothes, KY6 2DZ ☎ 01592 415383	47
5445124	**Saline Primary School** Oakley Road, Saline, Dunfermline, KY12 9TG ☎ 01383 852216	23
5402425	**South Parks Primary School** Napier Road, Glenrothes, KY6 1DS ☎ 01592 415300	40
5402522	**Southwood Primary School** Marchmont Crescent, Glenrothes, KY6 1JU ☎ 01592 752965	40
5425425	**Springfield Primary School** Main Street, Springfield, Cupar, KY15 5RZ ☎ 01334 653423	16
5405424	**St Agatha's R C Primary** Windygates Road, Leven, KY8 5BL ☎ 01333 592540	39
5420016	**St Andrews Nursery** Kilrymont Road, St Andrews, KY16 8DF ☎ 01334 412614	37
5441129	**St Bride's R C Primary School** Barclay Street, Cowdenbeath, KY4 9LD ☎ 01383 313070	31
5444128	**St Kenneth's R C Primary School** Hill Road, Ballingry, Lochgelly, KY5 8NP ☎ 01592 414366	20
5442826	**St Leonard's Primary School** St Leonard's Street, Dunfermline, KY11 3AL ☎ 01383 312940	26
5442729	**St Margaret's Primary School** Woodmill Road, Dunfermline, KY11 4BB ☎ 01383 312965	71
5425824	**St Monans Primary School** Hope Place, St Monans, Anstruther, KY10 2DH ☎ 01333 730226	30
5400821	**St Ninian's R C Primary School** 76-78 Derran Drive, Cardenden, Lochgelly, KY5 0JJ ☎ 01592 414790	54
5445426	**St Serf's R C Primary School** Preston Street, High Valleyfield, Dunfermline, KY12 8SE ☎ 01383 880406	15
5425727	**Strathmiglo Primary School** 111 High Street, Strathmiglo, Cupar, KY14 7PT ☎ 01337 860262	17
5447313	**Sunflower Nursery** Melgund Place, Lochgelly, KY5 9QU ☎ 01592 781585	94
5402727	**Tanshall Primary School** South Parks Road, Glenrothes, KY6 2JH ☎ 01592 415360	43
5405823	**Thornton Primary School** Station Road, Thornton, Kirkcaldy, KY1 4AY ☎ 01592 415870	23
5404320	**Torbain Primary School** Blairmore Road, Kirkcaldy, KY2 6NP ☎ 01592 412520	68
5445221	**Torryburn Primary School** Main Street, Newmills, Dunfermline, KY12 8SU ☎ 01383 880289	17
5442923	**Touch Primary School** Garvock Bank, Dunfermline, KY11 4JZ ☎ 01383 312970	49
5443024	**Townhill Primary School** Chisholm Street, Townhill, Dunfermline, KY12 0EX ☎ 01383 312979	33
5445329	**Tulliallan Primary School** Kirk Street, Kincardine, Alloa, FK10 4PT ☎ 01259 730288	28
5404428	**Valley Primary School** Valley Gardens, Kirkcaldy, KY2 6BL ☎ 01592 412531	36
5408210	**Viewforth Nursery** Mitchell Street, Leven, KY8 4HJ ☎ 01333 425087	77
5400716	**Woodlands Nursery** Methilhaven Road, Methil, Leven, KY8 3LE ☎ 01333 592595	86
5426022	**Wormit Primary School** Flass Road, Wormit, DD6 8LJ ☎ 01382 541548	39
INDEPENDENT		
5480523	**Inchkeith School** Balgownie House, Culross, KY12 8JJ ☎ 01383 880330	7
5480337	**New Park School** 98 Hepburn Gardens, St Andrews, KY16 9LN ☎ 01334 472017	17
5480027	**Sea View Private School** 102 Loughborough Road, Kirkcaldy, KY1 3DD ☎ 01592 652244	8

GLASGOW CITY

8408114	**Acredyke Nursery School** 1 Ferness Oval, Glasgow, G21 3SQ ☎ 0141 5586770	96
8408211	**Adelphi Nursery School** 40 Waddell Court, Glasgow, G5 0QA ☎ 0141 429 1474	68
8408319	**Anderson Street Nursery School** 20 Anderson Street, Partick, Glasgow, G11 6AZ ☎ 0141 3392388	70
8408416	**Ardencraig Nursery School** 25 Ardencraig Drive, Glasgow, G45 0HX ☎ 0141 6311550	86
8408513	**Ardnahoe Nursery School** 18 Ardnahoe Place, Glasgow, G42 0DG ☎ 0141 6478934	76
8408610	**Arnwood Nursery School** 72 Dougrie Road, Castlemilk, Glasgow, G45 9NW ☎ 0141 6342809	89
8400415	**Ashley Street Nursery School** c/o Willowbank Primary School, Willowbank Cres., Woodlands Road, Glasgow, G3 6NB ☎ 0141 332 358	53
8408815	**Baishagray Nursery School** c/o 11 Thornwood Avenue, Glasgow, G11 7AB ☎ 0141 339 7445	63
8408912	**Belhaven Nursery School** 54 Kelvinside Avenue, Glasgow, G20 6PY ☎ 0141 9463169	128

SOEID Number	School name, address and telephone number	No. of pupils in nursery class
8403813	**Bellrock Crescent Nursery School** 21 Bellrock Crescent,Cranhill, Glasgow, G33 3HJ ☎ 0141 774 8036	57
8445419	**Bonnybroom Nursery School** 233 Petershill Drive, Glasgow, G21 4QT ☎ 0141 557 2550	138
8409110	**Broomloan Nursery School** c/o St Gerards Secondary, 80 Vicarfield Street, Glasgow, G51 2DF ☎ 0141 4451762	130
8409218	**Buchlyvie Nursery School** 45 Aberdalgie Road,Easterhouse, Glasgow, G34 9LT ☎ 0141 771 1056	122
8459916	**Caldercuilt Nursery School** 101 Invershiel Road, Glasgow, G23 5JG ☎ 0141 946 7450	68
8409013	**Chesters Nursery School** 129 Drummore Road, Drumchapel, Glasgow, G15 7NH ☎ 0141·9441831	89
8409412	**Cloan Avenue Nursery School** 45 Cloan Avenue,Drumchapel, Glasgow, G15 6DF ☎ 0141 944 2191	127
8447519	**Cloverbank Nursery School** 193 Moraine Avenue, Glasgow, G15 6LG ☎ 0141 944 8678	100
8409617	**Craigbank Nursery School** 26 Glenlora Drive,Craigbank, Glasgow, G53 6BH ☎ 0141 881 9720	117
8409714	**Craigton Nursery School** 13 Montrave Street,Cardonald, Glasgow, G52 2TS ☎ 0141 882 7604	109
8409811	**Cranstonhill Nursery School** 3 Little Street,Anderston, Glasgow, G3 8DQ ☎ 0141 248 4899	72
8445516	**Deanpark Nursery School** 10 Deanston Drive,Shawlands, Glasgow, G41 3AE ☎ 0141 649 8949	107
8410119	**Dowanhill Nursery School** 30 Havelock Street, Glasgow, G11 5JE ☎ 0141 334 8741	59
8410216	**Easthall Nursery School** c/o Easthall Primary School, 33 Ware Road, Glasgow, G34 9AR ☎ 0141 771 4348	93
8400113	**Eastwood Nursery School** Bonnyrigg Drive, Glasgow, G43 1HW ☎ 0141 6329773	109
8400210	**Elba Lane Nursery School** 1346 Gallowgate, Parkhead, Glasgow, G31 4DJ ☎ 0141 5542174	59
8446911	**Elmcroft Nursery School** 40 Croftcroighn Road, Glasgow, G33 3SA ☎ 0141 774 9311	94
8412529	**Elmvale Primary School** 712 Hawthorn Street, Glasgow, G22 6ED ☎ 0141 5585238/5573991	45
8400318	**Fortrose Nursery School** 74 Peel Street, Glasgow, G11 5LR ☎ 0141 3391808	55
8400512	**Garscube Nursery School** 2 Manresa Place, Glasgow, G4 9NB ☎ 0141 3323170	33
8449015	**Govanhill Nursery School** 335 Allison Street, Glasgow, G53 7HT ☎ 0141 424 1063	143
8413126	**Greenfield Primary School** 29 Nimmo Drive, Govan, Glasgow, G51 3SZ ☎ 0141 445 1774/3552	54
8400717	**Halgreen Nursery School** 51 Halgreen Avenue, Glasgow, G15 8AL ☎ 0141 9442060	65
8449619	**Helenslea Nursery School** 36 Methven Street, Glasgow, G31 4RB ☎ 0141 551 0504	120
8400911	**Hilltop Nursery School** 44 Kingsbridge Drive, Glasgow, G44 4JS ☎ 0141 649 1786	140
8413924	**Holmlea Primary School** 352 Holmlea Road, Cathcart, G44 4BY ☎ 0141 637 3989	48
8447314	**Kelso Nursery School** c/o St Brendans Primary School, 170 Hawick Street, Glasgow, G13 4HG ☎ 0141 952 2502	74
8401012	**Kennedy Street** 45 Parson Street, Glasgow, G4 0PX ☎ 0141 5522484	52
8445311	**Keppoch Nursery School** 73 Mansion Street, Glasgow, G22 5NT ☎ 0141 336 7750	132
8445613	**Kincardine Nursery School** 60 Kimcardine Sq,Garthamlock, Glasgow, G33 5BU ☎ 0141 774 5677	109
8401217	**Kinning Park Nursery School** 540 Scotland Street, Glasgow, G41 1BZ ☎ 0141 429 6835	71
8401314	**Lamlash Nursery School** 5 Lamlash Crescent, Glasgow, G33 3LH ☎ 0141 7743541	97
8401411	**Langa Street Nursery School** 83 Langa Street, Glasgow, G20 0SG ☎ 0141 9463721	50
8401519	**Langside Nursery School** 44 Carmichael Place, Glasgow, G42 9UE ☎ 0141 649 5668	95
8401713	**Linthaugh Nursery School** 533 Crookston Road, Glasgow, G53 7TX ☎ 0141 8827105	84
8445710	**Lochview Nursery School** 145 Lochend Rd,Easterhouse, Glasgow, G34 0LW ☎ 0141 773 1842	54
8401810	**London Road Nursery School** 1147 London Road, Glasgow, G40 3RG ☎ 0141 5540578	79
8401918	**Lyoncross Nursery School** Lyoncross Road,Pollok, Glasgow, G53 5UR ☎ 0141 8822172	119
8447810	**Machrie Nursery School** 33 Machrie Road,Castlemilk, Glasgow, G45 0AG ☎ 0141 631 2255	68
8449414	**Maryhill Park Nursery School** 81 Kilmun Street,Maryhill, Glasgow, G20 0EL ☎ 0141 946 7752	119
8402019	**Merryland Nursery School** 70 Clifford Street, Glasgow, G51 1PZ ☎ 0141 427 6411	54
8402116	**Mile End Nursery School** c/o St Annes Primary School, 35 David Street, Glasgow, G40 2UN ☎ 0141 554 1675	45
8402213	**Molendinar Nursery School** 1210 Royston Road, Glasgow, G33 1HE ☎ 0141 7704312	107
8402310	**Newark Drive Nursery School** 10 Newark Drive, Glasgow, G41 4QE ☎ 0141 4230585	69
8445818	**Newhurst Nursery School** c/o Wellhouse Primary, 4 Balado Road, Glasgow, G33 4EZ ☎ 0141 771 2447	102
8402418	**Nithsdale Road Nursery School** 264 Nithsdale Road, Glasgow, G41 5LB ☎ 0141 4271896	75

SOEID Number	School name, address and telephone number	No. of pupils in nursery class
8445915	**Novar Nursery School** 5 Lauderdale Gardens,Hyndland, Glasgow, G12 9UA ☎ 0141 339 2938	107
8402515	**Oatlands Nursery School** 347 Caledonia Road, Glasgow, G5 0JY ☎ 0141 429 0053	71
8402612	**Penilee Nursery School** 25 Inkerman Road,Penilee, Glasgow, G52 2RW ☎ 0141 8827605	116
8447411	**Pikeman Nursery School** 21 Archerhill Road, Glasgow, G13 3NJ ☎ 0141 954 2971	155
8418721	**Pollokshields Primary School** 241 Albert Drive, Glasgow, G41 2NA ☎ 0141 423 1363	28
8402914	**Prospecthill Nursery School** 124 Prospecthill Road, Glasgow, G42 9LH ☎ 0141 6326682	63
8418829	**Provanhall Primary School** 32 Balcurvie Road, Glasgow, G34 9QL ☎ 0141 771 2910	36
8418926	**Quarry Brae Primary School** 139 Crail Street, Parkhead, G31 5RB ☎ 0141 5543419/3259	41
8403112	**Queen Mary Street Nursery School** 20 Queen Mary Street,Bridgeton, Glasgow, G40 3BB ☎ 0141 5547658	81
8403317	**Queens Cross Nursery School** 65 Dunard Street,Maryhill, Glasgow, G20 6RL ☎ 0141 9462808	42
8403414	**Renfrew Street Nursery School** 256 Renfrew Street, Glasgow, G3 6TT ☎ 0141 3323236	64
8403511	**Rosshall Nursery School** 35 Cronberry Quadrant, Glasgow, G52 3NU ☎ 0141 8823605	81
8403619	**Rowena Nursery School** 36 Knightscliffe Avenue, Glasgow, G13 2TE ☎ 0141 9594183	100
8403716	**Royston Nursery School** 40 Royston Road, Glasgow, G21 2NU ☎ 0141 552 1045	34
8403910	**Sandaig Nursery School** Usmore Place, Barlanark, Glasgow, G33 4TE ☎ 0141 7711898	122
8404011	**Scaraway Nursery School** Shapinsay Street,Milton, Glasgow, G22 7JN ☎ 0141 772 1604	138
8447616	**Shawbridge Nursery School** 132 Shawbridge Street, Glasgow, G43 1NP ☎ 0141 649 6464	120
8446318	**Sighthill Nursery School** 61 Fountainwell Road, Glasgow, G21 1RG ☎ 0141 557 0903	107
8404216	**Springburn Nursery School** 48 Gourlay Street, Glasgow, G21 1AE ☎ 0141 5585279	65
8448825	**St Angela's Primary School** 227 Glen Moriston Rd, Glasgow, G53 7HT ☎ 0141 638 9646	58
8455120	**St Bridget's Primary School** Swinton Road, Baillieston, Glasgow, G69 6DT ☎ 0141 771 1294	49
8404313	**Strathclyde Nursery School** 106 Allan Street, Glasgow, G40 4JD ☎ 0141 5540587	47
8446113	**Thornlaw Nursery School** 34 Kilmuir Road, Glasgow, G46 8BQ ☎ 0141 638 9712	116
8430721	**Victoria Primary School** 67 Batson Street, Govanhill, G42 7HD ☎ 0141 423 2759	59
8404410	**Wellfield Nursery School** 308 Edgefauld Road,Springburn, Glasgow, G21 4YT ☎ 0141 558 5128	122
8449813	**Westercommon Nursery School** 198 Auckland Street, Glasgow, G22 5NT ☎ 0141 336 6594	58
8404518	**Westercraigs Nursery School** c/o Golfhill Primary, 13 Circus Drive, Glasgow, G31 2JR ☎ 0141 5543180	60
8404615	**Westerhouse Nursery School** 55 Dubton Street,Easterhouse, Glasgow, G34 0NG ☎ 0141 7730055	103
8404712	**Whiteinch Nursery School** Glendore Street, Glasgow, G14 9RW ☎ 0141 9593823	161
8449511	**Woodacre Nursery School** 30 Willowford Rd.,Sth. Nitshill, Glasgow, G53 7LP ☎ 0141 881 9043	118
8405018	**Woodside Nursery School** 445 St George's Road, Glasgow, G3 6JX ☎ 0141 3327661	80
8446210	**Wyndford Nursery School** 33 Latherton Dr,Maryhill, Glasgow, G20 8JR ☎ 0141 945 1366	102
INDEPENDENT		
8482330	**Craigholme School for Girls** 72 St Andrews Drive, Glasgow, G41 4HS ☎ 0141 427 0375	41
8480223	**Dairsie House School** 54 Newlands Road, Newlands, Glasgow, G43 2JG ☎ 0141 632 0736	54
8483426	**Glasgow Steiner School** 52 Lumsden Street, Yorkhill, Glasgow, G3 8RH ☎ 0141 334 8855	15
8482535	**Kelvinside Academy** 33 Kirklee Road, Glasgow, G12 0SW ☎ 0141 357 3376	28
8483531	**Laurel Park School** 4 Lilybank Terrace, Glasgow, G12 8RX ☎ 0141 339 9127	30
8482837	**St Aloysius College** 45 Hill Street, Garnethill, Glasgow, G3 6RJ ☎ 0141 332 3190	37
8481830	**The Glasgow Academy** Colebrooke Street, Glasgow, G12 8HE ☎ 0141 334 8558	30
8481733	**The High School of Glasgow** 637 Crow Road, Glasgow, G13 1PL ☎ 0141 954 9628	51

SOEID Number	School name, address and telephone number	No. of pupils in nursery class
HIGHLAND		
5130220	**Ardgour Primary School**	11
5110920	**Assynt Primary School**	1
5128625	**Auchtertyre Primary**	16
5152526	**Auldearn Primary School**	17
5145228	**Aviemore Primary School**	22
5144027	**Beauly Primary School**	24
5107725	**Bonar Bridge Primary School**	18
5126029	**Borrodale Primary School**	2
5110726	**Brora Primary School**	21
5130611	**Caol Nursery School**	98
5100321	**Castletown Primary School**	20
5139627	**Cauldeen Primary School**	20
5152623	**Cawdor Primary School**	10
5139724	**Central Primary School**	19
5113822	**Conon Primary School**	17
5114020	**Contin Primary School**	28
5114225	**Coulhill Primary School**	53
5143527	**Cradlehall Primary School**	34
5120225	**Craighill Primary School**	83
5140021	**Dalneigh Primary School**	25
5114624	**Dingwall Primary School**	55
5110629	**Dornoch Primary**	25
5143624	**Duncan Forbes Primary School**	37
5110432	**Farr High School**	12
5133823	**Fort William Primary (RC)**	27
5108225	**Golspie Primary School**	17
5146127	**Grantown Primary School**	38
5110823	**Helmsdale Primary School**	8
5101824	**Hillhead Primary School**	22
5115329	**Hilton of Cadboll Primary School**	30
5140226	**Hilton Primary School**	34
5139120	**Holm Primary School**	20
5115523	**Inverasdale Primary School**	16
5100720	**Keiss Primary School**	11
5134420	**Kilmonivaig Primary School**	12
5115922	**Kiltearn Primary School**	24
5108527	**Kinbrace Primary School**	2
5146224	**Kingussie Primary School**	23
5135427	**Kinlochleven Primary School**	10
5142229	**Kinmylies Primary School**	26
5142326	**Kirkhill Primary School**	24
5123127	**Kyle Primary School**	11
5127025	**Kyleakin Primary School**	21
5109922	**Lairg Primary School**	18
5140323	**Lochardil Primary School**	23

SOEID Number	School name, address and telephone number	No. of pupils in nursery class
5100925	**Lybster Primary School**	13
5136423	**Mallaig Primary School**	19
5116422	**Maryburgh Primary School**	22
5139511	**Merkinch Nursery School**	80
5153026	**Millbank Primary School**	36
5101328	**Miller Academy Primary School**	42
5120624	**Milton Primary School**	15
5101425	**Mount Pleasant Primary School**	22
5136628	**Muck Primary School**	1
5143322	**Muirtown Primary School**	29
5114721	**North Kessock Primary School**	18
5101727	**North Primary School**	26
5110017	**Pals Family Nursery School**	72
5120527	**Park Primary School**	36
5101026	**Pennyland Primary School**	42
5128722	**Portree Primary**	24
5101921	**Pulteneytown Academy Primary**	43
5127424	**Raasay Primary School**	3
5140625	**Raigmore Primary School**	27
5153220	**Rosebank School**	37
5135028	**Rum Primary School**	1
5120829	**Scoraig Primary School**	2
5141621	**Smithton Primary School**	39
5115620	**South Lodge Primary School**	24
5102529	**South Primary School**	29
5134722	**St Bride's Primary School**	14
5108926	**Stoer Primary School**	2
5118522	**Tarradale Primary School**	20
5136121	**Upper Achintore Primary**	20

INVERCLYDE

8640017	**Aileymill Nursery School** Auchmead Road, Greenock, PA16 0RY ☏ 01475 633203	126
8640114	**Barmoss Nursery School** Auchenbothie Road, Port Glasgow, PA14 6HL ☏ 01475 704144	143
8646317	**Blairmore Nursery School** Strathblane Road, Greenock, PA15 3SJ ☏ 01475 781083	117
8631115	**Carsemeadow Nursery School** Quarrier's Village, Bridge of Weir, PA11 3SX ☏ 01505 613 251	116
8644225	**Highholm Primary School** Highholm Avenue, Port Glasgow, PA14 5JN ☏ 01475 741309	54
8641420	**Moorfoot Primary School** Moorfoot Drive, Gourock, PA19 1ES ☏ 01475 633055	20
8641226	**Overton Primary School** Peat Road, Greenock, PA16 7TU ☏ 01475 723346	21
8642427	**St Mungo's Primary School** Grosvenor Road, Greenock, PA15 2DP ☏ 01475 724794	39
8644721	**Wemyss Bay Primary School** Ardgowan Road, Wemyss Bay, PA18 6AT ☏ 01475 521792	29

MIDLOTHIAN

5544424	**Bryans Primary School** 24 Conifer Road, Mayfield, EH22 5BX ☏ 0131 6632049	35
5545919	**Cockpen Nursery School** Cockpen Road, Bonnyrigg, EH19 3HS ☏ 0131 663 5172	48
5544920	**Cornbank St James' Primary School** 34 Marchburn Drive, Penicuik, Midlothian, EH26 9HE ☏ 01968 673422	39
5547717	**Cuikenburn Nursery School** Queensway, Penicuik, EH26 0HE ☏ 01968 677748	91
5543126	**Danderhall Primary School** 59 Edmonstone Road, Danderhall, EH22 1QL ☏ 0131 6632400	45

SOEID Number	School name, address and telephone number	No. of pupils in nursery class
5543428	**Gorebridge Primary School** 80 Hunterfield Road, Gorebridge, EH23 4XA ☎ 01875 820529	72
5542820	**King's Park Primary School** 20 Croft Street, Dalkeith, EH22 3BA ☎ 0131 6632414	80
5544521	**Langlaw Primary School** Langlaw Road, Mayfield, EH22 5AU ☎ 0131 6632204	28
5543924	**Loanhead Primary School** 8 Academy Lane, Loanhead, EH20 9RP ☎ 0131 4400448	39
5547512	**Mayfield Nursery School** Stone Avenue, Mayfield, Dalkeith, EH22 5PB ☎ 0131 6602485	80
5543711	**Mount Esk Nursery School** Dalhousie Gardens, Bonnyrigg, EH19 2LS ☎ 0131 663 2364	110
5544629	**Newtongrange Primary School** Sixth Street, Newtongrange, EH22 4LB ☎ 0131 6633238	56
5544726	**Newtonloan St Andrew's Primary School** 121 Newhunterfield, Gorebridge, EH23 4NB ☎ 01875 820133	21
5547326	**Paradykes Primary School** 3 Mayburn Walk, Loanhead, EH20 9HG ☎ 0131 4403167	55
5544823	**Pathhead Primary School** 208 Main Street, Pathhead, Midlothian, EH37 5SG ☎ 01875 320279	29
5545420	**Rosewell Primary School** 85 Carnethie Street, Rosewell, EH24 9AN ☎ 0131 4402233	18
5545625	**Roslin Primary School** 8 Pentland View Place, Roslin, Midlothian, EH25 9ND ☎ 0131 4401871	38
5542324	**St Mary's Primary School** 62a Polton Street, Bonnyrigg, EH19 3DG ☎ 0131 6638646	48
5542111	**Strathesk Nursery School** Strathesk Road, Penicuik, EH26 8EE ☎ 01968 674081	93
5544211	**Thornybank Nursery School** Salters Road, Dalkeith, EH22 2DG ☎ 0131 6632696	81

MORAY

5206928	**Cullen School** Old Church Road, Cullen, Moray, AB56 4UZ ☎ 01542 840279	13
5207126	**Findochty School** Burnside Street, Findochty, Moray, AB56 2QZ ☎ 01542 832287	7
5201624	**Hopeman School** School Road, Hopeman, Moray, IV30 2TQ ☎ 01343 830281	37
5202124	**Hythehill School** Lossiemouth, Moray, IV31 6LW ☎ 01343 812014	63
5207525	**Keith Primary School** School Road, Keith, Moray, AB55 3ES ☎ 01542 882802	60
5201721	**Kinloss Primary School** Burghead Road, Kinloss, Moray, IV36 0UG ☎ 01309 690376	40
5201926	**Lhanbryde School** Garmouth Road, Lhanbryde, Moray, IV30 3PD ☎ 01343 842649	38
5206421	**Millbank School** McWilliam Crescent, Buckie, Moray, AB56 1LU ☎ 01542 831113	74
5202825	**Milne's Primary School** High Street, Fochabers, Moray, IV32 7EP ☎ 01343 820977	20
5202523	**New Elgin School** Bezack Street, New Elgin, Moray, IV30 3DW ☎ 01343 547587	67
5210127	**Pilmuir School** Pilmuir Road, Forres, Moray, IV36 0HD ☎ 01309 673034	79
5208122	**Portgordon School** Richmond Terrace, Portgordon, Moray, AB56 5RA ☎ 01542 831198	14
5201020	**Seafield School** Deanshaugh Terrace, Bishopmill, Elgin, Moray, IV30 2ES ☎ 01343 547792	112
5209919	**Speyside Nursery** c/o Rothes School, Green Street, Rothes, AB38 7BD ☎ 01340 831269	61
5206529	**St Peter's RC School** 37 St Peter's Terrace, Buckie, Moray, AB56 1QN ☎ 01542 831339	36
INDEPENDENT		
5282438	**Moray Steiner School** Drumduan, Clovenside Road, Forres, IV36 0BT ☎ 01309 676300	28
5280125	**Rosebrae School** Rosehaugh Farm, Elgin, Moray, IV30 3XT ☎ 01343 544841	47

NORTH AYRSHIRE

8212627	**Abbey Primary School** Claremont Crescent, Kilwinning, KA13 7HD ☎ 01294 552251	56
8214123	**Ardeer Primary School** Clark Crescent, Stevenston, KA20 3NX ☎ 01294 469785	20
8218129	**Brisbane Primary School** Holehouse Road, Largs, KA30 9DZ ☎ 01475 686601	56
8217920	**Broomlands Primary School** St Kilda Bank, Broomlands, Irvine, KA11 1LA ☎ 01294 214170	20
8200327	**Corrie Primary School** Corrie, Brodick, Isle Of Arran, KA27 8JB ☎ 01770 810244	9
8212821	**Corsehill Primary School** McGavin Avenue, Kilwinning, KA13 7LW ☎ 01294 552418	37
8218226	**Cumbrae Primary School** Bute Terrace, Millport, KA28 0BB ☎ 01475 530343	13
8210012	**Dalry Nursery School** Vennel Street, Dalry, Ayrshire, KA24 4AG ☎ 01294 832200	86
8211221	**Fairlie Primary School** Morton Way, Fairlie, KA29 0DE ☎ 01475 568441	15
8214328	**Glencairn Primary School** New Street, Stevenston, KA20 3HQ ☎ 01294 464376	30

SOEID Number	School name, address and telephone number	No. of pupils in nursery class
8214220	**Hayocks Primary School** Lumsden Place, Stevenston, KA20 4HG ☎ 01294 465283	43
8212023	**John Galt Primary School** Tollerton Drive, Irvine, KA12 0QD ☎ 01294 279487	67
8200424	**Kilmory Primary School** Kilmory, Brodick, Isle Of Arran, KA27 8PQ ☎ 01770 870262	3
8212120	**Loudoun-Montgomery Primary School** Ayr Road, Irvine, KA12 8DF ☎ 01294 279031	24
8211523	**Moorpark Primary School** Milton Road, Kilbirnie, KA25 7EP ☎ 01505 685386	30
8200629	**Shiskine Primary School** Shiskine, Isle of Arran, KA27 8EP ☎ 01770 860207	5
8213925	**Skelmorlie Primary School** Innes Park Road, Skelmorlie, Ayrshire, PA17 5BA ☎ 01475 520997	9
8214026	**Springside Primary School** Station Road, Springside, Irvine, KA11 3AZ ☎ 01294 211651	16
8210217	**Springvale Nursery School** McGillivray Avenue, Saltcoats, KA21 6BN ☎ 01294 464231	107
8211620	**St Bridget's Primary School** Hagthorn Avenue, Kilbirnie, KA25 6EJ ☎ 01505 683293	70
8217025	**St Luke's Primary School** Pennyburn Road, Kilwinning, KA13 6LF ☎ 01294 552131	38
8210721	**St Peter's Primary School** South Isle Road, Ardrossan, KA22 8EA ☎ 01294 462554	35
8217149	**Stanecastle School** Burns Crescent, Irvine, KA11 1AQ ☎ 01294 211914	27
8210527	**Stanley Primary School** Stanley Road, Ardrossan, KA22 7DH ☎ 01294 462531	87
8216827	**Towerlands Primary School** Heatherstane Way, Bourtreehill, Irvine, KA11 1DY ☎ 01294 211265	35
8212422	**Woodlands Primary School** Woodlands Avenue, Irvine, KA12 0PU ☎ 01294 279532	35

NORTH LANARKSHIRE

SOEID Number	School name, address and telephone number	No. of pupils in nursery class
8355118	**Abronhill Nursery School** 2/8 Hornbeam Road,Abronhill, Cumbernauld, Glasgow, G67 3NQ ☎ 01236 722171	115
8515328	**Berryhill Primary School** Hillcrest Avenue, Craigneuk, Wishaw, ML2 7RB ☎ 01698 375888	60
8510016	**Calderhead Nursery School** Kirk Road, Shotts, ML7 5ET ☎ 01501 822509	120
8515425	**Castlehill Primary School** Birkshaw Brae, Wishaw, ML2 0ND ☎ 01698 357497	80
8355711	**Cedar Road Nursery School** 196 Cedar Road, Cumbernauld, G67 3BL ☎ 01236 733604	129
8500118	**Coatholm Nursery School** Wallace St,Whifflet, Coatbridge, ML5 4DA ☎ 01236 423 684	85
8502021	**Corpus Christi Primary School** Crowwood Crescent, Calderbank, Airdrie, ML6 9TA ☎ 01236 763985	39
8355010	**Croy Nursery School** McSparran Road, Croy, G65 9HN ☎ 01236 823901	102
8507341	**Deanbank School** Tay Street, Coatbridge, ML5 2NA ☎ 01236 420471	15
8507147	**Drumpark School** Bargeddie, Baillieston, Glasgow, G69 7TW ☎ 01236 423955/428112	58
8512620	**Glencairn Primary School** Glencairn Street, Motherwell, ML1 1TT ☎ 01698 300281	65
8504822	**Glengowan Primary School** Drumfin Avenue, Caldercruix, Airdrie, ML6 7QP ☎ 01236 842308	57
8511926	**Harthill Primary School** West Main Street, Harthill, Shotts, ML7 5QE ☎ 01501 751289	46
8510210	**Hozier Nursery School** Cedar Drive,Viewpark, Uddingston, G71 5LE ☎	120
8502722	**Kirkshaws Primary School** Old Monkland Road, Coatbridge, ML5 5EJ ☎ 01236 424731	39
8513120	**Muirhouse Primary School** 66 Barons Road, Motherwell, ML1 2NB ☎ 01698 262337	39
8514224	**New Stevenston Primary School** Clydesdale Street, New Stevenston, Motherwell, ML1 4JG ☎ 01698 732579	80
8503028	**Old Monkland Primary School** Sharp Avenue, Coatbridge, ML5 5TJ ☎ 01236 424732	49
8510113	**Orbiston Nursery School** Liberty Road, Bellshill, ML4 2EU ☎ 01698 746153	114
8500215	**Richard Stewart Pr-5 Wing** Chapelside Centre, Airdrie, ML6 6LH ☎ 01236 767 359	122
8504121	**Sikeside Primary School** Sikeside Street, Coatbridge, ML5 4QH ☎ 01236 428082	100
8501025	**St Andrew's Primary School** Laggan Road, Airdrie, ML6 0LL ☎ 01236 762622	45
8515026	**St Columba's Primary School** Old Edinburgh Road, Uddingston, Glasgow, G71 6HF ☎ 01698 813804	91
8505128	**St David's Primary School** Meadowhead Road, Plains, Airdrie, ML6 7JF ☎ 01236 764623	52
8501122	**St Dominic's Primary School** Petersburn Road, Airdrie, ML6 8BX ☎ 01236 769663	60
8501327	**St Edward's Primary School** South Biggar Road, Airdrie, ML6 9LZ ☎ 01236 763748	79
8510822	**St Gerard's Primary School** Kelvin Road, Bellshill, ML4 1LN ☎ 01698 745555	82
8355320	**St Helen's Primary School** Lomond Drive, Condorrat, Cumbernauld, G67 4JL ☎ 01236 720070	66
8356920	**St Joseph's Primary School** Broomlands Road, Cumbernauld, G67 2ND ☎ 01236 726200	35

SOEID Number	School name, address and telephone number	No. of pupils in nursery class
8511829	**St Mary's Primary School** Chapel Street, Cleland, Motherwell, ML1 5QX ☎ 01698 860359	60
8341524	**St Michael's Primary School** Burnbrae Avenue, Moodiesburn, Chryston, G69 0ER ☎ 01236 872132	40
8358826	**St Patrick's Primary School** Backbrae Street, Kilsyth, G65 0NA ☎ 01236 822052	76
8503729	**St Patrick's Primary School** Kildonan Street, Coatbridge, ML5 3LG ☎ 01236 421869	38
8501424	**St Serf's Primary School** Thrashburn Road, Airdrie, ML6 6QU ☎ 01236 762781	40
8503923	**St Timothy's Primary School** Old Monkland Road, Coatbridge, ML5 5EA ☎ 01236 421835	38
8514828	**Tannochside Primary School** Douglas Street, Tannochside, Uddingston, G71 5RH ☎ 01698 813252/813275	80
8504229	**Townhead Primary School** Dochart Drive, Coatbridge, ML5 2PG ☎ 01236 421143	51
8501629	**Victoria Primary School** 79 Aitchison Street, Airdrie, ML6 0DB ☎ 01236 763113	48

ORKNEY ISLANDS

6000428	**Dounby Primary School** Dounby, Orkney, KW17 2HT ☎ 01856 771234	30
6002927	**Evie Primary School** Evie, Orkney, KW17 2PE ☎ 01856 751237	16
6003427	**Glaitness Primary School** Kirkwall, Orkney, KW15 1RP ☎ 01856 873648	28
6001521	**Hope Primary School** St Margaret's Hope, Orkney, KW17 2TN ☎ 01856 831217	14
6001629	**Papdale Primary School** Kirkwall, Orkney, KW15 1PJ ☎ 01856 872650	99
6003036	**Pierowall Junior High School** Westray, Orkney, KW17 2DH ☎ 01857 677353	5
6003729	**St Andrew's Primary School** Toab, Orkney, KW17 2QG ☎ 01856 861256	27
6002420	**Stenness Primary School** Stenness, Orkney, KW16 3LB ☎ 01856 850212	22
6002528	**Stromness Primary School** Stromness, Orkney, KW16 3AN ☎ 01856 850544	28

PERTH & KINROSS

5352223	**Alyth Primary School** Albert Street, Alyth, PH11 8AX ☎ 01828 632462/632784	30
5350034	**Auchterarder High School** New School Lane, Auchterarder, Perthshire, PH3 1BL ☎ 01764 662182/3	67
5340829	**Auchtergaven Primary School** Prieston Road, Bankfoot, Perth, PH1 4DE ☎ 01738 787227	20
5349834	**Breadalbane Academy** Crieff Road, Aberfeldy, PH15 2DU ☎ 01887 820428	40
5346525	**Caledonian Road Primary** Caledonian Road, Perth, PH2 8HH ☎ 01738 622139	40
5342627	**Comrie Primary School** School Road, Comrie, PH6 2LN ☎ 01764 670642	25
5350220	**Coupar Angus Primary School** School Road, Coupar Angus, Perthshire, PH13 9AS ☎ 01828 627356	60
5346827	**Craigie Primary School** 15 Abbot Road, Perth, PH2 0EE ☎ 01738 622155	31
5342724	**Crieff Primary School** Commissioner Street, Crieff, PH7 3AY ☎ 01764 652777	58
5340411	**Crieff Road Pre-School Centre** McCallum Court, Fairfield, Perth, PH1 2RT ☎ 01738 633054	130
5341825	**Dunbarney Primary School** Main Street, Bridge Of Earn, PH2 9DY ☎ 01738 812213	39
5340012	**Friarton Nursery School** Edinburgh Road, Perth, PH2 8BX ☎ 01738 625675	60
5346924	**Goodlyburn Primary School** Kingswell Terrace, Perth, PH1 2NT ☎ 01738 626656	32
5341426	**Hill Primary School** Upper Allan Street, Blairgowrie, PH10 6HL ☎ 01250 872815	70
5344727	**Inchture Primary School** Inchture, Perthshire, PH14 9RN ☎ 01828 686284	16
5339022	**Invergowrie Primary School** 4 Errol Road, Invergowrie, DD2 5AD ☎ 01382 562313	36
5345227	**Kinross School** Station Road, Kinross, KY13 7TG ☎ 01577 863515	71
5347122	**Letham Primary School** Struan Road, Perth, PH1 2NL ☎ 01738 625106	40
5346029	**Milnathort Primary School** Bridgefaulds Road, Milnathort, KY13 7XP ☎ 01577 863264	40
5352029	**North Muirton Primary School** Uist Place, Perth, PH1 3BY ☎ 01738 634681	73
5347424	**Oakbank Primary School** Viewlands Road West, Perth, PH1 1NA ☎ 01738 627508	39
5347521	**Our Lady's RC Primary** Garth Avenue, Perth, PH1 2LG ☎ 01738 625291	32
5347327	**Perth Northern District Primary School** Dunkeld Road, Perth, PH1 5DH ☎ 01738 624046	35
5351332	**Pitlochry High** East Moulin Road, Pitlochry, PH16 5ET ☎ 01796 472900	40
5348722	**Robert Douglas Memorial Primary School** Spoutwells Road, Scone, Perth, PH2 6RS ☎ 01738 551136	60
5342929	**Royal School Of Dunkeld Primary School** Dunkeld, PH8 0AB ☎ 01350 727237	19

SOEID Number	School name, address and telephone number	No. of pupils in nursery class
5347629	**St John's R C Primary School** Stormont Street, Perth, PH 1 5NW ☎ 01738 622142	37
5348625	**St Madoes Primary School** Sidlaw Terrace, St Madoes, Glencarse, PH2 7NH ☎ 01738 860332	27
5348927	**Stanley Primary School** The Square, Stanley, Perth, PH1 4LT ☎ 01738 828283	32
5347823	**Tulloch Primary School** Gillespie Place, Perth, PH1 2QX ☎ 01738 627500	36
5347920	**Viewlands Primary School** Oakbank Crescent, Perth, PH1 1BU ☎ 01738 621963	40
INDEPENDENT		
5380129	**Butterstone School** Arthurstone, Meigle, Blairgowrie, PH12 8QY ☎ 01828 640528	37
5380537	**Craigclowan School** Edinburgh Road, Perth, PH2 8PS ☎ 01738 626310	40

RENFREWSHIRE

SOEID Number	School name, address and telephone number	No. of pupils in nursery class
8622620	**Auchenlodment Primary School** Aspen Place, Johnstone, PA5 9QQ ☎ 01505 321464	39
8624623	**Bushes Primary School** Grampian Avenue, Glenburn, Paisley, PA2 8DW ☎ 0141 884 2497	63
8624720	**Craigielea Primary School** Blackstoun Road, Paisley, PA3 1EX ☎ 0141 889 5211	21
8624925	**Heriot Primary School** Heriot Avenue, Foxbar, Paisley, PA2 0DS ☎ 01505 813504	68
8623929	**Lochwinnoch Primary School** Calder Street, Lochwinnoch, PA12 4DG ☎ 01505 842583	40
8620512	**Springbank Nursery School** Fullerton Street, Paisley, PA3 2NN ☎ 0141 8892310	76
8625727	**St Catherine's Primary School** Brabloch Crescent, Paisley, PA3 4RG ☎ 0141 887 6085	60
8625824	**St Charles' Primary School** Rowan Street, Paisley, PA2 6RU ☎ 0141 884 4660	73
8625921	**St Fergus's Primary School** Blackstoun Road, Paisley, PA3 1NB ☎ 0141 889 0113	31
8627320	**St James's Primary School** Albert Road, Renfrew, PA4 8ET ☎ 0141 886 2497	38
8620113	**The Shaw Nursery School** Barrhill Road, Erskine, Renfrewshire, PA8 6BX ☎ 0141 812 2541	100
8626626	**Todholm Primary School** Lochfield Road, Paisley, PA2 7JE ☎ 0141 889 6949	47
8626723	**West Primary School** Newton Street, Paisley, PA1 2RL ☎ 0141 889 5350	47

SCOTTISH BORDERS

SOEID Number	School name, address and telephone number	No. of pupils in nursery class
5618320	**Balmoral Primary School** Balmoral Avenue, Galashiels, TD1 1JJ ☎ 01896 753400	42
5633222	**Broomlands Primary School** Ednam Road, Kelso, TD5 7SW ☎ 01573 223070	34
5630525	**Burnfoot Community School** Kenilworth Avenue, Hawick, TD9 8EQ ☎ 01450 373043	40
5645220	**Chirnside Primary School** Duns, Berwickshire, TD11 3HX ☎ 01890 818274	39
5645425	**Coldingham Primary School** Coldingham, Berwickshire, TD14 5NH ☎ 01890 771241	16
5645522	**Coldstream Primary School** Coldstream, Berwickshire, TD12 4DT ☎ 01890 882189	31
5630622	**Drumlanrig St Cuthbert's Primary School** The Loan, Hawick, TD9 0AU ☎ 01450 373521	39
5645824	**Duns Primary School** Duns, Berwickshire, TD11 3AG ☎ 01361 883797	40
5620724	**Earlston Primary School** Earlston, Berwickshire, TD4 6HF ☎ 0189 6848851	31
5631629	**Edenside Primary School** Inch Road, Kelso, Roxburghshire, TD5 7JP ☎ 01573 224264	38
5647827	**Eyemouth Primary School** Eyemouth, Berwickshire, TD14 5BY ☎ 01890 750692	33
5618827	**Glendinning Terrace Primary School** Glendinning Terrace, Galashiels, TD1 2JW ☎ 01896 753104	20
5631424	**Howdenburn Primary School** Lothian Road, Jedburgh, TD8 6LA ☎ 01835 862542	20
5600529	**Kingsland Primary School** Rosetta Road, Peebles, EH45 8HQ ☎ 01721 720025	43
5619424	**Knowepark Primary School** 1 Curror Street, Selkirk, TD7 4HF ☎ 01750 721736	40
5620627	**Langlee Primary School** Langlee Drive, Galashiels, TD1 2EB ☎ 01896 757892	66
5620120	**Melrose Grammar School** Huntly Road, Melrose, Roxburghshire, TD6 9SB ☎ 01896 822103	32
5631823	**Newcastleton Primary School** Montague Street, Newcastleton, Roxburghshire, TD9 0QZ ☎ 01387 375240	9
5620228	**Newtown Primary School** Sprouston Road, Newtown St Boswells, TD6 0RZ ☎ 01835 822263	16
5631521	**Parkside Primary School** Jedburgh, Roxburghshire, TD8 6HD ☎ 01835 863318	35
5619327	**Philiphaugh Community School** 2 Linglie Road, Selkirk, TD7 5JJ ☎ 01750 721774	32
5601126	**Priorsford Primary School** Marmion Road, Peebles, EH45 9BE ☎ 01721 721236	47
5618924	**St Peter's Primary School** Parsonage Road, Galashiels, TD1 3DS ☎ 01896 753185	20

SOEID Number	School name, address and telephone number	No. of pupils in nursery class
5600421	**St Ronan's Primary School** Innerleithen, Peeblesshire, EH44 6PB ☎ 01896 830349	39
5630924	**Trinity Primary School** Trinity Street, Hawick, TD9 9NR ☎ 01450 373434	40
5620424	**Tweedbank Primary School** Galashiels, TD1 3RR ☎ 01896 754807	21
5601827	**West Linton Primary School** West Linton, Peeblesshire, EH46 7DU ☎ 01968 660222	28
5647126	**Westruther Primary School** Westruther, Gordon, TD3 6NE ☎ 01578 740271	6
5631025	**Wilton Primary School** Wellfield Road, Hawick, Roxburghshire, TD9 7EN ☎ 01450 372075	39

SHETLAND ISLANDS

SOEID Number	School name, address and telephone number	No. of pupils in nursery class
6103030	**Aith Junior High School** Bixter, Shetland, ZE2 9NB ☎ 01595 810206	15
6101720	**Bell's Brae Primary School** Gilbertson Road, Lerwick, Shetland, ZE1 0QB ☎ 01595 692973	57
6103332	**Brae High School** Brae, Shetland, ZE2 9QJ ☎ 01806 522370	27
6100627	**Dunrossness Primary School** Dunrossness, Shetland, ZE2 9JG ☎ 01950 460488	26
6101429	**Happyhansel Primary School** Walls, Shetland, ZE2 9PG ☎ 01595 809217	18
6104428	**Mossbank Primary School** Mossbank, Shetland, ZE2 9RB ☎ 01806 242393	25
6103839	**Sandwick Junior High School** Sandwick, Shetland, ZE2 9HH ☎ 01950 431454/5/6	28
6104320	**Sound Primary School** Lerwick, Shetland, ZE1 0RQ ☎ 01595 694982	54
6104134	**Symbister House Junior High School** Symbister, Shetland, ZE2 9AQ ☎ 01806 566210	17
6101623	**Urafirth Primary School** Heylor, Shetland, ZE2 9RH ☎ 01806 503282	12

SOUTH AYRSHIRE

SOEID Number	School name, address and telephone number	No. of pupils in nursery class
8230323	**Annbank Primary School**	37
8230722	**Braehead Primary School**	57
8232628	**Coylton Primary School**	32
8233020	**Doonfoot Primary School**	50
8233926	**Gardenrose Primary School**	65
8230110	**Girvan Nursery School**	136
8234523	**Glenburn Primary School**	60
8237425	**Kincaidston Primary School**	35
8234620	**Kingcase Primary School**	98
8234221	**Monkton Primary School**	11
8235325	**Muirhead Primary School**	53
8237921	**Newton Primary School**	34
8234922	**Symington Primary School**	20
8230218	**Tarbolton Nursery School**	22
8235120	**Troon Primary School**	76
8230013	**Wallacetown Nursery School**	173
8237719	**Westwood Nursery School**	51

INDEPENDENT

SOEID Number	School name, address and telephone number	No. of pupils in nursery class
8280533	**Wellington School** Carleton Turrets, Craigweil Road, Ayr, KA7 2XH ☎ 01292 269321	37

SOUTH LANARKSHIRE

SOEID Number	School name, address and telephone number	No. of pupils in nursery class
8456720	**Bankhead Primary School** Bankhead Road, Rutherglen, G73 2BQ ☎ 0141 647 6967	46
8455821	**Cairns Primary School** Cairnswell Avenue, Halfway, Cambuslang, G72 8SW ☎ 0141 641 2218	61
8530726	**Castlefield Primary School** Maple Terrace, Greenhills, East Kilbride, G75 9EG ☎ 01355 230810	79
8457123	**Cathkin Primary School** Burnside Road, Rutherglen, G73 4AA ☎ 0141 634 4569	40
8546525	**Coalburn Primary School** Coalburn Road, Coalburn, Lanark, ML11 0LH ☎ 01555 820221	58
8547025	**Crawforddyke Primary School** Eastfield Road, Carluke, ML8 4NZ ☎ 01555 771215	101
8534225	**Crosshouse Primary School** Plover Drive, Greenhills, East Kilbride, G75 8UX ☎ 01355 245300	40

SOEID Number	School name, address and telephone number	No. of pupils in nursery class
8520321	**David Livingstone Memorial Primary School** Morven Avenue, Blantyre, G72 9JY ☎ 01698 823680	32
8530823	**East Milton Primary School** Vancouver Drive, Westwood, East Kilbride, G75 8LG ☎ 01355 222346	47
8547726	**Forth Primary School** Main Street, Forth, ML11 8AE ☎ 01555 811205	60
8520828	**Glenlee Primary School** Reid Street, Burnbank, Hamilton, ML3 0RQ ☎ 01698 823343	18
8530920	**Greenhills Primary School** Cedar Drive, East Kilbride, G75 9JD ☎ 01355 241646	72
8522928	**Hareleeshill Primary School** Myrtle Lane, Larkhall, ML9 2RQ ☎ 01698 883155	82
8520011	**Hollandbush Nursery School** Mill Road, Hamilton, ML3 8AA ☎ 01698 284005	166
8548129	**Lanark Primary School** Rhyber Avenue, Lanark, ML11 7HQ ☎ 01555 662806	71
8457220	**Loch Primary School** Lochaber Drive, Springhall, Rutherglen, G73 5HX ☎ 0141 634 7217	51
8531528	**Maxwellton Primary School** Maxwellton Avenue, Calderwood, East Kilbride, G74 3DU ☎ 01355 222521	52
8531722	**Murray Primary School** Napier Hill, Murray, East Kilbride, G75 0JP ☎ 01355 222566	42
8523320	**Netherburn Primary School** Draffan Road, Netherburn, Larkhall, ML9 3DE ☎ 01698 882484	37
8548927	**Robert Owen Memorial Primary** Smyllum Road, Lanark, ML11 7BZ ☎ 01555 662486	68
8523126	**Robert Smillie Memorial Primary School** Glen Avenue, Larkhall, ML9 1NJ ☎ 01698 882636	67
8457727	**Spittal Primary School** Lochlea Road, Spittal, Rutherglen, G73 4QJ ☎ 0141 634 5861	46
8520720	**St Bride's Primary School** Ailsa Road, Bothwell, G71 8LP ☎ 01698 853709	52
8521727	**St Cuthbert's Primary School** Greenfield Road, Burnbank, Hamilton, ML3 0RG ☎ 01698 282175	44
8532222	**St Leonard's Primary School** Brankumhall Road, Calderwood, East Kilbride, G74 3YA ☎ 01355 224800	70
8457522	**St Mark's Primary School** Kirkriggs Avenue, Blairbeth, Rutherglen, G73 4LY ☎ 0141 634 4238	44
8522227	**St Paul's Primary School** Backmuir Road, Whitehill, Hamilton, ML3 0PX ☎ 01698 284777	15
8549222	**Tinto Primary School** Main Street, Symington, Biggar, ML12 6LL ☎ 01899 308279	67
8518343	**Victoria Park School** Market Road, Carluke, ML8 4BE ☎ 01555 750591	17
8459517	**Westburn Nursery School** 50 Birch Drive, Cambuslang, Glasgow, G72 7LY ☎ 0141 641 7182	109
8533121	**Wester Overton Primary School** Ashkirk Road, Strathaven, ML10 6JT ☎ 01357 521870	62

STIRLING

5720028	**Aberfoyle Primary School** Lochard Road, Aberfoyle, FK8 3SZ ☎ 01877 382278	25
5724821	**Allan's Primary School** 29 Spittal Street, Stirling, FK8 1DU ☎ 01786 474757	41
5724929	**Borestone Primary School** Newpark Crescent, St.Ninians, Stirling, FK7 0QA ☎ 01786 472800	53
5725127	**Braehead Primary School** Springfield Road, Stirling, FK7 7RG ☎ 01786 462770	40
5723329	**Bridge Of Allan Primary** Pullar Avenue, Bridge Of Allan, Stirling, FK9 4SY ☎ 01786 832050	36
5720427	**Callander Primary School** Bridgend, Callendar, FK17 8AG ☎ 01877 331576	42
5723620	**Cambusbarron Primary School** Thomson Place, Cambusbarron, By Stirling, FK7 9PE ☎ 01786 472809	36
5725224	**Cornton Primary School** Cornton Road, Cornton, Stirling, FK9 5DZ ☎ 01786 832051	37
5723728	**Cowie Primary School** Main Street, Cowie, By Stirling, FK7 7BL ☎ 01786 813014	33
5725917	**Croftamie Nursery School** Glasgow Road, Croftamie, G63 0EU ☎ 01360 660 147	39
5720826	**Dunblane Primary School** Doune Road, Dunblane, FK15 9AU ☎ 01786 822351	45
5724023	**East Plean Primary School** Main Street, Plean, By Stirling, FK7 8BX ☎ 01786 813286	32
5724120	**Fallin Primary School** Lamont Crescent, Fallin, By Stirling, FK7 7EJ ☎ 01786 812063	39
5724627	**Killearn Primary School** Cross Head Road, Killearn, G63 9RN ☎ 01360 550430	54
5726018	**Killin Nursery School** Main Street, Killin, FK21 8UW ☎ 01567 820 889	43
5745829	**Newton Primary School** Newton Crescent, Dunblane, FK15 4DZ ☎ 01786 824484	52
5722314	**Park Drive Nursery** Park Drive, Bannockburn, Stirling, FK7 8JA ☎ 01786 816766	124
5726913	**Raploch Nursery School** Craighall Street, Raploch, Stirling, FK8 1TF ☎ 01786 470918	124
5725429	**Riverside Primary School** Forrest Road, Stirling, FK8 1UJ ☎ 01786 474128	39
5725623	**St Ninian's Primary School** Torbrex Road, St.Ninians, Stirling, FK7 9AS ☎ 01786 472024	52
INDEPENDENT		
5780136	**Beaconhurst** 52 Kenilworth Road, Bridge Of Allan, Stirling, FK9 4RR ☎ 01786 832146	35

SOEID Number	School name, address and telephone number	No. of pupils in nursery class
WEST DUNBARTONSHIRE		
8305617	**Andrew Cameron Nursery School** Broomhill Drive, Aitkenbar, Dumbarton, G82 3HQ ☎ 01389 762314	113
8300216	**Brucehill Nursery School** Ardoch Crescent, Dumbarton, G82 4EL ☎ 01389 762840	137
8300119	**Dalmonach Nursery School** First Avenue,Bonhill, Dunbartonshire, G83 9AU ☎ 01389 758208	105
8315019	**Dalmuir Nursery School** Castle Square, Dalmuir, G81 4HL ☎ 0141 9528305	118
8300410	**Jamestown Nursery School** Main Street, Jamestown, Alexandria, G83 8PN ☎ 01389 757729	108
8301328	**Ladyton Primary School** Ladyton, Bonhill, Alexandria, G83 9DZ ☎ 01389 753627	75
8312826	**Linnvale Primary School** Livingstone Street, Clydebank, G81 2RL ☎ 0141 9522625	88
8300518	**Renton Nursery School** Station Street, Renton, Dumbarton, G82 4NB ☎ 01389 754507	116
8313024	**St Eunan's Primary School** Melfort Avenue, Clydebank, G81 2HS ☎ 0141 9522831	70
8313725	**St Mary's Primary School** Chapel Road, Duntocher, Clydebank, G81 6DL ☎ 01389 873211	77
8302421	**St Peter's Primary School** Howatshaws Road, Bellsmyre, Dumbarton, G82 3DR ☎ 01389 762054	98
8312214	**Whitecrook Nursery School** Braes Avenue, Clydebank, G81 1QR ☎ 0141 9529201	96
PARTNERSHIP		
8315116	**Edinbarnet Nursery School** Faifley Road, Faifley, Clydebank, G81 5BQ ☎ 01389 879615	104
WEST LOTHIAN		
5500125	**Addiewell Primary School** Church Street, Addiewell, West Calder, EH55 8PG ☎ 01501 762794	18
5504627	**Armadale Primary School** Academy Street, Armadale, West Lothian, EH48 3JD ☎ 01501 730282	76
5502721	**Bankton Primary School** Kenilworth Rise, Livingston, EH54 6JL ☎ 01506 413001	37
5504015	**Bathgate West Nursery School** 63 Millburn Road, Bathgate, West Lothian, EH48 2AF ☎ 01506 652004	71
5505828	**Blackridge Primary School** Main Street, Blackridge, West Lothian, EH48 3RJ ☎ 01501 751223	29
5511917	**Bonnytoun Nursery School** 141 Springfield Road, Linlithgow, West Lothian, EH49 7SN ☎ 01506 847454	120
5505925	**Bridgend Primary School** Edinburgh Road, Bridgend, Linlithgow, EH49 6ND ☎ 01506 834204	10
5506026	**Broxburn Primary School** West Main Street, Broxburn, West Lothian, EH52 5RH ☎ 01506 852018	45
5502926	**Carmondean Primary School** Knightsridge Road West, Livingston, West Lothian, EH54 8PX ☎ 01506 432492	88
5508525	**Croftmalloch Primary School** Via Raeburn Crescent, Whitburn, West Lothian, EH47 8HQ ☎ 01501 740506	38
5506425	**Dechmont Infant School** Main Street, Dechmont, Broxburn, EH52 6LJ ☎ 01506 811264	9
5500524	**East Calder Primary School** 9 Langton Road, East Calder, EH53 0BL ☎ 01506 880810	55
5504511	**Eastertoun Nursery School** Manse Avenue, Armadale, West Lothian, EH48 3HS ☎ 01501 732299	62
5512018	**Fauldhouse Nursery School** Lanrigg Avenue, Fauldhouse, Bathgate, EH47 9JR ☎ 01501 770782	56
5502810	**Glenvue Nursery School** Dedridge East, Livingston, West Lothian, EH54 6JQ ☎ 01506 412333	85
5506921	**Greenrigg Primary School** Polkemmet Road, Harthill, Lanarkshire, ML7 5RF ☎ 01501 751334	18
5511712	**Hopefield Nursery School** Hopefield Road, Blackburn, West Lothian, EH47 7HZ ☎ 01506 630944	49
5510716	**Kirkhill Nursery School** Rashierigg Road, Broxburn, West Lothian, EH52 6AW ☎ 01506 853118	70
5500729	**Kirknewton Primary School** 21 Station Road, Kirknewton, West Lothian, EH27 8DD ☎ 01506 881461	38
5510813	**Knightsridge Nursery School** Ferguson Way, Livingston, West Lothian, EH54 8JF ☎ 01506 436364	70
5511410	**Ladywell Nursery School** Willowbank,Ladywell, Livingston, West Lothian, EH54 6HN ☎ 01506 434542	119
5501229	**Letham Primary School** Forth Drive, Livingston, EH54 5LZ ☎ 01506 432012	28
5507227	**Linlithgow Primary School** Preston Road, Linlithgow, West Lothian, EH49 6HB ☎ 01506 842686	98
5507723	**Longridge Primary School** School Road, Longridge, Bathgate, EH47 8AG ☎ 01501 770208	11
5501520	**Mid Calder Primary School** Mid Calder, Livingston, EH53 0RR ☎ 01506 882092	60
5505526	**Murrayfield Primary School** Catherine Terrace, Blackburn, West Lothian, EH47 7DX ☎ 01506 653400	43
5508029	**Our Lady's Primary School** 79 Main Street, Stoneyburn, EH47 8BA ☎ 01501 762265	46
5501628	**Parkhead Primary School** Harburn Road, West Calder, EH55 8AH ☎ 01506 871404	39
5511011	**Polbeth Nursery School** Polbeth Road, West Calder, West Lothian, EH55 8SR ☎ 01506 872511	63
5508622	**Polkemmet Primary School** The Avenue, Whitburn, West Lothian, EH47 0BX ☎ 01501 740319	45

SOEID Number	School name, address and telephone number	No. of pupils in nursery class
5501725	**Pumpherston Primary School** 18 Uphall Station Road, Pumpherston, Livingston, EH53 0LP ☎ 01506 432152	31
5501326	**Riverside Primary School** Maree Walk, Livingston, West Lothian, EH54 5EJ ☎ 01506 432248	44
5507820	**Seafield Infant School** Cousland Terrace, Seafield, by Bathgate, EH47 7BL ☎ 01506 652916	20
5505224	**St Columba's Primary School** Philip Avenue, Bathgate, West Lothian, EH48 1NQ ☎ 01506 653822	57
5505321	**St Mary's Primary School** Whitburn Road, Bathgate, West Lothian, EH48 2RD ☎ 01506 652511	60
5506220	**St Nicholas Primary School** West Mains Street, Broxburn, West Lothian, EH52 5LN ☎ 01506 853509	40
5511224	**St Ninian's Primary School** Douglas Rise, Dedridge, Livingston, EH54 6JR ☎ 01506 414612	50
5500621	**St Paul's Primary School** Main Street, East Calder, West Lothian, EH53 0ES ☎ 01506 881665	36
5501423	**Toronto Primary School** Howden East, Livingston, EH54 6BN ☎ 01506 431461	60
5511119	**Whitdale Nursery School** East Main Street, Whitburn, West Lothian, EH47 8JP ☎ 01501 743856	89
5509025	**Winchburgh Primary School** Glendevon Park, Winchburgh, West Lothian, EH52 6UE ☎ 01506 890202	43
5511313	**Woodlands Nursery School** Harburn Avenue, Deans, Livingston, West Lothian, EH54 8NQ ☎ 01506 412608	56

Names, addresses and telephone numbers and school rolls of all schools in Scotland, as per September 1998.
The School rolls are as per School Census September 1997.
(At the request of the education authorities of Highland and South Ayrshire the addresses and telephone numbers of the education authority schools in those areas are not supplied)
Source: The Scottish Office Education and Industry Department

Appendices

***Appendix 1:* Maps**

***Appendix 2:* Directory of Local Education Authorities**

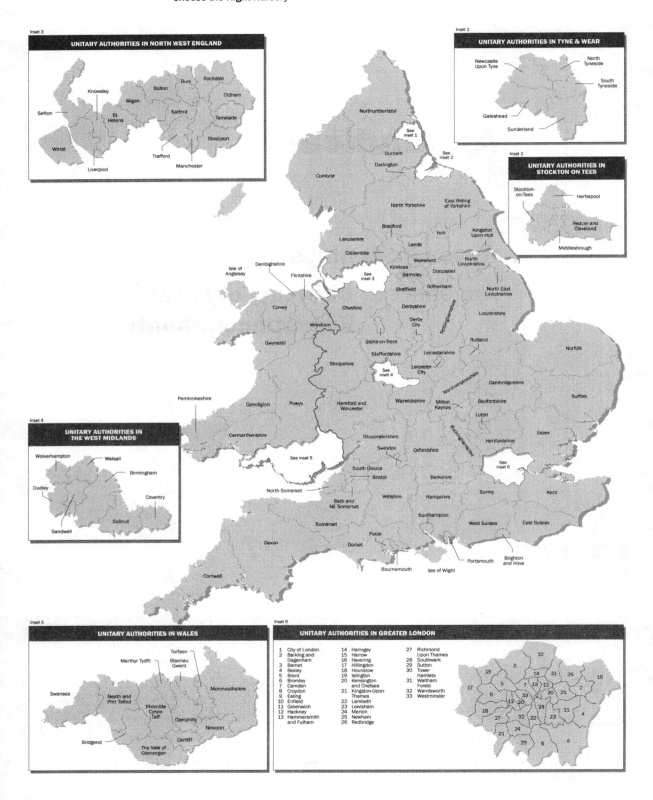

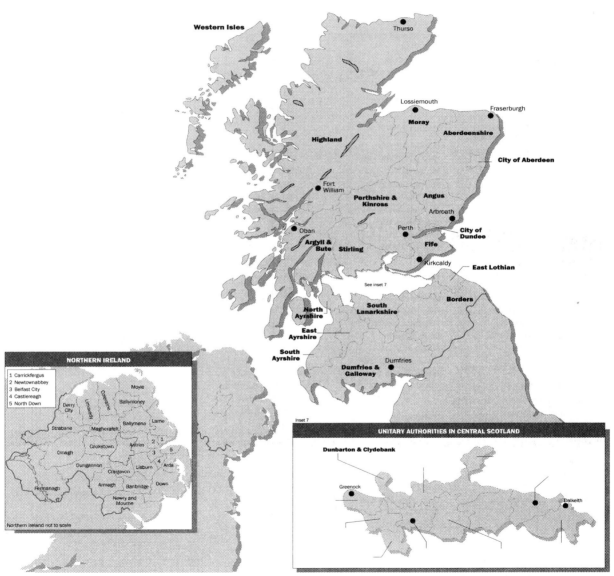

Directory of Local Education Authorities in England

A

Avon

See: Bath & North East Somerset,
Bristol, City of,
North Somerset,
South Gloucestershire.

B

Barking and Dagenham

(LEA code: 301)
Chief Education Officer
Education Offices
Town Hall, Barking
Essex IG11 7LU
Tel: 0181 592 4500
Fax: 0181 594 9837

Barnet

(LEA code: 302)
Director of Education Services
LBB Education Services (formerly
Friern Barnet Town Hall)
Friern Barnet Lane
London N11 3DL
Tel: 0181 359 2000
Fax: 0181 359 3057

Barnsley

(LEA code: 370)
Chief Education Officer
Education Offices
Berneslai Close, Barnsley
South Yorkshire S70 2HS
Tel: 01226 770770
Fax: 01226 773599

Bath & North East Somerset

(LEA code: 800)
Director of Education Cultural and
Community Service
Bath & North East Somerset
Council
Northgate House
Upper Borough, Walls
Bath BA1 2JD
Tel: 01225 460628
Fax: 01225 426990

Bedfordshire

(LEA code: 902)
Chief Education Officer
Education Department
County Hall
Bedford MK42 9AP
Tel: 01234 363222
Fax: 01234 228619

Berkshire

(LEA code: 903)
Chief Education Officer
Education Department
Shire Hall
Shinfield Park
Reading RG2 9XE
Tel: 01734 875444
Fax: 01734 750360

Bexley

(LEA code: 303)
Director of Education
Bexley
London Borough
Hill View
Hill View Drive, Welling
Kent DA16 3RY
Tel: 0181 303 7777
Fax: 0181 319 4302

Birmingham

(LEA code: 330)
Chief Education Officer
Education Department
Council House
Margaret Street
Birmingham B3 3BU
Tel: 0121 235 2590
Fax: 0121 235 1318

Bolton

(LEA code: 350)
Director of Education
PO Box 53
Paderborn House
Civic Centre, Bolton
Lancashire BL1 1JW
Tel: 01204 522311
Fax: 01204 365492

Bradford

(LEA code: 380)
Director of Education
Flockton House
Flockton Road, Bradford
West Yorkshire BD4 7RY
Tel: 01274 752111
Fax: 01274 390081

Brent

(LEA code: 304)
Chief Education Officer
Department of Education,
Arts and Libraries
Brent Council
Chesterfield House
9 Park Lane, Wembley
Middlesex HA9 7RW
Tel: 0181 937 3190
Fax: 0181 937 3023

Bristol, City of

(LEA code: 801)
Director of Education
Bristol City Council
The Council House
College Green
Bristol BS1 5TR
Tel: 0117 922 4401
Fax: 0117 922 2069

Bromley

(LEA code: 305)
Director of Education
London Borough of Bromley
Education Department
Bromley Civic Centre
Stockwell Close
Bromley BR1 3UH
Tel: 0181 464 3333
Fax: 0181 313 4049

Buckinghamshire

(LEA code: 904)
Chief Education Officer
County Hall
Aylesbury
Bucks HP20 1UZ
Tel: 01296 395000
Fax: 01296 383367

Bury

(LEA code: 351)
Director of Education
Education Department
Athenaeum House
Market Street, Bury
Lancashire BL9 0BN
Tel: 0161 705 5000
Fax: 0161 705 5653

C

Calderdale

(LEA code: 381)
Director of Education
Education Department
PO Box 33
Northgate House
Northgate, Halifax
West Yorkshire
HX1 1UN
Tel: 01422 357257
Fax: 01422 392515

Cambridgeshire

(LEA code: 905)
Director of Education
Castle Court
Shire Hall, Castle Hill
Cambridge CB3 0AP
Tel: 01223 317111
Fax: 01223 317201

Camden

(LEA code: 202)
Director of Education
London Borough of Camden
Education Department
Crowndale Centre
216-220 Eversholt Street
London NW1 1DE
Tel: 0171 911 1525
Fax: 0171 911 1536

Cheshire

(LEA code: 906)
Director of Educational Services
County Hall
Chester CH1 1SQ
Tel: 01244 602424
Fax: 01244 603800

Cleveland

See: Hartlepool, Middlesbrough,
Redcar and Cleveland,
Stockton-on-Tees.

Directory of Local Education Authorities in England

Cornwall

(LEA code: 908)

Secretary for Education
Education Offices
County Hall, Truro
Cornwall TR1 3BA
Tel: 01872 322000
Fax: 01872 323835

Corporation of London

(LEA code: 201)

City Education Officer
Corporation of London
Education Department
PO Box 270
Guildhall
London EC2P 2EJ
Tel: 0171 332 1750
Fax: 0171 332 1621

Only responsible for the one square mile City of London. Education in the rest of Greater London is the responsibility of the various boroughs - see the entry for London for details.

Coventry

(LEA code: 331)

Chief Education Officer
New Council Offices
Earl Street, Coventry CV1 5RS
Tel: 01203 833333
Fax: 01203 831620

Croydon

(LEA code: 306)

Director of Education
Taberner House
Park Lane, Croydon CR9 1TP
Tel: 0181 686 4433
Fax: 0181 760 0871

Cumbria

(LEA code: 909)

Director of Education
Education Offices
5 Portland Square
Carlisle CA1 1PU
Tel: 01228 23456
Fax: 01228 515189

D

Derbyshire

(LEA code: 910)

Chief Education Officer
County Offices, Matlock
Derbyshire DE4 3AG
Tel: 01629 580000
Fax: 01629 580350

Devon

(LEA code: 911)

Chief Education Officer
County Hall, Exeter EX2 4QG
Tel: 01392 382000
Fax: 01392 382203
Email:
education@ched.devon-cc.gov.uk

Doncaster

(LEA code: 371)

Director of Education
PO Box 266
The Council House, Doncaster
South Yorkshire DN1 3AD
Tel: 01302 737222
Fax: 01302 737223

Dorset

(LEA code: 912)

County Education Officer
Education Department
County Hall
Colliton Park, Dorchester
Dorset DT1 1XJ
Tel: 01305 251000
Fax: 01305 224499

Dudley

(LEA code: 332)

Chief Education Officer
Westox House
1 Trinity Road, Dudley
West Midlands DY1 1JB
Tel: 01384 456000
Fax: 01384 452216

Durham

(LEA code: 913)

Director of Education
Education Department
County Hall
Durham DH1 5UJ
Tel: 0191 386 4411
Fax: 0191 386 0487

E

Ealing

(LEA code: 307)

Director of Education
Perceval House
14-16 Uxbridge Road
Ealing
London W5 2HL
Tel: 0181 579 2424
Fax: 0181 566 2676

East Riding of Yorkshire

(LEA code: 811)

Chief Education Officer
East Riding of Yorkshire Council
County Hall, Beverley
East Riding of Yorkshire HU17 9BA
Tel: 01482 887700
Fax: 01482 871137

East Sussex

(LEA code: 914)

County Education Officer
PO Box 4, County Hall
St Anne's Crescent
Lewes
East Sussex BN7 1SG
Tel: 01273 481000
Fax: 01273 481261

Enfield

(LEA code: 308)

Director of Education
Education Department
PO Box 56
Civic Centre
Silver Street, Enfield
Middlesex EN1 3XQ
Tel: 0181 366 6565
Fax: 0181 982 7375

Essex

(LEA code: 915)

County Education Officer
Education Department
PO Box 47 A Block
County Hall, Victoria Road
Chelmsford CM1 1LD
Tel: 01245 492211
Fax: 01245 492759

FG

Gateshead

(LEA code: 390)

Director of Education
Education Offices
Civic Centre
Regent Street
Gateshead
Tyne and Wear NE8 1HH
Tel: 0191 477 1011
Fax: 0191 478 3495

Gloucestershire

(LEA code: 916)

Chief Education Officer
Shire Hall
Gloucester GL1 2TP
Tel: 01452 425300
Fax: 01452 425496

Greenwich

(LEA code: 203)

Director of Education
London Borough of Greenwich
9th Floor, Riverside House
Beresford Street
London SE18 6PW
Tel: 0181 854 8888
Fax: 0181 855 2427

H

Hackney

(LEA code: 204)

Director of Education
Hackney Education Directorate
Edith Cavell House
Enfield Road, London N1 5AZ
Tel: 0171 214 8400
Fax: 0171 214 8531

Hammersmith and Fulham

(LEA code: 205)

Director of Education
London Borough of Hammersmith and Fulham
Town Hall, King Street
London W6 9JU
(Visitors to Cambridge House, Cambridge Grove, London, W6 0LE)
Tel: 0181 748 3020 x 3621
Fax: 0181 741 0153

Directory of Local Education Authorities in England

Hampshire

(LEA code: 917)

County Education Officer
The Castle, Winchester
Hampshire SO23 8UG
Tel: 01962 841841
Fax: 01962 842355

Haringey

(LEA code: 309)

Director of Education Services
London Borough of Haringey
Education Offices
48 Station Road, Woodgreen
London N22 4TY
Tel: 0181 975 9700
Fax: 0181 862 3864

Harrow

(LEA code: 310)

Director of Education
PO Box 22
Civic Centre, Harrow
Middlesex HA1 2UW
Tel: 0181 863 5611
Fax: 0181 427 0810

Hartlepool

(LEA code: 805)

Director of Education and
Community Services
Hartlepool Council
Civic Centre
Hartlepool Council
Victoria Road, Hartlepool
Cleveland TS24 8AY
Tel: 01429 266522
Fax: 01429 869625

Havering

(LEA code: 311)

Director of Education and
Community Service
London Borough of Havering
The Broxhill Centre
Broxhill Road, Harold Hill
Romford RM14 1XN
Tel: 01708 772222
Fax: 01708 773850

Hereford and Worcester

(LEA code: 918)

County Education Officer
Castle Street
Worcester WR1 3AG
Tel: 01905 763763
Fax: 01905 766156

Hertfordshire

(LEA code: 919)

Director of Education
County Hall
Hertford SG13 8DF
Tel: 01992 555827
Fax: 01992 555644
Email:HCCEDCH
@ched.hertscc.gov.uk

Hillingdon

(LEA code: 312)

Director of Education
London Borough of Hillingdon
Civic Centre
Uxbridge
Middlesex UB8 1UW
Tel: 01895 250111
Fax: 01895 250878

Hounslow

(LEA code: 313)

Director of Education
Civic Centre
Lampton Road
Hounslow
Middlesex TW3 4DN
Tel: 0181 570 7728
Fax: 0181 572 4819
Email:info@lbhit.
parasoft.co.uk

Humberside

See: East Riding of Yorkshire,
Kingston-upon-Hull, City of,
North Lincolnshire,
North East Lincolnshire.

I

Isle of Wight

(LEA code: 921)

Director of Education
County Hall
Newport
Isle of Wight PO30 1UD
Tel: 01983 821000
Fax: 01983 521817

Isles of Scilly

(LEA code: 420)

Secretary for Education
Council of the Isles of Scilly
Town Hall
St Marys
Isles of Scilly TR21 0LW
Tel: 01720 22537
Fax: 01720 22202

Islington

(LEA code: 206)

Director of Education
London Borough of Islington
Laycock Street
London N1 1TH
Tel: 0171 226 1234
Fax: 0171 457 5555

J K

Kensington and Chelsea

(LEA code: 207)

Director of Education
Royal Borough of Kensington and
Chelsea Town Hall
Hornton Street
London W8 7NX
Tel: 0171 937 5464
Fax: 0171 937 0038

Kent

(LEA code: 922)

Director of Education Services
Education Department
Springfield
Maidstone
Kent ME14 2LJ
Tel: 01622 671411
Fax: 01622 690892

Kingston-upon-Hull, City of

(LEA code: 810)

Director of Education
Kingston-upon-Hull
City Council
Essex House
Manor Street
Kingston-upon-Hull
HU1 1YD
Tel: 01482 610610

Kingston-upon-Thames

(LEA code: 314)

Director of Education
Royal Borough of Kingston-upon-
Thames Guildhall
High Street
Kingston-upon-Thames
Surrey KT1 1EU
Tel: 0181 546 2121
Fax: 0181 547 5296

Kirklees

(LEA code: 382)

Chief Education Officer
Kirklees
Metropolitan Council
Oldgate House 2
Oldgate
Huddersfield HD1 6QW
Tel: 01484 422133
Fax: 01484 443336

Knowsley

(LEA code: 340)

Director of Education
Knowsley Borough Council
Education Office
Huyton Hey Road
Huyton
Merseyside L36 5YH
Tel: 0151 489 6000
Fax: 0151 449 3852

L

Lambeth

(LEA code: 208)

Director of Education
Lambeth Education Department
London Borough of Lambeth
Blue Star House
234/244 Stockwell Road
London SW9 9SP
Tel: 0171 926 1000
Fax: 0171 926 2633

Lancashire

(LEA code: 923)

Chief Education Officer
PO Box 61
County Hall
Preston PR1 8RJ
Tel: 01772 254868
Fax: 01772 261630

Directory of Local Education Authorities in England

Leeds

(LEA code: 383)

Chief Education Officer
Leeds Education Department
Selectapost
17 Merrion House
Merrion Centre
Leeds LS2 8DT
Tel: 0113 234 8080
Fax: 0113 234 1394

Leicestershire

(LEA code: 924)

Director of Education
Education Department
County Hall, Glenfield
Leicester LE3 8RF
Tel: 0116 232 3232
Fax: 0116 265 6634

Lewisham

(LEA code: 209)

Director of Education
London Borough of Lewisham
Laurence House
Town Hall, Catford
London SE6 4RU
Tel: 0181 695 6000
Fax: 0181 690 4392

Lincolnshire

(LEA code: 925)

Director of Education
County Offices, Newland
Lincoln LN1 1YQ
Tel: 01522 552222
Fax: 01522 553257

Liverpool

(LEA code: 341)

Director of Education
Education Offices
14 Sir Thomas Street
Liverpool L1 6BJ
Tel: 0151 227 3911
Fax: 0151 225 3029

London
Inner London

- See separate entries for Inner
London Education Authority (ILEA)
London Boroughs: Camden,
Corporation of London [covering
the one square mile of the City of
London], Greenwich, Hammersmith
and Fulham, Hackney, Islington,
Kensington and Chelsea, Lambeth,
Lewisham, Southwark, Tower Ham-
lets, Wandsworth, Westminster.

Outer London

- See separate entries for following
London Boroughs: Barking and
Dagenham, Barnet, Bexley, Brent,
Bromley, Croydon, Ealing, Enfield,
Haringey, Harrow, Havering,
Hillingdon, Hounslow, Kingston-
upon-Thames, Merton, Newham,
Redbridge, Richmond-upon-
Thames, Sutton, Waltham Forest.

M
Manchester

(LEA code: 352)

Chief Education Officer
Education Offices
Crown Square
Manchester M60 3BB
Tel: 0161 234 5000
Fax: 0161 234 7073

Merton

(LEA code: 315)

Director of Education Leisure and
Libraries
London Borough of Merton
Crown House
London Road
Morden, Surrey SM4 5DX
Tel: 0181 543 2222
Fax: 0181 543 7126

Middlesbrough

(LEA code: 806)

Director of Education
Middlesbrough Education Office
PO Box 191
2nd Floor, Civic Centre
Middlesbrough TS1 2XS
Tel: 01642 245432
Fax: 01642 262038

N
Newcastle-upon-Tyne

(LEA code: 391)

Chief Education Officer
Education Offices
Civic Centre
Barras Bridge
Newcastle-upon-Tyne NE1 8PU
Tel: 0191 232 8520
Fax: 0191 211 4983

Newham

(LEA code: 316)

Director of Education
London Borough of Newham
Education Offices
Broadway House
322 High Street
Stratford
London E15 1EP
Tel: 0181 534 4545
Fax: 0181 503 0014

Norfolk

(LEA code: 926)

County Education Officer
County Hall
Martineau Lane
Norwich NR1 2DL
Tel: 01603 222300
Fax: 01603 222119

North East Lincolnshire

(LEA code: 812)

Head of Professional Services
Education North East Lincolnshire
Council
Eleanor Street
Grimsby DN32 9DU
Tel: 01472 323051
Fax: 01472 323020

North Lincolnshire

(LEA code: 813)

Director of Education and Personal
Development
North Lincolnshire Council
Pittwood House
Asby Road
Scunthorpe
Humberside DN16 1AB
Tel: 0345 103103

North Somerset

(LEA code: 802)

Director of Education
North Somerset Council
PO Box 51
Weston-Super-Mare BS23 1ZZ
Tel: 01934 888829
Fax: 01934 888834

North Tyneside

(LEA code: 392)

Chief Education Officer
Education Department
Stephenson House
Stephenson Street
North Shields
Tyne and Wear NE30 1QA
Tel: 0191 257 5544
Fax: 0191 296 2439

North Yorkshire

(LEA code: 815)

[see also York, City of]
Director of Education, Libraries,
Archives, Museums and Arts
County Hall, Northallerton
North Yorkshire DL7 8AE
Tel: 01609 780780
Fax: 01609 778611

Northamptonshire

(LEA code: 928)

Director of Education and Libraries
Education Department
PO Box 149
County Hall, Guildhall Road
Northampton NN1 1AU
Tel: 01604 236236
Fax: 01604 236188

Northumberland

(LEA code: 929)

Director of Education
Education Department
County Hall, Morpeth
Northumberland NE61 2EF
Tel: 01670 533000
Fax: 01670 533750

Directory of Local Education Authorities in England

Nottinghamshire

(LEA code: 930)

Director of Education
County Hall, West Bridgford
Nottingham NG2 7QP
Tel: 0115 982 3823
Fax: 0115 981 2824

O

Oldham

(LEA code: 353)

Director of Education and Leisure
Education Department
Old Town Hall
Middleton Road
Chadderton
Oldham OL9 6PP
Tel: 0161 911 4260
Fax: 0161 628 0433

Oxfordshire

(LEA code: 931)

Chief Education Officer Education
Department
Macclesfield House
New Road
Oxford OX1 1NA
Tel: 01865 792422
Fax: 01865 791637

P Q R

Redbridge

(LEA code: 317)

Director of Education
Education Office
London Borough of Redbridge
Lynton House, 255-259 High Road
Ilford, Essex IG1 1NN
Tel: 0181 478 3020
Fax: 0181 553 0895

Redcar and Cleveland

(LEA code: 807)

Chief Education Officer
Redcar and Cleveland Borough
Council Redcar Council Offices
PO Box 83, Kirkleatham Street
Redcar TS10 1YA
Tel: 01642 444000
Fax: 01642 444122

Richmond-upon-Thames

(LEA code: 318)

Director of Education
London Borough of Richmond-
upon-Thames
Education Department
Regal House, London Road
Twickenham TW1 3QB
Tel: 0181 891 1411
Fax: 0181 891 7730

Rochdale

(LEA code: 354)

Director of Education
Education Department
PO Box 70
Municipal Offices
Smith Street
Rochdale OL16 1YD
Tel: 01706 47474
Fax: 01706 59475

Rotherham

(LEA code: 372)

Director of Education Services
Norfolk House,
Walker Place
Rotherham S60 1QT
Tel: 01709 382121
Fax: 01709 372056

S

St Helens

(LEA code: 342)

Director of Education
Community Education Department
The Rivington Centre
Rivington Road, St Helens
Merseyside WA10 4ND
Tel: 01744 456000
Fax: 01744 455350

Salford

(LEA code: 355)

Chief Education Officer
Education Office
Chapel Street, Salford M3 5LT
Tel: 0161 832 9751/8
Fax: 0161 835 1561

Sandwell

(LEA code: 333)

Director of Education
Sandwell
Metropolitan Borough Council
PO Box 41, Shaftesbury House
402 High Street
West Bromwich, Sandwell
West Midlands B70 9LT
Tel: 0121 525 7366
Fax: 0121 553 1528

Sefton

(LEA code: 343)

Director of Education
Sefton Borough Council
Education Department
Town Hall, Bootle
Merseyside L20 7AE
Tel: 0151 933 6003
Fax: 0151 934 3349

Sheffield
(LEA code: 373)
Director of Education
PO Box 67, Leopold Street
Sheffield S1 1RJ
Tel: 0114 272 6341
Fax: 0114 273 6279

Shropshire

(LEA code: 932)

Chief Education Officer
The Shirehall
Abbey Foregate
Shrewsbury SY2 6ND
Tel: 01743 2543017
Fax: 01743 254415

Solihull

(LEA code: 334)

Director of Education
PO Box 20
Council House
Solihull
West Midlands B91 3QU
Tel: 0121 704 6000
Fax: 0121 704 6669

Somerset

(LEA code: 933)

Chief Education Officer
County Hall, Taunton
Somerset TA1 4DY
Tel: 01823 333451
Fax: 01823 338139

South Gloucestershire

(LEA code: 803)

Director of Education
South Gloucestershire Offices
Bowling Hill
Chipping Sodbury
JBS17 6JX
Tel: 01454 863333
Fax: 01454 863264

South Tyneside

(LEA code: 393)

Director of Education
Education Department
Town Hall, Civic Offices
Westoe Road, South Shields
Tyne and Wear NE33 2RL
Tel: 0191 427 1717
Fax: 0191 455 0208

Southwark

(LEA code: 210)

Director of Education
London Borough of Southwark
1 Bradenham Close (off Albany
Road)
London SE17 2QA
Tel: 0171 525 5000
Fax: 0171 525 5025

Staffordshire

(LEA code: 934)

Chief Education Officer
County Buildings, Tipping Street
Stafford ST16 2DH
Tel: 01785 223121
Fax: 01785 56727

Stockport

(LEA code: 356)

Director of Education
Education Division
Stopford House
Stockport SK1 3XE
Tel: 0161 480 4949
Fax: 0161 477 9530

Stockton-on-Tees

(LEA code: 808)

Chief Education Officer
Stockton-on-Tees Council
PO Box 228, Municipal Buildings
Church Road, Stockton-on-Tees
TS18 1XE
Tel: 01642 393939
Fax: 01642 393479

Suffolk

(LEA code: 935)

Chief Education Officer
Education Department
St Andrew House
County Hall
Ipswich IP4 1LJ
Tel: 01473 230000
Fax: 01473 230395

Sunderland

(LEA code: 394)

Director of Education
Education Department
PO Box No 101
Town Hall and Civic Centre
Sunderland SR2 7DN
Tel: 0191 567 6161
Fax: 0191 510 9104

Surrey

(LEA code: 936)

County Education Officer
County Hall
Penrhyn Road
Kingston upon Thames KT1 2DJ
Tel: 0181 541 9501
Fax: 0181 541 9503

Sutton

(LEA code: 319)

Director of Education
London Borough of Sutton
The Grove
Carshalton SM5 3AL
Tel: 0181 770 5000
Fax: 0181 770 6545

T

Tameside

(LEA code: 357)

Director of Education
Tameside Metropolitan Borough
Council Education Department
Council Offices
Wellington Road
Ashton-under-Lyne
Lancashire OL6 6DL
Tel: 0161 342 8355
Fax: 0161 342 3260

Tower Hamlets

(LEA code: 211)

Chief Education Officer
London Borough of Tower Hamlets
Education Department
Mulberry Place
5 Clove Crescent
London E14 2BG
Tel: 0171 364 5000
Fax: 0171 364 4296

Trafford

(LEA code: 358)

Director of Education
Trafford Borough Council
PO Box 19
Education Department
Tatton Road
Sale M33 1YR
Tel: 0161 872 2101
Fax: 0161 969 8023

U V W

Wakefield

(LEA code: 384)

Chief Education Officer
Education Department
County Hall
Bond Street
Wakefield
West Yorkshire WF1 2QL
Tel: 01924 306090
Fax: 01924 305632

Walsall

(LEA code: 335)

Corporate Board Director for
Education and Culture
The Civic Centre
Darwall Street, Walsall
West Midlands WS1 1DQ
Tel: 01922 650000
Fax: 01922 722322

Waltham Forest

(LEA code: 320)

Chief Education Officer
London Borough of Waltham
Forest
Municipal Offices
High Road, Leyton
London E10 5QJ
Tel: 0181 527 5544
Fax: 0181 527 5544 x5163

Wandsworth

(LEA code: 212)

Director of Education
London Borough of Wandsworth
Town Hall
Wandsworth High Street
London SW18 2PU
Tel: 0181 871 8013
Fax: 0181 871 6609

Warwickshire

(LEA code: 937)

County Education Officer
22 Northgate Street
Warwick CV34 4SR
Tel: 01926 410410
Fax: 01926 412746

West Sussex

(LEA code: 938)

Director of Education
County Hall
West Street
Chichester
West Sussex PO19 1RF
Tel: 01243 777100
Fax: 01243 777229

Westminster

(LEA code: 213)

Director of Education and Leisure
Department
City of Westminster
PO Box 240
Westminster City Hall
Victoria Street
London SW1E 6QP
Tel: 0171 828 8070
Fax: 0171 798 3404

Wigan

(LEA code: 359)

Director of Education
Education Offices
Gateway House, Standishgate
Wigan WN1 1XL
Tel: 01942 44991
Fax: 01942 28811

Wiltshire

(LEA code: 939)

Chief Education Officer
County Hall
Bythesea Road
Trowbridge
Wiltshire BA14 8JB
Tel: 01225 713000
Fax: 01225 713982

Wirral

(LEA code: 344)

Director of Education
Wirral Metropolitan Borough
Council
Hamilton Building
Conway Street
Birkenhead L41 6FD
Tel: 0151 666 2121
Fax: 0151 666 4207

Wolverhampton

(LEA code: 336)

Director of Education
Education Department
Civic Centre
St Peter's Square
Wolverhampton WV1 1RR
Tel: 01902 27811
Fax: 01902 314218

X Y Z

York, City of

(LEA code: 816)

Director of Education
York City Council
Rougier House
George Hudson Street
York
Tel: 01904 613163 .

Directory of Local Education Authorities in Scotland

Aberdeen
Director of Education
Aberdeen City Council
Summerhill Education Centre
Stronsay Drive
Aberdeen AB15 6JA
Tel: 01224 522000
Fax: 01224 346061

Aberdeenshire
Director of Education
Aberdeenshire Council
Woodhill House
Westburn Road
Aberdeen AB16 5GB
Tel: 01224 665420
Fax: 01224 665445

Angus
Director of Education
Angus Council
County Buildings
Market Street
Forfar
DD8 3WE
Tel: 01307 461460
Fax: 01307 461848

Argyll and Bute
Director of Education
Argyll and Bute Council
Argyll House
Alexandra Parade
Dunoon
PA23 8AJ
Tel: 01369 704000
Fax: 01369 702614

Clackmannanshire
Director of Education &
Community Services
Clackmannanshire Council
Lime Tree House
Alloa
FK10 1EX
Tel: 01259 452435
Fax: 01259 452440

Dumfries & Galloway
Director of Education
Dumfries & Galloway Council
30 Edinburgh Road
Dumfries
DG1 1NW
Tel: 01387 260427
Fax: 01387 260453

Dundee
Director of Education
Dundee City Council
Tayside House
Crichton Street
Dundee
DD1 3RJ
Tel: 01382 433088
Fax: 01382 433080

East Ayrshire
Director of Education
East Ayrshire Council
Council Headquarters
London Road
Kilmarnock
KA3 7BU
Tel: 01563 576000
Fax: 01563 576210

East Dunbartonshire
Director of Education and Leisure
Services
East Dunbartonshire Council
Boclair House
100 Milngavie Road
Bearsden
Glasgow
G61 2TQ
Tel: 0141 942 9000
Fax: 0141 942 6814

East Lothian
Director of Education and
Community Services
East Lothian Council
Council Buildings
Haddington
EH41 3HA
Tel: 01620 827631
Fax: 01620 827291

East Renfrewshire
Director of Education
East Renfrewshire Council
Eastwood park
Rouken Glen Road
Giffnock
Glasgow
G46 6UG
Tel: 0141 577 3430
Fax: 0141 577 3405

Edinburgh
Director of Education
City of Edinburgh Council
Council Headquarters
Wellington Court
10 Waterloo Place
Edinburgh
EH1 3EG
Tel: 0131 469 3222
Fax: 0131 469 3320

Eilean Siar (Western Isles)
Director of Education and Leisure
Services
Comhairle nan Eilean Siar
Sandwick Road
Stornoway
Isle of Lewis
HS1 2BW
Tel: 01851 703773
Fax: 01851 705796

Falkirk
Director of Education
Flakirk Council
McClaren house
Marchmont Avenue
Polmont
FK2 0NZ
Tel: 01324 506600
Fax: 01324 506664

Fife
Head of Education
Fife Council
Fife House
North Street
Glenrothes
KY7 5LT
Tel: 01592 414141
Fax: 01592 416411

Glasgow
Director of Education
Glasgow City Council
House 1
Charing Cross Complex
20 India Street
Glasgow
G2 4PF
Tel: 0141 287 2000
Fax: 0141 287 6892

Highland
Director of Education
Highland Council
Glenurquhart Road
Inverness
IV3 5NX
Tel: 01463 702000
Fax: 01463 702828

Inverclyde
Director of Education Services
Inverclyde Council
Department of Education Services
105 Dalrymple Street
Greenock
PA15 1HT
Tel: 01475 712824
Fax: 01475 712875

Midlothian
Director of Education
Midlothian Council
Fairfield House
8 Lothian Road
Dalkeith
EH22 3ZG
Tel: 0131 271 3718
Fax: 0131 271 3751

Moray
Director of Education
Moray Council
High Street
Elgin
IV30 1BX
Tel: 01343 563134
Fax: 01343563416

North Ayrshire
Director of Education
North Ayrshire Council
Cunninghame House
Friars Croft
Irvine
KA12 8EE
Tel: 01294 324411
Fax: 01294 324444

North Lanarkshire
Director of Education
North Lanarkshire Council
Municipal Building
Kildonan Street
Coatbridge
ML5 3BT
Tel: 01236 812336
Fax: 01236 812335

Orkney
Director of Education
Orkney Islands Council
School Place
Kirkwall
Orkney
KE15 1NY
Tel: 01856 873535
Fax: 01856 870302

Perth & Kinross
Director of Education
Perth & Kinross Council
Blackfriars
Perth
PH1 5LT
Tel: 01738 476211
Fax: 01738 476210

Renfrewshire
Director of Education
Renfrewshire Council
Cotton Street
Paisley
PA1 1LE
Tel: 0141 842 5663
Fax: 0141 842 5655

Scottish Borders
Director of Education
Scottish Borders Council
Council Headquarters
Newtown St Boswells
Melrose
TD6 0SA
Tel: 01835 823095
Fax: 01835 825091

Shetland
Director of Education and
Community Services
Shetland Islands Council
Hayfield House
Hayfield Lane
Lerwick
Shetland
ZE1 0QD
Tel: 01595 744000
Fax: 01595 692810

South Ayrshire

Director of Educational Services
South Ayrshire Council
Wellington Square
Ayr
KA7 1DR
Tel: 01292 612201
Fax: 01292 612258

South Lanarkshire

Executive Director (Education Resources)
South Lanarkshire Council
Floor 5
Council Offices
Almada Street
Hamilton
ML3 0AE
Tel: 01698 454545
Fax: 01698 454465

Stirling

Director of Education
Stirling Council
Viewforth
Stirling
FK8 2ET
Tel: 01786 443322
Fax: 01786 442782

West Dunbartonshire

Director of Education
West Dunbartonshire Council
Council Offices
Garshake Road
Dumbarton
G82 3PU
Tel: 01389 737000
Fax: 01389 737348

West Lothian

Corporate Manager of Education Services
West Lothian Council
Lindsay House
South Bridge Street
Bathgate
EH48 1TS
Tel: 01506 776000
Fax: 01506 776378

Source: The Scottish Office

Clwyd

Director of Education
Education Offices
Education Department
Shire Hall
Mold CH7 6ND
Tel: 01352 752121
Fax: 01352 754202

Dyfed

Chief Education Officer
Education Offices
Education Department
Pibwrlwyd
Carmarthen SA31 2NH
Tel: 01267 2333333

Area Education Offices

Aberystwyth

Area Education Officer
County Offices
Marine Terrace
Aberystwyth SY23 2DE
Tel: 01970 617581

Carmarthen

Area Education Officer
1 Penlan Road
Carmarthen SA31 1DN

Haverfordwest

Area Education Officer
Education Offices
St Thomas Green
Haverfordwest SA61 1QZ
Tel: 01437 764591
Fax: 01437 769557

Llanelli

Area Education Officer
17 Goring Road
Llanelli SA15 3HF

Gwent

Director of Education
Education Offices
County Hall
Cwmbran
Gwent NP44 2XG
Tel: 01633 838838

Gwynedd

Director of Education
Education Offices
Castle Street
Caernarvon LL55 1SH
Tel: 01286 672255

Area Education Office

Ysgol Syr Hugh Owen
Caernarfon LL55 1HW
Tel: 01286 672255

Area Education Office

Parc Mount
Llangefni
Tel: 01248 750444

Area Education Office

Swyddfa Bro Meirion
Safle Y Gader
Dolgellau LL40 1HY
Tel: 01341 423191

Area Education Office

Ysgol Gogarth
Ffordd Nant-y-Gamar
Llandudno LL30 1YF
Tel: 01492 860777

Area Education Office

9 Llieniau Uchaf
Pwllheli LL53 5DT
Tel: 01758 701005

Mid-Glamorgan

Director of Education
Education Offices
County Hall
Cathays Park
Cardiff CF1 3NF
Tel: 01222 820820

Cynon Valley

District Manager
Education Offices
Old Boy's Grammar School
Trecynon
Aberdare CF44 8DY

Merthyr Tydfil

Education Offices
Gwernllwyn Road
Dowlais
Merthyr Tydfil CF48 3TA
Tel: 01685 722761

Ogwr

District Manager Education Offices
County Council Offices
Sunnyside
Bridgend CF31 4AR

Rhondda

Education Offices
Crawshay Street
Ton Pentre CF41 7ER

Rhymney Valley

Education Offices
Caerphilly Road
Ystrad Mynach
Hengoed CF8 7EP
Tel: 01443 816016

Taff Ely

Education Offices
The Grange
Tyfica Road

Pontypridd

CF37 2DD
Tel: 01443 486801

Powys

Director of Education
Education Offices
County Hall
Llandrindod Wells
Powys LD1 5LG
Tel: 01597 826000
Fax: 01597 826475

Area Education Offices

Mid Powys

Southfields
County Hall
Llandrindod Wells LD1 5LG
Tel: 01597 826715

North Powys

Old College off Station Road
Newton
Powys SY16 1BE
Tel: 01686 626395
Fax: 01686 629626

South Powys

Watton Mount
Brecon
Powys LD3 7BB
Tel: 01874 624411

South-Glamorgan

Director of Education and Cultural Services
Education Offices
County Hall
Atlantic Wharf
Cardiff CF1 5UW
Tel: 01874 624411
Fax: 01222 872777

West-Glamorgan

Director of Education
Education Offices
County Hall
Swansea SA1 3SN
Tel: 01792 471111

241

ISIS

National ISIS

56 Buckingham Gate
London
SW1E 6AG
Tel: 0171 630 8793/4
Fax: 0171 630 5013
email: national@isis.org.uk

London & South East

3 Vandon Street
London SW1H 0AH
Tel: 0171 222 7274
Fax: 0171 222 8795
email: southeast@isis.org.uk

Central England

Woodstock
Oxon OX7 1YF
Tel: 01993 813006
Fax: 01993 811400
email: isis-central@dial.pipex.com

North England & North Wales

2 Overhead Cottages
Capernwray
Carnforth LA6 1AD
Tel: 01524 735977
Fax: 01524 735977
email: north@isis.org.uk

Eastern England

Welcome Cottage
Wiveton, nr Holt,
Norfolk NR25 7TH
Tel: 01263 741333
Fax: 01263 741332
email: isis-east@dial.pipex.com

South & West England

Skippers
Shipton Lane
Burton Bradstock
Bridport
Dorset DT6 4NQ
Tel: 01308 898045
Fax: 01308 897221
email: southwest@isis.org.uk

Wales

3 Heol Crwys
Fishguard
Pembs SA62 6SB
Tel: 01348 874460
Fax: 01348 874624
email: isis-wales@dial.pipex.com

Scotland

21 Melville Street
Edinburgh EH3 7PE
Tel: 0131 220 2106
Fax: 0131 225 8594

The Montessori Society A.M.I. (UK)

All schools are run by AMI Diploma Holders

Head Office

26 Lyndhurst Gardens
London NW3 5NW
Tel: 0171 435 7874
Fax: 0171 431 8096

London East

E1

Bethnal Green Montessori School
68 Warner Place
Bethnal Green E2 7DA
Tel: 0171 739 4343 or
0171 739 5372
Ages: 2 1/2 to 5

London North

N4

Holly Park Montessori School
Holly Park Methodist Church
Crouch Hill N4 4BY
Tel: 0171 263 6563
Ages: 2 to 9

N10

The Montessori House
5 Princes Avenue
Muswell Hill N10 3LS
Tel: 0181 444 4399
Ages: 2 1/2 to 5+

N12

Lavendale Montessori
13 Michelham Down
Woodside Park N12 7JJ
Tel: 0181 343 9345
Ages: 2 1/2 to 5

London North West

NW2

**First Steps Montessori
Nursery School**
St Cuthbert's Church
Fordwich Road NW2 3TG
Tel: 0181 452 1257
Ages: 2 1/2 to 5

Neasdon Montessori School
St Catherine's Church Hall
Dudden Hill Lane
Neasden NW2 7RX
Tel: 0181 208 1631
Ages: 2 to 5

**St Michael's Montessori
Children's House**
St Michael's Church Hall
St Micheal's Road NW2 6XG
Tel: 0181 208 2554
Ages: Ages: 2 to 5+

NW3

Chalcot Montessori School
9 Chalcot Gardens
Belsize Park NW3 4YB
Tel: 0171 722 71386
Ages: 2 1/2 to 6

Maria Montessori Childrens House
26 Lyndhurst Gardens
Hampstead NW3 5NW
Tel: 0171 435 3646
Ages: 2 1/2 to 5

NW4

Hendon Montessori School
7 Denehurst Gardens
Hendon NW4 3QS
Tel: 0181 202 8516
Ages: 2 1/2 to 5

NW5

Kentish Town Montessori School
Methodist Church Hall
Fortess Road
Kentish Town NW5 1AH
Tel: 0171 209 5076
Ages: Ages: 2 1/2 to 5

NW11

**Hellenic College of London –
Bilingual Montessori Nursery
of St Michael's**
The Greek Orthodox Cathedral of
the Holy Cross and St Michael
Golders Green Road
Golders Green NW11 8DL
Ages: 2 1/2 to 5

London South East

SE1

**St Patrick';s Montessori
Nursery School**
91 Cornwall Road
Waterloo SE1
Tel: 0171 928 5557
Ages: 2 1/2 to 5

London South West

SW4

**Clapham Montessori School
(Old Town), St Paul's
Community Hall**
St Paul's Church
Rectory Grove
Clapham SW4 0DX
Tel: 0171 498 8324
Ages: Ages: 2 1/2 to 5+

Clapham Park Montessori
St Jame's Church House
10 West Road
Clapham SW4
Tel: 0171 627 0352
Ages: 2 to 5

SW11

Bridge Lane Montessori School
Bridge Lane
Battersea SW11
Tel: 0171 738 0509
or 0171 228 9403
Ages: 2 1/2 to 5+

**The South London Montessori
School**
Trott Street
Battersea
SW11 3DS
Tel: 0171 738 9546
Ages: 2 1/2 to 12

SW18

**Right Impressions Montessori
School**
All Saints Community Hall
Lebanon Road
Southfields
T: 0181 942 8026
Ages: 18 months to 6

SW19

**Wimbeldon Montessori
Childrens House**
St John's Ambulance Hall
122-124 Kingston Road
Wimbeldon
Tel: 0181 543 6353

London West

W1

**Great Beginnings Montessori
School**
The Welsh Church Hall
82A Chiltern Street
Marylebone
W1M 1PS
Tel: 0171 486 2276
Ages: 2 1/2 to 5+

W3

Ealing Montessori School
St Martin's Church Hall
Hale Gardens
Acton W3 9SQ
Tel: 0181 992 4513
Ages: 2 1/2 to 5+

W5

The Maria Montessori School
Church of Ascension
Beaufort Road
Ealing W5 3EB
Tel: 0181 997 6979
Ages: 2 1/2 to 5+

W11

**Maria Montessori Childrens House
- Notting Hill**
All Saints Church Hall
28 Powis Gardens
Notting Hill W11 1JE
Tel: 0171 435 3646
Ages: 2 to 5

Berks

Windsor Montessori School
Windsosr Cricket Club
Home Park
Datchet Road
Windsor
Berks
Tel: 01753 8868399 or
01344 8445592
Ages: 2 ¹/₂ to 6

Bucks

The Beehive Montessori School
1st Amersham Scouts Hall
White Lion Road
Little Chalfont
Bucks
Tel: 0181 992 1844
Ages: 2 ¹/₂ to 5¹/₂

Derbyshire

Littleover Montessori School
27 Gladstone Street
Derby DE23 6PQ
Tel: 01332 273297
Ages: 2 ¹/₂ to 5+

East Sussex

**Brighton and Hove
Montessori School**
67 Stamford Avenue
Brighton BN1 6FB
Tel: 01273 702485
Ages: 2 ¹/₂ to 9

Hampshire

Maria Montessori Nursery
Hawkley Village Hall
Hawkley
N Liss GU33 6NE
Tel: 01420 474481
Ages: 2 to 5

The Montessori Children's House
The Kingsley Centre
Kingsley
Nr Bordon GU35 9ND
Tel: 0962 732507
Ages: 2 ¹/₂ to 5

Herts

Albany Montessori School
Methodist Church Hall
133B Hatfield Road
St Albans AL1 4JS
Tel: 01727 832036
Ages: 2 ¹/₂ to 5

Fairview Montessori School
79 Waatling Street
St Albans AL1 2QF
Tel: 01727 842102
Ages: 2 ¹/₂ to 5

Highgate Montessori School
Wesley Hall
Stapylton Road
Barnet EN5 4JJ
Tel: 0181 883 6849

Little Acorns Montessori School
Bushey WD2 2LN
Tel: 01923 230705
Ages: 2 to 6

**St Christopher School –
Montessori Department**
Barrington Road
Letchworth SG6 3JZ
Tel: 01462 679301
Ages: 2 ¹/₂ to 5¹/₂

**The Chorley Wood
Montessori School**
Rickmansworth Road
Chorleywood WD3 5SL
Tel: 01923 285691
Ages: 2 ¹/₂ to 5

Middlesex

Alexander Montessori School
19 Mepham Gardens
Harrow Weald HA3 6QS
Tel: 0181 421 3102
Ages: 2 ¹/₂ to 5

Southall Montessori School
St John's Parish Centre
Church Avenue
Southall UB2 4DH
Tel: 0181 893 5355
Ages: 2 to 5

Norfolk

The Norwich Montessori School
The Colney Parish Room
Old Watton Road
Colney NR4 7TW
Tel: 01603 452522
Ages: 2 ¹/₂ to 6

Westacre Montessori School
Village Hall
Westacre
Kings Lynn PE32 1TX
Tel: 01760 755650
Ages: 2 ¹/₂ to 5

North Yorkshire

The Montessori School
Little Green
Piper Lane
Thirsk YO7 1AN
Tel: 01845 525953
Ages: 2 ¹/₂ to 6

Oxfordshire

Small World Montessori School
89 Bagley Wood Road
Kennington OX1 5NA
Tel: 01865 326660
Ages: 12 weeks to 5

Surrey

Weyhill Montessori School
Scout Headquarters
Youth Campus
Weyhill
Haslemere GU27 1BX
Tel: 01428 656840
or 0374 936960
Ages: 2 ¹/₂ to 5

Steiner Waldorf Education – Kindergartens

Steiner Waldorf Schools Fellowship

Kidbrooke Park
Forest Row
East Sussex RH18 5JA
Tel: 01342 822115
Fax: 01342 826004
email:
mail@waldorf.compulink.co.uk
http://www.compulink.co.uk/
waldorf

Kindergartens attached to Steiner Waldorf Schools

Aldergate Bridge School
Mill Lane
Padworth
Reading
Berkshire RG7 4JU
Tel: 01189 714471

Aberdeen Waldorf School
Craigton Road
Cults
Aberdeen AB15 9QD
Tel: 01224 868366

Brighton Steiner School
John Howard House
Roedean Road
Kemp Town
Brighton BN2 5RA
Tel: 01273 386300

Bristol Waldorf School
Windergarten
12D Cotham Road
Bristol BS6 6DR
Tel 0117 9734399

Botton Village School
Danby, nr. Whitby
North Yorkshire YO21 2NJ
Tel 01287 661206

Cooleenbridge School
Raheen
Tuamgraney
Co. Clare, Ireland
Tel 00 353 61 921494

Dublin Waldorf Kindergarten
47A Rathgar Road
Rathgar
Dublin 6
Tel 00 353 1 4960525

Edinburgh Ruldolf Steiner School
60-64 Spylaw Road
Edinburgh EH10 5BR
Tel 0131 337 3410

Elmfield School
Love Lane
Stourbridge
West Midlands DY8 2EA
Tel 01384 72933

Glasgow Steiner School
52 Lumsden Street
York Hill
Glasgow G3 8RH
Tel: 0141 334 8855

Hereford Waldorf School
Much Dewchurch
Herefordshire HR2 8DE
Tel: 01981 540221

Holywood Rudolf Steiner School
34 Croft Road
Holywood
Co. Down
N.Ireland BT18 0PR
Tel: 01232 428029

Iona School
310 Sneinton Dale
Nottingham NG3 7DN
Tel: 01159 587392

Kings Langley Rudolf Steiner School
Langely Hill
Kings Langley
Herts. WD4 9HG
Tel: 01923 263284

Micheal Hall School Kidbrooke Park
Forest Row
East Sussex RH18 5JA
Tel: 01342 823660

Micheal House School
The Field
Shipley
Heanor
Derby DE7 7JH
Tel: 01773 718050

Moray Steiner School
Drumduan
Clovenside Road
Forres
Moray IV36 0RD
Tel: 01309 676300

Nant-y-Cwm Steiner School
Llanycefn
Clunderwen
Pembs. SA66 7QJ Wales
Tel: 01437 563640

North London Steiner School
PO Box 280
London N8 7HT
Tel: 0181 348 5050/
0181 341 4455

Perry Court School
Garlinge Green
Chartham
Canterbury
Kent CT4 5RU
Tel: 01227 738285

Plas Tan yr Allt Waldorf School
Tremadog
Gwynedd LL49 9RG
Wales
Tel: 01766 512068

Reading Steiner Kindergarten
5 Christchurch Gardens
Reading RG2 7AH
Tel: 01189 866301

Ringwood Waldorf School
Ashley
Ringwood
Hampshire BH24 2NN
Tel: 01425 472664

South Devon Rudlof Steiner School
Hood Manor
Dartington
Totnes
Devon TQ9 6AB
Tel: 01803 762528

St Albans Steiner Kindergarten
Fleetville Community Centre
Royal Road
St Albans
Herts
Tel: 01923 400453

Waldorf School of South London
Cresset Kindergarten
12 Balham Park Road
London SW12 8DR
Tel: 0181 769 6587

Woodfields Kindergarten
16-18 Abbotswood Road
Streatham
London SW16 1AP
Tel: 0181 769 6587

York Steiner School
Danesmead
Fulford Cross
York YO1 4PB
Tel: 01904 654983

Wynstones School
Whaddon Green
Gloucester GL4 0UF
Tel: 01452 522475

Independent Steinder Waldorf Kindergartens

The Barn Nursery
The Pavillion
John Pear's Field
Ashurst Wood
Sussex
Tel: 01342 822640

Butterflies and Bumblebees
20 Nigel Playfair Avenue
Hammersmith
London W6
Tel: 0171 734 9501

Cherrytrees Kindergarten
Withgill House
Withgill Fold
Clitheroe BB7 3LW
Tel: 015242 22408

Hoathly Hill Kindergarten
The Barn
Hoathly Hill
West Hoathly
Sussex RH19 4SJ
Tel: 01342 810762

Rosebridge Steiner Kindergarten
24 Roseford Road
Cambridge CB4 2HD
Tel: 01223 516756

The Lindens Waldorf Kindergarten and Family Centre
Lower Street
Stroud
Glous. GL5
Tel: 01452 812393

The Meadow School
18-20 High Street
Bruton
Somerset BA10 0AA
Tel: 01749 813629/813176

The Merlin Kindergarten
2 Meadow Bank Road
Sheffield S11 9AH
Tel: 0114 250 8274

St Paul's School
1 St Paul's Road
Islington
London N1 2QH
Tel: 0171 226 4454

Primrose Nursery
34 Glenilla Road
London NW3 4AP
Tel: 0171 794 5865

Sunlands Kindergarten
57 Cainscross Road
Stroud
Glous. GL5 4EX
Tel: 01452 813795

Waldorf Kindergartens in Camphill in the UK and Ireland for severely handicapped children

John's Haven Kindergarten
Tangle'ha Cottage
Tangle'ha
Nr St Cyrus
Montrose
Angus DD10 0DG
Tel: 01674 850627

Mourne Grange
169 Newry Road
Kilkeel
Co Down BT34 4EX.

Newton Dee Kindergarten
Orion
Newton Dee
Bieldside
Aberdeen AB15 9DL
Tel: 01224 868270

Puddleduck Kindergarten
Clanabogin Camphill Community
Drudgeon
Omagh
Co Tyrone
N. Ireland
Tel: 0662 41627

The Croft Kindergarten
Camphill Community
Highfield Road
Old Malton
North Yorks. YO17 0EY
Tel: 01653 694323/694815

The Grange & Oaklands Kindergarten
Camphill Village
Newham on Severn
Nr Glous GL 14 1EF
Tel: 01452 813948.

Useful Contact Information

Advisory Centre for Education (ACE) Ltd

Department A
Unit 1B Aberdeen Studios
22 Highbury Grove
London N5 2DQ
Tel: 0171 354 8321
Fax: 0171 354 9069
email:
ace-ed@easynet.co.uk
http://www.agora.co.uk/domino/a
cehome.nsf

British Association for Early Childhood Education

111 City View House
463 Bethnal Green Road
London E2 9QY
Tel: 0171-739 7594
Fax: 0171-613 5330 (HQ)

Childcare Association

BO7 Coppergate House
16 Brune Street
London E1 7NJ
Tel: 0171 721 7960

Child Support Agency National Enquiry Line

Tel: 0345 133133

Education Otherwise

PO Box 7420
London N9 9SG
Tel: 0891 518303

Equal Opportunities Commission

Overseas House
Quay Street
Manchester M3 3HM
Tel: 0161 833 9244

Family Credit Helpline

Tel: 01253 500050

Federation of Recruitment and Employment Services

Tel: 0171 323 4300

Home Education Advisory Service

PO Box 98
Welwyn Garden City
Herts AL8 6AN
Tel: 01707 335825
Fax: 01707 335825

National Association for the Education of Sick Children

St Margaret's House
17 Old Ford Road
London E2 9PL

National Association of Nursery Nurses

17 Lamb Close
Garston
Watford
Herts WD2 6PB
Tel: 01923 893867

National Assoiation of Welsh-medium Nursery Schools and Playgroups/Mudiad Ysgolion Meithrin

145 Albany Road
Roath
Cardiff GF2 3NT
Tel: 01222 485510
Fax: 01222 470196

National Campaign for Nursery Education

BCM Box 6216
London WC1N 3XX

National Childminding Association

8 Masons Hill
Bromley
Kent BR2 9EY
Tel: 0181-464 6164
Fax: 0181-290 6834 (HQ)

National Childminding Association Information Line

(2pm to 4pm)
Tel: 0181 466 0200

National Childminding Association in Wales

Offices 4-5 Lighthouse
Business Park
Bastion Park
Prestatyn
Denbighshire LL19 7ND
Tel: 01745 852995
Fax: 01745 852995

National Private Day Nurseries Association

55 New Hey Road
Lindley
Huddersfield
W Yorks HD3 4AL
Tel: 01484 546502
Fax: 01484 546502 (HQ)

New Ways to Work

Advice line open 12pm to 3pm
Monday, Tuesday and Thursday
Tel: 0171 226 4026

Northern Ireland Childminding Association

Tel: 01247 811015

Parentline

Endway House
Endway
Hadleigh
Essex SS7 2AN
Tel: 01702 559900 (helpline)
Tel: 01702 554782 (admin)
Fax: 01702 554911 (HQ)

Parents at Work Information Line

Tel: 0171 628 3578

Pre-School Learning Alliance

69 Kings Cross Road
London WC1X 9LL
Tel: 0171 833 0991
Fax: 0171 837 4942

Professional Association of Nursery Nurses

2 St James' Court
Friar Gate
Derby DE1 1BT
Tel: 01332 343029
Fax: 01332 290310
& 292431 (HQ)

Scottish Childminding Association

Tel: 01786 445377

Scottish Independent Nurseries Association

32 Heriot Hill Terrace
Edinburgh EH7 4DY
Tel: 0131-467 8676

Society for Interactive Learning

11 Lloyd Street
Ryton
Tyne & Wear NE40 4DJ
Tel: 0191-413 2262
Fax: 0191-413 2262

Society of Nursery Nursing Administrators

40 Archdale Road
London SE22 9HJ
Tel: 0181-516 1366
Fax: 0171-274 5103 (HQ)

Working for Childcare

7 Holloway Road
London N7 8JZ
Tel: 0171-700 0281
Fax: 0171-700 1105 (HQ)